Young's Literal Translation c

by Robert Young

This section of the Old testament is the collection of the first five books often known as the Torah, it also contains the last 8 verses of Deuteronomy which were often omitted as they describe the death of Moses, and as tradition dictates that he wrote the books it is rather obvious that this cannot be so when we take the description of his death into account.

The majority of scholars today all agree that the Torah does not have a single author, and that it was complied over many centuries. There was a general consensus from the 19th century onwards about the documentary hypothesis, which suggests that the five books were created c.450 BCE by combining four originally independent sources, known as the Jahwist, or J (about 900 BCE), the Elohist, or E (about 800 BCE), the Deuteronomist, or D, (about 600 BCE), and the Priestly source, or P (about 500 BCE).This idea has been questioned since the 1970's, and today there are many more theories but no consensus.

This text is taken from the 'Robert Young's Literal Translation' published in 1862

It aimed to be a literal translation and remove the added poetic license given to the King James edition, this translation was made using the original Hebrew and Greek translations. Young even uses the present tense were most English translations use the past, because this conforms to the original Hebrew text.

This version is printed with students of the text in mind,printed in a large A4 format and each verse and chapter is placed at the start of a new line for easy reference

Genesis

"creation"

Exodus

"departure"

Leviticus

refers to the Levites and the regulations that apply to their presence and service in the Temple, which form the bulk of the third book.

Numbers

contains a record of the numbering of the Israelites in the wilderness of Sinai and later on the plain of Moab.

Deuteronomy

"second law"

refers to the fifth book's recapitulation of the commandments reviewed by Moses before his death.

Genesis

1:1 In the beginning of God's preparing the heavens and the earth –
1:2 the earth hath existed waste and void, and darkness [is] on the face of the deep, and the Spirit
of God fluttering on the face of the waters,
1:3 and God saith, `Let light be;' and light is.
1:4 And God seeth the light that [it is] good, and God separateth between the light and the
darkness,
1:5 and God calleth to the light `Day,' and to the darkness He hath called `Night;' and there is an
evening, and there is a morning -- day one.
1:6 And God saith, `Let an expanse be in the midst of the waters, and let it be separating between
waters and waters.'
1:7 And God maketh the expanse, and it separateth between the waters which [are] under the
expanse, and the waters which [are] above the expanse: and it is so.
1:8 And God calleth to the expanse `Heavens;' and there is an evening, and there is a morning --
day second.
1:9 And God saith, `Let the waters under the heavens be collected unto one place, and let the dry
land be seen:' and it is so.
1:10 And God calleth to the dry land `Earth,' and to the collection of the waters He hath called
`Seas;' and God seeth that [it is] good.
1:11 And God saith, `Let the earth yield tender grass, herb sowing seed, fruit-tree (whose seed [is]
in itself) making fruit after its kind, on the earth:' and it is so.
1:12 And the earth bringeth forth tender grass, herb sowing seed after its kind, and tree making
fruit (whose seed [is] in itself) after its kind; and God seeth that [it is] good;
1:13 and there is an evening, and there is a morning -- day third.
1:14 And God saith, `Let luminaries be in the expanse of the heavens, to make a separation
between the day and the night, then they have been for signs, and for seasons, and for days and
years,
1:15 and they have been for luminaries in the expanse of the heavens to give light upon the earth:'
and it is so.
1:16 And God maketh the two great luminaries, the great luminary for the rule of the day, and the
small luminary -- and the stars -- for the rule of the night;
1:17 and God giveth them in the expanse of the heavens to give light upon the earth,
1:18 and to rule over day and over night, and to make a separation between the light and the
darkness; and God seeth that [it is] good;

1:19 and there is an evening, and there is a morning -- day fourth.
1:20 And God saith, `Let the waters teem with the teeming living creature, and fowl let fly on the
earth on the face of the expanse of the heavens.'
1:21 And God prepareth the great monsters, and every living creature that is creeping, which the
waters have teemed with, after their kind, and every fowl with wing, after its kind, and God seeth
that [it is] good.
1:22 And God blesseth them, saying, `Be fruitful, and multiply, and fill the waters in the seas, and
the fowl let multiply in the earth:'
1:23 and there is an evening, and there is a morning -- day fifth.
1:24 And God saith, `Let the earth bring forth the living creature after its kind, cattle and creeping
thing, and beast of the earth after its kind:' and it is so.
1:25 And God maketh the beast of the earth after its kind, and the cattle after their kind, and every
creeping thing of the ground after its kind, and God seeth that [it is] good.
1:26 And God saith, `Let Us make man in Our image, according to Our likeness, and let them rule
over fish of the sea, and over fowl of the heavens, and over cattle, and over all the earth, and over
every creeping thing that is creeping on the earth.'
1:27 And God prepareth the man in His image; in the image of God He prepared him, a male and a
female He prepared them.
1:28 And God blesseth them, and God saith to them, `Be fruitful, and multiply, and fill the earth, and
subdue it, and rule over fish of the sea, and over fowl of the heavens, and over every living thing
that is creeping upon the earth.'
1:29 And God saith, `Lo, I have given to you every herb sowing seed, which [is] upon the face of all
the earth, and every tree in which [is] the fruit of a tree sowing seed, to you it is for food;
1:30 and to every beast of the earth, and to every fowl of the heavens, and to every creeping thing
on the earth, in which [is] breath of life, every green herb [is] for food:' and it is so.
1:31 And God seeth all that He hath done, and lo, very good; and there is an evening, and there is
a morning -- day the sixth.
2:1 And the heavens and the earth are completed, and all their host;
2:2 and God completeth by the seventh day His work which He hath made, and ceaseth by the
seventh day from all His work which He hath made.
2:3 And God blesseth the seventh day, and sanctifieth it, for in it He hath ceased from all His work
which God had prepared for making.
2:4 These [are] births of the heavens and of the earth in their being prepared, in the day of Jehovah
God's making earth and heavens;

2:5 and no shrub of the field is yet in the earth, and no herb of the field yet sprouteth, for Jehovah God hath not rained upon the earth, and a man there is not to serve the ground,
2:6 and a mist goeth up from the earth, and hath watered the whole face of the ground.
2:7 And Jehovah God formeth the man -- dust from the ground, and breatheth into his nostrils breath of life, and the man becometh a living creature.
2:8 And Jehovah God planteth a garden in Eden, at the east, and He setteth there the man whom He hath formed;
2:9 and Jehovah God causeth to sprout from the ground every tree desirable for appearance, and good for food, and the tree of life in the midst of the garden, and the tree of knowledge of good and evil.
2:10 And a river is going out from Eden to water the garden, and from thence it is parted, and hath become four chief [rivers];
2:11 the name of the one [is] Pison, it [is] that which is surrounding the whole land of the Havilah where the gold [is],
2:12 and the gold of that land [is] good, there [is] the bdolach and the shoham stone;
2:13 and the name of the second river [is] Gibon, it [is] that which is surrounding the whole land of Cush;
2:14 and the name of the third river [is] Hiddekel, it [is] that which is going east of Asshur; and the fourth river is Phrat.
2:15 And Jehovah God taketh the man, and causeth him to rest in the garden of Eden, to serve it, and to keep it.
2:16 And Jehovah God layeth a charge on the man, saying, `Of every tree of the garden eating thou dost eat;
2:17 and of the tree of knowledge of good and evil, thou dost not eat of it, for in the day of thine eating of it -- dying thou dost die.'
2:18 And Jehovah God saith, `Not good for the man to be alone, I do make to him an helper -- as his counterpart.'
2:19 And Jehovah God formeth from the ground every beast of the field, and every fowl of the heavens, and bringeth in unto the man, to see what he doth call it; and whatever the man calleth a living creature, that [is] its name.
2:20 And the man calleth names to all the cattle, and to fowl of the heavens, and to every beast of the field; and to man hath not been found an helper -- as his counterpart.
2:21 And Jehovah God causeth a deep sleep to fall upon the man, and he sleepeth, and He taketh one of his ribs, and closeth up flesh in its stead.

no - wrong Hebrew root - meant "Side" 2nd hebrew translation was not as clear as "side" and Greek flipped it to Rib.

2:22 And Jehovah God buildeth up the rib which He hath taken out of the man into a woman, and bringeth her in unto the man;
2:23 and the man saith, `This [is] the [proper] step! bone of my bone, and flesh of my flesh!' for this it is called Woman, for from a man hath this been taken;
2:24 therefore doth a man leave his father and his mother, and hath cleaved unto his wife, and they have become one flesh.
2:25 And they are both of them naked, the man and his wife, and they are not ashamed of themselves.
3:1 And the serpent hath been subtile above every beast of the field which Jehovah God hath made, and he saith unto the woman, `Is it true that God hath said, Ye do not eat of every tree of the garden?'
3:2 And the woman saith unto the serpent, `Of the fruit of the trees of the garden we do eat,
3:3 and of the fruit of the tree which [is] in the midst of the garden God hath said, Ye do not eat of it, nor touch it, lest ye die.'
3:4 And the serpent saith unto the woman, `Dying, ye do not die,
3:5 for God doth know that in the day of your eating of it -- your eyes have been opened, and ye have been as God, knowing good and evil.'
3:6 And the woman seeth that the tree [is] good for food, and that it [is] pleasant to the eyes, and the tree is desirable to make [one] wise, and she taketh of its fruit and eateth, and giveth also to her husband with her, and he doth eat;
3:7 and the eyes of them both are opened, and they know that they [are] naked, and they sew fig-leaves, and make to themselves girdles.
3:8 And they hear the sound of Jehovah God walking up and down in the garden at the breeze of the day, and the man and his wife hide themselves from the face of Jehovah God in the midst of the trees of the garden.
3:9 And Jehovah God calleth unto the man, and saith to him, `Where [art] thou?'
3:10 and he saith, `Thy sound I have heard in the garden, and I am afraid, for I am naked, and I hide myself.'
3:11 And He saith, `Who hath declared to thee that thou [art] naked? of the tree of which I have commanded thee not to eat, hast thou eaten?'
3:12 and the man saith, `The woman whom Thou didst place with me -- she hath given to me of the tree -- and I do eat.'
3:13 And Jehovah God saith to the woman, `What [is] this thou hast done?' and the woman saith, `The serpent hath caused me to forget -- and I do eat.'

3:14 And Jehovah God saith unto the serpent, `Because thou hast done this, cursed [art] thou above all the cattle, and above every beast of the field: on thy belly dost thou go, and dust thou dost eat, all days of thy life;
3:15 and enmity I put between thee and the woman, and between thy seed and her seed; he doth bruise thee -- the head, and thou dost bruise him -- the heel.'
3:16 Unto the woman He said, `Multiplying I multiply thy sorrow and thy conception, in sorrow dost thou bear children, and toward thy husband [is] thy desire, and he doth rule over thee.'
3:17 And to the man He said, `Because thou hast hearkened to the voice of thy wife, and dost eat of the tree concerning which I have charged thee, saying, Thou dost not eat of it, cursed [is] the ground on thine account; in sorrow thou dost eat of it all days of thy life,
3:18 and thorn and bramble it doth bring forth to thee, and thou hast eaten the herb of the field;
3:19 by the sweat of thy face thou dost eat bread till thy return unto the ground, for out of it hast thou been taken, for dust thou [art], and unto dust thou turnest back.'
3:20 And the man calleth his wife's name Eve: for she hath been mother of all living.
3:21 And Jehovah God doth make to the man and to his wife coats of skin, and doth clothe them.
3:22 And Jehovah God saith, `Lo, the man was as one of Us, as to the knowledge of good and evil; and now, lest he send forth his hand, and have taken also of the tree of life, and eaten, and lived to the age,' --
3:23 Jehovah God sendeth him forth from the garden of Eden to serve the ground from which he hath been taken;
3:24 yea, he casteth out the man, and causeth to dwell at the east of the garden of Eden the cherubs and the flame of the sword which is turning itself round to guard the way of the tree of life.
4:1 And the man knew Eve his wife, and she conceiveth and beareth Cain, and saith, `I have gotten a man by Jehovah;'
4:2 and she addeth to bear his brother, even Abel. And Abel is feeding a flock, and Cain hath been servant of the ground.
4:3 And it cometh to pass at the end of days that Cain bringeth from the fruit of the ground a present to Jehovah;
4:4 and Abel, he hath brought, he also, from the female firstlings of his flock, even from their fat ones; and Jehovah looketh unto Abel and unto his present,
4:5 and unto Cain and unto his present He hath not looked; and it is very displeasing to Cain, and his countenance is fallen.
4:6 And Jehovah saith unto Cain, `Why hast thou displeasure? and why hath thy countenance fallen?

4:7 Is there not, if thou dost well, acceptance? and if thou dost not well, at the opening a sin-offering is crouching, and unto thee its desire, and thou rulest over it.'
4:8 And Cain saith unto Abel his brother, [`Let us go into the field;'] and it cometh to pass in their being in the field, that Cain riseth up against Abel his brother, and slayeth him.
4:9 And Jehovah saith unto Cain, `Where [is] Abel thy brother?' and he saith, `I have not known; my brother's keeper -- I?'
4:10 And He saith, `What hast thou done? the voice of thy brother's blood is crying unto Me from the ground;
4:11 and now, cursed [art] thou from the ground, which hath opened her mouth to receive the blood of thy brother from thy hand;
4:12 when thou tillest the ground, it doth not add to give its strength to thee -- a wanderer, even a trembling one, thou art in the earth.'
4:13 And Cain saith unto Jehovah, `Greater is my punishment than to be borne;
4:14 lo, Thou hast driven me to-day from off the face of the ground, and from Thy face I am hid; and I have been a wanderer, even a trembling one, in the earth, and it hath been -- every one finding me doth slay me.'
4:15 And Jehovah saith to him, `Therefore -- of any slayer of Cain sevenfold it is required;' and Jehovah setteth to Cain a token that none finding him doth slay him.
4:16 And Cain goeth out from before Jehovah, and dwelleth in the land, moving about east of Eden;
4:17 and Cain knoweth his wife, and she conceiveth, and beareth Enoch; and he is building a city, and he calleth the name of the city, according to the name of his son -- Enoch.
4:18 And born to Enoch is Irad; and Irad hath begotten Mehujael; and Mehujael hath begotten Methusael; and Methusael hath begotten Lamech.
4:19 And Lamech taketh to himself two wives, the name of the one Adah, and the name of the second Zillah.
4:20 And Adah beareth Jabal, he hath been father of those inhabiting tents and purchased possessions;
4:21 and the name of his brother [is] Jubal, he hath been father of every one handling harp and organ.
4:22 And Zillah she also bare Tubal-Cain, an instructor of every artificer in brass and iron; and a sister of Tubal-Cain [is] Naamah.
4:23 And Lamech saith to his wives: -- `Adah and Zillah, hear my voice; Wives of Lamech, give ear [to] my saying: For a man I have slain for my wound, Even a young man for my hurt;

4:24 For sevenfold is required for Cain, And for Lamech seventy and sevenfold.'

4:25 And Adam again knoweth his wife, and she beareth a son, and calleth his name Seth, `for God hath appointed for me another seed instead of Abel:' for Cain had slain him.

4:26 And to Seth, to him also a son hath been born, and he calleth his name Enos; then a beginning was made of preaching in the name of Jehovah.

5:1 This [is] an account of the births of Adam: In the day of God's preparing man, in the likeness of God He hath made him;

5:2 a male and a female He hath prepared them, and He blesseth them, and calleth their name Man, in the day of their being prepared.

5:3 And Adam liveth an hundred and thirty years, and begetteth [a son] in his likeness, according to his image, and calleth his name Seth.

5:4 And the days of Adam after his begetting Seth are eight hundred years, and he begetteth sons and daughters.

5:5 And all the days of Adam which he lived are nine hundred and thirty years, and he dieth.

5:6 And Seth liveth an hundred and five years, and begetteth Enos.

5:7 And Seth liveth after his begetting Enos eight hundred and seven years, and begetteth sons and daughters.

5:8 And all the days of Seth are nine hundred and twelve years, and he dieth.

5:9 And Enos liveth ninety years, and begetteth Cainan.

5:10 And Enos liveth after his begetting Cainan eight hundred and fifteen years, and begetteth sons and daughters.

5:11 And all the days of Enos are nine hundred and five years, and he dieth.

5:12 And Cainan liveth seventy years, and begetteth Mahalaleel.

5:13 And Cainan liveth after his begetting Mahalaleel eight hundred and forty years, and begetteth sons and daughters.

5:14 And all the days of Cainan are nine hundred and ten years, and he dieth.

5:15 And Mahalaleel liveth five and sixty years, and begetteth Jared.

5:16 And Mahalaleel liveth after his begetting Jared eight hundred and thirty years, and begetteth sons and daughters.

5:17 And all the days of Mahalaleel are eight hundred and ninety and five years, and he dieth.

5:18 And Jared liveth an hundred and sixty and two years, and begetteth Enoch.

5:19 And Jared liveth after his begetting Enoch eight hundred years, and begetteth sons and daughters.

5:20 And all the days of Jared are nine hundred and sixty and two years, and he dieth.

5:21 And Enoch liveth five and sixty years, and begetteth Methuselah.
5:22 And Enoch walketh habitually with God after his begetting Methuselah three hundred years, and begetteth sons and daughters.
5:23 And all the days of Enoch are three hundred and sixty and five years.
5:24 And Enoch walketh habitually with God, and he is not, for God hath taken him.
5:25 And Methuselah liveth an hundred and eighty and seven years, and begetteth Lamech.
5:26 And Methuselah liveth after his begetting Lamech seven hundred and eighty and two years, and begetteth sons and daughters.
5:27 And all the days of Methuselah are nine hundred and sixty and nine years, and he dieth.
5:28 And Lamech liveth an hundred and eighty and two years, and begetteth a son,
5:29 and calleth his name Noah, saying, `This [one] doth comfort us concerning our work, and concerning the labour of our hands, because of the ground which Jehovah hath cursed.'
5:30 And Lamech liveth after his begetting Noah five hundred and ninety and five years, and begetteth sons and daughters.
5:31 And all the days of Lamech are seven hundred and seventy and seven years, and he dieth.
5:32 And Noah is a son of five hundred years, and Noah begetteth Shem, Ham, and Japheth.
6:1 And it cometh to pass that mankind have begun to multiply on the face of the ground, and daughters have been born to them,
6:2 and sons of God see the daughters of men that they [are] fair, and they take to themselves women of all whom they have chosen.
6:3 And Jehovah saith, `My Spirit doth not strive in man -- to the age; in their erring they [are] flesh:' and his days have been an hundred and twenty years.
6:4 The fallen ones were in the earth in those days, and even afterwards when sons of God come in unto daughters of men, and they have borne to them -- they [are] the heroes, who, from of old, [are] the men of name.
6:5 And Jehovah seeth that abundant [is] the wickedness of man in the earth, and every imagination of the thoughts of his heart only evil all the day;
6:6 and Jehovah repenteth that He hath made man in the earth, and He grieveth Himself -- unto His heart.
6:7 And Jehovah saith, `I wipe away man whom I have prepared from off the face of the ground, from man unto beast, unto creeping thing, and unto fowl of the heavens, for I have repented that I have made them.'
6:8 And Noah found grace in the eyes of Jehovah.
6:9 These [are] births of Noah: Noah [is] a righteous man; perfect he hath been among his

generations; with God hath Noah walked habitually.
6:10 And Noah begetteth three sons, Shem, Ham, and Japheth.
6:11 And the earth is corrupt before God, and the earth is filled [with] violence.
6:12 And God seeth the earth, and lo, it hath been corrupted, for all flesh hath corrupted its way on the earth.
6:13 And God said to Noah, `An end of all flesh hath come before Me, for the earth hath been full of violence from their presence; and lo, I am destroying them with the earth.
6:14 `Make for thyself an ark of gopher-wood; rooms dost thou make with the ark, and thou hast covered it within and without with cypress;
6:15 and this [is] that which thou dost with it: three hundred cubits [is] the length of the ark, fifty cubits its breadth, and thirty cubits its height;
6:16 a window dost thou make for the ark, and unto a cubit thou dost restrain it from above; and the opening of the ark thou dost put in its side, -- lower, second, and third [stories] dost thou make it.
6:17 `And I, lo, I am bringing in the deluge of waters on the earth to destroy all flesh, in which [is] a living spirit, from under the heavens; all that [is] in the earth doth expire.
6:18 `And I have established My covenant with thee, and thou hast come in unto the ark, thou, and thy sons, and thy wife, and thy son's wives with thee;
6:19 and of all that liveth, of all flesh, two of every [sort] thou dost bring in unto the ark, to keep alive with thee; male and female are they.
6:20 Of the fowl after its kind, and of the cattle after their kind, of every creeping thing of the ground after its kind, two of every [sort] they come in unto thee, to keep alive.
6:21 `And thou, take to thyself of all food that is eaten; and thou hast gathered unto thyself, and it hath been to thee and to them for food.'
6:22 And Noah doth according to all that God hath commanded him; so hath he done.
7:1 And Jehovah saith to Noah, `Come in, thou and all thy house, unto the ark, for thee I have seen righteous before Me in this generation;
7:2 of all the clean beasts thou dost take to thee seven pairs, a male and its female; and of the beasts which are not clean two, a male and its female;
7:3 also, of fowl of the heavens seven pairs, a male and a female, to keep alive seed on the face of all the earth;
7:4 for after other seven days I am sending rain on the earth forty days and forty nights, and have wiped away all the substance that I have made from off the face of the ground.'
7:5 And Noah doth according to all that Jehovah hath commanded him:
7:6 and Noah [is] a son of six hundred years, and the deluge of waters hath been upon the earth.

7:7 And Noah goeth in, and his sons, and his wife, and his sons' wives with him, unto the ark, from the presence of the waters of the deluge;
7:8 of the clean beasts and of the beasts that [are] not clean, and of the fowl, and of every thing that is creeping upon the ground,
7:9 two by two they have come in unto Noah, unto the ark, a male and a female, as God hath commanded Noah.
7:10 And it cometh to pass, after the seventh of the days, that waters of the deluge have been on the earth.
7:11 In the six hundredth year of the life of Noah, in the second month, in the seventeenth day of the month, in this day have been broken up all fountains of the great deep, and the net-work of the heavens hath been opened,
7:12 and the shower is on the earth forty days and forty nights.
7:13 In this self-same day went in Noah, and Shem, and Ham, and Japheth, sons of Noah, and Noah's wife and the three wives of his sons with them, unto the ark;
7:14 they, and every living creature after its kind, and every beast after its kind, and every creeping thing that is creeping on the earth after its kind, and every fowl after its kind, every bird -- every wing.
7:15 And they come in unto Noah, unto the ark, two by two of all the flesh in which [is] a living spirit;
7:16 and they that are coming in, male and female of all flesh, have come in as God hath commanded him, and Jehovah doth close [it] for him.
7:17 And the deluge is forty days on the earth, and the waters multiply, and lift up the ark, and it is raised up from off the earth;
7:18 and the waters are mighty, and multiply exceedingly upon the earth; and the ark goeth on the face of the waters.
7:19 And the waters have been very very mighty on the earth, and covered are all the high mountains which [are] under the whole heavens;
7:20 fifteen cubits upwards have the waters become mighty, and the mountains are covered;
7:21 and expire doth all flesh that is moving on the earth, among fowl, and among cattle, and among beasts, and among all the teeming things which are teeming on the earth, and all mankind;
7:22 all in whose nostrils [is] breath of a living spirit -- of all that [is] in the dry land -- have died.
7:23 And wiped away is all the substance that is on the face of the ground, from man unto beast, unto creeping thing, and unto fowl of the heavens; yea, they are wiped away from the earth, and only Noah is left, and those who [are] with him in the ark;
7:24 and the waters are mighty on the earth a hundred and fifty days.

8:1 And God remembereth Noah, and every living thing, and all the cattle which [are] with him in the ark, and God causeth a wind to pass over the earth, and the waters subside,
8:2 and closed are the fountains of the deep and the net-work of the heavens, and restrained is the shower from the heavens.
8:3 And turn back do the waters from off the earth, going on and returning; and the waters are lacking at the end of a hundred and fifty days.
8:4 And the ark resteth, in the seventh month, in the seventeenth day of the month, on mountains of Ararat;
8:5 and the waters have been going and becoming lacking till the tenth month; in the tenth [month], on the first of the month, appeared the heads of the mountains.
8:6 And it cometh to pass, at the end of forty days, that Noah openeth the window of the ark which he made,
8:7 and he sendeth forth the raven, and it goeth out, going out and turning back till the drying of the waters from off the earth.
8:8 And he sendeth forth the dove from him to see whether the waters have been lightened from off the face of the ground,
8:9 and the dove hath not found rest for the sole of her foot, and she turneth back unto him, unto the ark, for waters [are] on the face of all the earth, and he putteth out his hand, and taketh her, and bringeth her in unto him, unto the ark.
8:10 And he stayeth yet other seven days, and addeth to send forth the dove from the ark;
8:11 and the dove cometh in unto him at even-time, and lo, an olive leaf torn off in her mouth; and Noah knoweth that the waters have been lightened from off the earth.
8:12 And he stayeth yet other seven days, and sendeth forth the dove, and it added not to turn back unto him any more.
8:13 And it cometh to pass in the six hundredth and first year, in the first [month], in the first of the month, the waters have been dried from off the earth; and Noah turneth aside the covering of the ark, and looketh, and lo, the face of the ground hath been dried.
8:14 And in the second month, in the seven and twentieth day of the month, the earth hath become dry.
8:15 And God speaketh unto Noah, saying, `Go out from the ark, thou, and thy wife, and thy sons, and thy sons' wives with thee;
8:16 every living thing that [is] with thee, of all flesh, among fowl, and among cattle, and among every creeping thing which is creeping on the earth, bring out with thee;
8:17 and they have teemed in the earth, and been fruitful, and have multiplied on the earth.'

8:18 And Noah goeth out, and his sons, and his wife, and his sons' wives with him;
8:19 every beast, every creeping thing, and every fowl; every creeping thing on the earth, after their families, have gone out from the ark.
8:20 And Noah buildeth an altar to Jehovah, and taketh of every clean beast, and of every clean fowl, and causeth burnt-offerings to ascend on the altar;
8:21 and Jehovah smelleth the sweet fragrance, and Jehovah saith unto His heart, `I continue not to disesteem any more the ground because of man, though the imagination of the heart of man [is] evil from his youth; and I continue not to smite any more all living, as I have done;
8:22 during all days of the earth, seed-time and harvest, and cold and heat, and summer and winter, and day and night, do not cease.'
9:1 And God blesseth Noah, and his sons, and saith to them, `Be fruitful, and multiply, and fill the earth;
9:2 and your fear and your dread is on every beast of the earth, and on every fowl of the heavens, on all that creepeth on the ground, and on all fishes of the sea -- into your hand they have been given.
9:3 Every creeping thing that is alive, to you it is for food; as the green herb I have given to you the whole;
9:4 only flesh in its life -- its blood -- ye do not eat.
9:5 `And only your blood for your lives do I require; from the hand of every living thing I require it, and from the hand of man, from the hand of every man's brother I require the life of man;
9:6 whoso sheddeth man's blood, by man is his blood shed: for in the image of God hath He made man.
9:7 And ye, be fruitful and multiply, teem in the earth, and multiply in it.'
9:8 And God speaketh unto Noah, and unto his sons with him, saying,
9:9 `And I, lo, I am establishing My covenant with you, and with your seed after you,
9:10 and with every living creature which [is] with you, among fowl, among cattle, and among every beast of the earth with you, from all who are going out of the ark -- to every beast of the earth.
9:11 And I have established My covenant with you, and all flesh is not any more cut off by waters of a deluge, and there is not any more a deluge to destroy the earth.'
9:12 And God saith, `This is a token of the covenant which I am giving between Me and you, and every living creature that [is] with you, to generations age-during;
9:13 My bow I have given in the cloud, and it hath been for a token of a covenant between Me and the earth;
9:14 and it hath come to pass (in My sending a cloud over the earth) that the bow hath been seen

in the cloud,
9:15 and I have remembered My covenant which is between Me and you, and every living creature among all flesh, and the waters become no more a deluge to destroy all flesh;
9:16 and the bow hath been in the cloud, and I have seen it -- to remember the covenant age-during between God and every living creature among all flesh which [is] on the earth.'
9:17 And God saith unto Noah, `This [is] a token of the covenant which I have established between Me and all flesh that [is] upon the earth.'
9:18 And the sons of Noah who are going out of the ark are Shem, and Ham, and Japheth; and Ham is father of Canaan.
9:19 These three [are] sons of Noah, and from these hath all the earth been overspread.
9:20 And Noah remaineth a man of the ground, and planteth a vineyard,
9:21 and drinketh of the wine, and is drunken, and uncovereth himself in the midst of the tent.
9:22 And Ham, father of Canaan, seeth the nakedness of his father, and declareth to his two brethren without.
9:23 And Shem taketh -- Japheth also -- the garment, and they place on the shoulder of them both, and go backward, and cover the nakedness of their father; and their faces [are] backward, and their father's nakedness they have not seen.
9:24 And Noah awaketh from his wine, and knoweth that which his young son hath done to him,
9:25 and saith: `Cursed [is] Canaan, Servant of servants he is to his brethren.'
9:26 And he saith: `Blessed of Jehovah my God [is] Shem, And Canaan is servant to him.
9:27 God doth give beauty to Japheth, And he dwelleth in tents of Shem, And Canaan is servant to him.'
9:28 And Noah liveth after the deluge three hundred and fifty years;
9:29 and all the days of Noah are nine hundred and fifty years, and he dieth.
10:1 And these [are] births of the sons of Noah, Shem, Ham, and Japheth; and born to them are sons after the deluge.
10:2 `Sons of Japheth [are] Gomer, and Magog, and Madai, and Javan, and Tubal, and Meshech, and Tiras.
10:3 And sons of Gomer [are] Ashkenaz, and Riphath, and Togarmah.
10:4 And sons of Javan [are] Elishah, and Tarshish, Kittim, and Dodanim.
10:5 By these have the isles of the nations been parted in their lands, each by his tongue, by their families, in their nations.
10:6 And sons of Ham [are] Cush, and Mitzraim, and Phut, and Canaan.
10:7 And sons of Cush [are] Seba, and Havilah, and Sabtah, and Raamah, and Sabtechah; and

sons of Raamah [are] Sheba and Dedan.
10:8 And Cush hath begotten Nimrod;
10:9 he hath begun to be a hero in the land; he hath been a hero in hunting before Jehovah;
therefore it is said, `As Nimrod the hero [in] hunting before Jehovah.'
10:10 And the first part of his kingdom is Babel, and Erech, and Accad, and Calneh, in the land of
Shinar;
10:11 from that land he hath gone out to Asshur, and buildeth Nineveh, even the broad places of
the city, and Calah,
10:12 and Resen, between Nineveh and Calah; it [is] the great city.
10:13 And Mitzraim hath begotten the Ludim, and the Anamim, and the Lehabim, and the
Naphtuhim,
10:14 and the Pathrusim, and the Casluhim, (whence have come out Philistim,) and the Caphtorim.
10:15 And Canaan hath begotten Sidon his first-born, and Heth,
10:16 and the Jebusite, and the Amorite, and the Girgashite,
10:17 and the Hivite, and the Arkite, and the Sinite,
10:18 and the Arvadite, and the Zemarite, and the Hamathite; and afterwards have the families of
the Canaanite been scattered.
10:19 And the border of the Canaanite is from Sidon, [in] thy coming towards Gerar, unto Gaza; [in]
thy coming towards Sodom, and Gomorrah, and Admah, and Zeboim, unto Lasha.
10:20 These [are] sons of Ham, by their families, by their tongues, in their lands, in their nations.
10:21 As to Shem, father of all sons of Eber, brother of Japheth the elder, he hath also begotten:
10:22 Sons of Shem [are] Elam, and Asshur, and Arphaxad, and Lud, and Aram.
10:23 And sons of Aram [are] Uz, and Hul, and Gether, and Mash.
10:24 And Arphaxad hath begotten Salah, and Salah hath begotten Eber.
10:25 And to Eber have two sons been born; the name of the one [is] Peleg (for in his days hath
the earth been divided,) and his brother's name [is] Joktan.
10:26 And Joktan hath begotten Almodad, and Sheleph, and Hazarmaveth, and Jerah,
10:27 and Hadoram, and Uzal, and Diklah,
10:28 and Obal, and Abimael, and Sheba,
10:29 and Ophir, and Havilah, and Jobab; all these [are] sons of Joktan;
10:30 and their dwelling is from Mesha, [in] thy coming towards Sephar, a mount of the east.
10:31 These [are] sons of Shem, by their families, by their tongues, in their lands, by their nations.
10:32 These [are] families of the sons of Noah, by their births, in their nations, and by these have
the nations been parted in the earth after the deluge.

11:1 And the whole earth is of one pronunciation, and of the same words,
11:2 and it cometh to pass, in their journeying from the east, that they find a valley in the land of Shinar, and dwell there;
11:3 and they say each one to his neighbour, `Give help, let us make bricks, and burn [them] thoroughly:' and the brick is to them for stone, and the bitumen hath been to them for mortar.
11:4 And they say, `Give help, let us build for ourselves a city and tower, and its head in the heavens, and make for ourselves a name, lest we be scattered over the face of all the earth.'
11:5 And Jehovah cometh down to see the city and the tower which the sons of men have builded;
11:6 and Jehovah saith, `Lo, the people [is] one, and one pronunciation [is] to them all, and this it hath dreamed of doing; and now, nothing is restrained from them of that which they have purposed to do.
11:7 Give help, let us go down, and mingle there their pronunciation, so that a man doth not understand the pronunciation of his companion.'
11:8 And Jehovah doth scatter them from thence over the face of all the earth, and they cease to build the city;
11:9 therefore hath [one] called its name Babel, for there hath Jehovah mingled the pronunciation of all the earth, and from thence hath Jehovah scattered them over the face of all the earth.
11:10 These [are] births of Shem: Shem [is] a son of an hundred years, and begetteth Arphaxad two years after the deluge.
11:11 And Shem liveth after his begetting Arphaxad five hundred years, and begetteth sons and daughters.
11:12 And Arphaxad hath lived five and thirty years, and begetteth Salah.
11:13 And Arphaxad liveth after his begetting Salah four hundred and three years, and begetteth sons and daughters.
11:14 And Salah hath lived thirty years, and begetteth Eber.
11:15 And Salah liveth after his begetting Eber four hundred and three years, and begetteth sons and daughters.
11:16 And Eber liveth four and thirty years, and begetteth Peleg.
11:17 And Eber liveth after his begetting Peleg four hundred and thirty years, and begetteth sons and daughters.
11:18 And Peleg liveth thirty years, and begetteth Reu.
11:19 And Peleg liveth after his begetting Reu two hundred and nine years, and begetteth sons and daughters.
11:20 And Reu liveth two and thirty years, and begetteth Serug.

11:21 And Reu liveth after his begetting Serug two hundred and seven years, and begetteth sons and daughters.

11:22 And Serug liveth thirty years, and begetteth Nahor.

11:23 And Serug liveth after his begetting Nahor two hundred years, and begetteth sons and daughters.

11:24 And Nahor liveth nine and twenty years, and begetteth Terah.

11:25 And Nahor liveth after his begetting Terah an hundred and nineteen years, and begetteth sons and daughters.

11:26 And Terah liveth seventy years, and begetteth Abram, Nahor, and Haran.

11:27 And these [are] births of Terah: Terah hath begotten Abram, Nahor, and Haran; and Haran hath begotten Lot;

11:28 and Haran dieth in the presence of Terah his father, in the land of his birth, in Ur of the Chaldees.

11:29 And Abram and Nahor take to themselves wives; the name of Abram's wife [is] Sarai, and the name of Nahor's wife [is] Milcah, daughter of Haran, father of Milcah, and father of Iscah.

11:30 And Sarai is barren -- she hath no child.

11:31 And Terah taketh Abram his son, and Lot, son of Haran, his son's son, and Sarai his daughter-in-law, wife of Abram his son, and they go out with them from Ur of the Chaldees, to go towards the land of Canaan; and they come unto Charan, and dwell there.

11:32 And the days of Terah are two hundred and five years, and Terah dieth in Charan.

12:1 And Jehovah saith unto Abram, `Go for thyself, from thy land, and from thy kindred, and from the house of thy father, unto the land which I shew thee.

12:2 And I make thee become a great nation, and bless thee, and make thy name great; and be thou a blessing.

12:3 And I bless those blessing thee, and him who is disesteeming thee I curse, and blessed in thee have been all families of the ground.'

12:4 And Abram goeth on, as Jehovah hath spoken unto him, and Lot goeth with him, and Abram [is] a son of five and seventy years in his going out from Charan.

12:5 And Abram taketh Sarai his wife, and Lot his brother's son, and all their substance that they have gained, and the persons that they have obtained in Charan; and they go out to go towards the land of Canaan; and they come in to the land of Canaan.

12:6 And Abram passeth over into the land, unto the place Shechem, unto the oak of Moreh; and the Canaanite [is] then in the land.

12:7 And Jehovah appeareth unto Abram, and saith, `To thy seed I give this land;' and he buildeth

there an altar to Jehovah, who hath appeared unto him.
12:8 And he removeth from thence towards a mountain at the east of Beth-El, and stretcheth out the tent (Beth-El at the west, and Hai at the east), and he buildeth there an altar to Jehovah, and preacheth in the name of Jehovah.
12:9 And Abram journeyeth, going on and journeying towards the south.
12:10 And there is a famine in the land, and Abram goeth down towards Egypt to sojourn there, for the famine [is] grievous in the land;
12:11 and it cometh to pass as he hath drawn near to enter Egypt, that he saith unto Sarai his wife, `Lo, I pray thee, I have known that thou [art] a woman of beautiful appearance;
12:12 and it hath come to pass that the Egyptians see thee, and they have said, `This [is] his wife,' and they have slain me, and thee they keep alive:
12:13 say, I pray thee, thou [art] my sister, so that it is well with me because of thee, and my soul hath lived for thy sake.'
12:14 And it cometh to pass, at the entering of Abram into Egypt, that the Egyptians see the woman that she [is] exceeding fair;
12:15 and princes of Pharaoh see her, and praise her unto Pharaoh, and the woman is taken [to] Pharaoh's house;
12:16 and to Abram he hath done good because of her, and he hath sheep and oxen, and he-asses, and men-servants, and handmaids, and she-asses, and camels.
12:17 And Jehovah plagueth Pharaoh and his house -- great plagues -- for the matter of Sarai, Abram's wife.
12:18 And Pharaoh calleth for Abram, and saith, `What [is] this thou hast done to me? why hast thou not declared to me that she [is] thy wife?
12:19 Why hast thou said, She [is] my sister, and I take her to myself for a wife? and now, lo, thy wife, take and go.'
12:20 And Pharaoh chargeth men concerning him, and they send him away, and his wife, an all that he hath.
13:1 And Abram goeth up from Egypt (he and his wife, and all that he hath, and Lot with him) towards the south;
13:2 and Abram [is] exceedingly wealthy in cattle, in silver, and in gold.
13:3 And he goeth on his journeyings from the south, even unto Bethel, unto the place where his tent had been at the commencement, between Bethel and Hai --
13:4 unto the place of the altar which he made there at the first, and there doth Abram preach in the name of Jehovah.

13:5 And also to Lot, who is going with Abram, there hath been sheep and oxen and tents;
13:6 and the land hath not suffered them to dwell together, for their substance hath been much, and they have not been able to dwell together;
13:7 and there is a strife between those feeding Abram's cattle and those feeding Lot's cattle; and the Canaanite and the Perizzite [are] then dwelling in the land.
13:8 And Abram saith unto Lot, `Let there not, I pray thee, be strife between me and thee, and between my shepherds and thy shepherds, for we [are] men -- brethren.
13:9 Is not all the land before thee? be parted, I pray thee, from me; if to the left, then I to the right; and if to the right, then I to the left.'
13:10 And Lot lifteth up his eyes, and seeth the whole circuit of the Jordan that it [is] all a watered country (before Jehovah's destroying Sodom and Gomorrah, as Jehovah's garden, as the land of Egypt,) in thy coming toward Zoar,
13:11 and Lot chooseth for himself the whole circuit of the Jordan; and Lot journeyeth from the east, and they are parted -- a man from his companion;
13:12 Abram hath dwelt in the land of Canaan, and Lot hath dwelt in the cities of the circuit, and tenteth unto Sodom;
13:13 and the men of Sodom [are] evil, and sinners before Jehovah exceedingly.
13:14 And Jehovah said unto Abram, after Lot's being parted from him, `Lift up, I pray thee, thine eyes, and look from the place where thou [art], northward, and southward, and eastward, and westward;
13:15 for the whole of the land which thou are seeing, to thee I give it, and to thy seed -- to the age.
13:16 And I have set thy seed as dust of the earth, so that, if one is able to number the dust of the earth, even thy seed is numbered;
13:17 rise, go up and down through the land, to its length, and to its breadth, for to thee I give it.'
13:18 And Abram tenteth, and cometh, and dwelleth among the oaks of Mamre, which [are] in Hebron, and buildeth there an altar to Jehovah.
14:1 And it cometh to pass in the days of Amraphel king of Shinar, Arioch king of Ellasar, Chedorlaomer king of Elam, and Tidal king of Goyim,
14:2 they have made war with Bera king of Sodom, and with Birsha king of Gomorrah, Shinab king of Admah, and Shemeber king of Zeboim, and the king of Bela, which [is] Zoar.
14:3 All these have been joined together unto the valley of Siddim, which [is] the Salt Sea;
14:4 twelve years they served Chedorlaomer, and the thirteenth year they rebelled.
14:5 And in the fourteenth year came Chedorlaomer, and the kings who [are] with him, and they smite the Rephaim in Ashteroth Karnaim, and the Zuzim in Ham, and the Emim in Shaveh

Kiriathaim,
14:6 and the Horites in their mount Seir, unto El-Paran, which [is] by the wilderness;
14:7 and they turn back and come in unto En-Mishpat, which [is] Kadesh, and smite the whole field of the Amalekite, and also the Amorite who is dwelling in Hazezon-Tamar.
14:8 And the king of Sodom goeth out, and the king of Gomorrah, and the king of Admah, and the king of Zeboim, and the king of Bela, which [is] Zoar; and they set the battle in array with them in the valley of Siddim,
14:9 with Chedorlaomer king of Elam, and Tidal king of Goyim, and Amraphel king of Shinar, and Arioch king of Ellasar; four kings with the five.
14:10 And the valley of Siddim [is] full of bitumen-pits; and the kings of Sodom and Gomorrah flee, and fall there, and those left have fled to the mountain.
14:11 And they take the whole substance of Sodom and Gomorrah, and the whole of their food, and go away;
14:12 and they take Lot, Abram's brother's son (seeing he is dwelling in Sodom), and his substance, and go away.
14:13 And one who is escaping cometh and declareth to Abram the Hebrew, and he is dwelling among the oaks of Mamre the Amorite, brother of Eshcol, and brother of Aner, and they [are] Abram's allies.
14:14 And Abram heareth that his brother hath been taken captive, and he draweth out his trained domestics, three hundred and eighteen, and pursueth unto Dan.
14:15 And he divideth himself against them by night, he and his servants, and smiteth them, and pursueth them unto Hobah, which [is] at the left of Damascus;
14:16 and he bringeth back the whole of the substance, and also Lot his brother and his substance hath he brought back, and also the women and the people.
14:17 And the king of Sodom goeth out to meet him (after his turning back from the smiting of Chedorlaomer, and of the kings who [are] with him), unto the valley of Shaveh, which [is] the king's valley.
14:18 And Melchizedek king of Salem hath brought out bread and wine, and he [is] priest of God Most High;
14:19 and he blesseth him, and saith, `Blessed [is] Abram to God Most High, possessing heaven and earth;
14:20 and blessed [is] God Most High, who hath delivered thine adversaries into thy hand;' and he giveth to him a tenth of all.
14:21 And the king of Sodom saith unto Abram, `Give to me the persons, and the substance take to

thyself,'
14:22 and Abram saith unto the king of Sodom, `I have lifted up my hand unto Jehovah, God Most
High, possessing heaven and earth --
14:23 from a thread even unto a shoe-latchet I take not of anything which thou hast, that thou say
not, I -- I have made Abram rich;
14:24 save only that which the young men have eaten, and the portion of the men who have gone
with me -- Aner, Eshcol, and Mamre -- they take their portion.'
15:1 After these things hath the word of Jehovah been unto Abram in a vision, saying, `Fear not,
Abram, I [am] a shield to thee, thy reward [is] exceeding great.'
15:2 And Abram saith, `Lord Jehovah, what dost Thou give to me, and I am going childless? and
an acquired son in my house is Demmesek Eliezer.'
15:3 And Abram saith, `Lo, to me Thou hast not given seed, and lo, a domestic doth heir me.'
15:4 And lo, the word of Jehovah [is] unto him, saying, `This [one] doth not heir thee; but he who
cometh out from thy bowels, he doth heir thee;'
15:5 and He bringeth him out without, and saith, `Look attentively, I pray thee, towards the
heavens, and count the stars, if thou art able to count them;' and He saith to him, `Thus is thy
seed.'
15:6 And he hath believed in Jehovah, and He reckoneth it to him -- righteousness.
15:7 And He saith unto him, `I [am] Jehovah who brought thee out from Ur of the Chaldees, to give
to thee this land to possess it;'
15:8 and he saith, `Lord Jehovah, whereby do I know that I possess it?'
15:9 And He saith unto him, `Take for Me a heifer of three years, and a she-goat of three years,
and a ram of three years, and a turtle-dove, and a young bird;'
15:10 and he taketh to him all these, and separateth them in the midst, and putteth each piece over
against its fellow, but the bird he hath not divided;
15:11 and the ravenous birds come down upon the carcases, and Abram causeth them to turn
back.
15:12 And the sun is about to go in, and deep sleep hath fallen upon Abram, and lo, a terror of
great darkness is falling upon him;
15:13 and He saith to Abram, `knowing -- know that thy seed is a sojourner in a land not theirs, and
they have served them, and they have afflicted them four hundred years,
15:14 and the nation also whom they serve I judge, and after this they go out with great substance;
15:15 and thou -- thou comest in unto thy fathers in peace; thou art buried in a good old age;
15:16 and the fourth generation doth turn back hither, for the iniquity of the Amorite is not yet

complete.'
15:17 And it cometh to pass -- the sun hath gone in, and thick darkness hath been -- and lo, a furnace of smoke, and a lamp of fire, which hath passed over between those pieces.
15:18 In that day hath Jehovah made with Abram a covenant, saying, `To thy seed I have given this land, from the river of Egypt unto the great river, the river Phrat,
15:19 with the Kenite, and the Kenizzite, and the Kadmonite,
15:20 and the Hittite, and the Perizzite, and the Rephaim,
15:21 and the Amorite, and the Canaanite, and the Girgashite, and the Jebusite.'
16:1 And Sarai, Abram's wife, hath not borne to him, and she hath an handmaid, an Egyptian, and her name [is] Hagar;
16:2 and Sarai saith unto Abram, `Lo, I pray thee, Jehovah hath restrained me from bearing, go in, I pray thee, unto my handmaid; perhaps I am built up from her;' and Abram hearkeneth to the voice of Sarai.
16:3 And Sarai, Abram's wife, taketh Hagar the Egyptian, her handmaid, at the end of the tenth year of Abram's dwelling in the land of Canaan, and giveth her to Abram her husband, to him for a wife,
16:4 and he goeth in unto Hagar, and she conceiveth, and she seeth that she hath conceived, and her mistress is lightly esteemed in her eyes.
16:5 And Sarai saith unto Abram, `My violence [is] for thee; I -- I have given mine handmaid into thy bosom, and she seeth that she hath conceived, and I am lightly esteemed in her eyes; Jehovah doth judge between me and thee.'
16:6 And Abram saith unto Sarai, `Lo, thine handmaid [is] in thine hand, do to her that which is good in thine eyes;' and Sarai afflicted her, and she fleeth from her presence.
16:7 And a messenger of Jehovah findeth her by the fountain of water in the wilderness, by the fountain in the way [to] Shur,
16:8 and he saith, `Hagar, Sarai's handmaid, whence hast thou come, and whither dost thou go?' and she saith, `From the presence of Sarai, my mistress, I am fleeing.'
16:9 And the messenger of Jehovah saith to her, `Turn back unto thy mistress, and humble thyself under her hands;'
16:10 and the messenger of Jehovah saith to her, `Multiplying I multiply thy seed, and it is not numbered from multitude;'
16:11 and the messenger of Jehovah saith to her, `Behold thou [art] conceiving, and bearing a son, and hast called his name Ishmael, for Jehovah hath hearkened unto thine affliction;
16:12 and he is a wild-ass man, his hand against every one, and every one's hand against him --

and before the face of all his brethren he dwelleth.'
16:13 And she calleth the name of Jehovah who is speaking unto her, `Thou [art], O God, my beholder;' for she said, `Even here have I looked behind my beholder?'
16:14 therefore hath one called the well, `The well of the Living One, my beholder;' lo, between Kadesh and Bered.
16:15 And Hagar beareth to Abram a son; and Abram calleth the name of his son, whom Hagar hath borne, Ishmael;
16:16 and Abram [is] a son of eighty and six years in Hagar's bearing Ishmael to Abram.
17:1 And Abram is a son of ninety and nine years, and Jehovah appeareth unto Abram, and saith unto him, `I [am] God Almighty, walk habitually before Me, and be thou perfect;
17:2 and I give My covenant between Me and thee, and multiply thee very exceedingly.'
17:3 And Abram falleth upon his face, and God speaketh with him, saying,
17:4 `I -- lo, My covenant [is] with thee, and thou hast become father of a multitude of nations;
17:5 and thy name is no more called Abram, but thy name hath been Abraham, for father of a multitude of nations have I made thee;
17:6 and I have made thee exceeding fruitful, and made thee become nations, and kings go out from thee.
17:7 `And I have established My covenant between Me and thee, and thy seed after thee, to their generations, for a covenant age-during, to become God to thee, and to thy seed after thee;
17:8 and I have given to thee, and to thy seed after thee, the land of thy sojournings, the whole land of Canaan, for a possession age-during, and I have become their God.'
17:9 And God saith unto Abraham, `And thou dost keep My covenant, thou and thy seed after thee, to their generations;
17:10 this [is] My covenant which ye keep between Me and you, and thy seed after thee: Every male of you [is] to be circumcised;
17:11 and ye have circumcised the flesh of your foreskin, and it hath become a token of a covenant between Me and you.
17:12 `And a son of eight days is circumcised by you; every male to your generations, born in the house, or bought with money from any son of a stranger, who is not of thy seed;
17:13 he is certainly circumcised who [is] born in thine house, or bought with thy money; and My covenant hath become in your flesh a covenant age-during;
17:14 and an uncircumcised one, a male, the flesh of whose foreskin is not circumcised, even that person hath been cut off from his people; My covenant he hath broken.'
17:15 And God saith unto Abraham, `Sarai thy wife -- thou dost not call her name Sarai, for Sarah

[is] her name;
17:16 and I have blessed her, and have also given to thee a son from her; and I have blessed her, and she hath become nations -- kings of peoples are from her.'
17:17 And Abraham falleth upon his face, and laugheth, and saith in his heart, `To the son of an hundred years is one born? or doth Sarah -- daughter of ninety years -- bear?'
17:18 And Abraham saith unto God, `O that Ishmael may live before Thee;'
17:19 and God saith, `Sarah thy wife is certainly bearing a son to thee, and thou hast called his name Isaac, and I have established My covenant with him, for a covenant age-during, to his seed after him.
17:20 As to Ishmael, I have heard thee; lo, I have blessed him, and made him fruitful, and multiplied him, very exceedingly; twelve princes doth he beget, and I have made him become a great nation;
17:21 and My covenant I establish with Isaac, whom Sarah doth bear to thee at this appointed time in the next year;'
17:22 and He finisheth speaking with him, and God goeth up from Abraham.
17:23 And Abraham taketh Ishmael his son, and all those born in his house, and all those bought with his money -- every male among the men of Abraham's house -- and circumciseth the flesh of their foreskin, in this self-same day, as God hath spoken with him.
17:24 And Abraham [is] a son of ninety and nine years in the flesh of his foreskin being circumcised;
17:25 and Ishmael his son [is] a son of thirteen years in the flesh of his foreskin being circumcised;
17:26 in this self-same day hath Abraham been circumcised, and Ishmael his son;
17:27 and all the men of his house -- born in the house, and bought with money from the son of a stranger -- have been circumcised with him.
18:1 And Jehovah appeareth unto him among the oaks of Mamre, and he is sitting at the opening of the tent, about the heat of the day;
18:2 and he lifteth up his eyes and looketh, and lo, three men standing by him, and he seeth, and runneth to meet them from the opening of the tent, and boweth himself towards the earth,
18:3 And he saith, `My Lord, if, I pray thee, I have found grace in thine eyes, do not, I pray thee, pass on from thy servant;
18:4 let, I pray thee, a little water be accepted, and wash your feet, and recline under the tree;
18:5 and I bring a piece of bread, and support ye your heart; afterwards pass on, for therefore have ye passed over unto your servant;' and they say, `So mayest thou do as thou has spoken.'
18:6 And Abraham hasteth towards the tent, unto Sarah, and saith, `Hasten three measures of

flour-meal, knead, and make cakes;'
18:7 and Abraham ran unto the herd, and taketh a son of the herd, tender and good, and giveth unto the young man, and he hasteth to prepare it;
18:8 and he taketh butter and milk, and the son of the herd which he hath prepared, and setteth before them; and he is standing by them under the tree, and they do eat.
18:9 And they say unto him, `Where [is] Sarah thy wife?' and he saith, `Lo -- in the tent;'
18:10 and he saith, `returning I return unto thee, about the time of life, and lo, to Sarah thy wife a son.'
18:11 And Sarah is hearkening at the opening of the tent, which is behind him;
18:12 and Abraham and Sarah [are] aged, entering into days -- the way of women hath ceased to be to Sarah;
18:13 and Sarah laugheth in her heart, saying, `After I have waxed old I have had pleasure! -- my lord also [is] old!'
18:14 And Jehovah saith unto Abraham, `Why [is] this? Sarah hath laughed, saying, Is it true really -- I bear -- and I am aged? Is any thing too wonderful for Jehovah? at the appointed time I return unto thee, about the time of life, and Sarah hath a son.'
18:15 And Sarah denieth, saying, `I did not laugh;' for she hath been afraid; and He saith, `Nay, but thou didst laugh.'
18:16 And the men rise from thence, and look on the face of Sodom, and Abraham is going with them to send them away;
18:17 and Jehovah said, `Am I concealing from Abraham that which I am doing,
18:18 and Abraham certainly becometh a nation great and mighty, and blessed in him have been all nations of the earth?
18:19 for I have known him, that he commandeth his children, and his house after him (and they have kept the way of Jehovah), to do righteousness and judgment, that Jehovah may bring on Abraham that which He hath spoken concerning him.'
18:20 And Jehovah saith, `The cry of Sodom and Gomorrah -- because great; and their sin -- because exceeding grievous:
18:21 I go down now, and see whether according to its cry which is coming unto Me they have done completely -- and if not -- I know;'
18:22 and the men turn from thence, and go towards Sodom; and Abraham is yet standing before Jehovah.
18:23 And Abraham draweth nigh and saith, `Dost Thou also consume righteous with wicked?
18:24 peradventure there are fifty righteous in the midst of the city; dost Thou also consume, and

not bear with the place for the sake of the fifty -- the righteous who [are] in its midst?
18:25 Far be it from Thee to do according to this thing, to put to death the righteous with the wicked; that it hath been -- as the righteous so the wicked -- far be it from Thee; doth the Judge of all the earth not do justice?'
18:26 And Jehovah saith, `If I find in Sodom fifty righteous in the midst of the city, then have I borne with all the place for their sake.'
18:27 And Abraham answereth and saith, `Lo, I pray thee, I have willed to speak unto the Lord, and I -- dust and ashes;
18:28 peradventure there are lacking five of the fifty righteous -- dost Thou destroy for five the whole of the city?' and He saith, `I destroy [it] not, if I find there forty and five.'
18:29 And he addeth again to speak unto Him and saith, `Peradventure there are found there forty?' and He saith, `I do [it] not, because of the forty.'
18:30 And he saith, `Let it not be, I Pray thee, displeasing to the Lord, and I speak: peradventure there are found there thirty?' and He saith, `I do [it] not, if I find there thirty.'
18:31 And he saith, `Lo, I pray thee, I have willed to speak unto the Lord: peradventure there are found there twenty?' and He saith, `I do not destroy [it], because of the twenty.'
18:32 And he saith, `Let it not be, I pray Thee, displeasing to the Lord, and I speak only this time: peradventure there are found there ten?' and He saith, `I do not destroy [it], because of the ten.'
18:33 And Jehovah goeth on, when He hath finished speaking unto Abraham, and Abraham hath turned back to his place.
19:1 And two of the messengers come towards Sodom at even, and Lot is sitting at the gate of Sodom, and Lot seeth, and riseth to meet them, and boweth himself -- face to the earth,
19:2 and he saith, `Lo, I pray you, my lords, turn aside, I pray you, unto the house of your servant, and lodge, and wash your feet -- then ye have risen early and gone on your way;' and they say, `Nay, but in the broad place we do lodge.'
19:3 And he presseth on them greatly, and they turn aside unto him, and come in unto his house; and he maketh for them a banquet, and hath baked unleavened things; and they do eat.
19:4 Before they lie down, the men of the city -- men of Sodom -- have come round about against the house, from young even unto aged, all the people from the extremity;
19:5 and they call unto Lot and say to him, `Where [are] the men who have come in unto thee to-night? bring them out unto us, and we know them.'
19:6 And Lot goeth out unto them, to the opening, and the door hath shut behind him,
19:7 and saith, `Do not, I pray you, my brethren, do evil;
19:8 lo, I pray you, I have two daughters, who have not known any one; let me, I pray you, bring

them out unto you, and do to them as [is] good in your eyes; only to these men do not anything, for
therefore have they come in within the shadow of my roof.'
19:9 And they say, `Come nigh hither;' they say also, `This one hath come in to sojourn, and he
certainly judgeth! now, we do evil to thee more than [to] them;' and they press against the man,
against Lot greatly, and come nigh to break the door.
19:10 And the men put forth their hand, and bring in Lot unto them, into the house, and have shut
the door;
19:11 and the men who [are] at the opening of the house they have smitten with blindness, from
small even unto great, and they weary themselves to find the opening.
19:12 And the men say unto Lot, `Whom hast thou here still? son-in-law, thy sons also, and thy
daughters, and all whom thou hast in the city, bring out from this place;
19:13 for we are destroying this place, for their cry hath been great [before] the face of Jehovah,
and Jehovah doth send us to destroy it.'
19:14 And Lot goeth out, and speaketh unto his sons-in-law, those taking his daughters, and saith,
`Rise, go out from this place, for Jehovah is destroying the city;' and he is as [one] mocking in the
eyes of his sons-in-law.
19:15 And when the dawn hath ascended, then the messengers press upon Lot, saying, `Rise,
take thy wife, and thy two daughters who are found present, lest thou be consumed in the iniquity
of the city.'
19:16 And he lingereth, and the men lay hold on his hand, and on the hand of his wife, and on the
hand of his two daughters, through the mercy of Jehovah unto him, and they bring him out, and
cause him to rest without the city.
19:17 And it cometh to pass when he hath brought them out without, that he saith, `Escape for thy
life; look not expectingly behind thee, nor stand thou in all the circuit; to the mountain escape, lest
thou be consumed.'
19:18 And Lot saith unto them, `Not [so], I pray thee, my lord;
19:19 lo, I pray thee, thy servant hath found grace in thine eyes, and thou dost make great thy
kindness which thou hast done with me by saving my life, and I am unable to escape to the
mountain, lest the evil cleave [to] me, and I have died;
19:20 lo, I pray thee, this city [is] near to flee thither, and it [is] little; let me escape, I pray thee,
thither, (is it not little?) and my soul doth live.'
19:21 And he saith unto him, `Lo, I have accepted thy face also for this thing, without overthrowing
the city [for] which thou hast spoken;
19:22 haste, escape thither, for I am not able to do anything till thine entering thither;' therefore

hath he calleth the name of the city Zoar.
19:23 The sun hath gone out on the earth, and Lot hath entered into Zoar,
19:24 and Jehovah hath rained upon Sodom and upon Gomorrah brimstone and fire from Jehovah, from the heavens;
19:25 and He overthroweth these cities, and all the circuit, and all the inhabitants of the cities, and that which is shooting up from the ground.
19:26 And his wife looketh expectingly from behind him, and she is -- a pillar of salt!
19:27 And Abraham riseth early in the morning, unto the place where he hath stood [before] the face of Jehovah;
19:28 and he looketh on the face of Sodom and Gomorrah, and on all the face of the land of the circuit, and seeth, and lo, the smoke of the land went up as smoke of the furnace.
19:29 And it cometh to pass, in God's destroying the cities of the circuit, that God remembereth Abraham, and sendeth Lot out of the midst of the overthrow in the overthrowing of the cities in which Lot dwelt.
19:30 And Lot goeth up out of Zoar, and dwelleth in the mountain, and his two daughters with him, for he hath been afraid of dwelling in Zoar, and he dwelleth in a cave, he and his two daughters.
19:31 And the first-born saith unto the younger, `Our father [is] old, and a man there is not in the earth to come in unto us, as [is] the way of all the earth;
19:32 come, we cause our father to drink wine, and lie with him, and preserve from our father -- a seed.'
19:33 And they cause their father to drink wine on that night; and the first-born goeth in, and lieth with her father, and he hath not known in her lying down, or in her rising up.
19:34 And it cometh to pass, on the morrow, that the first-born saith unto the younger, `Lo, I have lain yesterday-night with my father: we cause him to drink wine also to-night, and go thou in, lie with him, and we preserve from our father -- a seed.'
19:35 And they cause their father to drink wine on that night also, and the younger riseth and lieth with him, and he hath not known in her lying down, or in her rising up.
19:36 And the two daughters of Lot conceive from their father,
19:37 and the first-born beareth a son, and calleth his name Moab; he [is] father of Moab unto this day;
19:38 as to the younger, she also hath born a son, and calleth his name Ben-Ammi: he [is] father of the Beni-Ammon unto this day.
20:1 And Abraham journeyeth from thence toward the land of the south, and dwelleth between Kadesh and Shur, and sojourneth in Gerar;

20:2 and Abraham saith concerning Sarah his wife, `She is my sister;' and Abimelech king of Gerar sendeth and taketh Sarah.

20:3 And God cometh in unto Abimelech in a dream of the night, and saith to him, `Lo, thou [art] a dead man, because of the woman whom thou hast taken -- and she married to a husband.'

20:4 And Abimelech hath not drawn near unto her, and he saith, `Lord, also a righteous nation dost thou slay?

20:5 hath not he himself said to me, She [is] my sister! and she, even she herself, said, He [is] my brother; in the integrity of my heart, and in the innocency of my hands, I have done this.'

20:6 And God saith unto him in the dream, `Yea, I -- I have known that in the integrity of thy heart thou hast done this, and I withhold thee, even I, from sinning against Me, therefore I have not suffered thee to come against her;

20:7 and now send back the man's wife, for he [is] inspired, and he doth pray for thee, and live thou; and if thou do not send back, know that dying thou dost die, thou, and all that thou hast.'

20:8 And Abimelech riseth early in the morning, and calleth for all his servants, and speaketh all these words in their ears; and the men fear exceedingly;

20:9 and Abimelech calleth for Abraham, and saith to him, `What hast thou done to us? and what have I sinned against thee, that thou hast brought upon me, and upon my kingdom, a great sin? works which are not done thou hast done with me.'

20:10 Abimelech also saith unto Abraham, `What hast thou seen that thou hast done this thing?'

20:11 And Abraham saith, `Because I said, `Surely the fear of God is not in this place, and they have slain me for the sake of my wife;

20:12 and also, truly she is my sister, daughter of my father, only not daughter of my mother, and she becometh my wife;

20:13 and it cometh to pass, when God hath caused me to wander from my father's house, that I say to her, This [is] thy kindness which thou dost with me: at every place whither we come, say of me, He [is] my brother.'

20:14 And Abimelech taketh sheep and oxen, and servants and handmaids, and giveth to Abraham, and sendeth back to him Sarah his wife;

20:15 and Abimelech saith, `Lo, my land [is] before thee, where it is good in thine eyes, dwell;'

20:16 and to Sarah he hath said, `Lo, I have given a thousand silverlings to thy brother; lo, it is to thee a covering of eyes, to all who are with thee;' and by all this she is reasoned with.

20:17 And Abraham prayeth unto God, and God healeth Abimelech and his wife, and his handmaids, and they bear:

20:18 for Jehovah restraining had restrained every womb of the house of Abimelech, because of

Sarah, Abraham's wife.

21:1 And Jehovah hath looked after Sarah as He hath said, and Jehovah doth to Sarah as He hath spoken;

21:2 and Sarah conceiveth, and beareth a son to Abraham, to his old age, at the appointed time that God hath spoken of with him;

21:3 and Abraham calleth the name of his son who is born to him, whom Sarah hath born to him -- Isaac;

21:4 and Abraham circumciseth Isaac his son, [being] a son of eight days, as God hath commanded him.

21:5 And Abraham [is] a son of a hundred years in Isaac his son being born to him,

21:6 and Sarah saith, `God hath made laughter for me; every one who is hearing laugheth for me.'

21:7 She saith also, `Who hath said to Abraham, Sarah hath suckled sons, that I have born a son for his old age?'

21:8 And the lad groweth, and is weaned, and Abraham maketh a great banquet in the day of Isaac's being weaned;

21:9 and Sarah seeth the son of Hagar the Egyptian, whom she hath borne to Abraham, mocking,

21:10 and she saith to Abraham, `Cast out this handmaid and her son; for the son of this handmaid hath no possession with my son -- with Isaac.'

21:11 And the thing is very wrong in the eyes of Abraham, for his son's sake;

21:12 and God saith unto Abraham, `Let it not be wrong in thine eyes because of the youth, and because of thy handmaid: all that Sarah saith unto thee -- hearken to her voice, for in Isaac is a seed called to thee.

21:13 As to the son of the handmaid also, for a nation I set him, because he [is] thy seed.'

21:14 And Abraham riseth early in the morning, and taketh bread, and a bottle of water, and giveth unto Hagar (placing [it] on her shoulder), also the lad, and sendeth her out; and she goeth on, and goeth astray in the wilderness of Beer-Sheba;

21:15 and the water is consumed from the bottle, and she placeth the lad under one of the shrubs.

21:16 And she goeth and sitteth by herself over-against, afar off, about a bow-shot, for she said, `Let me not look on the death of the lad;' and she sitteth over-against, and lifteth up her voice, and weepeth.

21:17 And God heareth the voice of the youth; and the messenger of God calleth unto Hagar from the heavens, and saith to her, `What to thee, Hagar? fear not; for God hath hearkened unto the voice of the youth where he [is];

21:18 rise, lift up the youth, and lay hold on him with thy hand, for for a great nation I set him.'

21:19 And God openeth her eyes, and she seeth a well of water, and she goeth and filleth the bottle [with] water, and causeth the youth to drink;
21:20 and God is with the youth, and he groweth, and dwelleth in the wilderness, and is an archer;
21:21 and he dwelleth in the wilderness of Paran, and his mother taketh for him a wife from the land of Egypt.
21:22 And it cometh to pass at that time that Abimelech speaketh -- Phichol also, head of his host -- unto Abraham, saying, `God [is] with thee in all that thou art doing;
21:23 and now, swear to me by God here: thou dost not lie to me, or to my continuator, or to my successor; according to the kindness which I have done with thee thou dost with me, and with the land in which thou hast sojourned.'
21:24 And Abraham saith, `I -- I do swear.'
21:25 And Abraham reasoned with Abimelech concerning the matter of a well of water which Abimelech's servants have taken violently away,
21:26 and Abimelech saith, `I have not known who hath done this thing, and even thou didst not declare to me, and I also, I have not heard save to-day.'
21:27 And Abraham taketh sheep and oxen, and giveth to Abimelech, and they make, both of them, a covenant;
21:28 and Abraham setteth seven Lambs of the flock by themselves.
21:29 And Abimelech saith unto Abraham, `What [are] they -- these seven lambs which thou hast set by themselves?'
21:30 And he saith, `For -- the seven lambs thou dost accept from my hand, so that it becometh a witness for me that I have digged this well;'
21:31 therefore hath he called that place `Beer-Sheba,' for there have both of them sworn.
21:32 And they make a covenant in Beer-Sheba, and Abimelech riseth -- Phichol also, head of his host -- and they turn back unto the land of the Philistines;
21:33 and [Abraham] planteth a tamarask in Beer-Sheba, and preacheth there in the name of Jehovah, God age-during;
21:34 and Abraham sojourneth in the land of the Philistines many days.
22:1 And it cometh to pass after these things that God hath tried Abraham, and saith unto him, `Abraham;' and he saith, `Here [am] I.'
22:2 And He saith, `Take, I pray thee, thy son, thine only one, whom thou hast loved, even Isaac, and go for thyself unto the land of Moriah, and cause him to ascend there for a burnt-offering on one of the mountains of which I speak unto thee.'
22:3 And Abraham riseth early in the morning, and saddleth his ass, and taketh two of his young

men with him, and Isaac his son, and he cleaveth the wood of the burnt-offering, and riseth and goeth unto the place of which God hath spoken to him.
22:4 On the third day -- Abraham lifteth up his eyes, and seeth the place from afar;
22:5 and Abraham saith unto his young men, `Remain by yourselves here with the ass, and I and the youth go yonder and worship, and turn back unto you.'
22:6 And Abraham taketh the wood of the burnt-offering, and placeth on Isaac his son, and he taketh in his hand the fire, and the knife; and they go on both of them together.
22:7 And Isaac speaketh unto Abraham his father, and saith, `My father,' and he saith, `Here [am] I, my son.' And he saith, `Lo, the fire and the wood, and where the lamb for a burnt-offering?'
22:8 and Abraham saith, `God doth provide for Himself the lamb for a burnt-offering, my son;' and they go on both of them together.
22:9 And they come in unto the place of which God hath spoken to him, and there Abraham buildeth the altar, and arrangeth the wood, and bindeth Isaac his son, and placeth him upon the altar above the wood;
22:10 and Abraham putteth forth his hand, and taketh the knife -- to slaughter his son.
22:11 And the messenger of Jehovah calleth unto him from the heavens, and saith, `Abraham, Abraham;' and he saith, `Here [am] I;'
22:12 and He saith, `Put not forth thine hand unto the youth, nor do anything to him, for now I have known that thou art fearing God, and hast not withheld thy son, thine only one, from Me.'
22:13 And Abraham lifteth up his eyes, and looketh, and lo, a ram behind, seized in a thicket by its horns; and Abraham goeth, and taketh the ram, and causeth it to ascend for a burnt-offering instead of his son;
22:14 and Abraham calleth the name of that place `Jehovah-Jireh,' because it is said this day in the mount, `Jehovah doth provide.'
22:15 And the messenger of Jehovah calleth unto Abraham a second time from the heavens,
22:16 and saith, `By Myself I have sworn -- the affirmation of Jehovah -- that because thou hast done this thing, and hast not withheld thy son, thine only one --
22:17 that blessing I bless thee, and multiplying I multiply thy seed as stars of the heavens, and as sand which [is] on the sea-shore; and thy seed doth possess the gate of his enemies;
22:18 and blessed themselves in thy seed have all nations of the earth, because that thou hast hearkened to My voice.'
22:19 And Abraham turneth back unto his young men, and they rise and go together unto Beer-Sheba; and Abraham dwelleth in Beer-Sheba.
22:20 And it cometh to pass after these things that it is declared to Abraham, saying, `Lo, Milcah

hath borne, even she, sons to Nahor thy brother:
22:21 Huz his first-born, and Buz his brother; and Kemuel father of Aram,
22:22 and Chesed, and Hazo, and Pildash, and Jidlaph, and Bethuel;
22:23 and Bethuel hath begotten Rebekah;' these eight hath Milcah borne to Nahor, Abraham's brother;
22:24 and his concubine, whose name [is] Reumah, she also hath borne Tebah, and Gaham, and Tahash, and Maachah.
23:1 And the life of Sarah is a hundred and twenty and seven years -- years of the life of Sarah;
23:2 and Sarah dieth in Kirjath-Arba, which [is] Hebron, in the land of Caanan, and Abraham goeth in to mourn for Sarah, and to bewail her.
23:3 And Abraham riseth up from the presence of his dead, and speaketh unto the sons of Heth, saying,
23:4 `A sojourner and a settler I [am] with you; give to me a possession of a burying-place with you, and I bury my dead from before me.'
23:5 And the sons of Heth answer Abraham, saying to him,
23:6 `Hear us, my lord; a prince of God [art] thou in our midst; in the choice of our burying-places bury thy dead: none of us his burying-place doth withhold from thee, from burying thy dead.'
23:7 And Abraham riseth and boweth himself to the people of the land, to the sons of Heth,
23:8 and he speaketh with them, saying, `If it is your desire to bury my dead from before me, hear me, and meet for me with Ephron, son of Zoar;
23:9 and he giveth to me the cave of Machpelah, which he hath, which [is] in the extremity of his field; for full money doth he give it to me, in your midst, for a possession of a burying-place.'
23:10 And Ephron is sitting in the midst of the sons of Heth, and Ephron the Hittite answereth Abraham in the ears of the sons of Heth, of all those entering the gate of his city, saying,
23:11 `Nay, my lord, hear me: the field I have given to thee, and the cave that [is] in it, to thee I have given it; before the eyes of the sons of my people I have given it to thee -- bury thy dead.'
23:12 And Abraham boweth himself before the people of the land,
23:13 and speaketh unto Ephron in the ears of the people of the land, saying, `Only -- if thou wouldst hear me -- I have given the money of the field -- accept from me, and I bury my dead there.'
23:14 And Ephron answereth Abraham, saying to him,
23:15 `My lord, hear me: the land -- four hundred shekels of silver; between me and thee, what [is] it? -- thy dead bury.'
23:16 And Abraham hearkeneth unto Ephron, and Abraham weigheth to Ephron the silver which he

hath spoken of in the ears of the sons of Heth, four hundred silver shekels, passing with the merchant.
23:17 And established are the field of Ephron, which [is] in Machpelah, which [is] before Mamre, the field and the cave which [is] in it, and all the trees which [are] in the field, which [are] in all its border round about,
23:18 to Abraham by purchase, before the eyes of the sons of Heth, among all entering the gate of his city.
23:19 And after this hath Abraham buried Sarah his wife at the cave of the field of Machpelah before Mamre (which [is] Hebron), in the land of Canaan;
23:20 and established are the field, and the cave which [is] in it, to Abraham for a possession of a burying-place, from the sons of Heth.
24:1 And Abraham [is] old, he hath entered into days, and Jehovah hath blessed Abraham in all [things];
24:2 and Abraham saith unto his servant, the eldest of his house, who is ruling over all that he hath, `Put, I pray thee, thy hand under my thigh,
24:3 and I cause thee to swear by Jehovah, God of the heavens, and God of the earth, that thou dost not take a wife for my son from the daughters of the Canaanite, in the midst of whom I am dwelling;
24:4 but unto my land and unto my kindred dost thou go, and hast taken a wife for my son, for Isaac.'
24:5 And the servant saith unto him, `It may be the woman is not willing to come after me unto this land; do I at all cause thy son to turn back unto the land from whence thou camest out?'
24:6 And Abraham saith unto him, `Take heed to thyself, lest thou cause my son to turn back thither;
24:7 Jehovah, God of the heavens, who hath taken me from the house of my father, and from the land of my birth, and who hath spoken to me, and who hath sworn to me, saying, To thy seed I give this land, He doth send His messenger before thee, and thou hast taken a wife for my son from thence;
24:8 and if the woman be not willing to come after thee, then thou hast been acquitted from this mine oath: only my son thou dost not cause to turn back thither.'
24:9 And the servant putteth his hand under the thigh of Abraham his lord, and sweareth to him concerning this matter.
24:10 And the servant taketh ten camels of the camels of his lord and goeth, also of all the goods of his lord in his hand, and he riseth, and goeth unto Aram-Naharaim, unto the city of Nahor;

24:11 and he causeth the camels to kneel at the outside of the city, at the well of water, at even-time, at the time of the coming out of the women who draw water.
24:12 And he saith, `Jehovah, God of my lord Abraham, cause to meet, I pray Thee, before me this day -- (and do kindness with my lord Abraham;
24:13 lo, I am standing by the fountain of water, and daughters of the men of the city are coming out to draw water;
24:14 and it hath been, the young person unto whom I say, Incline, I pray thee, thy pitcher, and I drink, and she hath said, Drink, and I water also thy camels) -- her Thou hast decided for Thy servant, for Isaac; and by it I know that Thou hast done kindness with my lord.'
24:15 And it cometh to pass, before he hath finished speaking, that lo, Rebekah (who was born to Bethuel, son of Milcah, wife of Nahor, brother of Abraham) is coming out, and her pitcher on her shoulder,
24:16 and the young person [is] of very good appearance, a virgin, and a man hath not known her; and she goeth down to the fountain, and filleth her pitcher, and cometh up.
24:17 And the servant runneth to meet her, and saith, `Let me swallow, I pray thee, a little water from thy pitcher;'
24:18 and she saith, `Drink, my lord;' and she hasteth, and letteth down her pitcher upon her hand, and giveth him drink.
24:19 And she finisheth giving him drink, and saith, `Also for thy camels I draw till they have finished drinking;'
24:20 and she hasteth, and emptieth her pitcher into the drinking-trough, and runneth again unto the well to draw, and draweth for all his camels.
24:21 And the man, wondering at her, remaineth silent, to know whether Jehovah hath made his way prosperous or not.
24:22 And it cometh to pass when the camels have finished drinking, that the man taketh a golden ring (whose weight [is] a bekah), and two bracelets for her hands (whose weight [is] ten [bekahs] of gold),
24:23 and saith, `Whose daughter [art] thou? declare to me, I pray thee, is the house of thy father a place for us to lodge in?'
24:24 And she saith unto him, `I [am] daughter of Bethuel, son of Milcah, whom she hath borne to Nahor.'
24:25 She saith also unto him, `Both straw and provender [are] abundant with us, also a place to lodge in.'
24:26 And the man boweth, and doth obeisance to Jehovah,

24:27 and saith, `Blessed [is] Jehovah, God of my lord Abraham, who hath not left off His kindness and His truth with my lord; -- I [being] in the way, Jehovah hath led me to the house of my lord's brethren.'
24:28 And the young person runneth, and declareth to the house of her mother according to these words.
24:29 And Rebekah hath a brother, and his name [is] Laban, and Laban runneth unto the man who [is] without, unto the fountain;
24:30 yea, it cometh to pass, when he seeth the ring, and the bracelets on the hands of his sister, and when he heareth the words of Rebekah his sister, saying, `Thus hath the man spoken unto me,' that he cometh in unto the man, and lo, he is standing by the camels by the fountain.
24:31 And he saith, `Come in, O blessed one of Jehovah, why standest thou without, and I -- I have prepared the house and place for the camels!'
24:32 And he bringeth in the man into the house, and looseth the camels, and giveth straw and provender for the camels, and water to wash his feet, and the feet of the men who [are] with him:
24:33 and setteth before him to eat; but he saith, `I do not eat till I have spoken my word;' and he saith, `Speak.'
24:34 And he saith, `I [am] Abraham's servant;
24:35 and Jehovah hath blessed my lord exceedingly, and he is great; and He giveth to him flock, and herd, and silver, and gold, and men-servants, and maid-servants, and camels, and asses;
24:36 and Sarah, my lord's wife, beareth a son to my lord, after she hath been aged, and he giveth to him all that he hath.
24:37 `And my lord causeth me to swear, saying, Thou dost not take a wife to my son from the daughters of the Canaanite, in whose land I am dwelling.
24:38 If not -- unto the house of my father thou dost go, and unto my family, and thou hast taken a wife for my son.
24:39 `And I say unto my lord, It may be the woman doth not come after me;
24:40 and he saith unto me, Jehovah, before whom I have walked habitually, doth send His messenger with thee, and hath prospered thy way, and thou hast taken a wife for my son from my family, and from the house of my father;
24:41 then art thou acquitted from my oath, when thou comest unto my family, and if they give not [one] to thee; then thou hast been acquitted from my oath.
24:42 `And I come to-day unto the fountain, and I say, Jehovah, God of my lord Abraham, if Thou art, I pray Thee, making prosperous my way in which I am going --
24:43 (lo, I am standing by the fountain of water), then the virgin who is coming out to draw, and I

have said unto her, Let me drink, I pray thee, a little water from thy pitcher,
24:44 and she hath said unto me, Both drink thou, and also for thy camels I draw -- she is the woman whom Jehovah hath decided for my lord's son.
24:45 `Before I finish speaking unto my heart, then lo, Rebekah is coming out, and her pitcher on her shoulder, and she goeth down to the fountain, and draweth; and I say unto her, Let me drink, I pray thee,
24:46 and she hasteth and letteth down her pitcher from off her and saith, Drink, and thy camels also I water; and I drink, and the camels also she hath watered.
24:47 `And I ask her, and say, Whose daughter [art] thou? and she saith, Daughter of Bethuel, son of Nahor, whom Milcah hath borne to him, and I put the ring on her nose, and the bracelets on her hands,
24:48 and I bow, and do obeisance before Jehovah, and I bless Jehovah, God of my lord Abraham, who hath led me in the true way to receive the daughter of my lord's brother for his son.
24:49 `And now, if ye are dealing kindly and truly with my lord, declare to me; and if not, declare to me; and I turn unto the right or unto the left.'
24:50 And Laban answereth -- Bethuel also -- and they say, `The thing hath gone out from Jehovah; we are not able to speak unto thee bad or good;
24:51 lo, Rebekah [is] before thee, take and go, and she is a wife to thy lord's son, as Jehovah hath spoken.'
24:52 And it cometh to pass, when the servant of Abraham hath heard their words, that he boweth himself towards the earth before Jehovah;
24:53 and the servant taketh out vessels of silver, and vessels of gold, and garments, and giveth to Rebekah; precious things also he hath given to her brother and to her mother.
24:54 And they eat and drink, he and the men who [are] with him, and lodge all night; and they rise in the morning, and he saith, `Send me to my lord;'
24:55 and her brother saith -- her mother also -- `Let the young person abide with us a week or ten days, afterwards doth she go.'
24:56 And he saith unto them, `Do not delay me, seeing Jehovah hath prospered my way; send me away, and I go to my lord;'
24:57 and they say, `Let us call for the young person, and ask at her mouth;'
24:58 and they call for Rebekah, and say unto her, `Dost thou go with this man?' and she saith, `I go.'
24:59 And they send away Rebekah their sister, and her nurse, and Abraham's servant, and his men;

24:60 and they bless Rebekah, and say to her, `Thou [art] our sister; become thou thousands of
myriads, and thy seed doth possess the gate of those hating it.'
24:61 And Rebekah and her young women arise, and ride on the camels, and go after the man;
and the servant taketh Rebekah and goeth.
24:62 And Isaac hath come in from the entrance of the Well of the Living One, my Beholder; and
he is dwelling in the land of the south,
24:63 and Isaac goeth out to meditate in the field, at the turning of the evening, and he lifteth up his
eyes, and looketh, and lo, camels are coming.
24:64 And Rebekah lifteth up her eyes, and seeth Isaac, and alighteth from off the camel;
24:65 and she saith unto the servant, `Who [is] this man who is walking in the field to meet us?'
and the servant saith, `It [is] my lord;' and she taketh the veil, and covereth herself.
24:66 And the servant recounteth to Isaac all the things that he hath done,
24:67 and Isaac bringeth her in unto the tent of Sarah his mother, and he taketh Rebekah, and she
becometh his wife, and he loveth her, and Isaac is comforted after [the death of] his mother.
25:1 And Abraham addeth and taketh a wife, and her name [is] Keturah;
25:2 and she beareth to him Zimran, and Jokshan, and Medan, and Midian, and Ishbak, and
Shuah.
25:3 And Jokshan hath begotten Sheba and Dedan; and the sons of Dedan were Asshurim, and
Letushim, and Leummim;
25:4 and the sons of Midian [are] Ephah, and Epher, and Hanoch, and Abidah, and Eldaah: all
these [are] sons of Keturah.
25:5 And Abraham giveth all that he hath to Isaac;
25:6 and to the sons of the concubines whom Abraham hath, Abraham hath given gifts, and
sendeth them away from Isaac his son (in his being yet alive) eastward, unto the east country.
25:7 And these [are] the days of the years of the life of Abraham, which he lived, a hundred and
seventy and five years;
25:8 and Abraham expireth, and dieth in a good old age, aged and satisfied, and is gathered unto
his people.
25:9 And Isaac and Ishmael his sons bury him at the cave of Machpelah, at the field of Ephron, son
of Zoar the Hittite, which [is] before Mamre --
25:10 the field which Abraham bought from the sons of Heth -- there hath Abraham been buried,
and Sarah his wife.
25:11 And it cometh to pass after the death of Abraham, that God blesseth Isaac his son; and Isaac
dwelleth by the Well of the Living One, my Beholder.

25:12 And these [are] births of Ishmael, Abraham's son, whom Hagar the Egyptian, Sarah's handmaid, hath borne to Abraham;
25:13 and these [are] the names of the sons of Ishmael, by their names, according to their births: first-born of Ishmael, Nebajoth; and Kedar, and Adbeel, and Mibsam,
25:14 and Mishma, and Dumah, and Massa,
25:15 Hadar, and Tema, Jetur, Naphish, and Kedemah:
25:16 these are sons of Ishmael, and these their names, by their villages, and by their towers; twelve princes according to their peoples.
25:17 And these [are] the years of the life of Ishmael, a hundred and thirty and seven years; and he expireth, and dieth, and is gathered unto his people;
25:18 and they tabernacle from Havilah unto Shur, which [is] before Egypt, in [thy] going towards Asshur; in the presence of all his brethren hath he fallen.
25:19 And these [are] births of Isaac, Abraham's son: Abraham hath begotten Isaac;
25:20 and Isaac is a son of forty years in his taking Rebekah, daughter of Bethuel the Aramaean, from Padan-Aram, sister of Laban the Aramaean, to him for a wife.
25:21 And Isaac maketh entreaty to Jehovah before his wife, for she [is] barren: and Jehovah is entreated of him, and Rebekah his wife conceiveth,
25:22 and the children struggle together within her, and she saith, `If [it is] right -- why [am] I thus?' and she goeth to seek Jehovah.
25:23 And Jehovah saith to her, `Two nations [are] in thy womb, and two peoples from thy bowels are parted; and the [one] people than the [other] people is stronger; and the elder doth serve the younger.'
25:24 And her days to bear are fulfilled, and lo, twins [are] in her womb;
25:25 and the first cometh out all red as a hairy robe, and they call his name Esau;
25:26 and afterwards hath his brother come out, and his hand is taking hold on Esau's heel, and one calleth his name Jacob; and Isaac [is] a son of sixty years in her bearing them.
25:27 And the youths grew, and Esau is a man acquainted [with] hunting, a man of the field; and Jacob [is] a plain man, inhabiting tents;
25:28 and Isaac loveth Esau, for [his] hunting [is] in his mouth; and Rebekah is loving Jacob.
25:29 And Jacob boileth pottage, and Esau cometh in from the field, and he [is] weary;
25:30 and Esau saith unto Jacob, `Let me eat, I pray thee, some of this red red thing, for I [am] weary;' therefore hath [one] called his name Edom [Red];
25:31 and Jacob saith, `Sell to-day thy birthright to me.'
25:32 And Esau saith, `Lo, I am going to die, and what is this to me -- birthright?'

25:33 and Jacob saith, `Swear to me to-day:' and he sweareth to him, and selleth his birthright to Jacob;
25:34 and Jacob hath given to Esau bread and pottage of lentiles, and he eateth, and drinketh, and riseth, and goeth; and Esau despiseth the birthright.
26:1 And there is a famine in the land, besides the first famine which was in the days of Abraham, and Isaac goeth unto Abimelech king of the Philistines, to Gerar.
26:2 And Jehovah appeareth unto him, and saith, `Go not down towards Egypt, tabernacle in the land concerning which I speak unto thee,
26:3 sojourn in this land, and I am with thee, and bless thee, for to thee and to thy seed I give all these lands, and I have established the oath which I have sworn to Abraham thy father;
26:4 and I have multiplied thy seed as stars of the heavens, and I have given to thy seed all these lands; and blessed themselves in thy seed have all nations of the earth;
26:5 because that Abraham hath hearkened to My voice, and keepeth My charge, My commands, My statutes, and My laws.'
26:6 And Isaac dwelleth in Gerar;
26:7 and men of the place ask him of his wife, and he saith, `She [is] my sister:' for he hath been afraid to say, `My wife -- lest the men of the place kill me for Rebekah, for she [is] of good appearance.'
26:8 And it cometh to pass, when the days have been prolonged to him there, that Abimelech king of the Philistines looketh through the window, and seeth, and lo, Isaac is playing with Rebekah his wife.
26:9 And Abimelech calleth for Isaac, and saith, `Lo, she [is] surely thy wife; and how hast thou said, She [is] my sister?' and Isaac saith unto him, `Because I said, Lest I die for her.'
26:10 And Abimelech saith, `What [is] this thou hast done to us? as a little thing one of the people had lain with thy wife, and thou hadst brought upon us guilt;'
26:11 and Abimelech commandeth all the people, saying, `He who cometh against this man or against his wife, dying doth die.'
26:12 And Isaac soweth in that land, and findeth in that year a hundredfold, and Jehovah blesseth him;
26:13 and the man is great, and goeth on, going on and becoming great, till that he hath been very great,
26:14 and he hath possession of a flock, and possession of a herd, and an abundant service; and the Philistines envy him,
26:15 and all the wells which his father's servants digged in the days of Abraham his father, the

Philistines have stopped them, and fill them with dust.
26:16 And Abimelech saith unto Isaac, `Go from us; for thou hast become much mightier than we;'
26:17 and Isaac goeth from thence, and encampeth in the valley of Gerar, and dwelleth there;
26:18 and Isaac turneth back, and diggeth the wells of water which they digged in the days of Abraham his father, which the Philistines do stop after the death of Abraham, and he calleth to them names according to the names which his father called them.
26:19 And Isaac's servants dig in the valley, and find there a well of living water,
26:20 and shepherds of Gerar strive with shepherds of Isaac, saying, `The water [is] ours;' and he calleth the name of the well `Strife,' because they have striven habitually with him;
26:21 and they dig another well, and they strive also for it, and he calleth its name `Hatred.'
26:22 And he removeth from thence, and diggeth another well, and they have not striven for it, and he calleth its name Enlargements, and saith, `For -- now hath Jehovah given enlargement to us, and we have been fruitful in the land.'
26:23 And he goeth up from thence [to] Beer-Sheba,
26:24 and Jehovah appeareth unto him during that night, and saith, `I [am] the God of Abraham thy father, fear not, for I [am] with thee, and have blessed thee, and have multiplied thy seed, because of Abraham My servant;'
26:25 and he buildeth there an altar, and preacheth in the name of Jehovah, and stretcheth out there his tent, and there Isaac's servants dig a well.
26:26 And Abimelech hath gone unto him from Gerar, and Ahuzzath his friend, and Phichol head of his host;
26:27 and Isaac saith unto them, `Wherefore have ye come unto me, and ye have hated me, and ye send me away from you?'
26:28 And they say, `We have certainly seen that Jehovah hath been with thee, and we say, `Let there be, we pray thee, an oath between us, between us and thee, and let us make a covenant with thee;
26:29 do not evil with us, as we have not touched thee, and as we have only done good with thee, and send thee away in peace; thou [art] now blessed of Jehovah.'
26:30 And he maketh for them a banquet, and they eat and drink,
26:31 and rise early in the morning, and swear one to another, and Isaac sendeth them away, and they go from him in peace.
26:32 And it cometh to pass during that day that Isaac's servants come and declare to him concerning the circumstances of the well which they have digged, and say to him, `We have found water;'

26:33 and he calleth it Shebah, [oath,] therefore the name of the city [is] Beer-Sheba, [well of the oath,] unto this day.
26:34 And Esau is a son of forty years, and he taketh a wife, Judith, daughter of Beeri the Hittite, and Bashemath, daughter of Elon the Hittite,
26:35 and they are a bitterness of spirit to Isaac and to Rebekah.
27:1 And it cometh to pass that Isaac [is] aged, and his eyes are too dim for seeing, and he calleth Esau his elder son, and saith unto him, `My son;' and he saith unto him, `Here [am] I.'
27:2 And he saith, `Lo, I pray thee, I have become aged, I have not known the day of my death;
27:3 and now, take up, I pray thee, thy instruments, thy quiver, and thy bow, and go out to the field, and hunt for me provision,
27:4 and make for me tasteful things, [such] as I have loved, and bring in to me, and I do eat, so that my soul doth bless thee before I die.'
27:5 And Rebekah is hearkening while Isaac is speaking unto Esau his son; and Esau goeth to the field to hunt provision -- to bring in;
27:6 and Rebekah hath spoken unto Jacob her son, saying, `Lo, I have heard thy father speaking unto Esau thy brother, saying,
27:7 Bring for me provision, and make for me tasteful things, and I do eat, and bless thee before Jehovah before my death.
27:8 `And now, my son, hearken to my voice, to that which I am commanding thee:
27:9 Go, I pray thee, unto the flock, and take for me from thence two good kids of the goats, and I make them tasteful things for thy father, [such] as he hath loved;
27:10 and thou hast taken in to thy father, and he hath eaten, so that his soul doth bless thee before his death.
27:11 And Jacob saith unto Rebekah his mother, `Lo, Esau my brother [is] a hairy man, and I a smooth man,
27:12 it may be my father doth feel me, and I have been in his eyes as a deceiver, and have brought upon me disesteem, and not a blessing;'
27:13 and his mother saith to him, `On me thy disesteem, my son; only hearken to my voice, and go, take for me.'
27:14 And he goeth, and taketh, and bringeth to his mother, and his mother maketh tasteful things, [such] as his father hath loved;
27:15 and Rebekah taketh the desirable garments of Esau her elder son, which [are] with her in the house, and doth put on Jacob her younger son;
27:16 and the skins of the kids of the goats she hath put on his hands, and on the smooth of his

neck,
27:17 and she giveth the tasteful things, and the bread which she hath made, into the hand of Jacob her son.
27:18 And he cometh in unto his father, and saith, `My father;' and he saith, `Here [am] I; who [art] thou, my son?'
27:19 And Jacob saith unto his father, `I [am] Esau thy first-born; I have done as thou hast spoken unto me; rise, I pray thee, sit, and eat of my provision, so that thy soul doth bless me.'
27:20 And Isaac saith unto his son, `What [is] this thou hast hasted to find, my son?' and he saith, `That which Jehovah thy God hath caused to come before me.'
27:21 And Isaac saith unto Jacob, `Come nigh, I pray thee, and I feel thee, my son, whether thou [art] he, my son Esau, or not.'
27:22 And Jacob cometh nigh unto Isaac his father, and he feeleth him, and saith, `The voice [is] the voice of Jacob, and the hands hands of Esau.'
27:23 And he hath not discerned him, for his hands have been hairy, as the hands of Esau his brother, and he blesseth him,
27:24 and saith, `Thou art he -- my son Esau?' and he saith, `I [am].'
27:25 And he saith, `Bring nigh to me, and I do eat of my son's provision, so that my soul doth bless thee;' and he bringeth nigh to him, and he eateth; and he bringeth to him wine, and he drinketh.
27:26 And Isaac his father saith to him, `Come nigh, I pray thee, and kiss me, my son;'
27:27 and he cometh nigh, and kisseth him, and he smelleth the fragrance of his garments, and blesseth him, and saith, `See, the fragrance of my son [is] as the fragrance of a field which Jehovah hath blessed;
27:28 and God doth give to thee of the dew of heaven, and of the fatness of the earth, and abundance of corn and wine;
27:29 peoples serve thee, and nations bow themselves to thee, be thou mighty over thy brethren, and the sons of thy mother bow themselves to thee; those who curse thee [are] cursed, and those who bless thee [are] blessed.'
27:30 And it cometh to pass, as Isaac hath finished blessing Jacob, and Jacob is only just going out from the presence of Isaac his father, that Esau his brother hath come in from his hunting;
27:31 and he also maketh tasteful things, and bringeth to his father, and saith to his father, `Let my father arise, and eat of his son's provision, so that thy soul doth bless me.'
27:32 And Isaac his father saith to him, `Who [art] thou?' and he saith, `I [am] thy son, thy first-born, Esau;'

27:33 and Isaac trembleth a very great trembling, and saith, `Who, now, [is] he who hath provided provision, and bringeth in to me, and I eat of all before thou comest in, and I bless him? -- yea, blessed is he.'

27:34 When Esau heareth the words of his father, then he crieth a very great and bitter cry, and saith to his father, `Bless me, me also, O my father;'

27:35 and he saith, `Thy brother hath come with subtilty, and taketh thy blessing.'

27:36 And he saith, `Is it because [one] called his name Jacob that he doth take me by the heel these two times? my birthright he hath taken; and lo, now, he hath taken my blessing;' he saith also, `Hast thou not kept back a blessing for me?'

27:37 And Isaac answereth and saith to Esau, `Lo, a mighty one have I set him over thee, and all his brethren have I given to him for servants, and [with] corn and wine have I sustained him; and for thee now, what shall I do, my son?'

27:38 And Esau saith unto his father, `One blessing hast thou my father? bless me, me also, O my father;' and Esau lifteth up his voice, and weepeth.

27:39 And Isaac his father answereth and saith unto him, `Lo, of the fatness of the earth is thy dwelling, and of the dew of the heavens from above;

27:40 and by thy sword dost thou live, and thy brother dost thou serve; and it hath come to pass when thou rulest, that thou hast broken his yoke from off thy neck.'

27:41 And Esau hateth Jacob, because of the blessing with which his father blessed him, and Esau saith in his heart, `The days of mourning [for] my father draw near, and I slay Jacob my brother.'

27:42 And the words of Esau her elder son are declared to Rebekah, and she sendeth and calleth for Jacob her younger son, and saith unto him, `Lo, Esau thy brother is comforting himself in regard to thee -- to slay thee;

27:43 and now, my son, hearken to my voice, and rise, flee for thyself unto Laban my brother, to Haran,

27:44 and thou hast dwelt with him some days, till thy brother's fury turn back,

27:45 till thy brother's anger turn back from thee, and he hath forgotten that which thou hast done to him, and I have sent and taken thee from thence; why am I bereaved even of you both the same day?'

27:46 And Rebekah saith unto Isaac, `I have been disgusted with my life because of the presence of the daughters of Heth; if Jacob take a wife of the daughters of Heth, like these -- from the daughters of the land -- why do I live?'

28:1 And Isaac calleth unto Jacob, and blesseth him, and commandeth him, and saith to him, `Thou dost not take a wife of the daughters of Caanan;

28:2 rise, go to Padan-Aram, to the house of Bethuel, thy mother's father, and take for thyself from
thence a wife, of the daughters of Laban, thy mother's brother;
28:3 and God Almighty doth bless thee, and make thee fruitful, and multiply thee, and thou hast
become an assembly of peoples;
28:4 and He doth give to thee the blessing of Abraham, to thee and to thy seed with thee, to cause
thee to possess the land of thy sojournings, which God gave to Abraham.'
28:5 And Isaac sendeth away Jacob, and he goeth to Padan-Aram, unto Laban, son of Bethuel the
Aramaean, brother of Rebekah, mother of Jacob and Esau.
28:6 And Esau seeth that Isaac hath blessed Jacob, and hath sent him to Padan-Aram to take to
himself from thence a wife -- in his blessing him that he layeth a charge upon him, saying, Thou
dost not take a wife from the daughters of Canaan --
28:7 that Jacob hearkeneth unto his father and unto his mother, and goeth to Padan-Aram --
28:8 and Esau seeth that the daughters of Canaan are evil in the eyes of Isaac his father,
28:9 and Esau goeth unto Ishmael, and taketh Mahalath, daughter of Ishmael, Abraham's son,
sister of Nebajoth, unto his wives, to himself, for a wife.
28:10 And Jacob goeth out from Beer-Sheba, and goeth toward Haran,
28:11 and he toucheth at a [certain] place, and lodgeth there, for the sun hath gone in, and he
taketh of the stones of the place, and maketh [them] his pillows, and lieth down in that place.
28:12 And he dreameth, and lo, a ladder set up on the earth, and its head is touching the heavens;
and lo, messengers of God are going up and coming down by it;
28:13 and lo, Jehovah is standing upon it, and He saith, `I [am] Jehovah, God of Abraham thy
father, and God of Isaac; the land on which thou art lying, to thee I give it, and to thy seed;
28:14 and thy seed hath been as the dust of the land, and thou hast broken forth westward, and
eastward, and northward, and southward, and all families of the ground have been blessed in thee
and in thy seed.
28:15 `And lo, I [am] with thee, and have kept thee whithersoever thou goest, and have caused
thee to turn back unto this ground; for I leave thee not till that I have surely done that which I have
spoken to thee.'
28:16 And Jacob awaketh out of his sleep, and saith, `Surely Jehovah is in this place, and I knew
not;'
28:17 and he feareth, and saith, `How fearful [is] this place; this is nothing but a house of God, and
this a gate of the heavens.'
28:18 And Jacob riseth early in the morning, and taketh the stone which he hath made his pillows,
and maketh it a standing pillar, and poureth oil upon its top,

28:19 and he calleth the name of that place Bethel, [house of God,] and yet, Luz [is] the name of the city at the first.
28:20 And Jacob voweth a vow, saying, `Seeing God is with me, and hath kept me in this way which I am going, and hath given to me bread to eat, and a garment to put on --
28:21 when I have turned back in peace unto the house of my father, and Jehovah hath become my God,
28:22 then this stone which I have made a standing pillar is a house of God, and all that Thou dost give to me -- tithing I tithe to Thee.'
29:1 And Jacob lifteth up his feet, and goeth towards the land of the sons of the east;
29:2 and he looketh, and lo, a well in the field, and lo, there three droves of a flock crouching by it, for from that well they water the droves, and the great stone [is] on the mouth of the well.
29:3 (When thither have all the droves been gathered, and they have rolled the stone from off the mouth of the well, and have watered the flock, then they have turned back the stone on the mouth of the well to its place.)
29:4 And Jacob saith to them, `My brethren, from whence [are] ye?' and they say, `We [are] from Haran.'
29:5 And he saith to them, `Have ye known Laban, son of Nahor?' and they say, `We have known.'
29:6 And he saith to them, `Hath he peace?' and they say, `Peace; and lo, Rachel his daughter is coming with the flock.'
29:7 And he saith, `Lo, the day [is] still great, [it is] not time for the cattle to be gathered; water ye the flock, and go, delight yourselves.'
29:8 And they say, `We are not able, till that all the droves be gathered together, and they have rolled away the stone from the mouth of the well, and we have watered the flock.'
29:9 He is yet speaking with them, and Rachel hath come with the flock which her father hath, for she [is] shepherdess;
29:10 and it cometh to pass when Jacob hath seen Rachel, daughter of Laban his mother's brother, and the flock of Laban his mother's brother, that Jacob cometh nigh and rolleth the stone from off the mouth of the well, and watereth the flock of Laban his mother's brother.
29:11 And Jacob kisseth Rachel, and lifteth up his voice, and weepeth,
29:12 and Jacob declareth to Rachel that he [is] her father's brother, and that he [is] Rebekah's son, and she runneth and declareth to her father.
29:13 And it cometh to pass, when Laban heareth the report of Jacob his sister's son, that he runneth to meet him, and embraceth him, and kisseth him, and bringeth him in unto his house; and he recounteth to Laban all these things,

29:14 and Laban saith to him, `Only my bone and my flesh [art] thou;' and he dwelleth with him a month of days.
29:15 And Laban saith to Jacob, `Is it because thou [art] my brother that thou hast served me for nought? declare to me what [is] thy hire.'
29:16 And Laban hath two daughters, the name of the elder [is] Leah, and the name of the younger Rachel,
29:17 and the eyes of Leah [are] tender, and Rachel hath been fair of form and fair of appearance.
29:18 And Jacob loveth Rachel, and saith, `I serve thee seven years for Rachel thy younger daughter:'
29:19 and Laban saith, `It is better for me to give her to thee than to give her to another man; dwell with me;'
29:20 and Jacob serveth for Rachel seven years; and they are in his eyes as some days, because of his loving her.
29:21 And Jacob saith unto Laban, `Give up my wife, for my days have been fulfilled, and I go in unto her;'
29:22 and Laban gathereth all the men of the place, and maketh a banquet.
29:23 And it cometh to pass in the evening, that he taketh Leah, his daughter, and bringeth her in unto him, and he goeth in unto her;
29:24 and Laban giveth to her Zilpah, his maid-servant, to Leah his daughter, a maid-servant.
29:25 And it cometh to pass in the morning, that lo, it [is] Leah; and he saith unto Laban, `What [is] this thou hast done to me? for Rachel have I not served with thee? and why hast thou deceived me?'
29:26 And Laban saith, `It is not done so in our place, to give the younger before the first-born;
29:27 fulfil the week of this one, and we give to thee also this one, for the service which thou dost serve with me yet seven other years.'
29:28 And Jacob doth so, and fulfilleth the week of this one, and he giveth to him Rachel his daughter, to him for a wife;
29:29 and Laban giveth to Rachel his daughter Bilhah his maid-servant, for a maid-servant to her.
29:30 And he goeth in also unto Rachel, and he also loveth Rachel more than Leah; and he serveth with him yet seven other years.
29:31 And Jehovah seeth that Leah [is] the hated one, and He openeth her womb, and Rachel [is] barren;
29:32 and Leah conceiveth, and beareth a son, and calleth his name Reuben, for she said, `Because Jehovah hath looked on mine affliction; because now doth my husband love me.'

29:33 And she conceiveth again, and beareth a son, and saith, `Because Jehovah hath heard that I [am] the hated one, He also giveth to me even this [one];' and she calleth his name Simeon.
29:34 And she conceiveth again, and beareth a son, and saith, `Now [is] the time, my husband is joined unto me, because I have born to him three sons,' therefore hath [one] called his name Levi.
29:35 And she conceiveth again, and beareth a son, and saith this time, `I praise Jehovah;' therefore hath she called his name Judah; and she ceaseth from bearing.
30:1 And Rachel seeth that she hath not borne to Jacob, and Rachel is envious of her sister, and saith unto Jacob, `Give me sons, and if there is none -- I die.'
30:2 And Jacob's anger burneth against Rachel, and he saith, `Am I in stead of God who hath withheld from thee the fruit of the womb?'
30:3 And she saith, `Lo, my handmaid Bilhah, go in unto her, and she doth bear on my knees, and I am built up, even I, from her;'
30:4 and she giveth to him Bilhah her maid-servant for a wife, and Jacob goeth in unto her;
30:5 and Bilhah conceiveth, and beareth to Jacob a son,
30:6 and Rachel saith, `God hath decided for me, and also hath hearkened to my voice, and giveth to me a son;' therefore hath she called his name Dan.
30:7 And Bilhah, Rachel's maid-servant, conceiveth again, and beareth a second son to Jacob,
30:8 and Rachel saith, `With wrestlings of God I have wrestled with my sister, yea, I have prevailed;' and she calleth his name Napthali.
30:9 And Leah seeth that she hath ceased from bearing, and she taketh Zilpah her maid-servant, and giveth her to Jacob for a wife;
30:10 and Zilpah, Leah's maid-servant, beareth to Jacob a son,
30:11 and Leah saith, `A troop is coming;' and she calleth his name Gad.
30:12 And Zilpah, Leah's maid-servant, beareth a second son to Jacob,
30:13 and Leah saith, `Because of my happiness, for daughters have pronounced me happy;' and she calleth his name Asher.
30:14 And Reuben goeth in the days of wheat-harvest, and findeth love-apples in the field, and bringeth them in unto Leah, his mother, and Rachel saith unto Leah, `Give to me, I pray thee, of the love-apples of thy son.'
30:15 And she saith to her, `Is thy taking my husband a little thing, that thou hast taken also the love-apples of my son?' and Rachel saith, `Therefore doth he lie with thee to-night, for thy son's love-apples.'
30:16 And Jacob cometh in from the field at evening; and Leah goeth to meet him, and saith, `Unto me dost thou come in, for hiring I have hired thee with my son's love-apples;' and he lieth with her

during that night.
30:17 And God hearkeneth unto Leah, and she conceiveth, and beareth to Jacob a son, a fifth,
30:18 and Leah saith, `God hath given my hire, because I have given my maid-servant to my husband;' and she calleth his name Issachar.
30:19 And conceive again doth Leah, and she beareth a sixth son to Jacob,
30:20 and Leah saith, `God hath endowed me -- a good dowry; this time doth my husband dwell with me, for I have borne to him six sons;' and she calleth his name Zebulun;
30:21 and afterwards hath she born a daughter, and calleth her name Dinah.
30:22 And God remembereth Rachel, and God hearkeneth unto her, and openeth her womb,
30:23 and she conceiveth and beareth a son, and saith, `God hath gathered up my reproach;'
30:24 and she calleth his name Joseph, saying, `Jehovah is adding to me another son.'
30:25 And it cometh to pass, when Rachel hath borne Joseph, that Jacob saith unto Laban, `Send me away, and I go unto my place, and to my land;
30:26 give up my wives and my children, for whom I have served thee, and I go; for thou -- thou hast known my service which I have served thee.'
30:27 And Laban saith unto him, `If, I pray thee, I have found grace in thine eyes -- I have observed diligently that Jehovah doth bless me for thy sake.'
30:28 He saith also, `Define thy hire to me, and I give.'
30:29 And he saith unto him, `Thou -- thou hast known that which I have served thee [in], and that which thy substance was with me;
30:30 for [it is] little which thou hast had at my appearance, and it breaketh forth into a multitude, and Jehovah blesseth thee at my coming; and now, when do I make, I also, for mine own house?'
30:31 And he saith, `What do I give to thee?' And Jacob saith, `Thou dost not give me anything; if thou do for me this thing, I turn back; I have delight; thy flock I watch;
30:32 I pass through all thy flock to-day to turn aside from thence every sheep speckled and spotted, and every brown sheep among the lambs, and speckled and spotted among the goats -- and it hath been my hire;
30:33 and my righteousness hath answered for me in the day to come, when it cometh in for my hire before thy face; -- every one which is not speckled and spotted among [my] goats, and brown among [my] lambs -- it is stolen with me.'
30:34 And Laban saith, `Lo, O that it were according to thy word;'
30:35 and he turneth aside during that day the ring-straked and the spotted he-goats, and all the speckled and the spotted she-goats, every one that [hath] white in it, and every brown one among the lambs, and he giveth into the hand of his sons,

30:36 and setteth a journey of three days between himself and Jacob; and Jacob is feeding the rest of the flock of Laban.
30:37 And Jacob taketh to himself a rod of fresh poplar, and of the hazel and chesnut, and doth peel in them white peelings, making bare the white that [is] on the rods,
30:38 and setteth up the rods which he hath peeled in the gutters in the watering troughs (when the flock cometh in to drink), over-against the flock, that they may conceive in their coming in to drink;
30:39 and the flocks conceive at the rods, and the flock beareth ring-straked, speckled, and spotted ones.
30:40 And the lambs hath Jacob parted, and he putteth the face of the flock towards the ring-straked, also all the brown in the flock of Laban, and he setteth his own droves by themselves, and hath not set them near Laban's flock.
30:41 And it hath come to pass whenever the strong ones of the flock conceive, that Jacob set the rods before the eyes of the flock in the gutters, to cause them to conceive by the rods,
30:42 and when the flock is feeble, he doth not set [them]; and the feeble ones have been Laban's, and the strong ones Jacob's.
30:43 And the man increaseth very exceedingly, and hath many flocks, and maid-servants, and men-servants, and camels, and asses.
31:1 And he heareth the words of Laban's sons, saying, `Jacob hath taken all that our father hath; yea, from that which our father hath, he hath made all this honour;'
31:2 and Jacob seeth the face of Laban, and lo, it is not with him as heretofore.
31:3 And Jehovah saith unto Jacob, `Turn back unto the land of thy fathers, and to thy kindred, and I am with thee.'
31:4 And Jacob sendeth and calleth for Rachel and for Leah to the field unto his flock;
31:5 and saith to them, `I am beholding your father's face -- that it is not towards me as heretofore, and the God of my father hath been with me,
31:6 and ye -- ye have known that with all my power I have served your father,
31:7 and your father hath played upon me, and hath changed my hire ten times; and God hath not suffered him to do evil with me.
31:8 `If he say thus: The speckled are thy hire, then bare all the flock speckled ones; and if he say thus: The ring-straked are thy hire, then bare all the flock ring-straked;
31:9 and God taketh away the substance of your father, and doth give to me.
31:10 `And it cometh to pass at the time of the flock conceiving, that I lift up mine eyes and see in a dream, and lo, the he-goats, which are going up on the flock, [are] ring-straked, speckled, and grisled;

31:11 and the messenger of God saith unto me in the dream, Jacob, and I say, Here [am] I.
31:12 `And He saith, Lift up, I pray thee, thine eyes, and see -- all the he-goats which are going up on the flock [are] ring-straked, speckled, and grisled, for I have seen all that Laban is doing to thee;
31:13 I [am] the God of Bethel where thou hast anointed a standing pillar, where thou hast vowed a vow to me; now, arise, go out from this land, and turn back unto the land of thy birth.'
31:14 And Rachel answereth -- Leah also -- and saith to him, `Have we yet a portion and inheritance in the house of our father?
31:15 have we not been reckoned strangers to him? for he hath sold us, and he also utterly consumeth our money;
31:16 for all the wealth which God hath taken away from our father, it [is] ours, and our children's; and now, all that God hath said unto thee -- do.'
31:17 And Jacob riseth, and lifteth up his sons and his wives on the camels,
31:18 and leadeth all his cattle, and all his substance which he hath acquired, the cattle of his getting, which he hath acquired in Padan-Aram, to go unto Isaac his father, to the land of Canaan.
31:19 And Laban hath gone to shear his flock, and Rachel stealeth the teraphim which her father hath;
31:20 and Jacob deceiveth the heart of Laban the Aramaean, because he hath not declared to him that he is fleeing;
31:21 and he fleeth, he and all that he hath, and riseth, and passeth over the River, and setteth his face [toward] the mount of Gilead.
31:22 And it is told to Laban on the third day that Jacob hath fled,
31:23 and he taketh his brethren with him, and pursueth after him a journey of seven days, and overtaketh him in the mount of Gilead.
31:24 And God cometh in unto Laban the Aramaean in a dream of the night, and saith to him, `Take heed to thyself lest thou speak with Jacob from good unto evil.'
31:25 And Laban overtaketh Jacob; and Jacob hath fixed his tent in the mount; and Laban with his brethren have fixed [theirs] in the mount of Gilead.
31:26 And Laban saith to Jacob, `What hast thou done that thou dost deceive my heart, and lead away my daughters as captives of the sword?
31:27 Why hast thou hidden thyself to flee, and deceivest me, and hast not declared to me, and I send thee away with joy and with songs, with tabret and with harp,
31:28 and hast not suffered me to kiss my sons and my daughters? -- now thou hast acted foolishly in doing [so];
31:29 my hand is to God to do evil with you, but the God of your father yesternight hath spoken

unto me, saying, Take heed to thyself from speaking with Jacob from good unto evil.
31:30 `And now, thou hast certainly gone, because thou hast been very desirous for the house of thy father; why hast thou stolen my gods?'
31:31 And Jacob answereth and saith to Laban, `Because I was afraid, for I said, Lest thou take violently away thy daughters from me;
31:32 with whomsoever thou findest thy gods -- he doth not live; before our brethren discern for thyself what [is] with me, and take to thyself:' and Jacob hath not known that Rachel hath stolen them.
31:33 And Laban goeth into the tent of Jacob, and into the tent of Leah, and into the tent of the two handmaidens, and hath not found; and he goeth out from the tent of Leah, and goeth into the tent of Rachel.
31:34 And Rachel hath taken the teraphim, and putteth them in the furniture of the camel, and sitteth upon them; and Laban feeleth all the tent, and hath not found;
31:35 and she saith unto her father, `Let it not be displeasing in the eyes of my lord that I am not able to rise at thy presence, for the way of women [is] on me;' and he searcheth, and hath not found the teraphim.
31:36 And it is displeasing to Jacob, and he striveth with Laban; and Jacob answereth and saith to Laban, `What [is] my transgression? what my sin, that thou hast burned after me?
31:37 for thou hast felt all my vessels: what hast thou found of all the vessels of thy house? set here before my brethren, and thy brethren, and they decide between us both.
31:38 `These twenty years I [am] with thee: thy ewes and thy she-goats have not miscarried, and the rams of thy flock I have not eaten;
31:39 the torn I have not brought in unto thee -- I, I repay it -- from my hand thou dost seek it; I have been deceived by day, and I have been deceived by night;
31:40 I have been [thus]: in the day consumed me hath drought, and frost by night, and wander doth my sleep from mine eyes.
31:41 `This [is] to me twenty years in thy house: I have served thee fourteen years for thy two daughters, and six years for thy flock; and thou changest my hire ten times;
31:42 unless the God of my father, the God of Abraham, and the Fear of Isaac, had been for me, surely now empty thou hadst sent me away; mine affliction and the labour of my hands hath God seen, and reproveth yesternight.'
31:43 And Laban answereth and saith unto Jacob, `The daughters [are] my daughters, and the sons my sons, and the flock my flock, and all that thou art seeing [is] mine; and to my daughters -- what do I to these to-day, or to their sons whom they have born?

31:44 and now, come, let us make a covenant, I and thou, and it hath been for a witness between me and thee.'
31:45 And Jacob taketh a stone, and lifteth it up [for] a standing pillar;
31:46 and Jacob saith to his brethren, `Gather stones,' and they take stones, and make a heap; and they eat there on the heap;
31:47 and Laban calleth it Jegar-Sahadutha; and Jacob hath called it Galeed.
31:48 And Laban saith, `This heap [is] witness between me and thee to-day;' therefore hath he called its name Galeed;
31:49 Mizpah also, for he said, `Jehovah doth watch between me and thee, for we are hidden one from another;
31:50 if thou afflict my daughters, or take wives beside my daughters -- there is no man with us -- see, God [is] witness between me and thee.'
31:51 And Laban saith to Jacob, `Lo, this heap, and lo, the standing pillar which I have cast between me and thee;
31:52 this heap [is] witness, and the standing pillar [is] witness, that I do not pass over this heap unto thee, and that thou dost not pass over this heap and this standing pillar unto me -- for evil;
31:53 the God of Abraham and the God of Nahor, doth judge between us -- the God of their father,' and Jacob sweareth by the Fear of his father Isaac.
31:54 And Jacob sacrificeth a sacrifice in the mount, and calleth to his brethren to eat bread, and they eat bread, and lodge in the mount;
31:55 and Laban riseth early in the morning, and kisseth his sons and his daughters, and blesseth them; and Laban goeth on, and turneth back to his place.
32:1 And Jacob hath gone on his way, and messengers of God come upon him;
32:2 and Jacob saith, when he hath seen them, `This [is] the camp of God;' and he calleth the name of that place `Two Camps.'
32:3 And Jacob sendeth messengers before him unto Esau his brother, towards the land of Seir, the field of Edom,
32:4 and commandeth them, saying, `Thus do ye say to my lord, to Esau: Thus said thy servant Jacob, With Laban I have sojourned, and I tarry until now;
32:5 and I have ox, and ass, flock, and man-servant, and maid-servant, and I send to declare to my lord, to find grace in his eyes.'
32:6 And the messengers turn back unto Jacob, saying, `We came in unto thy brother, unto Esau, and he also is coming to meet thee, and four hundred men with him;'
32:7 and Jacob feareth exceedingly, and is distressed, and he divideth the people who [are] with

him, and the flock, and the herd, and the camels, into two camps,
32:8 and saith, `If Esau come in unto the one camp, and have smitten it -- then the camp which is left hath been for an escape.'
32:9 And Jacob saith, `God of my father Abraham, and God of my father Isaac, Jehovah who saith unto me, Turn back to thy land, and to thy kindred, and I do good with thee:
32:10 I have been unworthy of all the kind acts, and of all the truth which Thou hast done with thy servant -- for, with my staff I passed over this Jordan, and now I have become two camps.
32:11 `Deliver me, I pray Thee, from the hand of my brother, from the hand of Esau: for I am fearing him, less he come and have smitten me -- mother beside sons;
32:12 and Thou -- Thou hast said, I certainly do good with thee, and have set thy seed as the sand of the sea, which is not numbered because of the multitude.'
32:13 And he lodgeth there during that night, and taketh from that which is coming into his hand, a present for Esau his brother:
32:14 she-goats two hundred, and he-goats twenty, ewes two hundred, and rams twenty,
32:15 suckling camels and their young ones thirty, cows forty, and bullocks ten, she-asses twenty, and foals ten;
32:16 and he giveth into the hand of his servants, every drove by itself, and saith unto his servants, `Pass over before me, and a space ye do put between drove and drove.'
32:17 And he commandeth the first, saying, `When Esau my brother meeteth thee, and hath asked thee, saying, Whose [art] thou? and whither goest thou? and whose [are] these before thee?
32:18 then thou hast said, Thy servant Jacob's: it [is] a present sent to my lord, to Esau; and lo, he also [is] behind us.'
32:19 And he commandeth also the second, also the third, also all who are going after the droves, saying, `According to this manner do ye speak unto Esau in your finding him,
32:20 and ye have said also, Lo, thy servant Jacob [is] behind us;' for he said, `I pacify his face with the present which is going before me, and afterwards I see his face; it may be he lifteth up my face;'
32:21 and the present passeth over before his face, and he hath lodged during that night in the camp.
32:22 And he riseth in that night, and taketh his two wives, and his two maid-servants, and his eleven children, and passeth over the passage of Jabbok;
32:23 and he taketh them, and causeth them to pass over the brook, and he causeth that which he hath to pass over.
32:24 And Jacob is left alone, and one wrestleth with him till the ascending of the dawn;

32:25 and he seeth that he is not able for him, and he cometh against the hollow of his thigh, and the hollow of Jacob's thigh is disjointed in his wrestling with him;
32:26 and he saith, `Send me away, for the dawn hath ascended:' and he saith, `I send thee not away, except thou hast blessed me.'
32:27 And he saith unto him, `What [is] thy name?' and he saith, `Jacob.'
32:28 And he saith, `Thy name is no more called Jacob, but Israel; for thou hast been a prince with God and with men, and dost prevail.'
32:29 And Jacob asketh, and saith, `Declare, I pray thee, thy name;' and he saith, `Why [is] this, thou askest for My name?' and He blesseth him there.
32:30 And Jacob calleth the name of the place Peniel: for `I have seen God face unto face, and my life is delivered;'
32:31 and the sun riseth on him when he hath passed over Penuel, and he is halting on his thigh;
32:32 therefore the sons of Israel do not eat the sinew which shrank, which [is] on the hollow of the thigh, unto this day, because He came against the hollow of Jacob's thigh, against the sinew which shrank.
33:1 And Jacob lifteth up his eyes, and looketh, and lo, Esau is coming, and with him four hundred men; and he divideth the children unto Leah, and unto Rachel, and unto the two maid-servants;
33:2 and he setteth the maid-servants and their children first, and Leah and her children behind, and Rachel and Joseph last.
33:3 And he himself passed over before them, and boweth himself to the earth seven times, until his drawing nigh unto his brother,
33:4 and Esau runneth to meet him, and embraceth him, and falleth on his neck, and kisseth him, and they weep;
33:5 and he lifteth up his eyes, and seeth the women and the children, and saith, `What [are] these to thee?' And he saith, `The children with whom God hath favoured thy servant.'
33:6 And the maid-servants draw nigh, they and their children, and bow themselves;
33:7 and Leah also draweth nigh, and her children, and they bow themselves; and afterwards Joseph hath drawn nigh with Rachel, and they bow themselves.
33:8 And he saith, `What to thee [is] all this camp which I have met?' and he saith, `To find grace in the eyes of my lord.'
33:9 And Esau saith, `I have abundance, my brother, let it be to thyself that which thou hast.'
33:10 And Jacob saith, `Nay, I pray thee, if, I pray thee, I have found grace in thine eyes, then thou hast received my present from my hand, because that I have seen thy face, as the seeing of the face of God, and thou art pleased with me;

33:11 receive, I pray thee, my blessing, which is brought to thee, because God hath favoured me, and because I have all [things];' and he presseth on him, and he receiveth,
33:12 and saith, `Let us journey and go on, and I go on before thee.'
33:13 And he saith unto him, `My lord knoweth that the children [are] tender, and the suckling flock and the herd [are] with me; when they have beaten them one day, then hath all the flock died.
33:14 Let my lord, I pray thee, pass over before his servant, and I -- I lead on gently, according to the foot of the work which [is] before me, and to the foot of the children, until that I come unto my lord, to Seir.'
33:15 And Esau saith, `Let me, I pray thee, place with thee some of the people who [are] with me;' and he said, `Why [is] this? I find grace in the eyes of my lord.'
33:16 And turn back on that day doth Esau on his way to Seir;
33:17 and Jacob hath journeyed to Succoth, and buildeth to himself a house, and for his cattle hath made booths, therefore hath he called the name of the place Succoth.
33:18 And Jacob cometh in to Shalem, a city of Shechem, which [is] in the land of Canaan, in his coming from Padan-Aram, and encampeth before the city,
33:19 and he buyeth the portion of the field where he hath stretched out his tent, from the hand of the sons of Hamor, father of Shechem, for a hundred kesitah;
33:20 and he setteth up there an altar, and proclaimeth at it God -- the God of Israel.
34:1 And Dinah, daughter of Leah, whom she hath borne to Jacob, goeth out to look on the daughters of the land,
34:2 and Shechem, son of Hamor the Hivite, a prince of the land, seeth her, and taketh her, and lieth with her, and humbleth her;
34:3 and his soul cleaveth to Dinah, daughter of Jacob, and he loveth the young person, and speaketh unto the heart of the young person.
34:4 And Shechem speaketh unto Hamor his father, saying, `Take for me this damsel for a wife.'
34:5 And Jacob hath heard that he hath defiled Dinah his daughter, and his sons were with his cattle in the field, and Jacob kept silent till their coming.
34:6 And Hamor, father of Shechem, goeth out unto Jacob to speak with him;
34:7 and the sons of Jacob came in from the field when they heard, and the men grieve themselves, and it [is] very displeasing to them, for folly he hath done against Israel, to lie with the daughter of Jacob -- and so it is not done.
34:8 And Hamor speaketh with them, saying, `Shechem, my son, his soul hath cleaved to your daughter; give her, I pray you, to him for a wife,
34:9 and join ye in marriage with us; your daughters ye give to us, and our daughters ye take to

yourselves,
34:10 and with us ye dwell, and the land is before you; dwell ye and trade [in] it, and have
possessions in it.'
34:11 And Shechem saith unto her father, and unto her brethren, `Let me find grace in your eyes,
and that which ye say unto me, I give;
34:12 multiply on me exceedingly dowry and gift, and I give as ye say unto me, and give to me the
young person for a wife.'
34:13 And the sons of Jacob answer Shechem and Hamor his father deceitfully, and they speak
(because he defiled Dinah their sister),
34:14 and say unto them, `We are not able to do this thing, to give our sister to one who hath a
foreskin: for it [is] a reproach to us.
34:15 `Only for this we consent to you; if ye be as we, to have every male of you circumcised,
34:16 then we have given our daughters to you, and your daughters we take to ourselves, and we
have dwelt with you, and have become one people;
34:17 and if ye hearken not unto us to be circumcised, then we have taken our daughter, and have
gone.'
34:18 And their words are good in the eyes of Hamor, and in the eyes of Shechem, Hamor's son;
34:19 and the young man delayed not to do the thing, for he had delight in Jacob's daughter, and
he is honourable above all the house of his father.
34:20 And Hamor cometh -- Shechem his son also -- unto the gate of their city, and they speak
unto the men of their city, saying,
34:21 `These men are peaceable with us; then let them dwell in the land, and trade [in] it; and the
land, lo, [is] wide before them; their daughters let us take to ourselves for wives, and our daughters
give to them.
34:22 `Only for this do the men consent to us, to dwell with us, to become one people, in every
male of us being circumcised, as they are circumcised;
34:23 their cattle, and their substance, and all their beasts -- are they not ours? only let us consent
to them, and they dwell with us.'
34:24 And unto Hamor, and unto Shechem his son, hearken do all those going out of the gate of
his city, and every male is circumcised, all those going out of the gate of his city.
34:25 And it cometh to pass, on the third day, in their being pained, that two of the sons of Jacob,
Simeon and Levi, Dinah's brethren, take each his sword, and come in against the city confidently,
and slay every male;
34:26 and Hamor, and Shechem his son, they have slain by the mouth of the sword, and they take

Dinah out of Shechem's house, and go out.
34:27 Jacob's sons have come in upon the wounded, and they spoil the city, because they had defiled their sister;
34:28 their flock and their herd, and their asses, and that which [is] in the city, and that which [is] in the field, have they taken;
34:29 and all their wealth, and all their infants, and their wives they have taken captive, and they spoil also all that [is] in the house.
34:30 And Jacob saith unto Simeon and unto Levi, `Ye have troubled me, by causing me to stink among the inhabitants of the land, among the Canaanite, and among the Perizzite: and I [am] few in number, and they have been gathered against me, and have smitten me, and I have been destroyed, I and my house.'
34:31 And they say, `As a harlot doth he make our sister?'
35:1 And God saith unto Jacob, `Rise, go up to Bethel, and dwell there, and make there an altar to God, who appeared unto thee in thy fleeing from the face of Esau thy brother.'
35:2 And Jacob saith unto his household, and unto all who [are] with him, `Turn aside the gods of the stranger which [are] in your midst, and cleanse yourselves, and change your garments;
35:3 and we rise, and go up to Bethel, and I make there an altar to God, who is answering me in the day of my distress, and is with me in the way that I have gone.'
35:4 And they give unto Jacob all the gods of the stranger that [are] in their hand, and the rings that [are] in their ears, and Jacob hideth them under the oak which [is] by Shechem;
35:5 and they journey, and the terror of God is on the cities which [are] round about them, and they have not pursued after the sons of Jacob.
35:6 And Jacob cometh in to Luz which [is] in the land of Canaan (it [is] Bethel), he and all the people who [are] with him,
35:7 and he buildeth there an altar, and proclaimeth at the place the God of Bethel: for there had God been revealed unto him, in his fleeing from the face of his brother.
35:8 And Deborah, Rebekah's nurse, dieth, and she is buried at the lower part of Bethel, under the oak, and he calleth its name `Oak of weeping.'
35:9 And God appeareth unto Jacob again, in his coming from Padan-Aram, and blesseth him;
35:10 and God saith to him, `Thy name [is] Jacob: thy name is no more called Jacob, but Israel is thy name;' and He calleth his name Israel.
35:11 And God saith to him, `I [am] God Almighty; be fruitful and multiply, a nation and an assembly of nations is from thee, and kings from thy loins go out;
35:12 and the land which I have given to Abraham and to Isaac -- to thee I give it, yea to thy seed

after thee I give the land.'
35:13 And God goeth up from him, in the place where He hath spoken with him.
35:14 And Jacob setteth up a standing pillar in the place where He hath spoken with him, a
standing pillar of stone, and he poureth on it an oblation, and he poureth on it oil;
35:15 and Jacob calleth the name of the place where God spake with him Bethel.
35:16 And they journey from Bethel, and there is yet a kibrath of land before entering Ephratha,
and Rachel beareth, and is sharply pained in her bearing;
35:17 and it cometh to pass, in her being sharply pained in her bearing, that the midwife saith to
her, `Fear not, for this also [is] a son for thee.'
35:18 And it cometh to pass in the going out of her soul (for she died), that she calleth his name
Ben-Oni; and his father called him Benjamin;
35:19 and Rachel dieth, and is buried in the way to Ephratha, which [is] Bethlehem,
35:20 and Jacob setteth up a standing pillar over her grave; which [is] the standing pillar of
Rachel's grave unto this day.
35:21 And Israel journeyeth, and stretcheth out his tent beyond the tower of Edar;
35:22 and it cometh to pass in Israel's dwelling in that land, that Reuben goeth, and lieth with
Bilhah his father's concubine; and Israel heareth.
35:23 And the sons of Jacob are twelve. Sons of Leah: Jacob's first-born Reuben, and Simeon,
and Levi, and Judah, and Issachar, and Zebulun.
35:24 Sons of Rachel: Joseph and Benjamin.
35:25 And sons of Bilhah, Rachel's maid-servant: Dan and Naphtali.
35:26 And sons of Zilpah, Leah's maid-servant: Gad and Asher. These [are] sons of Jacob, who
have been born to him in Padan-Aram.
35:27 And Jacob cometh unto Isaac his father, at Mamre, the city of Arba (which [is] Hebron),
where Abraham and Isaac have sojourned.
35:28 And the days of Isaac are a hundred and eighty years,
35:29 and Isaac expireth, and dieth, and is gathered unto his people, aged and satisfied with days;
and bury him do Esau and Jacob his sons.
36:1 And these [are] births of Esau, who [is] Edom.
36:2 Esau hath taken his wives from the daughters of Canaan: Adah daughter of Elon the Hittite,
and Aholibamah daughter of Anah, daughter of Zibeon the Hivite,
36:3 and Bashemath daughter of Ishmael, sister of Nebajoth.
36:4 And Adah beareth to Esau, Eliphaz; and Bashemath hath born Reuel;
36:5 and Aholibamah hath born Jeush, and Jaalam, and Korah. These [are] sons of Esau, who

were born to him in the land of Canaan.
36:6 And Esau taketh his wives, and his sons, and his daughters, and all the persons of his house, and his cattle, and all his beasts, and all his substance which he hath acquired in the land of Canaan, and goeth into the country from the face of Jacob his brother;
36:7 for their substance was more abundant than to dwell together, and the land of their sojournings was not able to bear them because of their cattle;
36:8 and Esau dwelleth in mount Seir: Esau is Edom.
36:9 And these [are] births of Esau, father of Edom, in mount Seir.
36:10 These [are] the names of the sons of Esau: Eliphaz son of Adah, wife of Esau; Reuel son of Bashemath, wife of Esau.
36:11 And the sons of Eliphaz are Teman, Omar, Zepho, and Gatam, and Kenaz;
36:12 and Timnath hath been concubine to Eliphaz son of Esau, and she beareth to Eliphaz, Amalek; these [are] sons of Adah wife of Esau.
36:13 And these [are] sons of Reuel: Nahath and Zerah, Shammah and Mizzah; these were sons of Bashemath wife of Esau.
36:14 And these have been the sons of Aholibamah daughter of Anah, daughter of Zibeon, wife of Esau; and she beareth to Esau, Jeush and Jaalam and Korah.
36:15 These [are] chiefs of the sons of Esau: sons of Eliphaz, first-born of Esau: chief Teman, chief Omar, chief Zepho, chief Kenaz,
36:16 chief Korah, chief Gatam, chief Amalek; these [are] chiefs of Eliphaz, in the land of Edom; these [are] sons of Adah.
36:17 And these [are] sons of Reuel son of Esau: chief Nahath, chief Zerah, chief Shammah, chief Mizzah; these [are] chiefs of Reuel, in the land of Edom; these [are] sons of Bashemath wife of Esau.
36:18 And these [are] sons of Aholibamah wife of Esau: chief Jeush, chief Jaalam, chief Korah; these [are] chiefs of Aholibamah daughter of Anah, wife of Esau.
36:19 These [are] sons of Esau (who [is] Edom), and these their chiefs.
36:20 These [are] sons of Seir the Horite, the inhabitants of the land: Lotan, and Shobal, and Zibeon, and Anah,
36:21 and Dishon, and Ezer, and Dishan; these [are] chiefs of the Horites, sons of Seir, in the land of Edom.
36:22 And the sons of Lotan are Hori and Heman; and a sister of Lotan [is] Timna.
36:23 And these [are] sons of Shobal: Alvan and Manahath, and Ebal, Shepho and Onam.
36:24 And these [are] sons of Zibeon, both Ajah and Anah: it [is] Anah that hath found the Imim in

the wilderness, in his feeding the asses of Zibeon his father.
36:25 And these [are] sons of Anah: Dishon, and Aholibamah daughter of Anah.
36:26 And these [are] sons of Dishon: Hemdan, and Eshban, and Ithran, and Cheran.
36:27 These [are] sons of Ezer: Bilhan, and Zaavan, and Akan.
36:28 These [are] sons of Dishan: Uz and Aran.
36:29 These [are] chiefs of the Horite: chief Lotan, chief Shobal, chief Zibeon, chief Anah,
36:30 chief Dishon, chief Ezer, chief Dishan: these [are] chiefs of the Horite in reference to their chiefs in the land of Seir.
36:31 And these [are] the kings who have reigned in the land of Edom before the reigning of a king over the sons of Israel.
36:32 And Bela son of Beor reigneth in Edom, and the name of his city [is] Dinhabah;
36:33 and Bela dieth, and reign in his stead doth Jobab son of Zerah from Bozrah;
36:34 and Jobab dieth, and reign in his stead doth Husham from the land of the Temanite.
36:35 And Husham dieth, and reign in his stead doth Hadad son of Bedad (who smiteth Midian in the field of Moab), and the name of his city [is] Avith;
36:36 and Hadad dieth, and reign in his stead doth Samlah of Masrekah;
36:37 and Samlah dieth, and reign in his stead doth Saul from Rehoboth of the River;
36:38 and Saul dieth, and reign in his stead doth Baal-hanan son of Achbor;
36:39 and Baal-hanan son of Achbor dieth, and reign in his stead doth Hadar, and the name of his city [is] Pau; and his wife's name [is] Mehetabel daughter of Matred, daughter of Me-zahab.
36:40 And these [are] the names of the chiefs of Esau, according to their families, according to their places, by their names: chief Timnah, chief Alvah, chief Jetheth,
36:41 chief Aholibamah, chief Elah, chief Pinon,
36:42 chief Kenaz, chief Teman, chief Mibzar,
36:43 chief Magdiel, chief Iram: these [are] chiefs of Edom, in reference to their dwellings, in the land of their possession; he [is] Esau father of Edom.
37:1 And Jacob dwelleth in the land of his father's sojournings -- in the land of Canaan.
37:2 These [are] births of Jacob: Joseph, a son of seventeen years, hath been enjoying himself with his brethren among the flock, (and he [is] a youth,) with the sons of Bilhah, and with the sons of Zilpah, his father's wives, and Joseph bringeth in an account of their evil unto their father.
37:3 And Israel hath loved Joseph more than any of his sons, for he [is] a son of his old age, and hath made for him a long coat;
37:4 and his brethren see that their father hath loved him more than any of his brethren, and they hate him, and have not been able to speak [to] him peaceably.

37:5 And Joseph dreameth a dream, and declareth to his brethren, and they add still more to hate him.
37:6 And he saith unto them, `Hear ye, I pray you, this dream which I have dreamed:
37:7 that, lo, we are binding bundles in the midst of the field, and lo, my bundle hath arisen, and hath also stood up, and lo, your bundles are round about, and bow themselves to my bundle.'
37:8 And his brethren say to him, `Dost thou certainly reign over us? dost thou certainly rule over us?' and they add still more to hate him, for his dreams, and for his words.
37:9 And he dreameth yet another dream, and recounteth it to his brethren, and saith, `Lo, I have dreamed a dream again, and lo, the sun and the moon, and eleven stars, are bowing themselves to me.'
37:10 And he recounteth unto his father, and unto his brethren; and his father pusheth against him, and saith to him, `What [is] this dream which thou hast dreamt? do we certainly come -- I, and thy mother, and thy brethren -- to bow ourselves to thee, to the earth?'
37:11 and his brethren are zealous against him, and his father hath watched the matter.
37:12 And his brethren go to feed the flock of their father in Shechem,
37:13 and Israel saith unto Joseph, `Are not thy brethren feeding in Shechem? come, and I send thee unto them;' and he saith to him, `Here [am] I;'
37:14 and he saith to him, `Go, I pray thee, see the peace of thy brethren, and the peace of the flock, and bring me back word;' and he sendeth him from the valley of Hebron, and he cometh to Shechem.
37:15 And a man findeth him, and lo, he is wandering in the field, and the man asketh him, saying, `What seekest thou?'
37:16 and he saith, `My brethren I am seeking, declare to me, I pray thee, where they are feeding?'
37:17 And the man saith, `They have journeyed from this, for I have heard some saying, Let us go to Dothan,' and Joseph goeth after his brethren, and findeth them in Dothan.
37:18 And they see him from afar, even before he draweth near unto them, and they conspire against him to put him to death.
37:19 And they say one unto another, `Lo, this man of the dreams cometh;
37:20 and now, come, and we slay him, and cast him into one of the pits, and have said, An evil beast hath devoured him; and we see what his dreams are.'
37:21 And Reuben heareth, and delivereth him out of their hand, and saith, `Let us not smite the life;'
37:22 and Reuben saith unto them, `Shed no blood; cast him into this pit which [is] in the wilderness, and put not forth a hand upon him,' -- in order to deliver him out of their hand, to bring

him back unto his father.
37:23 And it cometh to pass, when Joseph hath come unto his brethren, that they strip Joseph of
his coat, the long coat which [is] upon him,
37:24 and take him and cast him into the pit, and the pit [is] empty, there is no water in it.
37:25 And they sit down to eat bread, and they lift up their eyes, and look, and lo, a company of
Ishmaelites coming from Gilead, and their camels bearing spices, and balm, and myrrh, going to
take [them] down to Egypt.
37:26 And Judah saith unto his brethren, `What gain when we slay our brother, and have
concealed his blood?
37:27 Come, and we sell him to the Ishmaelites, and our hands are not on him, for he [is] our
brother -- our flesh;' and his brethren hearken.
37:28 And Midianite merchantmen pass by and they draw out and bring up Joseph out of the pit,
and sell Joseph to the Ishmaelites for twenty silverlings, and they bring Joseph into Egypt.
37:29 And Reuben returneth unto the pit, and lo, Joseph is not in the pit, and he rendeth his
garments,
37:30 and he returneth unto his brethren, and saith, `The lad is not, and I -- whither am I going?'
37:31 And they take the coat of Joseph, and slaughter a kid of the goats, and dip the coat in the
blood,
37:32 and send the long coat, and they bring [it] in unto their father, and say, `This have we found;
discern, we pray thee, whether it [is] thy son's coat or not?'
37:33 And he discerneth it, and saith, `My son's coat! an evil beast hath devoured him; torn -- torn
is Joseph!'
37:34 And Jacob rendeth his raiment, and putteth sackcloth on his loins, and becometh a mourner
for his son many days,
37:35 and all his sons and all his daughters rise to comfort him, and he refuseth to comfort himself,
and saith, `For -- I go down mourning unto my son, to Sheol,' and his father weepeth for him.
37:36 And the Medanites have sold him unto Egypt, to Potiphar, a eunuch of Pharaoh, head of the
executioners.
38:1 And it cometh to pass, at that time, that Judah goeth down from his brethren, and turneth
aside unto a man, an Adullamite, whose name [is] Hirah;
38:2 and Judah seeth there the daughter of a man, a Canaanite, whose name [is] Shuah, and
taketh her, and goeth in unto her.
38:3 And she conceiveth, and beareth a son, and he calleth his name Er;
38:4 and she conceiveth again, and beareth a son, and calleth his name Onan;

38:5 and she addeth again, and beareth a son, and calleth his name Shelah; and he was in Chezib in her bearing him.
38:6 And Judah taketh a wife for Er, his first-born, and her name [is] Tamar;
38:7 and Er, Judah's first-born, is evil in the eyes of Jehovah, and Jehovah doth put him to death.
38:8 And Judah saith to Onan, `Go in unto the wife of thy brother, and marry her, and raise up seed to thy brother;'
38:9 and Onan knoweth that the seed is not [reckoned] his; and it hath come to pass, if he hath gone in unto his brother's wife, that he hath destroyed [it] to the earth, so as not to give seed to his brother;
38:10 and that which he hath done is evil in the eyes of Jehovah, and He putteth him also to death.
38:11 And Judah saith to Tamar his daughter-in-law, `Abide a widow at thy father's house, till Shelah my son groweth up;' for he said, `Lest he die -- even he -- like his brethren;' and Tamar goeth and dwelleth at her father's house.
38:12 And the days are multiplied, and the daughter of Shuah, Judah's wife, dieth; and Judah is comforted, and goeth up unto his sheep-shearers, he and Hirah his friend the Adullamite, to Timnath.
38:13 And it is declared to Tamar, saying, `Lo, thy husband's father is going up to Timnath to shear his flock;'
38:14 and she turneth aside the garments of her widowhood from off her, and covereth herself with a vail, and wrappeth herself up, and sitteth in the opening of Enayim, which [is] by the way to Timnath, for she hath seen that Shelah hath grown up, and she hath not been given to him for a wife.
38:15 And Judah seeth her, and reckoneth her for a harlot, for she hath covered her face,
38:16 and he turneth aside unto her by the way, and saith, `Come, I pray thee, let me come in unto thee,' (for he hath not known that she [is] his daughter-in-law); and she saith, `What dost thou give to me, that thou mayest come in unto me?'
38:17 and he saith, `I -- I send a kid of the goats from the flock.' And she saith, `Dost thou give a pledge till thou send [it]?'
38:18 and he saith, `What [is] the pledge that I give to thee?' and she saith, `Thy seal, and thy ribbon, and thy staff which [is] in thy hand;' and he giveth to her, and goeth in unto her, and she conceiveth to him;
38:19 and she riseth, and goeth, and turneth aside her vail from off her, and putteth on the garments of her widowhood.
38:20 And Judah sendeth the kid of the goats by the hand of his friend the Adullamite, to receive

the pledge from the hand of the woman, and he hath not found her.
38:21 And he asketh the men of her place, saying, `Where [is] the separated one -- she in Enayim,
by the way?' and they say, `There hath not been in this [place] a separated one.'
38:22 And he turneth back unto Judah, and saith, `I have not found her; and the men of the place
also have said, There hath not been in this [place] a separated one,'
38:23 and Judah saith, `Let her take to herself, lest we become despised; lo, I sent this kid, and
thou hast not found her.'
38:24 And it cometh to pass about three months [after], that it is declared to Judah, saying, `Tamar
thy daughter-in-law hath committed fornication; and also, lo, she hath conceived by fornication:'
and Judah saith, `Bring her out -- and she is burnt.'
38:25 She is brought out, and she hath sent unto her husband's father, saying, `To a man whose
these [are], I [am] pregnant;' and she saith, `Discern, I pray thee, whose [are] these -- the seal, and
the ribbons, and the staff.'
38:26 And Judah discerneth and saith, `She hath been more righteous than I, because that I did
not give her to Shelah my son;' and he hath not added to know her again.
38:27 And it cometh to pass in the time of her bearing, that lo, twins [are] in her womb;
38:28 and it cometh to pass in her bearing, that [one] giveth out a hand, and the midwife taketh and
bindeth on his hand a scarlet thread, saying, `This hath come out first.'
38:29 And it cometh to pass as he draweth back his hand, that lo, his brother hath come out, and
she saith, `What! thou hast broken forth -- on thee [is] the breach;' and he calleth his name Pharez;
38:30 and afterwards hath his brother come out, on whose hand [is] the scarlet thread, and he
calleth his name Zarah.
39:1 And Joseph hath been brought down to Egypt, and Potiphar, a eunuch of Pharaoh, head of
the executioners, an Egyptian man, buyeth him out of the hands of the Ishmaelites who have
brought him thither.
39:2 And Jehovah is with Joseph, and he is a prosperous man, and he is in the house of his lord
the Egyptian,
39:3 and his lord seeth that Jehovah is with him, and all that he is doing Jehovah is causing to
prosper in his hand,
39:4 and Joseph findeth grace in his eyes and serveth him, and he appointeth him over his house,
and all that he hath he hath given into his hand.
39:5 And it cometh to pass from the time that he hath appointed him over his house, and over all
that he hath, that Jehovah blesseth the house of the Egyptian for Joseph's sake, and the blessing
of Jehovah is on all that he hath, in the house, and in the field;

39:6 and he leaveth all that he hath in the hand of Joseph, and he hath not known anything that he hath, except the bread which he is eating. And Joseph is of a fair form, and of a fair appearance.
39:7 And it cometh to pass after these things, that his lord's wife lifteth up her eyes unto Joseph, and saith, `Lie with me;'
39:8 and he refuseth, and saith unto his lord's wife, `Lo, my lord hath not known what [is] with me in the house, and all that he hath he hath given into my hand;
39:9 none is greater in this house than I, and he hath not withheld from me anything, except thee, because thou [art] his wife; and how shall I do this great evil? -- then have I sinned against God.'
39:10 And it cometh to pass at her speaking unto Joseph day [by] day, that he hath not hearkened unto her, to lie near her, to be with her;
39:11 and it cometh to pass about this day, that he goeth into the house to do his work, and there is none of the men of the house there in the house,
39:12 and she catcheth him by his garment, saying, `Lie with me;' and he leaveth his garment in her hand, and fleeth, and goeth without.
39:13 And it cometh to pass when she seeth that he hath left his garment in her hand, and fleeth without,
39:14 that she calleth for the men of her house, and speaketh to them, saying, `See, he hath brought in to us a man, a Hebrew, to play with us; he hath come in unto me, to lie with me, and I call with a loud voice,
39:15 and it cometh to pass, when he heareth that I have lifted up my voice and call, that he leaveth his garment near me, and fleeth, and goeth without.'
39:16 And she placeth his garment near her, until the coming in of his lord unto his house.
39:17 And she speaketh unto him according to these words, saying, `The Hebrew servant whom thou hast brought unto us, hath come in unto me to play with me;
39:18 and it cometh to pass, when I lift my voice and call, that he leaveth his garment near me, and fleeth without.'
39:19 And it cometh to pass when his lord heareth the words of his wife, which she hath spoken unto him, saying, `According to these things hath thy servant done to me,' that his anger burneth;
39:20 and Joseph's lord taketh him, and putteth him unto the round-house, a place where the king's prisoners [are] bound; and he is there in the round-house.
39:21 And Jehovah is with Joseph, and stretcheth out kindness unto him, and putteth his grace in the eyes of the chief of the round-house;
39:22 and the chief of the round-house giveth into the hand of Joseph all the prisoners who [are] in the round-house, and of all that they are doing there, he hath been doer;

39:23 the chief of the round-house seeth not anything under his hand, because Jehovah [is] with him, and that which he is doing Jehovah is causing to prosper.
40:1 And it cometh to pass, after these things -- the butler of the king of Egypt and the baker have sinned against their lord, against the king of Egypt;
40:2 and Pharaoh is wroth against his two eunuchs, against the chief of the butlers, and against the chief of the bakers,
40:3 and giveth them in charge in the house of the chief of the executioners, unto the round-house, the place where Joseph [is] a prisoner,
40:4 and the chief of the executioners chargeth Joseph with them, and he serveth them; and they are days in charge.
40:5 And they dream a dream both of them, each his dream in one night, each according to the interpretation of his dream, the butler and the baker whom the king of Egypt hath, who [are] prisoners in the round-house.
40:6 And Joseph cometh in unto them in the morning, and seeth them, and lo, they [are] morose;
40:7 and he asketh Pharaoh's eunuchs who [are] with him in charge in the house of his lord, saying, `Wherefore [are] your faces sad to-day?'
40:8 And they say unto him, `A dream we have dreamed, and there is no interpreter of it;' and Joseph saith unto them, `Are not interpretations with God? recount, I pray you, to me.'
40:9 And the chief of the butlers recounteth his dream to Joseph, and saith to him, `In my dream, then lo, a vine [is] before me!
40:10 and in the vine [are] three branches, and it [is] as it were flourishing; gone up hath its blossom, its clusters have ripened grapes;
40:11 and Pharaoh's cup [is] in my hand, and I take the grapes and press them into the cup of Pharaoh, and I give the cup into the hand of Pharaoh.'
40:12 And Joseph saith to him, `This [is] its interpretation: the three branches are three days;
40:13 yet, within three days doth Pharaoh lift up thy head, and hath put thee back on thy station, and thou hast given the cup of Pharaoh into his hand, according to the former custom when thou wast his butler.
40:14 `Surely if thou hast remembered me with thee, when it is well with thee, and hast done (I pray thee) kindness with me, and hast made mention of me unto Pharaoh, then hast thou brought me out from this house,
40:15 for I was really stolen from the land of the Hebrews; and here also have I done nothing that they have put me in the pit.'
40:16 And the chief of the bakers seeth that he hath interpreted good, and he saith unto Joseph, `I

also [am] in a dream, and lo, three baskets of white bread [are] on my head,
40:17 and in the uppermost basket [are] of all [kinds] of Pharaoh's food, work of a baker; and the birds are eating them out of the basket, from off my head.'
40:18 And Joseph answereth and saith, `This [is] its interpretation: the three baskets are three days;
40:19 yet, within three days doth Pharaoh lift up thy head from off thee, and hath hanged thee on a tree, and the birds have eaten thy flesh from off thee.'
40:20 And it cometh to pass, on the third day, Pharaoh's birthday, that he maketh a banquet to all his servants, and lifteth up the head of the chief of the butlers, and the head of the chief of the bakers among his servants,
40:21 and he putteth back the chief of the butlers to his butlership, and he giveth the cup into the hand of Pharaoh;
40:22 and the chief of the bakers he hath hanged, as Joseph hath interpreted to them;
40:23 and the chief of the butlers hath not remembered Joseph, but forgetteth him.
41:1 And it cometh to pass, at the end of two years of days that Pharaoh is dreaming, and lo, he is standing by the River,
41:2 and lo, from the River coming up are seven kine, of fair appearance, and fat [in] flesh, and they feed among the reeds;
41:3 and lo, seven other kine are coming up after them out of the River, of bad appearance, and lean [in] flesh, and they stand near the kine on the edge of the River,
41:4 and the kine of bad appearance and lean [in] flesh eat up the seven kine of fair appearance, and fat -- and Pharaoh awaketh.
41:5 And he sleepeth, and dreameth a second time, and lo, seven ears are coming up on one stalk, fat and good,
41:6 and lo, seven ears, thin, and blasted with an east wind, are springing up after them;
41:7 and the thin ears swallow the seven fat and full ears -- and Pharaoh awaketh, and lo, a dream.
41:8 And it cometh to pass in the morning, that his spirit is moved, and he sendeth and calleth all the scribes of Egypt, and all its wise men, and Pharaoh recounteth to them his dream, and there is no interpreter of them to Pharaoh.
41:9 And the chief of the butlers speaketh with Pharaoh, saying, `My sin I mention this day:
41:10 Pharaoh hath been wroth against his servants, and giveth me into charge in the house of the chief of the executioners, me and the chief of the bakers;
41:11 and we dream a dream in one night, I and he, each according to the interpretation of his dream we have dreamed.

41:12 And there [is] with us a youth, a Hebrew, servant to the chief of the executioners, and we recount to him, and he interpreteth to us our dreams, [to] each according to his dream hath he interpreted,
41:13 and it cometh to pass, as he hath interpreted to us so it hath been, me he put back on my station, and him he hanged.'
41:14 And Pharaoh sendeth and calleth Joseph, and they cause him to run out of the pit, and he shaveth, and changeth his garments, and cometh in unto Pharaoh.
41:15 And Pharaoh saith unto Joseph, `A dream I have dreamed, and there is no interpreter of it, and I -- I have heard concerning thee, saying, Thou understandest a dream to interpret it,'
41:16 and Joseph answereth Pharaoh, saying, `Without me -- God doth answer Pharaoh with peace.'
41:17 And Pharaoh speaketh unto Joseph: `In my dream, lo, I am standing by the edge of the River,
41:18 and lo, out of the River coming up are seven kine, fat [in] flesh, and of fair form, and they feed among the reeds;
41:19 and lo, seven other kine are coming up after them, thin, and of very bad form, and lean [in] flesh; I have not seen like these in all the land of Egypt for badness.
41:20 `And the lean and the bad kine eat up the first seven fat kine,
41:21 and they come in unto their midst, and it hath not been known that they have come in unto their midst, and their appearance [is] bad as at the commencement; and I awake.
41:22 `And I see in my dream, and lo, seven ears are coming up on one stalk, full and good;
41:23 and lo, seven ears, withered, thin, blasted with an east wind, are springing up after them;
41:24 and the thin ears swallow the seven good ears; and I tell unto the scribes, and there is none declaring to me.'
41:25 And Joseph saith unto Pharaoh, `The dream of Pharaoh is one: that which God is doing he hath declared to Pharaoh;
41:26 the seven good kine are seven years, and the seven good ears are seven years, the dream is one;
41:27 and the seven thin and bad kine which are coming up after them are seven years, and the seven empty ears, blasted with an east wind, are seven years of famine;
41:28 this [is] the thing which I have spoken unto Pharaoh: That which God is doing, he hath shewn Pharaoh.
41:29 `Lo, seven years are coming of great abundance in all the land of Egypt,
41:30 and seven years of famine have arisen after them, and all the plenty is forgotten in the land

of Egypt, and the famine hath finished the land,
41:31 and the plenty is not known in the land because of that famine afterwards, for it [is] very
grievous.
41:32 `And because of the repeating of the dream unto Pharaoh twice, surely the thing is
established by God, and God is hastening to do it.
41:33 `And now, let Pharaoh provide a man, intelligent and wise, and set him over the land of
Egypt;
41:34 let Pharaoh make and appoint overseers over the land, and receive a fifth of the land of
Egypt in the seven years of plenty,
41:35 and they gather all the food of these good years that are coming, and heap up corn under
the hand of Pharaoh -- food in the cities; and they have kept [it],
41:36 and the food hath been for a store for the land, for the seven years of famine which are in the
land of Egypt; and the land is cut off by the famine.'
41:37 And the thing is good in the eyes of Pharaoh, and in the eyes of all his servants,
41:38 and Pharaoh saith unto his servants, `Do we find like this, a man in whom the spirit of God
[is]?'
41:39 and Pharaoh saith unto Joseph, `After God's causing thee to know all this, there is none
intelligent and wise as thou;
41:40 thou -- thou art over my house, and at thy mouth do all my people kiss; only in the throne I
am greater than thou.'
41:41 And Pharaoh saith unto Joseph, `See, I have put thee over all the land of Egypt.'
41:42 And Pharaoh turneth aside his seal-ring from off his hand, and putteth it on the hand of
Joseph, and clotheth him [with] garments of fine linen, and placeth a chain of gold on his neck,
41:43 and causeth him to ride in the second chariot which he hath, and they proclaim before him,
`Bow the knee!' and -- to put him over all the land of Egypt.
41:44 And Pharaoh saith unto Joseph, `I [am] Pharaoh, and without thee a man doth not lift up his
hand and his foot in all the land of Egypt;'
41:45 and Pharaoh calleth Joseph's name Zaphnath-Paaneah, and he giveth to him Asenath
daughter of Poti-Pherah, priest of On, for a wife, and Joseph goeth out over the land of Egypt.
41:46 And Joseph [is] a son of thirty years in his standing before Pharaoh king of Egypt, and
Joseph goeth out from the presence of Pharaoh, and passeth over through all the land of Egypt;
41:47 and the land maketh in the seven years of plenty by handfuls.
41:48 And he gathereth all the food of the seven years which have been in the land of Egypt, and
putteth food in the cities; the food of the field which [is] round about [each] city hath he put in its

midst;
41:49 and Joseph gathereth corn as sand of the sea, multiplying exceedingly, until that he hath
ceased to number, for there is no number.
41:50 And to Joseph were born two sons before the year of famine cometh, whom Asenath
daughter of Poti-Pherah, priest of On, hath borne to him,
41:51 and Joseph calleth the name of the first-born Manasseh: `for, God hath made me to forget all
my labour, and all the house of my father;'
41:52 and the name of the second he hath called Ephraim: `for, God hath caused me to be fruitful
in the land of mine affliction.'
41:53 And the seven years of plenty are completed which have been in the land of Egypt,
41:54 and the seven years of famine begin to come, as Joseph said, and famine is in all the lands,
but in all the land of Egypt hath been bread;
41:55 and all the land of Egypt is famished, and the people crieth unto Pharaoh for bread, and
Pharaoh saith to all the Egyptians, `Go unto Joseph; that which he saith to you -- do.'
41:56 And the famine has been over all the face of the land, and Joseph openeth all [places] which
have [corn] in them, and selleth to the Egyptians; and the famine is severe in the land of Egypt,
41:57 and all the earth hath come to Egypt, to buy, unto Joseph, for the famine was severe in all
the earth.
42:1 And Jacob seeth that there is corn in Egypt, and Jacob saith to his sons, `Why do you look at
each other?'
42:2 he saith also, `Lo, I have heard that there is corn in Egypt, go down thither, and buy for us
from thence, and we live and do not die;'
42:3 and the ten brethren of Joseph go down to buy corn in Egypt,
42:4 and Benjamin, Joseph's brother, Jacob hath not sent with his brethren, for he said, `Lest
mischief meet him.'
42:5 And the sons of Israel come to buy in the midst of those coming, for the famine hath been in
the land of Canaan,
42:6 and Joseph is the ruler over the land, he who is selling to all the people of the land, and
Joseph's brethren come and bow themselves to him -- face to the earth.
42:7 And Joseph seeth his brethren, and discerneth them, and maketh himself strange unto them,
and speaketh with them sharp things, and saith unto them, `From whence have ye come?' and
they say, `From the land of Canaan -- to buy food.'
42:8 And Joseph discerneth his brethren, but they have not discerned him,
42:9 and Joseph remembereth the dreams which he dreamed of them, and saith unto them, `Ye

[are] spies; to see the nakedness of the land ye have come.'
42:10 And they say unto him, `No, my lord, but thy servants have come to buy food;
42:11 we [are] all of us sons of one man, we [are] right men; thy servants have not been spies;'
42:12 and he saith unto them, `No, but the nakedness of the land ye have come to see;'
42:13 and they say, `Thy servants [are] twelve brethren; we [are] sons of one man in the land of
Canaan, and lo, the young one [is] with our father to-day, and the one is not.'
42:14 And Joseph saith unto them, `This [is] that which I have spoken unto you, saying, Ye [are]
spies,
42:15 by this ye are proved: Pharaoh liveth! if ye go out from this -- except by your young brother
coming hither;
42:16 send one of you, and let him bring your brother, and ye, remain ye bound, and let your words
be proved, whether truth be with you: and if not -- Pharaoh liveth! surely ye [are] spies;'
42:17 and he removeth them unto charge three days.
42:18 And Joseph saith unto them on the third day, `This do and live; God I fear!
42:19 if ye [are] right men, let one of your brethren be bound in the house of your ward, and ye, go,
carry in corn [for] the famine of your houses,
42:20 and your young brother ye bring unto me, and your words are established, and ye die not;'
and they do so.
42:21 And they say one unto another, `Verily we [are] guilty concerning our brother, because we
saw the distress of his soul, in his making supplication unto us, and we did not hearken: therefore
hath this distress come upon us.'
42:22 And Reuben answereth them, saying, `Spake I not unto you, saying, Sin not against the lad?
and ye hearkened not; and his blood also, lo, it is required.'
42:23 And they have not known that Joseph understandeth, for the interpreter [is] between them;
42:24 and he turneth round from them, and weepeth, and turneth back unto them, and speaketh
unto them, and taketh from them Simeon, and bindeth him before their eyes.
42:25 And Joseph commandeth, and they fill their vessels [with] corn, also to put back the money
of each unto his sack, and to give to them provision for the way; and one doth to them so.
42:26 And they lift up their corn upon their asses, and go from thence,
42:27 and the one openeth his sack to give provender to his ass at a lodging-place, and he seeth
his money, and lo, it [is] in the mouth of his bag,
42:28 and he saith unto his brethren, `My money hath been put back, and also, lo, in my bag:' and
their heart goeth out, and they tremble, one to another saying, `What [is] this God hath done to us!'
42:29 And they come in unto Jacob their father, to the land of Canaan, and they declare to him all

the things meeting them, saying,
42:30 `The man, the lord of the land, hath spoken with us sharp things, and maketh us as spies of the land;
42:31 and we say unto him, We [are] right men, we have not been spies,
42:32 we [are] twelve brethren, sons of our father, the one is not, and the young one [is] to-day with our father in the land of Canaan.
42:33 `And the man, the lord of the land, saith unto us, By this I know that ye [are] right men -- one of your brethren leave with me, and [for] the famine of your houses take ye and go,
42:34 and bring your young brother unto me, and I know that ye [are] not spies, but ye [are] right men; your brother I give to you, and ye trade with the land.'
42:35 And it cometh to pass, they are emptying their sacks, and lo, the bundle of each man's silver [is] in his sack, and they see their bundles of silver, they and their father, and are afraid;
42:36 and Jacob their father saith unto them, `Me ye have bereaved; Joseph is not, and Simeon is not, and Benjamin ye take -- against me have been all these.'
42:37 And Reuben speaketh unto his father, saying, `My two sons thou dost put to death, if I bring him not in unto thee; give him into my hand, and I -- I bring him back unto thee;'
42:38 and he saith, `My son doth not go down with you, for his brother [is] dead, and he by himself is left; when mischief hath met him in the way in which ye go, then ye have brought down my grey hairs in sorrow to sheol.'
43:1 And the famine [is] severe in the land;
43:2 and it cometh to pass, when they have finished eating the corn which they brought from Egypt, that their father saith unto them, `Turn back, buy for us a little food.'
43:3 And Judah speaketh unto him, saying, `The man protesting protested to us, saying, Ye do not see my face without your brother [being] with you;
43:4 if thou art sending our brother with us, we go down, and buy for thee food,
43:5 and if thou art not sending -- we do not go down, for the man said unto us, Ye do not see my face without your brother [being] with you.'
43:6 And Israel saith, `Why did ye evil to me, by declaring to the man that ye had yet a brother?'
43:7 and they say, `The man asked diligently concerning us, and concerning our kindred, saying, Is your father yet alive? have ye a brother? and we declare to him according to the tenor of these things; do we certainly know that he will say, Bring down your brother?'
43:8 And Judah saith unto Israel his father, `Send the youth with me, and we arise, and go, and live, and do not die, both we, and thou, and our infants.
43:9 I -- I am surety [for] him, from my hand thou dost require him; if I have not brought him in unto

thee, and set him before thee -- then I have sinned against thee all the days;
43:10 for if we had not lingered, surely now we had returned these two times.'
43:11 And Israel their father saith unto them, `If so, now, this do: take of the praised thing of the land in your vessels, and take down to the man a present, a little balm, and a little honey, spices and myrrh, nuts and almonds;
43:12 and double money take in your hand, even the money which is brought back in the mouth of your bags, ye take back in your hand, it may be it [is] an oversight.
43:13 `And take your brother, and rise, turn back unto the man;
43:14 and God Almighty give to you mercies before the man, so that he hath sent to you your other brother and Benjamin; and I, when I am bereaved -- I am bereaved.'
43:15 And the men take this present, double money also they have taken in their hand, and Benjamin; and they rise, and go down to Egypt, and stand before Joseph;
43:16 and Joseph seeth Benjamin with them, and saith to him who [is] over his house, `Bring the men into the house, and slaughter an animal, and make ready, for with me do the men eat at noon.'
43:17 And the man doth as Joseph hath said, and the man bringeth in the men into the house of Joseph,
43:18 and the men are afraid because they have been brought into the house of Joseph, and they say, `For the matter of the money which was put back in our bags at the commencement are we brought in -- to roll himself upon us, and to throw himself on us, and to take us for servants -- our asses also.'
43:19 And they come nigh unto the man who [is] over the house of Joseph, and speak unto him at the opening of the house,
43:20 and say, `O, my lord, we really come down at the commencement to buy food;
43:21 and it cometh to pass, when we have come in unto the lodging-place, and open our bags, that lo, each one's money [is] in the mouth of his bag, our money in its weight, and we bring it back in our hand;
43:22 and other money have we brought down in our hand to buy food; we have not known who put our money in our bags.'
43:23 And he saith, `Peace to you, fear not: your God and the God of your father hath given to you hidden treasure in your bags, your money came unto me;' and he bringeth out Simeon unto them.
43:24 And the man bringeth in the men into Joseph's house, and giveth water, and they wash their feet; and he giveth provender for their asses,
43:25 and they prepare the present until the coming of Joseph at noon, for they have heard that there they do eat bread.

43:26 And Joseph cometh into the house, and they bring to him the present which [is] in their hand, into the house, and bow themselves to him, to the earth;
43:27 and he asketh of them of peace, and saith, `Is your father well? the aged man of whom ye have spoken, is he yet alive?'
43:28 and they say, `Thy servant our father [is] well, he is yet alive;' and they bow, and do obeisance.
43:29 And he lifteth up his eyes, and seeth Benjamin his brother, his mother's son, and saith, `Is this your young brother, of whom ye have spoken unto me?' and he saith, `God favour thee, my son.'
43:30 And Joseph hasteth, for his bowels have been moved for his brother, and he seeketh to weep, and entereth the inner chamber, and weepeth there;
43:31 and he washeth his face, and goeth out, and refraineth himself, and saith, `Place bread.'
43:32 And they place for him by himself, and for them by themselves, and for the Egyptians who are eating with him by themselves: for the Egyptians are unable to eat bread with the Hebrews, for it [is] an abomination to the Egyptians.
43:33 And they sit before him, the first-born according to his birthright, and the young one according to his youth, and the men wonder one at another;
43:34 and he lifteth up gifts from before him unto them, and the gift of Benjamin is five hands more than the gifts of all of them; and they drink, yea, they drink abundantly with him.
44:1 And he commandeth him who [is] over his house, saying, `Fill the bags of the men [with] food, as they are able to bear, and put the money of each in the mouth of his bag;
44:2 and my cup, the silver cup, thou dost put in the mouth of the bag of the young one, and his corn-money;' and he doth according to the word of Joseph which he hath spoken.
44:3 The morning is bright, and the men have been sent away, they and their asses --
44:4 they have gone out of the city -- they have not gone far off -- and Joseph hath said to him who [is] over his house, `Rise, pursue after the men; and thou hast overtaken them, and thou hast said unto them, Why have ye recompensed evil for good?
44:5 Is not this that with which my lord drinketh? and he observeth diligently with it; ye have done evil [in] that which ye have done.'
44:6 And he overtaketh them, and speaketh unto them these words,
44:7 and they say unto him, `Why doth my lord speak according to these words? far be it from thy servants to do according to this word;
44:8 lo, the money which we found in the mouth of our bags we brought back unto thee from the land of Canaan, and how do we steal from the house of thy lord silver or gold?

44:9 with whomsoever of thy servants it is found, he hath died, and we also are to my lord for servants.'

44:10 And he saith, `Now, also, according to your words, so it [is]; he with whom it is found becometh my servant, and ye are acquitted;'

44:11 and they hasten and take down each his bag to the earth, and each openeth his bag;

44:12 and he searcheth -- at the eldest he hath begun, and at the youngest he hath completed -- and the cup is found in the bag of Benjamin;

44:13 and they rend their garments, and each ladeth his ass, and they turn back to the city.

44:14 And Judah -- his brethren also -- cometh in unto the house of Joseph, and he is yet there, and they fall before him to the earth;

44:15 and Joseph saith to them, `What [is] this deed that ye have done? have ye not known that a man like me doth diligently observe?'

44:16 And Judah saith, `What do we say to my lord? what do we speak? and what -- do we justify ourselves? God hath found out the iniquity of thy servants; lo, we [are] servants to my lord, both we, and he in whose hand the cup hath been found;'

44:17 and he saith, `Far be it from me to do this; the man in whose hand the cup hath been found, he becometh my servant; and ye, go ye up in peace unto your father.'

44:18 And Judah cometh nigh unto him, and saith, `O, my lord, let thy servant speak, I pray thee, a word in the ears of my lord, and let not thine anger burn against thy servant -- for thou art as Pharaoh.

44:19 My lord hath asked his servants, saying, Have ye a father or brother?

44:20 and we say unto my lord, We have a father, an aged one, and a child of old age, a little one; and his brother died, and he is left alone of his mother, and his father hath loved him.

44:21 `And thou sayest unto thy servants, Bring him down unto me, and I set mine eye upon him;

44:22 and we say unto my lord, The youth is not able to leave his father, when he hath left his father, then he hath died;

44:23 and thou sayest unto thy servants, If your young brother come not down with you, ye add not to see my face.

44:24 `And it cometh to pass, that we have come up unto thy servant my father, that we declare to him the words of my lord;

44:25 and our father saith, Turn back, buy for us a little food,

44:26 and we say, We are not able to go down; if our young brother is with us, then we have gone down; for we are not able to see the man's face, and our young brother not with us.

44:27 `And thy servant my father saith unto us, Ye -- ye have known that two did my wife bare to

me,
44:28 and the one goeth out from me, and I say, Surely he is torn -- torn! and I have not seen him since;
44:29 when ye have taken also this from my presence, and mischief hath met him, then ye have brought down my grey hairs with evil to sheol.
44:30 `And now, at my coming in unto thy servant my father, and the youth not with us (and his soul is bound up in his soul),
44:31 then it hath come to pass when he seeth that the youth is not, that he hath died, and thy servants have brought down the grey hairs of thy servant our father with sorrow to sheol;
44:32 for thy servant obtained the youth by surety from my father, saying, If I bring him not in unto thee -- then I have sinned against my father all the days.
44:33 `And now, let thy servant, I pray thee, abide instead of the youth a servant to my lord, and the youth goeth up with his brethren,
44:34 for how do I go up unto my father, and the youth not with me? lest I look on the evil which doth find my father.'
45:1 And Joseph hath not been able to refrain himself before all those standing by him, and he calleth, `Put out every man from me;' and no man hath stood with him when Joseph maketh himself known unto his brethren,
45:2 and he giveth forth his voice in weeping, and the Egyptians hear, and the house of Pharaoh heareth.
45:3 And Joseph saith unto his brethren, `I [am] Joseph, is my father yet alive?' and his brethren have not been able to answer him, for they have been troubled at his presence.
45:4 And Joseph saith unto his brethren, `Come nigh unto me, I pray you,' and they come nigh; and he saith, `I [am] Joseph, your brother, whom ye sold into Egypt;
45:5 and now, be not grieved, nor let it be displeasing in your eyes that ye sold me hither, for to preserve life hath God sent me before you.
45:6 `Because these two years the famine [is] in the heart of the land, and yet [are] five years, [in] which there is neither ploughing nor harvest;
45:7 and God sendeth me before you, to place of you a remnant in the land, and to give life to you by a great escape;
45:8 and now, ye -- ye have not sent me hither, but God, and He doth set me for a father to Pharaoh, and for lord to all his house, and ruler over all the land of Egypt.
45:9 `Haste, and go up unto my father, then ye have said to him, Thus said Joseph thy son, God hath set me for lord to all Egypt; come down unto me, stay not,

45:10 and thou hast dwelt in the land of Goshen, and been near unto me, thou and thy sons, and
thy son's sons, and thy flock, and thy herd, and all that thou hast,
45:11 and I have nourished thee there -- for yet [are] five years of famine -- lest thou become poor,
thou and thy household, and all that thou hast.
45:12 `And lo, your eyes are seeing, and the eyes of my brother Benjamin, that [it is] my mouth
which is speaking unto you;
45:13 and ye have declared to my father all my honour in Egypt, and all that ye have seen, and ye
have hasted, and have brought down my father hither.'
45:14 And he falleth on the neck of Benjamin his brother, and weepeth, and Benjamin hath wept on
his neck;
45:15 and he kisseth all his brethren, and weepeth over them; and afterwards have his brethren
spoken with him.
45:16 And the sound hath been heard in the house of Pharaoh, saying, `Come have the brethren of
Joseph;' and it is good in the eyes of Pharaoh, and in the eyes of his servants,
45:17 and Pharaoh saith unto Joseph, `Say unto thy brethren, This do ye: lade your beasts, and
go, enter ye the land of Canaan,
45:18 and take your father, and your households, and come unto me, and I give to you the good of
the land of Egypt, and eat ye the fat of the land.
45:19 `Yea, thou -- thou hast been commanded: this do ye, take for yourselves out of the land of
Egypt, waggons for your infants, and for your wives, and ye have brought your father, and come;
45:20 and your eye hath no pity on your vessels, for the good of all the land of Egypt [is] yours.'
45:21 And the sons of Israel do so, and Joseph giveth waggons to them by the command of
Pharaoh, and he giveth to them provision for the way;
45:22 to all of them hath he given -- to each changes of garments, and to Benjamin he hath given
three hundred silverlings, and five changes of garments;
45:23 and to his father he hath sent thus: ten asses bearing of the good things of Egypt, and ten
she-asses bearing corn and bread, even food for his father for the way.
45:24 And he sendeth his brethren away, and they go; and he saith unto them, `Be not angry in the
way.'
45:25 And they go up out of Egypt, and come in to the land of Canaan, unto Jacob their father,
45:26 and they declare to him, saying, `Joseph [is] yet alive,' and that he [is] ruler over all the land
of Egypt; and his heart ceaseth, for he hath not given credence to them.
45:27 And they speak unto him all the words of Joseph, which he hath spoken unto them, and he
seeth the waggons which Joseph hath sent to bear him away, and live doth the spirit of Jacob their

father;
45:28 and Israel saith, `Enough! Joseph my son [is] yet alive; I go and see him before I die.'
46:1 And Israel journeyeth, and all that he hath, and cometh in to Beer-Sheba, and sacrificeth
sacrifices to the God of his father Isaac;
46:2 and God speaketh to Israel in visions of the night, and saith, `Jacob, Jacob;' and he saith,
`Here [am] I.'
46:3 And He saith, `I [am] God, God of thy father, be not afraid of going down to Egypt, for for a
great nation I set thee there;
46:4 I -- I go down with thee to Egypt, and I -- I also certainly bring thee up, and Joseph doth put
his hand on thine eyes.'
46:5 And Jacob riseth from Beer-Sheba, and the sons of Israel bear away Jacob their father, And
their infants, and their wives, in the waggons which Pharaoh hath sent to bear him,
46:6 and they take their cattle, and their goods which they have acquired in the land of Canaan,
and come into Egypt -- Jacob, and all his seed with him,
46:7 his sons, and his sons' sons with him, his daughters, and his sons' daughters, yea, all his
seed he brought with him into Egypt.
46:8 And these [are] the names of the sons of Israel who are coming into Egypt: Jacob and his
sons, Jacob's first-born, Reuben.
46:9 And sons of Reuben: Hanoch, and Phallu, and Hezron, and Carmi.
46:10 And sons of Simeon: Jemuel, and Jamin, and Ohad, and Jachin, and Zohar, and Shaul son
of the Canaanitess.
46:11 And sons of Levi: Gershon, Kohath, and Merari.
46:12 And sons of Judah: Er, and Onan, and Shelah, and Pharez, and Zarah, (and Er and Onan
die in the land of Canaan.) And sons of Pharez are Hezron and Hamul.
46:13 And sons of Issachar: Tola, and Phuvah, and Job, and Shimron.
46:14 And sons of Zebulun: Sered, and Elon, and Jahleel.
46:15 These [are] sons of Leah whom she bare to Jacob in Padan-Aram, and Dinah his daughter;
all the persons of his sons and his daughters [are] thirty and three.
46:16 And sons of Gad: Ziphion, and Haggi, Shuni, and Ezbon, Eri, and Arodi, and Areli.
46:17 And sons of Asher: Jimnah, and Ishuah, and Isui, and Beriah, and Serah their sister. And
sons of Beriah: Heber and Malchiel.
46:18 These [are] sons of Zilpah, whom Laban gave to Leah his daughter, and she beareth these
to Jacob -- sixteen persons.
46:19 Sons of Rachel, Jacob's wife: Joseph and Benjamin.

46:20 And born to Joseph in the land of Egypt (whom Asenath daughter of Poti-Pherah, priest of On, hath borne to him) [are] Manasseh and Ephraim.
46:21 And sons of Benjamin: Belah, and Becher, and Ashbel, Gera, and Naaman, Ehi, and Rosh, Muppim, and Huppim, and Ard.
46:22 These [are] sons of Rachel, who were born to Jacob; all the persons [are] fourteen.
46:23 And sons of Dan: Hushim.
46:24 And sons of Naphtali: Jahzeel, and Guni, and Jezer, and Shillem.
46:25 These [are] sons of Bilhah, whom Laban gave to Rachel his daughter; and she beareth these to Jacob -- all the persons [are] seven.
46:26 All the persons who are coming to Jacob to Egypt, coming out of his thigh, apart from the wives of Jacob's sons, all the persons [are] sixty and six.
46:27 And the sons of Joseph who have been born to him in Egypt [are] two persons. All the persons of the house of Jacob who are coming into Egypt [are] seventy.
46:28 And Judah he hath sent before him unto Joseph, to direct before him to Goshen, and they come into the land of Goshen;
46:29 and Joseph harnesseth his chariot, and goeth up to meet Israel his father, to Goshen, and appeareth unto him, and falleth on his neck, and weepeth on his neck again;
46:30 and Israel saith unto Joseph, `Let me die this time, after my seeing thy face, for thou [art] yet alive.'
46:31 And Joseph saith unto his brethren, and unto the house of his father, `I go up, and declare to Pharaoh, and say unto him, My brethren, and the house of my father who [are] in the land of Canaan have come in unto me;
46:32 and the men [are] feeders of a flock, for they have been men of cattle; and their flock, and their herd, and all that they have, they have brought.'
46:33 `And it hath come to pass when Pharaoh calleth for you, and hath said, What [are] your works?
46:34 that ye have said, Thy servants have been men of cattle from our youth, even until now, both we and our fathers, -- in order that ye may dwell in the land of Goshen, for the abomination of the Egyptians is every one feeding a flock.'
47:1 And Joseph cometh, and declareth to Pharaoh, and saith, `My father, and my brethren, and their flock, and their herd, and all they have, have come from the land of Canaan, and lo, they [are] in the land of Goshen.'
47:2 And out of his brethren he hath taken five men, and setteth them before Pharaoh;
47:3 and Pharaoh saith unto his brethren, `What [are] your works?' and they say unto Pharaoh,

`Thy servants [are] feeders of a flock, both we and our fathers;'
47:4 and they say unto Pharaoh, `To sojourn in the land we have come, for there is no pasture for
the flock which thy servants have, for grievous [is] the famine in the land of Canaan; and now, let
thy servants, we pray thee, dwell in the land of Goshen.'
47:5 And Pharaoh speaketh unto Joseph, saying, `Thy father and thy brethren have come unto
thee:
47:6 the land of Egypt is before thee; in the best of the land cause thy father and thy brethren to
dwell -- they dwell in the land of Goshen, and if thou hast known, and there are among them men
of ability, then thou hast set them heads over the cattle I have.'
47:7 And Joseph bringeth in Jacob his father, and causeth him to stand before Pharaoh; and Jacob
blesseth Pharaoh.
47:8 And Pharaoh saith unto Jacob, `How many [are] the days of the years of thy life?'
47:9 And Jacob saith unto Pharaoh, `The days of the years of my sojournings [are] an hundred and
thirty years; few and evil have been the days of the years of my life, and they have not reached the
days of the years of the life of my fathers, in the days of their sojournings.'
47:10 And Jacob blesseth Pharaoh, and goeth out from before Pharaoh.
47:11 And Joseph settleth his father and his brethren, and giveth to them a possession in the land
of Egypt, in the best of the land, in the land of Rameses, as Pharaoh commanded;
47:12 and Joseph nourisheth his father, and his brethren, and all the house of his father [with]
bread, according to the mouth of the infants.
47:13 And there is no bread in all the land, for the famine [is] very grievous, and the land of Egypt
and the land of Canaan are feeble because of the famine;
47:14 and Joseph gathereth all the silver that is found in the land of Egypt, and in the land of
Canaan, for the corn that they are buying, and Joseph bringeth the silver into the house of
Pharaoh.
47:15 And the silver is consumed out of the land of Egypt, and out of the land of Canaan, and all
the Egyptians come in unto Joseph, saying, `Give to us bread -- why do we die before thee, though
the money hath ceased?'
47:16 and Joseph saith, `Give your cattle; and I give to you for your cattle, if the money hath
ceased.'
47:17 And they bring in their cattle unto Joseph, and Joseph giveth to them bread, for the horses,
and for the cattle of the flock, and for the cattle of the herd, and for the asses; and he tendeth them
with bread, for all their cattle, during that year.
47:18 And that year is finished, and they come in unto him on the second year, and say to him, `We

do not hide from my lord, that since the money hath been finished, and possession of the cattle [is] unto my lord, there hath not been left before my lord save our bodies, and our ground;

47:19 why do we die before thine eyes, both we and our ground? buy us and our ground for bread, and we and our ground are servants to Pharaoh; and give seed, and we live, and die not, and the ground is not desolate.'

47:20 And Joseph buyeth all the ground of Egypt for Pharaoh, for the Egyptians have sold each his field, for the famine hath been severe upon them, and the land becometh Pharaoh's;

47:21 as to the people he hath removed them to cities from the [one] end of the border of Egypt even unto its [other] end.

47:22 Only the ground of the priests he hath not bought, for the priests have a portion from Pharaoh, and they have eaten their portion which Pharaoh hath given to them, therefore they have not sold their ground.

47:23 And Joseph saith unto the people, `Lo, I have bought you to-day and your ground for Pharaoh; lo, seed for you, and ye have sown the ground,

47:24 and it hath come to pass in the increases, that ye have given a fifth to Pharaoh, and four of the parts are for yourselves, for seed of the field, and for your food, and for those who [are] in your houses, and for food for your infants.'

47:25 And they say, `Thou hast revived us; we find grace in the eyes of my lord, and have been servants to Pharaoh;'

47:26 and Joseph setteth it for a statute unto this day, concerning the ground of Egypt, [that] Pharaoh hath a fifth; only the ground of the priests alone hath not become Pharaoh's.

47:27 And Israel dwelleth in the land of Egypt, in the land of Goshen, and they have possession in it, and are fruitful, and multiply exceedingly;

47:28 and Jacob liveth in the land of Egypt seventeen years, and the days of Jacob, the years of his life, are an hundred and forty and seven years.

47:29 And the days of Israel are near to die, and he calleth for his son, for Joseph, and saith to him, `If, I pray thee, I have found grace in thine eyes, put, I pray thee, thy hand under my thigh, and thou hast done with me kindness and truth; bury me not, I pray thee, in Egypt,

47:30 and I have lain with my fathers, and thou hast borne me out of Egypt, and buried me in their burying-place.' And he saith, `I -- I do according to thy word;'

47:31 and he saith, `Swear to me;' and he sweareth to him, and Israel boweth himself on the head of the bed.

48:1 And it cometh to pass, after these things, that [one] saith to Joseph, `Lo, thy father is sick;' and he taketh his two sons with him, Manasseh and Ephraim.

48:2 And [one] declareth to Jacob, and saith, `Lo, thy son Joseph is coming unto thee;' and Israel doth strengthen himself, and sit upon the bed.
48:3 And Jacob saith unto Joseph, `God Almighty hath appeared unto me, in Luz, in the land of Canaan, and blesseth me,
48:4 and saith unto me, Lo, I am making thee fruitful, and have multiplied thee, and given thee for an assembly of peoples, and given this land to thy seed after thee, a possession age-during.
48:5 `And now, thy two sons, who are born to thee in the land of Egypt, before my coming unto thee to Egypt, mine they [are]; Ephraim and Manasseh, as Reuben and Simeon they are mine;
48:6 and thy family which thou hast begotten after them are thine; by the name of their brethren they are called in their inheritance.
48:7 `And I -- in my coming in from Padan-[Aram] Rachel hath died by me in the land of Canaan, in the way, while yet a kibrath of land to enter Ephrata, and I bury her there in the way of Ephrata, which [is] Bethlehem.'
48:8 And Israel seeth the sons of Joseph, and saith, `Who [are] these?'
48:9 and Joseph saith unto his father, `They [are] my sons, whom God hath given to me in this [place];' and he saith, `Bring them, I pray thee, unto me, and I bless them.'
48:10 And the eyes of Israel have been heavy from age, he is unable to see; and he bringeth them nigh unto him, and he kisseth them, and cleaveth to them;
48:11 and Israel saith unto Joseph, `To see thy face I had not thought, and lo, God hath shewed me also thy seed.'
48:12 And Joseph bringeth them out from between his knees, and boweth himself on his face to the earth;
48:13 and Joseph taketh them both, Ephraim in his right hand towards Israel's left, and Manasseh in his left towards Israel's right, and bringeth [them] nigh to him.
48:14 And Israel putteth out his right hand, and placeth [it] upon the head of Ephraim, who [is] the younger, and his left hand upon the head of Manasseh; he hath guided his hands wisely, for Manasseh [is] the first-born.
48:15 And he blesseth Joseph, and saith, `God, before whom my fathers Abraham and Isaac walked habitually: God who is feeding me from my being unto this day:
48:16 the Messenger who is redeeming me from all evil doth bless the youths, and my name is called upon them, and the name of my fathers Abraham and Isaac; and they increase into a multitude in the midst of the land.'
48:17 And Joseph seeth that his father setteth his right hand on the head of Ephraim, and it is wrong in his eyes, and he supporteth the hand of his father to turn it aside from off the head of

Ephraim to the head of Manasseh;
48:18 and Joseph saith unto his father, `Not so, my father, for this [is] the first-born; set thy right hand on his head.'
48:19 And his father refuseth, and saith, `I have known, my son, I have known; he also becometh a people, and he also is great, and yet, his young brother is greater than he, and his seed is the fulness of the nations;'
48:20 and he blesseth them in that day, saying, `By thee doth Israel bless, saying, God set thee as Ephraim and as Manasseh;' and he setteth Ephraim before Manasseh.
48:21 And Israel saith unto Joseph, `Lo, I am dying, and God hath been with you, and hath brought you back unto the land of your fathers;
48:22 and I -- I have given to thee one portion above thy brethren, which I have taken out of the hand of the Amorite by my sword and by my bow.'
49:1 And Jacob calleth unto his sons and saith, `Be gathered together, and I declare to you that which doth happen with you in the latter end of the days.
49:2 `Be assembled, and hear, sons of Jacob, And hearken unto Israel your father.
49:3 Reuben! my first-born thou, My power, and beginning of my strength, The abundance of exaltation, And the abundance of strength;
49:4 Unstable as water, thou art not abundant; For thou hast gone up thy father's bed; Then thou hast polluted: My couch he went up!
49:5 Simeon and Levi [are] brethren! Instruments of violence -- their espousals!
49:6 Into their secret, come not, O my soul! Unto their assembly be not united, O mine honour; For in their anger they slew a man, And in their self-will eradicated a prince.
49:7 Cursed [is] their anger, for [it is] fierce, And their wrath, for [it is] sharp; I divide them in Jacob, And I scatter them in Israel.
49:8 Judah! thou -- thy brethren praise thee! Thy hand [is] on the neck of thine enemies, Sons of thy father bow themselves to thee.
49:9 A lion's whelp [is] Judah, For prey, my son, thou hast gone up; He hath bent, he hath crouched as a lion, And as a lioness; who causeth him to arise?
49:10 The sceptre turneth not aside from Judah, And a lawgiver from between his feet, Till his Seed come; And his [is] the obedience of peoples.
49:11 Binding to the vine his ass, And to the choice vine the colt of his ass, He hath washed in wine his clothing, And in the blood of grapes his covering;
49:12 Red [are] eyes with wine, And white [are] teeth with milk!
49:13 Zebulun at a haven of the seas doth dwell, And he [is] for a haven of ships; And his side [is]

unto Zidon.
49:14 Issacher [is] a strong ass, Crouching between the two folds;
49:15 And he seeth rest that [it is] good, And the land that [it is] pleasant, And he inclineth his shoulder to bear, And is to tribute a servant.
49:16 Dan doth judge his people, As one of the tribes of Israel;
49:17 Dan is a serpent by the way, An adder by the path, Which is biting the horse's heels, And its rider falleth backward.
49:18 For Thy salvation I have waited, Jehovah!
49:19 Gad! a troop assaulteth him, But he assaulteth last.
49:20 Out of Asher his bread [is] fat; And he giveth dainties of a king.
49:21 Naphtali [is] a hind sent away, Who is giving beauteous young ones.
49:22 Joseph [is] a fruitful son; A fruitful son by a fountain, Daughters step over the wall;
49:23 And embitter him -- yea, they have striven, Yea, hate him do archers;
49:24 And his bow abideth in strength, And strengthened are the arms of his hands By the hands of the Mighty One of Jacob, Whence is a shepherd, a son of Israel.
49:25 By the God of thy father who helpeth thee, And the Mighty One who blesseth thee, Blessings of the heavens from above, Blessings of the deep lying under, Blessings of breasts and womb; --
49:26 Thy father's blessings have been mighty Above the blessings of my progenitors, Unto the limit of the heights age-during They are for the head of Joseph, And for the crown of the one Separate [from] his brethren.
49:27 Benjamin! a wolf teareth; In the morning he eateth prey, And at evening he apportioneth spoil.'
49:28 All these [are] the twelve tribes of Israel, and this [is] that which their father hath spoken unto them, and he blesseth them; each according to his blessing he hath blessed them.
49:29 And he commandeth them, and saith unto them, `I am being gathered unto my people; bury me by my fathers, at the cave which [is] in the field of Ephron the Hittite;
49:30 in the cave which [is] in the field of Machpelah, which [is] on the front of Mamre, in the land of Canaan, which Abraham bought with the field from Ephron the Hittite for a possession of a burying-place;
49:31 (there they buried Abraham and Sarah his wife; there they buried Isaac and Rebekah his wife; and there I buried Leah);
49:32 the purchase of the field and of the cave which [is] in it, [is] from Sons of Heth.'
49:33 And Jacob finisheth commanding his sons, and gathereth up his feet unto the bed, and expireth, and is gathered unto his people.

50:1 And Joseph falleth on his father's face, and weepeth over him, and kisseth him;
50:2 and Joseph commandeth his servants, the physicians, to embalm his father, and the physicians embalm Israel;
50:3 and they fulfil for him forty days, for so they fulfil the days of the embalmed, and the Egyptians weep for him seventy days.
50:4 And the days of his weeping pass away, and Joseph speaketh unto the house of Pharaoh, saying, `If, I pray you, I have found grace in your eyes, speak, I pray you, in the ears of Pharaoh, saying,
50:5 My father caused me to swear, saying, Lo, I am dying; in my burying-place which I have prepared for myself in the land of Canaan, there dost thou bury me; and now, let me go up, I pray thee, and bury my father, and return;'
50:6 and Pharaoh saith, `Go up and bury thy father, as he caused thee to swear.'
50:7 And Joseph goeth up to bury his father, and go up with him do all the servants of Pharaoh, elders of his house, and all the elders of the land of Egypt,
50:8 and all the house of Joseph, and his brethren, and the house of his father; only their infants, and their flock, and their herd, have they left in the land of Goshen;
50:9 and there go up with him both chariot and horsemen, and the camp is very great.
50:10 And they come unto the threshing-floor of Atad, which [is] beyond the Jordan, and they lament there, a lamentation great and very grievous; and he maketh for his father a mourning seven days,
50:11 and the inhabitant of the land, the Canaanite, see the mourning in the threshing-floor of Atad, and say, `A grievous mourning [is] this to the Egyptians;' therefore hath [one] called its name `The mourning of the Egyptians,' which [is] beyond the Jordan.
50:12 And his sons do to him so as he commanded them,
50:13 and his sons bear him away to the land of Canaan, and bury him in the cave of the field of Machpelah, which Abraham bought with the field for a possession of a burying-place, from Ephron the Hittite, on the front of Mamre.
50:14 And Joseph turneth back to Egypt, he and his brethren, and all who are going up with him to bury his father, after his burying his father.
50:15 And the brethren of Joseph see that their father is dead, and say, `Peradventure Joseph doth hate us, and doth certainly return to us all the evil which we did with him.'
50:16 And they give a charge for Joseph, saying, `Thy father commanded before his death, saying,
50:17 Thus ye do say to Joseph, I pray thee, bear, I pray thee, with the transgression of thy brethren, and their sin, for they have done thee evil; and now, bear, we pray thee, with the

transgression of the servants of the God of thy father;' and Joseph weepeth in their speaking unto him.

50:18 And his brethren also go and fall before him, and say, `Lo, we [are] to thee for servants.'

50:19 And Joseph saith unto them, `Fear not, for [am] I in the place of God?

50:20 As for you, ye devised against me evil -- God devised it for good, in order to do as [at] this day, to keep alive a numerous people;

50:21 and now, fear not: I do nourish you and your infants;' and he comforteth them, and speaketh unto their heart.

50:22 And Joseph dwelleth in Egypt, he and the house of his father, and Joseph liveth a hundred and ten years,

50:23 and Joseph looketh on Ephraim's sons of the third [generation]; sons also of Machir, son of Manasseh, have been born on the knees of Joseph.

50:24 And Joseph saith unto his brethren, `I am dying, and God doth certainly inspect you, and hath caused you to go up from this land, unto the land which He hath sworn to Abraham, to Isaac, and to Jacob.'

50:25 And Joseph causeth the sons of Israel to swear, saying, `God doth certainly inspect you, and ye have brought up my bones from this [place].'

50:26 And Joseph dieth, a son of an hundred and ten years, and they embalm him, and he is put into a coffin in Egypt.

Exodus

1:1 And these [are] the names of the sons of Israel who are coming into Egypt with Jacob; a man
and his household have they come;
1:2 Reuben, Simeon, Levi, and Judah,
1:3 Issachar, Zebulun, and Benjamin,
1:4 Dan, and Naphtali, Gad, and Asher.
1:5 And all the persons coming out of the thigh of Jacob are seventy persons; as to Joseph, he was
in Egypt.
1:6 And Joseph dieth, and all his brethren, and all that generation;
1:7 and the sons of Israel have been fruitful, and they teem, and multiply, and are very very mighty,
and the land is filled with them.
1:8 And there riseth a new king over Egypt, who hath not known Joseph,
1:9 and he saith unto his people, `Lo, the people of the sons of Israel [is] more numerous and
mighty than we;
1:10 give help! let us act wisely concerning it, lest it multiply, and it hath come to pass, when war
happeneth, that it hath been joined, even it, unto those hating us, and hath fought against us, and
hath gone out up of the land.'
1:11 And they set over it princes of tribute, so as to afflict it with their burdens, and it buildeth store-
cities for Pharaoh, Pithom and Raamses;
1:12 and as they afflict it, so it multiplieth, and so it breaketh forth, and they are vexed because of
the sons of Israel;
1:13 and the Egyptians cause the sons of Israel to serve with rigour,
1:14 and make their lives bitter in hard service, in clay, and in brick, and in every [kind] of service in
the field; all their service in which they have served [is] with rigour.
1:15 And the king of Egypt speaketh to the midwives, the Hebrewesses, (of whom the name of the
one [is] Shiphrah, and the name of the second Puah),
1:16 and saith, `When ye cause the Hebrew women to bear, and have looked on the children; if it
[is] a son -- then ye have put him to death; and if it [is] a daughter -- then she hath lived.'
1:17 And the midwives fear God, and have not done as the king of Egypt hath spoken unto them,
and keep the lads alive;
1:18 and the king of Egypt calleth for the midwives, and saith to them, `Wherefore have ye done
this thing, and keep the lads alive?'
1:19 And the midwives say unto Pharaoh, `Because the Hebrew women [are] not as the Egyptian
women, for they [are] lively; before the midwife cometh in unto them -- they have borne!'

1:20 And God doth good to the midwives, and the people multiply, and are very mighty;
1:21 and it cometh to pass, because the midwives have feared God, that He maketh for them households;
1:22 and Pharaoh layeth a charge on all his people, saying, `Every son who is born -- into the River ye do cast him, and every daughter ye do keep alive.'
2:1 And there goeth a man of the house of Levi, and he taketh the daughter of Levi,
2:2 and the woman conceiveth, and beareth a son, and she seeth him that he [is] fair, and she hideth him three months,
2:3 and she hath not been able any more to hide him, and she taketh for him an ark of rushes, and daubeth it with bitumen and with pitch, and putteth the lad in it, and putteth [it] in the weeds by the edge of the River;
2:4 and his sister stationeth herself afar off, to know what is done to him.
2:5 And a daughter of Pharaoh cometh down to bathe at the River, and her damsels are walking by the side of the River, and she seeth the ark in the midst of the weeds, and sendeth her handmaid, and she taketh it,
2:6 and openeth, and seeth him -- the lad, and lo, a child weeping! and she hath pity on him, and saith, `This is [one] of the Hebrews' children.'
2:7 And his sister saith unto the daughter of Pharaoh, `Do I go? when I have called for thee a suckling woman of the Hebrews, then she doth suckle the lad for thee;'
2:8 and the daughter of Pharaoh saith to her, `Go;' and the virgin goeth, and calleth the mother of the lad,
2:9 and the daughter of Pharaoh saith to her, `Take this lad away, and suckle him for me, and I -- I give thy hire;' and the woman taketh the lad, and suckleth him.
2:10 And the lad groweth, and she bringeth him in to the daughter of Pharaoh, and he is to her for a son, and she calleth his name Moses, and saith, `Because -- from the water I have drawn him.'
2:11 And it cometh to pass, in those days, that Moses is grown, and he goeth out unto his brethren, and looketh on their burdens, and seeth a man, an Egyptian, smiting a man, a Hebrew, [one] of his brethren,
2:12 and he turneth hither and thither, and seeth that there is no man, and smiteth the Egyptian, and hideth him in the sand.
2:13 And he goeth out on the second day, and lo, two men, Hebrews, striving! and he saith to the wrong-doer, `Why dost thou smite thy neighbour?'
2:14 and he saith, `Who set thee for a head and a judge over us? to slay me art thou saying [it], as thou hast slain the Egyptian?' and Moses feareth, and saith, `Surely the thing hath been known.'

2:15 And Pharaoh heareth of this thing, and seeketh to slay Moses, and Moses fleeth from the face of Pharaoh, and dwelleth in the land of Midian, and dwelleth by the well.
2:16 And to a priest of Midian [are] seven daughters, and they come and draw, and fill the troughs, to water the flock of their father,
2:17 and the shepherds come and drive them away, and Moses ariseth, and saveth them, and watereth their flock.
2:18 And they come in to Reuel their father, and he saith, `Wherefore have ye hastened to come in to-day?'
2:19 and they say, `A man, an Egyptian, hath delivered us out of the hand of the shepherds, and also hath diligently drawn for us, and watereth the flock;'
2:20 and he saith unto his daughters, `And where [is] he? why [is] this? -- ye left the man! call for him, and he doth eat bread.'
2:21 And Moses is willing to dwell with the man, and he giveth Zipporah his daughter to Moses,
2:22 and she beareth a son, and he calleth his name Gershom, for he said, `A sojourner I have been in a strange land.'
2:23 And it cometh to pass during these many days, that the king of Egypt dieth, and the sons of Israel sigh because of the service, and cry, and their cry goeth up unto God, because of the service;
2:24 and God heareth their groaning, and God remembereth His covenant with Abraham, with Isaac, and with Jacob;
2:25 and God seeth the sons of Israel, and God knoweth.
3:1 And Moses hath been feeding the flock of Jethro his father-in-law, priest of Midian, and he leadeth the flock behind the wilderness, and cometh in unto the mount of God, to Horeb;
3:2 and there appeareth unto him a messenger of Jehovah in a flame of fire, out of the midst of the bush, and he seeth, and lo, the bush is burning with fire, and the bush is not consumed.
3:3 And Moses saith, `Let me turn aside, I pray thee, and I see this great appearance; wherefore is the bush not burned?'
3:4 and Jehovah seeth that he hath turned aside to see, and God calleth unto him out of the midst of the bush, and saith, `Moses, Moses;' and he saith, `Here [am] I.'
3:5 And He saith, `Come not near hither: cast thy shoes from off thy feet, for the place on which thou art standing is holy ground.'
3:6 He saith also, `I [am] the God of thy father, God of Abraham, God of Isaac, and God of Jacob;' and Moses hideth his face, for he is afraid to look towards God.
3:7 And Jehovah saith, `I have certainly seen the affliction of My people who [are] in Egypt, and

their cry I have heard, because of its exactors, for I have known its pains;
3:8 and I go down to deliver it out of the hand of the Egyptians, and to cause it to go up out of the land, unto a land good and broad, unto a land flowing with milk and honey -- unto the place of the Canaanite, and the Hittite, and the Amorite, and the Perizzite, and the Hivite, and the Jebusite.
3:9 `And now, lo, the cry of the sons of Israel hath come in unto Me, and I have also seen the oppression with which the Egyptians are oppressing them,
3:10 and now, come, and I send thee unto Pharaoh, and bring thou out My people, the sons of Israel, out of Egypt.'
3:11 And Moses saith unto God, `Who [am] I, that I go unto Pharaoh, and that I bring out the sons of Israel from Egypt?'
3:12 and He saith, `Because I am with thee, and this [is] to thee the sign that I have sent thee: in thy bringing out the people from Egypt -- ye do serve God on this mount.'
3:13 And Moses saith unto God, `Lo, I am coming unto the sons of Israel, and have said to them, The God of your fathers hath sent me unto you, and they have said to me, What [is] His name? what do I say unto them?'
3:14 And God saith unto Moses, `I AM THAT WHICH I AM;' He saith also, `Thus dost thou say to the sons of Israel, I AM hath sent me unto you.'
3:15 And God saith again unto Moses, `Thus dost thou say unto the sons of Israel, Jehovah, God of your fathers, God of Abraham, God of Isaac, and God of Jacob, hath sent me unto you; this [is] My name -- to the age, and this My memorial, to generation -- generation.
3:16 `Go, and thou hast gathered the elders of Israel, and hast said unto them: Jehovah, God of your fathers, hath appeareth unto me, God of Abraham, Isaac, and Jacob, saying, I have certainly inspected you, and that which is done to you in Egypt;
3:17 and I say, I bring you up out of the affliction of Egypt, unto the land of the Canaanite, and the Hittite, and the Amorite, and the Perizzite, and the Hivite, and the Jebusite, unto a land flowing [with] milk and honey.
3:18 `And they have hearkened to thy voice, and thou hast entered, thou and the elders of Israel, unto the king of Egypt, and ye have said unto him, Jehovah, God of the Hebrews, hath met with us; and now, let us go, we pray thee, a journey of three days into the wilderness, and we sacrifice to Jehovah our God.
3:19 `And I -- I have known that the king of Egypt doth not permit you to go, unless by a strong hand,
3:20 and I have put forth My hand, and have smitten Egypt with all My wonders, which I do in its midst -- and afterwards he doth send you away.

3:21 `And I have given the grace of this people in the eyes of the Egyptians, and it hath come to pass, when ye go, ye go not empty;
3:22 and [every] woman hath asked from her neighbour, and from her who is sojourning in her house, vessels of silver, and vessels of gold, and garments, and ye have put [them] on your sons and on your daughters, and have spoiled the Egyptians.'
4:1 And Moses answereth and saith, `And, if they do not give credence to me, nor hearken to my voice, and say, Jehovah hath not appeared unto thee?'
4:2 And Jehovah saith unto him, `What [is] this in thy hand?' and he saith, `A rod;'
4:3 and He saith, `Cast it to the earth;' and he casteth it to the earth, and it becometh a serpent -- and Moses fleeth from its presence.
4:4 And Jehovah saith unto Moses, `Put forth thy hand, and lay hold on the tail of it;' and he putteth forth his hand, and layeth hold on it, and it becometh a rod in his hand --
4:5 `-- so that they believe that Jehovah, God of their fathers, hath appeared unto thee, God of Abraham, God of Isaac, and God of Jacob.'
4:6 And Jehovah saith to him again, `Put in, I pray thee, thy hand into thy bosom;' and he putteth in his hand into his bosom, and he bringeth it out, and lo, his hand [is] leprous as snow;
4:7 and He saith, `Put back thy hand unto thy bosom;' and he putteth back his hand unto his bosom, and he bringeth it out from his bosom, and lo, it hath turned back as his flesh --
4:8 `-- and it hath come to pass, if they do not give credence to thee, and hearken not to the voice of the first sign, that they have given credence to the voice of the latter sign.
4:9 `And it hath come to pass, if they do not give credence even to these two signs, nor hearken to thy voice, that thou hast taken of the waters of the River, and hast poured on the dry land, and the waters which thou takest from the River have been, yea, they have become -- blood on the dry land.'
4:10 And Moses saith unto Jehovah, `O, my Lord, I [am] not a man of words, either yesterday, or before, or since Thy speaking unto Thy servant, for I [am] slow of mouth, and slow of tongue.'
4:11 And Jehovah saith unto him, `Who appointed a mouth for man? or who appointeth the dumb, or deaf, or open, or blind? is it not I, Jehovah?
4:12 and now, go, and I -- I am with thy mouth, and have directed thee that which thou speakest;'
4:13 and he saith, `O, my Lord, send, I pray thee, by the hand Thou dost send.'
4:14 And the anger of Jehovah burneth against Moses, and He saith, `Is not Aaron the Levite thy brother? I have known that he speaketh well, and also, lo, he is coming out to meet thee; when he hath seen thee, then he hath rejoiced in his heart,
4:15 and thou hast spoken unto him, and hast set the words in his mouth, and I -- I am with thy

mouth, and with his mouth, and have directed you that which ye do;
4:16 and he, he hath spoken for thee unto the people, and it hath come to pass, he -- he is to thee for a mouth, and thou -- thou art to him for God;
4:17 and this rod thou dost take in thy hand, with which thou doest the signs.'
4:18 And Moses goeth and turneth back unto Jethro his father-in-law, and saith to him, `Let me go, I pray thee, and I turn back unto my brethren who [are] in Egypt, and I see whether they are yet alive.' And Jethro saith to Moses, `Go in peace.'
4:19 And Jehovah saith unto Moses in Midian, `Go, turn back to Egypt, for all the men have died who seek thy life;'
4:20 and Moses taketh his wife, and his sons, and causeth them to ride on the ass, and turneth back to the land of Egypt, and Moses taketh the rod of God in his hand.
4:21 And Jehovah saith unto Moses, `In thy going to turn back to Egypt, see -- all the wonders which I have put in thy hand -- that thou hast done them before Pharaoh, and I -- I strengthen his heart, and he doth not send the people away;
4:22 and thou hast said unto Pharaoh, Thus said Jehovah, My son, My first-born [is] Israel,
4:23 and I say unto thee, Send away My son, and he doth serve Me; and -- thou dost refuse to send him away -- lo, I am slaying thy son, thy first-born.'
4:24 And it cometh to pass in the way, in a lodging place, that Jehovah meeteth him, and seeketh to put him to death;
4:25 and Zipporah taketh a flint, and cutteth off the foreskin of her son, and causeth [it] to touch his feet, and saith, `Surely a bridegroom of blood [art] thou to me;'
4:26 and He desisteth from him: then she said, `A bridegroom of blood,' in reference to the circumcision.
4:27 And Jehovah saith unto Aaron, `Go to meet Moses into the wilderness;' and he goeth, and meeteth him in the mount of God, and kisseth him,
4:28 and Moses declareth to Aaron all the words of Jehovah with which He hath sent him, and all the signs with which He hath charged him.
4:29 And Moses goeth -- Aaron also -- and they gather all the elders of the sons of Israel,
4:30 and Aaron speaketh all the words which Jehovah hath spoken unto Moses, and doth the signs before the eyes of the people;
4:31 and the people believe when they hear that Jehovah hath looked after the sons of Israel, and that He hath seen their affliction; and they bow and do obeisance.
5:1 And afterwards have Moses and Aaron entered, and they say unto Pharaoh, `Thus said Jehovah, God of Israel, Send My people away, and they keep a feast to Me in the wilderness;'

5:2 and Pharaoh saith, `Who [is] Jehovah, that I hearken to His voice, to send Israel away? I have not known Jehovah, and Israel also I do not send away.'
5:3 And they say, `The God of the Hebrews hath met with us, let us go, we pray thee, a journey of three days into the wilderness, and we sacrifice to Jehovah our God, lest He meet us with pestilence or with sword.'
5:4 And the king of Egypt saith unto them, `Why, Moses and Aaron, do ye free the people from its works? go to your burdens.'
5:5 Pharaoh also saith, `Lo, numerous now [is] the people of the land, and ye have caused them to cease from their burdens!'
5:6 And Pharaoh commandeth, on that day, the exactors among the people and its authorities, saying,
5:7 `Ye do not add to give straw to the people for the making of the bricks, as heretofore -- they go and have gathered straw for themselves;
5:8 and the proper quantity of the bricks which they are making heretofore ye do put on them, ye do not diminish from it, for they are remiss, therefore they are crying, saying, Let us go, let us sacrifice to our God;
5:9 let the service be heavy on the men, and let them work at it, and not be dazzled by lying words.'
5:10 And the exactors of the people, and its authorities, go out, and speak unto the people, saying, `Thus said Pharaoh, I do not give you straw,
5:11 ye -- go ye, take for yourselves straw where ye find [it], for there is nothing of your service diminished.'
5:12 And the people is scattered over all the land of Egypt, to gather stubble for straw,
5:13 and the exactors are making haste, saying, `Complete your works, the matter of a day in its day, as when there is straw.'
5:14 And the authorities of the sons of Israel, whom the exactors of Pharaoh have placed over them, are beaten, saying, `Wherefore have ye not completed your portion in making brick as heretofore, both yesterday and to-day?'
5:15 And the authorities of the sons of Israel come in and cry unto Pharaoh, saying, `Why dost thou thus to thy servants?
5:16 Straw is not given to thy servants, and they are saying to us, Make bricks, and lo, thy servants are smitten -- and thy people hath sinned.'
5:17 And he saith, `Remiss -- ye are remiss, therefore ye are saying, Let us go, let us sacrifice to Jehovah;
5:18 and now, go, serve; and straw is not given to you, and the measure of bricks ye do give.'

5:19 And the authorities of the sons of Israel see them in affliction, saying, `Ye do not diminish from your bricks; the matter of a day in its day.'
5:20 And they meet Moses and Aaron standing to meet them, in their coming out from Pharaoh,
5:21 and say unto them, `Jehovah look upon you, and judge, because ye have caused our fragrance to stink in the eyes of Pharaoh, and in the eyes of his servants -- to give a sword into their hand to slay us.'
5:22 And Moses turneth back unto Jehovah, and saith, `Lord, why hast Thou done evil to this people? why [is] this? -- Thou hast sent me!
5:23 and since I have come unto Pharaoh, to speak in Thy name, he hath done evil to this people, and Thou hast not at all delivered Thy people.'
6:1 And Jehovah saith unto Moses, `Now dost thou see that which I do to Pharaoh, for with a strong hand he doth send them away, yea, with a strong hand he doth cast them out of his land.'
6:2 And God speaketh unto Moses, and saith unto him, `I [am] Jehovah,
6:3 and I appear unto Abraham, unto Isaac, and unto Jacob, as God Almighty; as to My name Jehovah, I have not been known to them;
6:4 and also I have established My covenant with them, to give to them the land of Canaan, the land of their sojournings, wherein they have sojourned;
6:5 and also I have heard the groaning of the sons of Israel, whom the Egyptians are causing to serve, and I remember My covenant.
6:6 `Therefore say to the sons of Israel, I [am] Jehovah, and I have brought you out from under the burdens of the Egyptians, and have delivered you from their service, and have redeemed you by a stretched-out arm, and by great judgments,
6:7 and have taken you to Me for a people, and I have been to you for God, and ye have known that I [am] Jehovah your God, who is bringing you out from under the burdens of the Egyptians;
6:8 and I have brought you in unto the land which I have lifted up My hand to give it to Abraham, to Isaac, and to Jacob, and have given it to you -- a possession; I [am] Jehovah.'
6:9 And Moses speaketh so unto the sons of Israel, and they hearkened not unto Moses, for anguish of spirit, and for harsh service.
6:10 And Jehovah speaketh unto Moses, saying,
6:11 `Go in, speak unto Pharaoh king of Egypt, and he doth send the sons of Israel out of his land;
6:12 and Moses speaketh before Jehovah, saying, `Lo, the sons of Israel have not hearkened unto me, and how doth Pharaoh hear me, and I of uncircumcised lips?'
6:13 And Jehovah speaketh unto Moses, and unto Aaron, and chargeth them for the sons of Israel, and for Pharaoh king of Egypt, to bring out the sons of Israel from the land of Egypt.

6:14 These [are] heads of the house of their fathers: Sons of Reuben first-born of Israel [are] Hanoch, and Phallu, Hezron, and Carmi: these [are] families of Reuben.
6:15 And sons of Simeon [are] Jemuel, and Jamin, and Ohad, and Jachin, and Zohar, and Shaul, son of the Canaanitess: these [are] families of Simeon.
6:16 And these [are] the names of the sons of Levi, as to their births: Gershon, and Kohath, and Merari: and the years of the life of Levi [are] a hundred and thirty and seven years.
6:17 The sons of Gershon [are] Libni, and Shimi, as to their families.
6:18 And the sons of Kohath [are] Amram, and Izhar, and Hebron, and Uzziel: and the years of the life of Kohath [are] a hundred and thirty and three years.
6:19 And the sons of Merari [are] Mahli and Mushi: these [are] families of Levi, as to their births.
6:20 And Amram taketh Jochebed his aunt to himself for a wife, and she beareth to him Aaron and Moses: and the years of the life of Amram [are] a hundred and thirty and seven years.
6:21 And sons of Izhar [are] Korah, and Nepheg, and Zichri.
6:22 And sons of Uzziel [are] Mishael, and Elzaphan, and Sithri.
6:23 And Aaron taketh Elisheba daughter of Amminadab, sister of Naashon, to himself for a wife, and she beareth to him Nadab, and Abihu, Eleazar, and Ithamar.
6:24 And sons of Korah [are] Assir, and Elkanah, and Abiasaph: these [are] families of the Korhite.
6:25 And Eleazar, Aaron's son, hath taken to him [one] of the daughters of Putiel for a wife to himself, and she beareth to him Phinehas: these [are] heads of the fathers of the Levites, as to their families.
6:26 This [is] Aaron -- and Moses -- to whom Jehovah said, `Bring ye out the sons of Israel from the land of Egypt, by their hosts;'
6:27 these are they who are speaking unto Pharaoh king of Egypt, to bring out the sons of Israel from Egypt, this [is] Moses -- and Aaron.
6:28 And it cometh to pass in the day of Jehovah's speaking unto Moses in the land of Egypt,
6:29 that Jehovah speaketh unto Moses, saying, `I [am] Jehovah, speak unto Pharaoh king of Egypt all that I am speaking unto thee.'
6:30 And Moses saith before Jehovah, `Lo, I [am] of uncircumcised lips, and how doth Pharaoh hearken unto me?'
7:1 And Jehovah saith unto Moses, `See, I have given thee a god to Pharaoh, and Aaron thy brother is thy prophet;
7:2 thou -- thou dost speak all that I command thee, and Aaron thy brother doth speak unto Pharaoh, and he hath sent the sons of Israel out of his land.
7:3 `And I harden the heart of Pharaoh, and have multiplied My signs and My wonders in the land

of Egypt,
7:4 and Pharaoh doth not hearken, and I have put My hand on Egypt, and have brought out My hosts, My people, the sons of Israel, from the land of Egypt by great judgments;
7:5 and the Egyptians have known that I [am] Jehovah, in My stretching out My hand against Egypt; and I have brought out the sons of Israel from their midst.'
7:6 And Moses doth -- Aaron also -- as Jehovah commanded them; so have they done;
7:7 and Moses [is] a son of eighty years, and Aaron [is] a son of eighty and three years, in their speaking unto Pharaoh.
7:8 And Jehovah speaketh unto Moses and unto Aaron, saying,
7:9 `When Pharaoh speaketh unto you, saying, Give for yourselves a wonder; then thou hast said unto Aaron, Take thy rod, and cast before Pharaoh -- it becometh a monster.'
7:10 And Moses goeth in -- Aaron also -- unto Pharaoh, and they do so as Jehovah hath commanded; and Aaron casteth his rod before Pharaoh, and before his servants, and it becometh a monster.
7:11 And Pharaoh also calleth for wise men, and for sorcerers; and the scribes of Egypt, they also, with their flashings, do so,
7:12 and they cast down each his rod, and they become monsters, and the rod of Aaron swalloweth their rods;
7:13 and the heart of Pharaoh is strong, and he hath not hearkened unto them, as Jehovah hath spoken.
7:14 And Jehovah saith unto Moses, `The heart of Pharaoh hath been hard, he hath refused to send the people away;
7:15 go unto Pharaoh in the morning, lo, he is going out to the water, and thou hast stood to meet him by the edge of the River, and the rod which was turned to a serpent thou dost take in thy hand,
7:16 and thou hast said unto him: Jehovah, God of the Hebrews, hath sent me unto thee, saying, Send My people away, and they serve Me in the wilderness; and lo, thou hast not hearkened hitherto.
7:17 `Thus said Jehovah: By this thou knowest that I [am] Jehovah; lo, I am smiting with the rod which [is] in my hand, on the waters which [are] in the River, and they have been turned to blood,
7:18 and the fish that [are] in the River die, and the River hath stank, and the Egyptians have been wearied of drinking waters from the River.'
7:19 And Jehovah saith unto Moses, `Say unto Aaron, Take thy rod, and stretch out thy hand against the waters of Egypt, against their streams, against their rivers, and against their ponds, and against all their collections of waters; and they are blood -- and there hath been blood in all the land

of Egypt, both in [vessels of] wood, and in [those of] stone.'
7:20 And Moses and Aaron do so, as Jehovah hath commanded, and he lifteth up [his hand] with
the rod, and smiteth the waters which [are] in the River, before the eyes of Pharaoh, and before the
eyes of his servants, and all the waters which [are] in the River are turned to blood,
7:21 and the fish which [is] in the River hath died, and the River stinketh, and the Egyptians have
not been able to drink water from the River; and the blood is in all the land of Egypt.
7:22 And the scribes of Egypt do so with their flashings, and the heart of Pharaoh is strong, and he
hath not hearkened unto them, as Jehovah hath spoken,
7:23 and Pharaoh turneth and goeth in unto his house, and hath not set his heart even to this;
7:24 and all the Egyptians seek water round about the river to drink, for they have not been able to
drink of the waters of the River.
7:25 And seven days are completed after Jehovah's smiting the River,
8:1 And Jehovah saith unto Moses, `Go in unto Pharaoh: and thou hast said unto him, Thus said
Jehovah, Send My people away, and they serve Me;
8:2 and if thou art refusing to send away, lo, I am smiting all thy border with frogs;
8:3 and the River hath teemed [with] frogs, and they have gone up and gone into thy house, and
into the inner-chamber of thy bed, and on thy couch, and into the house of thy servants, and
among thy people, and into thine ovens, and into thy kneading-troughs;
8:4 yea, on thee, and on thy people, and on all thy servants do the frogs go up.'
8:5 And Jehovah saith unto Moses, `Say unto Aaron, Stretch out thy hand, with thy rod, against the
streams, against the rivers, and against the ponds, and cause the frogs to come up against the
land of Egypt.'
8:6 And Aaron stretcheth out his hand against the waters of Egypt, and the frog cometh up, and
covereth the land of Egypt;
8:7 and the scribes do so with their flashings, and cause the frogs to come up against the land of
Egypt.
8:8 And Pharaoh calleth for Moses and for Aaron, and saith, `Make supplication unto Jehovah, that
he turn aside the frogs from me, and from my people, and I send the people away, and they
sacrifice to Jehovah.'
8:9 And Moses saith to Pharaoh, `Beautify thyself over me; when do I make supplication for thee,
and for thy servants, and for thy people, to cut off the frogs from thee and from thy houses -- only in
the River they do remain?'
8:10 and he saith, `To-morrow.' And he saith, According to thy word [it is], so that thou knowest that
there is none like Jehovah our God,

8:11 and the frogs have turned aside from thee, and from thy houses, and from thy servants, and from thy people; only in the River they do remain.'

8:12 And Moses -- Aaron also -- goeth out from Pharaoh, and Moses crieth unto Jehovah, concerning the matter of the frogs which He hath set on Pharaoh;

8:13 and Jehovah doth according to the word of Moses, and the frogs die out of the houses, out of the courts, and out of the fields,

8:14 and they heap them up together, and the land stinketh.

8:15 And Pharaoh seeth that there hath been a respite, and he hath hardened his heart, and hath not hearkened unto them, as Jehovah hath spoken.

8:16 And Jehovah saith unto Moses, `Say unto Aaron, Stretch out thy rod, and smite the dust of the land, and it hath become gnats in all the land of Egypt.'

8:17 And they do so, and Aaron stretcheth out his hand with his rod, and smiteth the dust of the land, and the gnats are on man and on beast; all the dust of the land hath been gnats in all the land of Egypt.

8:18 And the scribes do so with their flashings, to bring out the gnats, and they have not been able, and the gnats are on man and on beast;

8:19 and the scribes say unto Pharaoh, `It [is] the finger of God;' and the heart of Pharaoh is strong, and he hath not hearkened unto them, as Jehovah hath spoken.

8:20 And Jehovah saith unto Moses, `Rise early in the morning, and station thyself before Pharaoh, lo, he is going out to the waters, and thou hast said unto him, Thus said Jehovah, Send My people away, and they serve Me;

8:21 for, if thou art not sending My people away, lo, I am sending against thee, and against thy servants, and against thy people, and against thy houses, the beetle, and the houses of the Egyptians have been full of the beetle, and also the ground on which they are.

8:22 `And I have separated in that day the land of Goshen, in which My people are staying, that the beetle is not there, so that thou knowest that I [am] Jehovah in the midst of the land,

8:23 and I have put a division between My people and thy people: to-morrow is this sign.'

8:24 And Jehovah doth so, and the grievous beetle entereth the house of Pharaoh, and the house of his servants, and in all the land of Egypt the land is corrupted from the presence of the beetle.

8:25 And Pharaoh calleth unto Moses and to Aaron, and saith, `Go, sacrifice to your God in the land;'

8:26 and Moses saith, `Not right to do so, for the abomination of the Egyptians we do sacrifice to Jehovah our God; lo, we sacrifice the abomination of the Egyptians before their eyes -- and they do not stone us!

8:27 A journey of three days we go into the wilderness, and have sacrificed to Jehovah our God, as
He saith unto us.'
8:28 And Pharaoh saith, `I send you away, and ye have sacrificed to Jehovah your God in the
wilderness, only go not very far off; make ye supplication for me;'
8:29 and Moses saith, `Lo, I am going out from thee, and have made supplication unto Jehovah,
and the beetle hath turned aside from Pharaoh, from his servants, and from his people -- to-
morrow, only let not Pharaoh add to deceive -- in not sending the people away to sacrifice to
Jehovah.'
8:30 And Moses goeth out from Pharaoh, and maketh supplication unto Jehovah,
8:31 and Jehovah doth according to the word of Moses, and turneth aside the beetle from Pharaoh,
from his servants, and from his people -- there hath not been left one;
8:32 and Pharaoh hardeneth his heart also at this time, and hath not sent the people away.
9:1 And Jehovah saith unto Moses, `Go in unto Pharaoh, and thou hast spoken unto him, Thus
said Jehovah, God of the Hebrews, Send My people away, and they serve me,
9:2 for, if thou art refusing to send away, and art still keeping hold upon them,
9:3 lo, the hand of Jehovah is on thy cattle which [are] in the field, on horses, on asses, on camels,
on herd, and on flock -- a pestilence very grievous.
9:4 `And Jehovah hath separated between the cattle of Israel and the cattle of Egypt, and there
doth not die a thing of all the sons of Israel's;
9:5 and Jehovah setteth an appointed time, saying, To-morrow doth Jehovah do this thing in the
land.'
9:6 And Jehovah doth this thing on the morrow, and all the cattle of Egypt die, and of the cattle of
the sons of Israel not one hath died;
9:7 and Pharaoh sendeth, and lo, not even one of the cattle of Israel hath died, and the heart of
Pharaoh is hard, and he hath not sent the people away.
9:8 And Jehovah saith unto Moses and unto Aaron, `Take to you the fulness of your hands [of] soot
of a furnace, and Moses hath sprinkled it towards the heavens, before the eyes of Pharaoh,
9:9 and it hath become small dust over all the land of Egypt, and it hath become on man and on
cattle a boil breaking forth [with] blains, in all the land of Egypt.'
9:10 And they take the soot of the furnace, and stand before Pharaoh, and Moses sprinkleth it
towards the heavens, and it is a boil [with] blains, breaking forth, on man and on beast;
9:11 and the scribes have not been able to stand before Moses, because of the boil, for the boil
hath been on the scribes, and on all the Egyptians.
9:12 And Jehovah strengtheneth the heart of Pharaoh, and he hath not hearkened unto them, as

Jehovah hath spoken unto Moses.
9:13 And Jehovah saith unto Moses, `Rise early in the morning, and station thyself before Pharaoh, and thou hast said unto him, Thus said Jehovah, God of the Hebrews, Send My people away, and they serve Me,
9:14 for, at this time I am sending all My plagues unto thy heart, and on thy servants, and on thy people, so that thou knowest that there is none like Me in all the earth,
9:15 for now I have put forth My hand, and I smite thee, and thy people, with pestilence, and thou art hidden from the earth.
9:16 `And yet for this I have caused thee to stand, so as to show thee My power, and for the sake of declaring My Name in all the earth;
9:17 still thou art exalting thyself against My people -- so as not to send them away;
9:18 lo, I am raining about [this] time to-morrow hail very grievous, such as hath not been in Egypt, even from the day of its being founded, even until now.
9:19 `And, now, send, strengthen thy cattle and all that thou hast in the field; every man and beast which is found in the field, and is not gathered into the house -- come down on them hath the hail, and they have died.'
9:20 He who is fearing the word of Jehovah among the servants of Pharaoh hath caused his servants and his cattle to flee unto the houses;
9:21 and he who hath not set his heart unto the word of Jehovah leaveth his servants and his cattle in the field.
9:22 And Jehovah saith unto Moses, `Stretch forth thy hand towards the heavens, and there is hail in all the land of Egypt, on man, and on beast, and on every herb of the field in the land of Egypt.'
9:23 And Moses stretcheth out his rod towards the heavens, and Jehovah hath given voices and hail, and fire goeth towards the earth, and Jehovah raineth hail on the land of Egypt,
9:24 and there is hail, and fire catching itself in the midst of the hail, very grievous, such as hath not been in all the land of Egypt since it hath become a nation.
9:25 And the hail smiteth in all the land of Egypt all that [is] in the field, from man even unto beast, and every herb of the field hath the hail smitten, and every tree of the field it hath broken;
9:26 only in the land of Goshen, where the sons of Israel [are], there hath been no hail.
9:27 And Pharaoh sendeth, and calleth for Moses and for Aaron, and saith unto them, `I have sinned this time, Jehovah [is] the Righteous, and I and my people [are] the Wicked,
9:28 make ye supplication unto Jehovah, and plead that there be no voices of God and hail, and I send you away, and ye add not to remain.'
9:29 And Moses saith unto him, `At my going out of the city, I spread my palms unto Jehovah -- the

voices cease, and the hail is not any more, so that thou knowest that the earth [is] Jehovah's;
9:30 but thou and thy servants -- I have known that ye are not yet afraid of the face of Jehovah
God.'
9:31 And the flax and the barley have been smitten, for the barley [is] budding, and the flax forming
flowers,
9:32 and the wheat and the rye have not been smitten, for they are late.
9:33 And Moses goeth out from Pharaoh, [from] the city, and spreadeth his hands unto Jehovah,
and the voices and the hail cease, and rain hath not been poured out to the earth;
9:34 and Pharaoh seeth that the rain hath ceased, and the hail and the voices, and he continueth
to sin, and hardeneth his heart, he and his servants;
9:35 and the heart of Pharaoh is strong, and he hath not sent the sons of Israel away, as Jehovah
hath spoken by the hand of Moses.
10:1 And Jehovah saith unto Moses, `Go in unto Pharaoh, for I have declared hard his heart, and
the heart of his servants, so that I set these My signs in their midst,
10:2 and so that thou recountest in the ears of thy son, and of thy son's son, that which I have done
in Egypt, and My signs which I have set among them, and ye have known that I [am] Jehovah.'
10:3 And Moses cometh in -- Aaron also -- unto Pharaoh, and they say unto him, `Thus said
Jehovah, God of the Hebrews, Until when hast thou refused to be humbled at My presence? send
My people away, and they serve Me,
10:4 for if thou art refusing to send My people away, lo, I am bringing in to-morrow the locust into
thy border,
10:5 and it hath covered the eye of the land, and none is able to see the land, and it hath eaten the
remnant of that which is escaped, which is left to you from the hail, and it hath eaten every tree
which is springing for you out of the field;
10:6 and they have filled thy houses, and the houses of all thy servants, and the houses of all the
Egyptians, which neither thy fathers nor thy father's fathers have seen, since the day of their being
on the ground unto this day,' -- and he turneth and goeth out from Pharaoh.
10:7 And the servants of Pharaoh say unto him, `Until when doth this [one] become a snare to us?
send the men away, and they serve Jehovah their God; knowest thou not yet that Egypt hath
perished?'
10:8 And Moses is brought back -- Aaron also -- unto Pharaoh, and he saith unto them, `Go, serve
Jehovah your God; -- who and who [are] those going?'
10:9 And Moses saith, `With our young ones, and with our aged ones, we go, with our sons, and
with our daughters, with our flock, and our herd, we go, for we have a festival to Jehovah.'

10:10 And he saith unto them, `Be it so, Jehovah [be] with you when I send you and your infants
away; see -- for evil [is] before your faces;
10:11 not so! go now, ye who [are] men, and serve Jehovah, for that ye are seeking;' and [one]
casteth them out from the presence of Pharaoh.
10:12 And Jehovah saith unto Moses, `Stretch out thy hand against the land of Egypt for the locust,
and it goeth up against the land of Egypt, and doth eat every herb of the land -- all that the hail hath
left.'
10:13 And Moses stretcheth out his rod against the land of Egypt, and Jehovah hath led an east
wind over the land all that day, and all the night; the morning hath been, and the east wind hath
lifted up the locust.
10:14 And the locust goeth up against all the land of Egypt, and resteth in all the border of Egypt --
very grievous: before it there hath not been such a locust as it, and after it there is none such;
10:15 and it covereth the eye of all the land, and the land is darkened; and it eateth every herb of
the land, and all the fruit of the trees which the hail hath left, and there hath not been left any green
thing in the trees, or in the herb of the field, in all the land of Egypt.'
10:16 And Pharaoh hasteth to call for Moses and for Aaron, and saith, `I have sinned against
Jehovah your God, and against you,
10:17 and now, bear with, I pray you, my sin, only this time, and make ye supplication to Jehovah
your God, that He turn aside from off me only this death.'
10:18 And he goeth out from Pharaoh, and maketh supplication unto Jehovah,
10:19 and Jehovah turneth a very strong sea wind, and it lifteth up the locust, and bloweth it into
the Red Sea -- there hath not been left one locust in all the border of Egypt;
10:20 and Jehovah strengtheneth the heart of Pharaoh, and he hath not sent the sons of Israel
away.
10:21 And Jehovah saith unto Moses, `Stretch out thy hand towards the heavens, and there is
darkness over the land of Egypt, and the darkness is felt.'
10:22 And Moses stretcheth out his hand towards the heavens, and there is darkness -- thick
darkness in all the land of Egypt three days;
10:23 they have not seen one another, and none hath risen from his place three days; and to all the
sons of Israel there hath been light in their dwellings.'
10:24 And Pharaoh calleth unto Moses and saith, `Go ye, serve Jehovah, only your flock and your
herd are stayed, your infants also go with you;'
10:25 and Moses saith, `Thou also dost give in our hand sacrifices and burnt-offerings, and we
have prepared for Jehovah our God;

10:26 and also our cattle doth go with us, there is not left a hoof, for from it we do take to serve
Jehovah our God; and we -- we know not how we do serve Jehovah till our going thither.'
10:27 And Jehovah strengtheneth the heart of Pharaoh, and he hath not been willing to send them
away;
10:28 and Pharaoh saith to him, `Go from me, take heed to thyself, add not to see my face, for in
the day thou seest my face thou diest;'
10:29 and Moses saith, `Rightly hast thou spoken, I add not any more to see thy face.'
11:1 And Jehovah saith unto Moses, `One plague more I do bring in on Pharaoh, and on Egypt,
afterwards he doth send you away from this; when he is sending you away, he surely casteth you
out altogether from this [place];
11:2 speak, I pray thee, in the ears of the people, and they ask -- each man from his neighbour,
and each woman from her neighbour, vessels of silver, and vessels of gold.'
11:3 And Jehovah giveth the grace of the people in the eyes of the Egyptians; also the man Moses
[is] very great in the land of Egypt, in the eyes of the servants of Pharaoh, and in the eyes of the
people.
11:4 And Moses saith, `Thus said Jehovah, About midnight I am going out into the midst of Egypt,
11:5 and every first-born in the land of Egypt hath died, from the first-born of Pharaoh who is sitting
on his throne, unto the first-born of the maid-servant who [is] behind the millstones, and all the first-
born of beasts;
11:6 and there hath been a great cry in all the land of Egypt, such as there hath not been, and such
as there is not again.
11:7 `And against all the sons of Israel a dog sharpeneth not its tongue, from man even unto beast,
so that ye know that Jehovah doth make a separation between the Egyptians and Israel;
11:8 and all these thy servants have come down unto me, and bowed themselves to me, saying,
Go out, thou and all the people who [are] at thy feet; and afterwards I do go out;' -- and he goeth
out from Pharaoh in the heat of anger.
11:9 And Jehovah saith unto Moses, `Pharaoh doth not hearken unto you, so as to multiply My
wonders in the land of Egypt;'
11:10 and Moses and Aaron have done all these wonders before Pharaoh, and Jehovah
strengtheneth Pharaoh's heart, and he hath not sent the sons of Israel out of his land.
12:1 And Jehovah speaketh unto Moses and unto Aaron, in the land of Egypt, saying,
12:2 `This month [is] to you the chief of months -- it [is] the first to you of the months of the year;
12:3 speak ye unto all the company of Israel, saying, In the tenth of this month -- they take to them
each man a lamb for the house of the fathers, a lamb for a house.

12:4 `(And if the household be too few for a lamb, then hath he taken, he and his neighbour who is near unto his house, for the number of persons, each according to his eating ye do count for the lamb,)
12:5 a lamb, a perfect one, a male, a son of a year, let be to you; from the sheep or from the goats ye do take [it].
12:6 `And it hath become a charge to you, until the fourteenth day of this month, and the whole assembly of the company of Israel have slaughtered it between the evenings;
12:7 and they have taken of the blood, and have put on the two side-posts, and on the lintel over the houses in which they eat it.
12:8 `And they have eaten the flesh in this night, roast with fire; with unleavened things and bitters they do eat it;
12:9 ye do not eat of it raw, or boiled at all in water, but roast with fire, its head with its legs, and with its inwards;
12:10 and ye do not leave of it till morning, and that which is remaining of it till morning with fire ye do burn.
12:11 `And thus ye do eat it: your loins girded, your sandals on your feet, and your staff in your hand, and ye have eaten it in haste; it is Jehovah's passover,
12:12 and I have passed over through the land of Egypt during this night, and have smitten every first-born in the land of Egypt, from man even unto beast, and on all the gods of Egypt I do judgments; I [am] Jehovah.
12:13 `And the blood hath become a sign for you on the houses where ye [are], and I have seen the blood, and have passed over you, and a plague is not on you for destruction in My smiting in the land of Egypt.
12:14 `And this day hath become to you a memorial, and ye have kept it a feast to Jehovah to your generations; -- a statute age-during; ye keep it a feast.
12:15 Seven days ye eat unleavened things; only -- in the first day ye cause leaven to cease out of your houses; for any one eating anything fermented from the first day till the seventh day, even that person hath been cut off from Israel.
12:16 `And in the first day [is] a holy convocation, and in the seventh day ye have a holy convocation; any work is not done in them, only that which is eaten by any person -- it alone is done by you,
12:17 and ye have observed the unleavened things, for in this self-same day I have brought out your hosts from the land of Egypt, and ye have observed this day to your generations -- a statute age-during.

12:18 `In the first [month], in the fourteenth day of the month, in the evening, ye do eat unleavened things until the one and twentieth day of the month, at evening;
12:19 seven days leaven is not found in your houses, for any [one] eating anything fermented -- that person hath been cut off from the company of Israel, among the sojourners or among the natives of the land;
12:20 anything fermented ye do not eat, in all your dwellings ye do eat unleavened things.'
12:21 And Moses calleth for all the elders of Israel, and saith unto them, `Draw out and take for yourselves [from] the flock, for your families, and slaughter the passover-sacrifice;
12:22 and ye have taken a bunch of hyssop, and have dipped [it] in the blood which [is] in the basin, and have struck [it] on the lintel, and on the two side-posts, from the blood which [is] in the basin, and ye, ye go not out each from the opening of his house till morning.
12:23 `And Jehovah hath passed on to smite the Egyptians, and hath seen the blood on the lintel, and on the two side-posts, and Jehovah hath passed over the opening, and doth not permit the destruction to come into your houses to smite.
12:24 `And ye have observed this thing, for a statute to thee, and to thy sons -- unto the age;
12:25 and it hath been, when ye come in unto the land which Jehovah giveth to you, as He hath spoken, that ye have kept this service;
12:26 and it hath come to pass when your sons say unto you, What [is] this service ye have?
12:27 that ye have said, A sacrifice of passover it [is] to Jehovah, who passed over the houses of the sons of Israel in Egypt, in His smiting the Egyptians, and our houses He delivered.'
12:28 And the people bow and do obeisance, and the sons of Israel go and do as Jehovah commanded Moses and Aaron; so have they done.
12:29 And it cometh to pass, at midnight, that Jehovah hath smitten every first-born in the land of Egypt, from the first-born of Pharaoh who is sitting on his throne, unto the first-born of the captive who [is] in the prison-house, and every first-born of beasts.
12:30 And Pharaoh riseth by night, he and all his servants, and all the Egyptians, and there is a great cry in Egypt, for there is not a house where there is not [one] dead,
12:31 and he calleth for Moses and for Aaron by night, and saith, `Rise, go out from the midst of my people, both ye and the sons of Israel, and go, serve Jehovah according to your word;
12:32 both your flock and your herd take ye, as ye have spoken, and go; then ye have blessed also me.'
12:33 And the Egyptians are urgent on the people, hasting to send them away out of the land, for they said, `We are all dead;'
12:34 and the people taketh up its dough before it is fermented, their kneading-troughs [are] bound

up in their garments on their shoulder.
12:35 And the sons of Israel have done according to the word of Moses, and they ask from the Egyptians vessels of silver and vessels of gold, and garments;
12:36 and Jehovah hath given the grace of the people in the eyes of the Egyptians, and they cause them to ask, and they spoil the Egyptians.
12:37 And the sons of Israel journey from Rameses to Succoth, about six hundred thousand men on foot, apart from infants;
12:38 and a great rabble also hath gone up with them, and flock and herd -- very much cattle.
12:39 And they bake with the dough which they have brought out from Egypt unleavened cakes, for it hath not fermented; for they have been cast out of Egypt, and have not been able to delay, and also provision they have not made for themselves.
12:40 And the dwelling of the sons of Israel which they have dwelt in Egypt [is] four hundred and thirty years;
12:41 and it cometh to pass, at the end of four hundred and thirty years -- yea, it cometh to pass in this self-same day -- all the hosts of Jehovah have gone out from the land of Egypt.
12:42 A night of watchings it [is] to Jehovah, to bring them out from the land of Egypt; it [is] this night to Jehovah of watchings to all the sons of Israel to their generations.
12:43 And Jehovah saith unto Moses and Aaron, `This [is] a statute of the passover; Any son of a stranger doth not eat of it;
12:44 and any man's servant, the purchase of money, when thou hast circumcised him -- then he doth eat of it;
12:45 a settler or hired servant doth not eat of it;
12:46 in one house it is eaten, thou dost not carry out of the house [any] of the flesh without, and a bone ye do not break of it;
12:47 all the company of Israel do keep it.
12:48 `And when a sojourner sojourneth with thee, and hath made a passover to Jehovah, every male of his [is] to be circumcised, and then he doth come near to keep it, and he hath been as a native of the land, but any uncircumcised one doth not eat of it;
12:49 one law is to a native, and to a sojourner who is sojourning in your midst.'
12:50 And all the sons of Israel do as Jehovah commanded Moses and Aaron; so have they done.
12:51 And it cometh to pass in this self-same day, Jehovah hath brought out the sons of Israel from the land of Egypt, by their hosts.
13:1 And Jehovah speaketh unto Moses, saying,
13:2 `Sanctify to Me every first-born, opening any womb among the sons of Israel, among man and

among beast; it [is] Mine.'

13:3 And Moses saith unto the people, `Remember this day [in] which ye have gone out from Egypt, from the house of servants, for by strength of hand hath Jehovah brought you out from this, and any thing fermented is not eaten;

13:4 To-day ye are going out, in the month of Abib.

13:5 `And it hath been, when Jehovah bringeth thee in unto the land of the Canaanite, and of the Hittite, and of the Amorite, and of the Hivite, and of the Jebusite, which He hath sworn to thy fathers to give to thee, a land flowing with milk and honey, that thou hast done this service in this month.

13:6 `Seven days thou dost eat unleavened things, and in the seventh day [is] a feast to Jehovah;

13:7 unleavened things are eaten the seven days, and any thing fermented is not seen with thee; yea, leaven is not seen with thee in all thy border.

13:8 `And thou hast declared to thy son in that day, saying, `[It is] because of what Jehovah did to me, in my going out from Egypt,

13:9 and it hath been to thee for a sign on thy hand, and for a memorial between thine eyes, so that the law of Jehovah is in thy mouth, for by a strong hand hath Jehovah brought thee out from Egypt;

13:10 and thou hast kept this statute at its appointed season from days to days.

13:11 `And it hath been, when Jehovah bringeth thee in unto the land of the Canaanite, as He hath sworn to thee and to thy fathers, and hath given it to thee,

13:12 that thou hast caused every one opening a womb to pass over to Jehovah, and every firstling -- the increase of beasts which thou hast: the males [are] Jehovah's.

13:13 `And every firstling of an ass thou dost ransom with a lamb, and if thou dost not ransom [it], then thou hast beheaded it: and every first-born of man among thy sons thou dost ransom.

13:14 `And it hath been, when thy son asketh thee hereafter, saying, What [is] this? that thou hast said unto him, By strength of hand hath Jehovah brought us out from Egypt, from a house of servants;

13:15 yea, it cometh to pass, when Pharaoh hath been pained to send us away, that Jehovah doth slay every first-born in the land of Egypt, from the first-born of man even unto the first-born of beast; therefore I am sacrificing to Jehovah all opening a womb who [are] males, and every first-born of my sons I ransom;

13:16 and it hath been for a token on thy hand, and for frontlets between thine eyes, for by strength of hand hath Jehovah brought us out of Egypt.'

13:17 And it cometh to pass in Pharaoh's sending the people away, that God hath not led them the way of the land of the Philistines, for it [is] near; for God said, `Lest the people repent in their

seeing war, and have turned back towards Egypt;'
13:18 and God turneth round the people the way of the wilderness of the Red Sea, and by fifties have the sons of Israel gone up from the land of Egypt.
13:19 And Moses taketh the bones of Joseph with him, for he certainly caused the sons of Israel to swear, saying, `God doth certainly inspect you, and ye have brought up my bones from this with you.'
13:20 And they journey from Succoth, and encamp in Etham at the extremity of the wilderness,
13:21 and Jehovah is going before them by day in a pillar of a cloud, to lead them in the way, and by night in a pillar of fire, to give light to them, to go by day and by night;
13:22 He removeth not the pillar of the cloud by day, and the pillar of the fire by night, [from] before the people.
14:1 And Jehovah speaketh unto Moses, saying,
14:2 `Speak unto the sons of Israel, and they turn back and encamp before Pi-Hahiroth, between Migdol and the sea, before Baal-Zephon; over-against it ye do encamp by the sea,
14:3 and Pharaoh hath said of the sons of Israel, They are entangled in the land, the wilderness hath shut upon them;
14:4 and I have strengthened the heart of Pharaoh, and he hath pursued after them, and I am honoured on Pharaoh, and on all his force, and the Egyptians have known that I [am] Jehovah;' and they do so.
14:5 And it is declared to the king of Egypt that the people hath fled, and the heart of Pharaoh and of his servants is turned against the people, and they say, `What [is] this we have done? that we have sent Israel away from our service.'
14:6 And he harnesseth his chariot, and his people he hath taken with him,
14:7 and he taketh six hundred chosen chariots, even all the chariots of Egypt, and captains over them all;
14:8 and Jehovah strengtheneth the heart of Pharaoh king of Egypt, and he pursueth after the sons of Israel, and the sons of Israel are going out with a high hand,
14:9 and the Egyptians pursue after them, and all the chariot horses of Pharaoh, and his horsemen, and his force, overtake them, encamping by the sea, by Pi-Hahiroth, before Baal-Zephon.
14:10 And Pharaoh hath drawn near, and the sons of Israel lift up their eyes, and lo, the Egyptians are journeying after them, and they fear exceedingly, and the sons of Israel cry unto Jehovah.
14:11 And they say unto Moses, `Because there are no graves in Egypt, hast thou taken us away to die in a wilderness? what is this thou hast done to us -- to bring us out from Egypt?

14:12 Is not this the word which we spake unto thee in Egypt, saying, Cease from us, and we serve the Egyptians; for better for us to serve the Egyptians than to die in a wilderness?'
14:13 And Moses saith unto the people, `Fear not, station yourselves, and see the salvation of Jehovah, which He doth for you to-day; for, as ye have seen the Egyptians to-day, ye add no more to see them -- to the age;
14:14 Jehovah doth fight for you, and ye keep silent.'
14:15 And Jehovah saith unto Moses, `What? thou criest unto Me -- speak unto the sons of Israel, and they journey;
14:16 and thou, lift up thy rod, and stretch out thy hand towards the sea, and cleave it, and the sons of Israel go into the midst of the sea on dry land.
14:17 `And I -- lo, I am strengthening the heart of the Egyptians, and they go in after them, and I am honoured on Pharaoh, and on all his force, on his chariots, and on his horsemen;
14:18 and the Egyptians have known that I [am] Jehovah, in My being honoured on Pharaoh, on his chariots, and on his horsemen.'
14:19 And the messenger of God, who is going before the camp of Israel, journeyeth and goeth at their rear; and the pillar of the cloud journeyeth from their front, and standeth at their rear,
14:20 and cometh in between the camp of the Egyptians and the camp of Israel, and the cloud and the darkness are, and he enlighteneth the night, and the one hath not drawn near unto the other all the night.
14:21 And Moses stretcheth out his hand towards the sea, and Jehovah causeth the sea to go on by a strong east wind all the night, and maketh the sea become dry ground, and the waters are cleaved,
14:22 and the sons of Israel go into the midst of the sea, on dry land, and the waters [are] to them a wall, on their right and on their left.
14:23 And the Egyptians pursue, and go in after them (all the horses of Pharaoh, his chariots, and his horsemen) unto the midst of the sea,
14:24 and it cometh to pass, in the morning watch, that Jehovah looketh unto the camp of the Egyptians through the pillar of fire and of the cloud, and troubleth the camp of the Egyptians,
14:25 and turneth aside the wheels of their chariots, and they lead them with difficulty, and the Egyptians say, `Let us flee from the face of Israel, for Jehovah is fighting for them against the Egyptians.'
14:26 And Jehovah saith unto Moses, `Stretch out thy hand toward the sea, and the waters turn back on the Egyptians, on their chariots, and on their horsemen.'
14:27 And Moses stretcheth out his hand towards the sea, and the sea turneth back, at the turning

of the morning, to its perennial flow, and the Egyptians are fleeing at its coming, and Jehovah shaketh off the Egyptians in the midst of the sea,
14:28 and the waters turn back, and cover the chariots and the horsemen, even all the force of Pharaoh, who are coming in after them into the sea -- there hath not been left of them even one.
14:29 And the sons of Israel have gone on dry land in the midst of the sea, and the waters [are] to them a wall, on their right and on their left;
14:30 and Jehovah saveth Israel in that day out of the hand of the Egyptians, and Israel seeth the Egyptians dead on the sea-shore,
14:31 and Israel seeth the great hand with which Jehovah hath wrought against the Egyptians, and the people fear Jehovah, and remain stedfast in Jehovah, and in Moses His servant.
15:1 Then singeth Moses and the sons of Israel this song to Jehovah, and they speak, saying: -- `I sing to Jehovah, For triumphing He hath triumphed; The horse and its rider He hath thrown into the sea.
15:2 My strength and song is JAH, And He is become my salvation: This [is] my God, and I glorify Him; God of my father, and I exalt Him.
15:3 Jehovah [is] a man of battle; Jehovah [is] His name.
15:4 Chariots of Pharaoh and his force He hath cast into the sea; And the choice of his captains Have sunk in the Red Sea!
15:5 The depths do cover them; They went down into the depths as a stone.
15:6 Thy right hand, O Jehovah, Is become honourable in power; Thy right hand, O Jehovah, Doth crush an enemy.
15:7 And in the abundance of Thine excellency Thou throwest down Thy withstanders, Thou sendest forth Thy wrath -- It consumeth them as stubble.
15:8 And by the spirit of Thine anger Have waters been heaped together; Stood as a heap have flowings; Congealed have been depths In the heart of a sea.
15:9 The enemy said, I pursue, I overtake; I apportion spoil; Filled is my soul with them; I draw out my sword; My hand destroyeth them: --
15:10 Thou hast blown with Thy wind The sea hath covered them; They sank as lead in mighty waters.
15:11 Who [is] like Thee among the gods, O Jehovah? Who [is] like Thee -- honourable in holiness -- Fearful in praises -- doing wonders?
15:12 Thou hast stretched out Thy right hand -- Earth swalloweth them!
15:13 Thou hast led forth in Thy kindness The people whom Thou hast redeemed. Thou hast led on in Thy strength Unto Thy holy habitation.

15:14 Peoples have heard, they are troubled; Pain hath seized inhabitants of Philistia.
15:15 Then have chiefs of Edom been troubled: Mighty ones of Moab -- Trembling doth seize them! Melted have all inhabitants of Canaan!
15:16 Fall on them doth terror and dread; By the greatness of Thine arm They are still as a stone, Till Thy people pass over, O Jehovah; Till the people pass over Whom Thou hast purchased.
15:17 Thou dost bring them in, And dost plant them In a mountain of Thine inheritance, A fixed place for Thy dwelling Thou hast made, O Jehovah; A sanctuary, O Lord, Thy hands have established;
15:18 Jehovah reigneth -- to the age, and for ever!'
15:19 For the horse of Pharaoh hath gone in with his chariots and with his horsemen into the sea, and Jehovah turneth back on them the waters of the sea, and the sons of Israel have gone on dry land in the midst of the sea.
15:20 And Miriam the inspired one, sister of Aaron, taketh the timbrel in her hand, and all the women go out after her, with timbrels and with choruses;
15:21 and Miriam answereth to them: -- `Sing ye to Jehovah, For Triumphing He hath triumphed; The horse and its rider He hath thrown into the sea!'
15:22 And Moses causeth Israel to journey from the Red Sea, and they go out unto the wilderness of Shur, and they go three days in the wilderness, and have not found water,
15:23 and they come in to Marah, and have not been able to drink the waters of Marah, for they [are] bitter; therefore hath [one] called its name Marah.
15:24 And the people murmur against Moses, saying, `What do we drink?'
15:25 and he crieth unto Jehovah, and Jehovah sheweth him a tree, and he casteth unto the waters, and the waters become sweet. There He hath made for them a statute, and an ordinance, and there He hath tried them,
15:26 and He saith, `If thou dost really hearken to the voice of Jehovah thy God, and dost that which is right in His eyes, and hast hearkened to His commands, and kept all His statutes: none of the sickness which I laid on the Egyptians do I lay on thee, for I, Jehovah, am healing thee.
15:27 And they come to Elim, and there [are] twelve fountains of water, and seventy palm trees; and they encamp there by the waters.
16:1 And they journey from Elim, and all the company of the sons of Israel come in unto the wilderness of Sin, which [is] between Elim and Sinai, on the fifteenth day of the second month of their going out from the land of Egypt.
16:2 And all the company of the sons of Israel murmur against Moses and against Aaron in the wilderness;

16:3 and the sons of Israel say unto them, `Oh that we had died by the hand of Jehovah in the land of Egypt, in our sitting by the flesh-pot, in our eating bread to satiety -- for ye have brought us out unto this wilderness to put all this assembly to death with hunger.'
16:4 And Jehovah saith unto Moses, `Lo, I am raining to you bread from the heavens -- and the people have gone out and gathered the matter of a day in its day -- so that I try them whether they walk in My law, or not;
16:5 and it hath been on the sixth day, that they have prepared that which they bring in, and it hath been double above that which they gather day [by] day.'
16:6 And Moses saith -- Aaron also -- unto all the sons of Israel, `Evening -- and ye have known that Jehovah hath brought you out from the land of Egypt;
16:7 and morning -- and ye have seen the honour of Jehovah, in His hearing your murmurings against Jehovah, and what [are] we, that ye murmur against us?'
16:8 And Moses saith, `In Jehovah's giving to you in the evening flesh to eat, and bread in the morning to satiety -- in Jehovah's hearing your murmurings, which ye are murmuring against Him, and what [are] we? your murmurings [are] not against us, but against Jehovah.'
16:9 And Moses saith unto Aaron, `Say unto all the company of the sons of Israel, Come ye near before Jehovah, for He hath heard your murmurings;'
16:10 and it cometh to pass, when Aaron is speaking unto all the company of the sons of Israel, that they turn towards the wilderness, and lo, the honour of Jehovah is seen in the cloud.
16:11 And Jehovah speaketh unto Moses, saying,
16:12 `I have heard the murmurings of the sons of Israel; speak unto them, saying, Between the evenings ye eat flesh, and in the morning ye are satisfied [with] bread, and ye have known that I [am] Jehovah your God.'
16:13 And it cometh to pass in the evening, that the quail cometh up, and covereth the camp, and in the morning there hath been the lying of dew round about the camp,
16:14 and the lying of the dew goeth up, and lo, on the face of the wilderness a thin, bare thing, thin as hoar-frost on the earth.
16:15 And the sons of Israel see, and say one unto another, `What [is] it?' for they have not known what it [is]; and Moses saith unto them, `It [is] the bread which Jehovah hath given to you for food.
16:16 `This [is] the thing which Jehovah hath commanded: Gather of it each according to his eating, an omer for a poll; and the number of your persons, take ye each for those in his tent.'
16:17 And the sons of Israel do so, and they gather, he who is [gathering] much, and he who is [gathering] little;
16:18 and they measure with an omer, and he who is [gathering] much hath nothing over, and he

who is [gathering] little hath no lack, each according to his eating they have gathered.
16:19 And Moses saith unto them, `Let no man leave of it till morning;'
16:20 and they have not hearkened unto Moses, and some of them do leave of it till morning, and it bringeth up worms and stinketh; and Moses is wroth with them.
16:21 And they gather it morning by morning, each according to his eating; when the sun hath been warm, then it hath melted.
16:22 And it cometh to pass on the sixth day, they have gathered a second bread, two omers for one, and all the princes of the company come in, and declare to Moses.
16:23 And he saith unto them, `It [is] that which Jehovah hath spoken [of]; a rest -- a holy sabbath to Jehovah -- [is] to-morrow; that which ye bake, bake; and that which ye boil, boil; and all that is over, let rest for yourselves in charge till the morning.'
16:24 And they let it rest until the morning, as Moses hath commanded, and it hath not stank, and a worm hath not been in it.
16:25 And Moses saith, `Eat it to-day, for to-day [is] a sabbath to Jehovah; to-day ye find it not in the field:
16:26 six days ye do gather it, and in the seventh day -- the sabbath -- in it there is none.'
16:27 And it cometh to pass on the seventh day, some of the people have gone out to gather, and have not found.
16:28 And Jehovah saith unto Moses, `How long have ye refused to keep My commands, and My laws?
16:29 see, because Jehovah hath given to you the sabbath, therefore He is giving to you on the sixth day bread of two days; abide ye each [in] his place, no one doth go out from his place on the seventh day.'
16:30 And the people rest on the seventh day,
16:31 and the house of Israel call its name Manna, and it [is] as coriander seed, white; and its taste [is] as a cake with honey.
16:32 And Moses saith, `This [is] the thing which Jehovah hath commanded: Fill the omer with it, for a charge for your generations, so that they see the bread which I have caused you to eat in the wilderness, in My bringing you out from the land of Egypt.'
16:33 And Moses saith unto Aaron, `Take one pot, and put there the fulness of the omer of manna, and let it rest before Jehovah, for a charge for your generations;'
16:34 as Jehovah hath given commandment unto Moses, so doth Aaron let it rest before the Testimony, for a charge.
16:35 And the sons of Israel have eaten the manna forty years, until their coming in unto the land

to be inhabited; the manna they have eaten till their coming in unto the extremity of the land of Canaan.
16:36 and the omer is a tenth of the ephah.
17:1 And all the company of the sons of Israel journey from the wilderness of Sin, on their journeyings, by the command of Jehovah, and encamp in Rephidim, and there is no water for the people to drink;
17:2 and the people strive with Moses, and say, `Give us water, and we drink.' And Moses saith to them, `What? -- ye strive with me, what? -- ye try Jehovah?'
17:3 and the people thirst there for water, and the people murmur against Moses, and say, `Why [is] this? -- thou hast brought us up out of Egypt, to put us to death, also our sons and our cattle, with thirst.'
17:4 And Moses crieth to Jehovah, saying, `What do I to this people? yet a little, and they have stoned me.'
17:5 And Jehovah saith unto Moses, `Pass over before the people, and take with thee of the elders of Israel, and thy rod with which thou hast smitten the River take in thy hand, and thou hast gone:
17:6 Lo, I am standing before thee there on the rock in Horeb, and thou hast smitten on the rock, and waters have come out from it, and the people have drunk.' And Moses doth so before the eyes of the elders of Israel,
17:7 and he calleth the name of the place Massah, and Meribah, because of the `strife' of the sons of Israel, and because of their `trying' Jehovah, saying, `Is Jehovah in our midst or not?'
17:8 And Amalek cometh, and fighteth with Israel in Rephidim,
17:9 and Moses saith unto Joshua, `Choose for us men, and go out, fight with Amalek: to-morrow I am standing on the top of the hill, and the rod of God in my hand.'
17:10 And Joshua doth as Moses hath said to him, to fight with Amalek, and Moses, Aaron, and Hur, have gone up [to] the top of the height;
17:11 and it hath come to pass, when Moses lifteth up his hand, that Israel hath been mighty, and when he letteth his hands rest, that Amalek hath been mighty.
17:12 And the hands of Moses [are] heavy, and they take a stone, and set [it] under him, and he sitteth on it: and Aaron and Hur have taken hold on his hands, on this side one, and on that one, and his hands are stedfast till the going in of the sun;
17:13 and Joshua weakeneth Amalek and his people by the mouth of the sword.
17:14 And Jehovah saith unto Moses, `Write this, a memorial in a Book, and set [it] in the ears of Joshua, that I do utterly wipe away the remembrance of Amalek from under the heavens;'
17:15 and Moses buildeth an altar, and calleth its name Jehovah-Nissi,

17:16 and saith, `Because a hand [is] on the throne of Jah, war [is] to Jehovah with Amalek from generation -- generation.'
18:1 And Jethro priest of Midian, father-in-law of Moses, heareth all that God hath done for Moses, and for Israel his people, that Jehovah hath brought out Israel from Egypt,
18:2 and Jethro, father-in-law of Moses, taketh Zipporah, wife of Moses, besides her parents,
18:3 and her two sons, of whom the name of the one [is] Gershom, for he said, `a sojourner I have been in a strange land:'
18:4 and the name of the other [is] Eliezer, for, `the God of my father [is] for my help, and doth deliver me from the sword of Pharaoh.'
18:5 And Jethro, father-in-law of Moses, cometh, and his sons, and his wife, unto Moses, unto the wilderness where he is encamping -- the mount of God;
18:6 and he saith unto Moses, `I, thy father-in-law, Jethro, am coming unto thee, and thy wife, and her two sons with her.'
18:7 And Moses goeth out to meet his father-in-law, and boweth himself, and kisseth him, and they ask one at another of welfare, and come into the tent;
18:8 and Moses recounteth to his father-in-law all that Jehovah hath done to Pharaoh, and to the Egyptians, on account of Israel, all the travail which hath found them in the way, and Jehovah doth deliver them.
18:9 And Jethro rejoiceth for all the good which Jehovah hath done to Israel, whom He hath delivered from the hand of the Egyptians;
18:10 and Jethro saith, `Blessed [is] Jehovah, who hath delivered you from the hand of the Egyptians, and from the hand of Pharaoh -- who hath delivered this people from under the hand of the Egyptians;
18:11 now I have known that Jehovah [is] greater than all the gods, for in the thing they have acted proudly -- [He is] above them!'
18:12 And Jethro, father-in-law of Moses, taketh a burnt-offering and sacrifices for God; and Aaron cometh in, and all the elders of Israel, to eat bread with the father-in-law of Moses, before God.
18:13 And it cometh to pass on the morrow, that Moses sitteth to judge the people, and the people stand before Moses, from the morning unto the evening;
18:14 and the father-in-law of Moses seeth all that he is doing to the people, and saith, `What [is] this thing which thou art doing to the people? wherefore art thou sitting by thyself, and all the people standing by thee from morning till evening?'
18:15 And Moses saith to his father-in-law, `Because the people come unto me to seek God;
18:16 when they have a matter, it hath come unto me, and I have judged between a man and his

neighbour, and made known the statutes of God, and His laws.'
18:17 And the father-in-law of Moses saith unto him, `The thing which thou art doing [is] not good;
18:18 thou dost surely wear away, both thou, and this people which [is] with thee, for the thing is
too heavy for thee, thou art not able to do it by thyself.
18:19 `Now, hearken to my voice, I counsel thee, and God is with thee: be thou for the people over-
against God, and thou hast brought in the things unto God;
18:20 and thou hast warned them [concerning] the statutes and the laws, and hast made known to
them the way in which they go, and the work which they do.
18:21 `And thou -- thou dost provide out of all the people men of ability, fearing God, men of truth,
hating dishonest gain, and hast placed [these] over them, heads of thousands, heads of hundreds,
heads of fifties, and heads of tens,
18:22 and they have judged the people at all times; and it hath come to pass, every great matter
they bring in unto thee, and every small matter they judge themselves; and lighten it from off
thyself, and they have borne with thee.
18:23 If thou dost this thing, and God hath commanded thee, then thou hast been able to stand,
and all this people also goeth in unto its place in peace.'
18:24 And Moses hearkeneth to the voice of his father-in-law, and doth all that he said,
18:25 and Moses chooseth men of ability out of all Israel, and maketh them chiefs over the people,
heads of thousands, heads of hundreds, heads of fifties, and heads of tens,
18:26 and they have judged the people at all times; the hard matter they bring in unto Moses, and
every small matter they judge themselves.
18:27 And Moses sendeth his father-in-law away, and he goeth away unto his own land.
19:1 In the third month of the going out of the sons of Israel from the land of Egypt, in this day they
have come into the wilderness of Sinai,
19:2 and they journey from Rephidim, and enter the wilderness of Sinai, and encamp in the
wilderness; and Israel encampeth there before the mount.
19:3 And Moses hath gone up unto God, and Jehovah calleth unto him out of the mount, saying,
`Thus dost thou say to the house of Jacob, and declare to the sons of Israel,
19:4 Ye -- ye have seen that which I have done to the Egyptians, and I bear you on eagles' wings,
and bring you in unto Myself.
19:5 `And now, if ye really hearken to My voice, then ye have kept My covenant, and been to Me a
peculiar treasure more than all the peoples, for all the earth [is] Mine;
19:6 and ye -- ye are to Me a kingdom of priests and a holy nation: these [are] the words which
thou dost speak unto the sons of Israel.'

19:7 And Moses cometh, and calleth for the elders of the people, and setteth before them all these words which Jehovah hath commanded him;
19:8 and all the people answer together and say, `All that Jehovah hath spoken we do;' and Moses returneth the words of the people unto Jehovah.
19:9 And Jehovah saith unto Moses, `Lo, I am coming unto thee in the thickness of the cloud, so that the people hear in My speaking with thee, and also believe in thee to the age;' and Moses declareth the words of the people unto Jehovah.
19:10 And Jehovah saith unto Moses, `Go unto the people; and thou hast sanctified them to-day and to-morrow, and they have washed their garments,
19:11 and have been prepared for the third day; for on the third day doth Jehovah come down before the eyes of all the people, on mount Sinai.
19:12 `And thou hast made a border [for] the people round about, saying, Take heed to yourselves, going up into the mount, or coming against its extremity; whoever is coming against the mount is certainly put to death;
19:13 a hand cometh not against him, for he is certainly stoned or shot through, whether beast or man it liveth not; in the drawing out of the jubilee cornet they go up into the mount.'
19:14 And Moses cometh down from the mount unto the people, and sanctifieth the people, and they wash their garments;
19:15 and he saith unto the people, `Be ye prepared for the third day, come not nigh unto a woman.'
19:16 And it cometh to pass, on the third day, while it is morning, that there are voices, and lightnings, and a heavy cloud, on the mount, and the sound of a trumpet very strong; and all the people who [are] in the camp do tremble.
19:17 And Moses bringeth out the people to meet God from the camp, and they station themselves at the lower part of the mount,
19:18 and mount Sinai [is] wholly a smoke from the presence of Jehovah, who hath come down on it in fire, and its smoke goeth up as smoke of the furnace, and the whole mount trembleth exceedingly;
19:19 and the sound of the trumpet is going on, and very strong; Moses speaketh, and God doth answer him with a voice.
19:20 And Jehovah cometh down on mount Sinai, unto the top of the mount, and Jehovah calleth for Moses unto the top of the mount, and Moses goeth up.
19:21 And Jehovah saith unto Moses, `Go down, protest to the people, lest they break through unto Jehovah to see, and many of them have fallen;

19:22 and also the priests who are coming nigh unto Jehovah do sanctify themselves, lest Jehovah break forth on them.'

19:23 And Moses saith unto Jehovah, `The people [is] unable to come up unto mount Sinai, for Thou -- Thou hast protested to us, saying, Make a border [for] the mount, then thou hast sanctified it.'

19:24 And Jehovah saith unto him, `Go, descend, then thou hast come up, thou, and Aaron with thee; and the priests and the people do not break through, to come up unto Jehovah, lest He break forth upon them.'

19:25 And Moses goeth down unto the people, and saith unto them: --

20:1 `And God speaketh all these words, saying,

20:2 I [am] Jehovah thy God, who hath brought thee out of the land of Egypt, out of a house of servants.

20:3 `Thou hast no other Gods before Me.

20:4 `Thou dost not make to thyself a graven image, or any likeness which [is] in the heavens above, or which [is] in the earth beneath, or which [is] in the waters under the earth.

20:5 Thou dost not bow thyself to them, nor serve them: for I, Jehovah thy God, [am] a zealous God, charging iniquity of fathers on sons, on the third [generation], and on the fourth, of those hating Me,

20:6 and doing kindness to thousands, of those loving Me and keeping My commands.

20:7 `Thou dost not take up the name of Jehovah thy God for a vain thing, for Jehovah acquitteth not him who taketh up His name for a vain thing.

20:8 `Remember the Sabbath-day to sanctify it;

20:9 six days thou dost labour, and hast done all thy work,

20:10 and the seventh day [is] a Sabbath to Jehovah thy God; thou dost not do any work, thou, and thy son, and thy daughter, thy man-servant, and thy handmaid, and thy cattle, and thy sojourner who is within thy gates, --

20:11 for six days hath Jehovah made the heavens and the earth, the sea, and all that [is] in them, and resteth in the seventh day; therefore hath Jehovah blessed the Sabbath-day, and doth sanctify it.

20:12 `Honour thy father and thy mother, so that thy days are prolonged on the ground which Jehovah thy God is giving to thee.

20:13 `Thou dost not murder.

20:14 `Thou dost not commit adultery.

20:15 `Thou dost not steal.

20:16 `Thou dost not answer against thy neighbour a false testimony.
20:17 `Thou dost not desire the house of thy neighbour, thou dost not desire the wife of thy neighbour, or his man-servant, or his handmaid, or his ox, or his ass, or anything which [is] thy neighbour's.'
20:18 And all the people are seeing the voices, and the flames, and the sound of the trumpet, and the mount smoking; and the people see, and move, and stand afar off,
20:19 and say unto Moses, `Speak thou with us, and we hear, and let not God speak with us, lest we die.'
20:20 And Moses saith unto the people, `Fear not, for to try you hath God come, and in order that His fear may be before your faces -- that ye sin not.'
20:21 And the people stand afar off, and Moses hath drawn nigh unto the thick darkness where God [is].
20:22 And Jehovah saith unto Moses, `Thus dost thou say unto the sons of Israel: Ye -- ye have seen that from the heavens I have spoken with you;
20:23 ye do not make with Me gods of silver, even gods of gold ye do not make to yourselves.
20:24 `An altar of earth thou dost make for Me, and thou hast sacrificed on it thy burnt-offerings and thy peace-offerings, thy flock and thy herd; in every place where I cause My name to be remembered I come in unto thee, and have blessed thee.
20:25 `And if an altar of stones thou dost make to Me, thou dost not build them of hewn work; when thy tool thou hast waved over it, then thou dost pollute it;
20:26 neither dost thou go up by steps on Mine altar, that thy nakedness be not revealed upon it.
21:1 `And these [are] the judgments which thou dost set before them:
21:2 `When thou buyest a Hebrew servant -- six years he doth serve, and in the seventh he goeth out as a freeman for nought;
21:3 if by himself he cometh in, by himself he goeth out; if he [is] owner of a wife, then his wife hath gone out with him;
21:4 if his lord give to him a wife, and she hath borne to him sons or daughters -- the wife and her children are her lord's, and he goeth out by himself.
21:5 `And if the servant really say: I have loved my lord, my wife, and my sons -- I do not go out free;
21:6 then hath his lord brought him nigh unto God, and hath brought him nigh unto the door, or unto the side-post, and his lord hath bored his ear with an awl, and he hath served him -- to the age.
21:7 `And when a man selleth his daughter for a handmaid, she doth not go out according to the

going out of the men-servants;
21:8 if evil in the eyes of her lord, so that he hath not betrothed her, then he hath let her be ransomed; to a strange people he hath not power to sell her, in his dealing treacherously with her.
21:9 `And if to his son he betroth her, according to the right of daughters he doth to her.
21:10 `If another [woman] he take for him, her food, her covering, and her habitation, he doth not withdraw;
21:11 and if these three he do not to her, then she hath gone out for nought, without money.
21:12 `He who smiteth a man so that he hath died, is certainly put to death;
21:13 as to him who hath not laid wait, and God hath brought to his hand, I have even set for thee a place whither he doth flee.
21:14 `And when a man doth presume against his neighbour to slay him with subtilty, from Mine altar thou dost take him to die.
21:15 `And he who smiteth his father or his mother is certainly put to death.
21:16 `And he who stealeth a man, and hath sold him, and he hath been found in his hand, is certainly put to death.
21:17 `And he who is reviling his father or his mother is certainly put to death.
21:18 `And when men contend, and a man hath smitten his neighbour with a stone, or with the fist, and he die not, but hath fallen on the bed;
21:19 if he rise, and hath gone up and down without on his staff, then hath the smiter been acquitted; only his cessation he giveth, and he is thoroughly healed.
21:20 `And when a man smiteth his man-servant or his handmaid, with a rod, and he hath died under his hand -- he is certainly avenged;
21:21 only if he remain a day, or two days, he is not avenged, for he [is] his money.
21:22 `And when men strive, and have smitten a pregnant woman, and her children have come out, and there is no mischief, he is certainly fined, as the husband of the woman doth lay upon him, and he hath given through the judges;
21:23 and if there is mischief, then thou hast given life for life,
21:24 eye for eye, tooth for tooth, hand for hand, foot for foot,
21:25 burning for burning, wound for wound, stripe for stripe.
21:26 `And when a man smiteth the eye of his man-servant, or the eye of his handmaid, and hath destroyed it, as a freeman he doth send him away for his eye;
21:27 and if a tooth of his man-servant or a tooth of his handmaid he knock out, as a freeman he doth send him away for his tooth.
21:28 `And when an ox doth gore man or woman, and they have died, the ox is certainly stoned,

and his flesh is not eaten, and the owner of the ox [is] acquitted;
21:29 and if the ox is [one] accustomed to gore heretofore, and it hath been testified to its owner, and he doth not watch it, and it hath put to death a man or woman, the ox is stoned, and its owner also is put to death.
21:30 `If atonement is laid upon him, then he hath given the ransom of his life, according to all that is laid upon him;
21:31 whether it gore a son or gore a daughter, according to this judgment it is done to him.
21:32 `If the ox gore a man-servant or a handmaid, thirty silver shekels he doth give to their lord, and the ox is stoned.
21:33 `And when a man doth open a pit, or when a man doth dig a pit, and doth not cover it, and an ox or ass hath fallen thither, --
21:34 the owner of the pit doth repay, money he doth give back to its owner, and the dead is his.
21:35 `And when a man's ox doth smite the ox of his neighbour, and it hath died, then they have sold the living ox, and halved its money, and also the dead one they do halve;
21:36 or, it hath been known that the ox is [one] accustomed to gore heretofore, and its owner doth not watch it, he certainly repayeth ox for ox, and the dead is his.
22:1 `When a man doth steal an ox or sheep, and hath slaughtered it or sold it, five of the herd he doth repay for the ox, and four of the flock for the sheep.
22:2 `If in the breaking through, the thief is found, and he hath been smitten, and hath died, there is no blood for him;
22:3 if the sun hath risen upon him, blood [is] for him, he doth certainly repay; if he have nothing, then he hath been sold for his theft;
22:4 if the theft is certainly found in his hand alive, whether ox, or ass, or sheep -- double he repayeth.
22:5 `When a man depastureth a field or vineyard, and hath sent out his beast, and it hath pastured in the field of another, [of] the best of his field, and the best of his vineyard, he doth repay.
22:6 `When fire goeth forth, and hath found thorns, and a stack, or the standing corn, or the field, hath been consumed, he who causeth the burning doth certainly repay.
22:7 `When a man doth give unto his neighbour silver, or vessels to keep, and it hath been stolen out of the man's house; if the thief is found, he repayeth double.
22:8 `If the thief is not found, then the master of the house hath been brought near unto God, whether he hath not put forth his hand against the work of his neighbour;
22:9 for every matter of transgression, for ox, for ass, for sheep, for raiment, for any lost thing of which it is said that it is his; unto God cometh the matter of them both; he whom God doth

condemn, he repayeth double to his neighbour.
22:10 `When a man doth give unto his neighbour an ass, or ox, or sheep, or any beast to keep, and it hath died, or hath been hurt, or taken captive, none seeing --
22:11 an oath of Jehovah is between them both, that he hath not put forth his hand against the work of his neighbour, and its owner hath accepted, and he doth not repay;
22:12 but if it is certainly stolen from him, he doth repay to its owner;
22:13 if it is certainly torn, he bringeth it in -- a witness; the torn thing he doth not repay.
22:14 `And when a man doth ask [anything] from his neighbour, and it hath been hurt or hath died -- its owner not being with it -- he doth certainly repay;
22:15 if its owner [is] with it, he doth not repay, -- if it [is] a hired thing, it hath come for its hire.
22:16 `And when a man doth entice a virgin who [is] not betrothed, and hath lain with her, he doth certainly endow her to himself for a wife;
22:17 if her father utterly refuse to give her to him, money he doth weigh out according to the dowry of virgins.
22:18 `A witch thou dost not keep alive.
22:19 `Whoever lieth with a beast is certainly put to death.
22:20 `He who is sacrificing to a god, save to Jehovah alone, is devoted.
22:21 `And a sojourner thou dost not oppress, nor crush him, for sojourners ye have been in the land of Egypt.
22:22 `Any widow or orphan ye do not afflict;
22:23 if thou dost really afflict him, surely if he at all cry unto Me, I certainly hear his cry;
22:24 and Mine anger hath burned, and I have slain you by the sword, and your wives have been widows, and your sons orphans.
22:25 `If thou dost lend My poor people with thee money, thou art not to him as a usurer; thou dost not lay on him usury;
22:26 if thou dost at all take in pledge the garment of thy neighbour, during the going in of the sun thou dost return it to him:
22:27 for it alone is his covering, it [is] his garment for his skin; wherein doth he lie down? and it hath come to pass, when he doth cry unto Me, that I have heard, for I [am] gracious.
22:28 `God thou dost not revile, and a prince among thy people thou dost not curse.
22:29 `Thy fulness and thy liquids thou dost not delay; the first-born of thy sons thou dost give to Me;
22:30 so thou dost to thine ox, to thy sheep; seven days it is with its dam, on the eighth day thou dost give it to Me.

22:31 `And ye are holy men to Me, and flesh torn in the field ye do not eat, to a dog ye do cast it.
23:1 `Thou dost not lift up a vain report; thou dost not put thy hand with a wicked man to be a violent witness.
23:2 `Thou art not after many to evil, nor dost thou testify concerning a strife, to turn aside after many to cause [others] to turn aside;
23:3 and a poor man thou dost not honour in his strife.
23:4 `When thou meetest thine enemy's ox or his ass going astray, thou dost certainly turn it back to him;
23:5 when thou seest the ass of him who is hating thee crouching under its burden, then thou hast ceased from leaving [it] to it -- thou dost certainly leave [it] with him.
23:6 `Thou dost not turn aside the judgment of thy needy one in his strife;
23:7 from a false matter thou dost keep far off, and an innocent and righteous man thou dost not slay; for I do not justify a wicked man.
23:8 `And a bribe thou dost not take; for the bribe bindeth the open-[eyed], and perverteth the words of the righteous.
23:9 `And a sojourner thou dost not oppress, and ye -- ye have known the soul of the sojourner, for sojourners ye have been in the land of Egypt.
23:10 `And six years thou dost sow thy land, and hast gathered its increase;
23:11 and the seventh thou dost release it, and hast left it, and the needy of thy people have eaten, and their leaving doth the beast of the field eat; so dost thou to thy vineyard -- to thine olive-yard.
23:12 `Six days thou dost do thy work, and on the seventh day thou dost rest, so that thine ox and thine ass doth rest, and the son of thine handmaid and the sojourner is refreshed;
23:13 and in all that which I have said unto you ye do take heed; and the name of other gods ye do not mention; it is not heard on thy mouth.
23:14 `Three times thou dost keep a feast to Me in a year;
23:15 the Feast of Unleavened things thou dost keep; seven days thou dost eat unleavened things, as I have commanded thee, at the time appointed [in] the month of Abib; for in it thou hast come forth out of Egypt, and ye do not appear [in] My presence empty;
23:16 and the Feast of Harvest, the first fruits of thy works which thou sowest in the field; and the Feast of the In-Gathering, in the outgoing of the year, in thy gathering thy works out of the field.
23:17 `Three times in a year do all thy males appear before the face of the Lord Jehovah.
23:18 `Thou dost not sacrifice on a fermented thing the blood of My sacrifice, and the fat of My festival doth not remain till morning;
23:19 the beginning of the first-fruits of thy ground thou dost bring into the house of Jehovah thy

God; thou dost not boil a kid in its mother's milk.
23:20 `Lo, I am sending a messenger before thee to keep thee in the way, and to bring thee in unto the place which I have prepared;
23:21 be watchful because of his presence, and hearken to his voice, rebel not against him, for he beareth not with your transgression, for My name [is] in his heart;
23:22 for, if thou diligently hearken to his voice, and hast done all that which I speak, then I have been at enmity with thine enemies, and have distressed those distressing thee.
23:23 `For My messenger goeth before thee, and hath brought thee in unto the Amorite, and the Hittite, and the Perizzite, and the Canaanite, the Hivite, and the Jebusite, and I have cut them off.
23:24 `Thou dost not bow thyself to their gods, nor serve them, nor do according to their doings, but dost utterly devote them, and thoroughly break their standing pillars.
23:25 `And ye have served Jehovah your God, and He hath blessed thy bread and thy water, and I have turned aside sickness from thine heart;
23:26 there is not a miscarrying and barren one in thy land; the number of thy days I fulfil:
23:27 My terror I send before thee, and I have put to death all the people among whom thou comest, and I have given the neck of all thine enemies unto thee.
23:28 `And I have sent the hornet before thee, and it hath cast out the Hivite, the Canaanite, and the Hittite, from before thee;
23:29 I cast them not out from before thee in one year, lest the land be a desolation, and the beast of the field hath multiplied against thee;
23:30 little [by] little I cast them out from before thee, till thou art fruitful, and hast inherited the land.
23:31 `And I have set thy border from the Red Sea, even unto the sea of the Philistines, and from the wilderness unto the River: for I give into your hand the inhabitants of the land, and thou hast cast them out from before thee;
23:32 thou dost not make a covenant with them, and with their gods;
23:33 they do not dwell in thy land, lest they cause thee to sin against Me when thou servest their gods, when it becometh a snare to thee.'
24:1 And unto Moses He said, `Come up unto Jehovah, thou, and Aaron, Nadab, and Abihu, and seventy of the elders of Israel, and ye have bowed yourselves afar off;'
24:2 and Moses hath drawn nigh by himself unto Jehovah; and they draw not nigh, and the people go not up with him.
24:3 And Moses cometh in, and recounteth to the people all the words of Jehovah, and all the judgments, and all the people answer -- one voice, and say, `All the words which Jehovah hath spoken we do.'

24:4 And Moses writeth all the words of Jehovah, and riseth early in the morning, and buildeth an altar under the hill, and twelve standing pillars for the twelve tribes of Israel;
24:5 and he sendeth the youths of the sons of Israel, and they cause burnt-offerings to ascend, and sacrifice sacrifices of peace-offerings to Jehovah -- calves.
24:6 And Moses taketh half of the blood, and putteth in basins, and half of the blood hath he sprinkled on the altar;
24:7 and he taketh the Book of the Covenant, and proclaimeth in the ears of the people, and they say, `All that which Jehovah hath spoken we do, and obey.'
24:8 And Moses taketh the blood, and sprinkleth on the people, and saith, `Lo, the blood of the covenant which Jehovah hath made with you, concerning all these things.'
24:9 And Moses goeth up, Aaron also, Nadab and Abihu, and seventy of the elders of Israel,
24:10 and they see the God of Israel, and under His feet [is] as the white work of the sapphire, and as the substance of the heavens for purity;
24:11 and unto those of the sons of Israel who are near He hath not put forth His hand, and they see God, and eat and drink.
24:12 And Jehovah saith unto Moses, `Come up unto Me to the mount, and be there, and I give to thee the tables of stone, and the law, and the command, which I have written to direct them.'
24:13 And Moses riseth -- Joshua his minister also -- and Moses goeth up unto the mount of God;
24:14 and unto the elders he hath said, `Abide ye for us in this [place], until that we turn back unto you, and lo, Aaron and Hur [are] with you -- he who hath matters doth come nigh unto them.'
24:15 And Moses goeth up unto the mount, and the cloud covereth the mount;
24:16 and the honour of Jehovah doth tabernacle on mount Sinai, and the cloud covereth it six days, and He calleth unto Moses on the seventh day from the midst of the cloud.
24:17 And the appearance of the honour of Jehovah [is] as a consuming fire on the top of the mount, before the eyes of the sons of Israel;
24:18 and Moses goeth into the midst of the cloud, and goeth up unto the mount, and Moses is on the mount forty days and forty nights.
25:1 And Jehovah speaketh unto Moses, saying,
25:2 `Speak unto the sons of Israel, and they take for Me a heave-offering; from every man whose heart impelleth him ye do take My heave-offering.
25:3 `And this [is] the heave-offering which ye take from them; gold, and silver, and brass,
25:4 and blue, and purple, and scarlet, and linen, and goats' [hair],
25:5 and rams' skins made red, and badgers' skins, and shittim wood,
25:6 oil for the light, spices for the anointing oil, and for the perfume of the spices,

25:7 shoham stones, and stones for setting for an ephod, and for a breastplate.
25:8 `And they have made for Me a sanctuary, and I have tabernacled in their midst;
25:9 according to all that which I am shewing thee, the pattern of the tabernacle, and the pattern of all its vessels, even so ye do make [it].
25:10 `And they have made an ark of shittim wood; two cubits and a half its length, and a cubit and a half its breadth, and a cubit and a half its height;
25:11 and thou hast overlaid it [with] pure gold, within and without thou dost overlay it, and thou hast made on it a ring of gold round about.
25:12 `And thou hast cast for it four rings of gold, and hast put [them] on its four feet, even two rings on its one side, and two rings on its second side;
25:13 and thou hast made staves of shittim wood, and hast overlaid them [with] gold,
25:14 and hast brought the staves into the rings on the sides of the ark, to bear the ark by them,
25:15 in the rings of the ark are the staves, they are not turned aside from it;
25:16 and thou hast put unto the ark the testimony which I give unto thee.
25:17 `And thou hast made a mercy-seat of pure gold, two cubits and a half its length, and a cubit and a half its breadth;
25:18 and thou hast made two cherubs of gold, beaten work dost thou make them, at the two ends of the mercy-seat;
25:19 and make thou one cherub at the end on this side, and one cherub at the end on that; at the mercy-seat ye do make the cherubs on its two ends.
25:20 `And the cherubs have been spreading out wings on high, covering the mercy-seat over with their wings, and their faces [are] one towards another -- towards the mercy-seat are the faces of the cherubs.
25:21 `And thou hast put the mercy-seat on the ark above, and unto the ark thou dost put the testimony which I give unto thee;
25:22 and I have met with thee there, and have spoken with thee from off the mercy-seat (from between the two cherubs, which [are] on the ark of the testimony) all that which I command thee concerning the sons of Israel.
25:23 `And thou hast made a table of shittim wood, two cubits its length, and a cubit its breadth, and a cubit and a half its height,
25:24 and hast overlaid it [with] pure gold, and hast made for it a crown of gold round about,
25:25 and hast made for it a border of a handbreadth round about, and hast made a crown of gold to its border round about.
25:26 `And thou hast made to it four rings of gold, and hast put the rings on the four corners, which

[are] to its four feet;
25:27 over-against the border are the rings for places for staves to bear the table;
25:28 and thou hast made the staves of shittim wood, and hast overlaid them with gold, and the table hath been borne with them;
25:29 and thou hast made its dishes, and its bowls, and its covers, and its cups, with which they pour out; of pure gold thou dost make them;
25:30 and thou hast put on the table bread of the presence before Me continually.
25:31 `And thou hast made a candlestick of pure gold, of beaten work is the candlestick made; its base, and its branch, its calyxes, its knops, and its flowers are of the same;
25:32 and six branches are coming out of its sides, three branches of the candlestick out of the one side, and three branches of the candlestick out of the second side;
25:33 three calyxes made like almonds in the one branch, a knop and a flower, and three calyxes made like almonds in one branch, a knop and a flower; so for the six branches which are coming out from the candlestick.
25:34 `And in the candlestick [are] four calyxes made like almonds, its knops and its flowers;
25:35 and a knop under two branches of the same, and a knop under two branches of the same, and a knop under two branches of the same, [are] to the six branches which are coming out of the candlestick;
25:36 their knops and their branches are of the same, all of it one beaten work of pure gold;
25:37 and thou hast made its seven lamps, and [one] hath caused its lights to go up, and it hath given light over-against its front.
25:38 `And its snuffers and its snuff dishes [are] of pure gold;
25:39 of a talent of pure gold he doth make it, with all these vessels.
25:40 And see thou and do [them] by their pattern which thou art shewn in the mount.
26:1 `And thou dost make the tabernacle: ten curtains of twined linen, and blue, and purple, and scarlet; [with] cherubs, work of a designer, thou dost make them;
26:2 the length of the one curtain [is] eight and twenty by the cubit, and the breadth of the one curtain four by the cubit, one measure [is] to all the curtains;
26:3 five of the curtains are joining one unto another, and five curtains are joining one to another.
26:4 `And thou hast made loops of blue upon the edge of the one curtain, at the end in the joining; and so thou makest in the edge of the outermost curtain, in the joining of the second.
26:5 fifty loops thou dost make in the one curtain, and fifty loops thou dost make in the edge of the curtain which [is] in the joining of the second, causing the loops to take hold one unto another;
26:6 and thou hast made fifty hooks of gold, and hast joined the curtains one to another by the

hooks, and the tabernacle hath been one.
26:7 `And thou hast made curtains of goats' [hair], for a tent over the tabernacle; thou dost make eleven curtains:
26:8 the length of the one curtain [is] thirty by the cubit, and the breadth of the one curtain four by the cubit; one measure [is] to the eleven curtains;
26:9 and thou hast joined the five curtains apart, and the six curtains apart, and hast doubled the six curtains over-against the front of the tent.
26:10 `And thou hast made fifty loops on the edge of the one curtain, the outermost in the joining, and fifty loops on the edge of the curtain which is joining the second;
26:11 and thou hast made fifty hooks of brass, and hast brought in the hooks into the loops, and hast joined the tent, and it hath been one.
26:12 `And the superfluity in the curtains of the tent -- the half of the curtain which is superfluous -- hath spread over the hinder part of the tabernacle;
26:13 and the cubit on this side, and the cubit on that, in the superfluity in the length of the curtains of the tent, is spread out over the sides of the tabernacle, on this and on that, to cover it;
26:14 and thou hast made a covering for the tent, of rams' skins made red, and a covering of badgers' skins above.
26:15 `And thou hast made the boards for the tabernacle, of shittim wood, standing up;
26:16 ten cubits [is] the length of the board, and a cubit and a half the breadth of the one board;
26:17 two handles [are] to the one board, joined one unto another; so thou dost make for all the boards of the tabernacle;
26:18 and thou hast made the boards of the tabernacle: twenty boards for the south side southward;
26:19 and forty sockets of silver thou dost make under the twenty boards, two sockets under the one board for its two handles, and two sockets under the other board for its two handles.
26:20 `And for the second side of the tabernacle, for the north side, [are] twenty boards,
26:21 and their forty sockets of silver, two sockets under the one board, and two sockets under another board.
26:22 And for the sides of the tabernacle westward, thou dost make six boards.
26:23 And two boards thou dost make for the corners of the tabernacle in the two sides.
26:24 And they are pairs beneath, and together they are pairs above its head unto the one ring; so is it for them both, they are for the two corners.
26:25 And they have been eight boards, and their sockets of silver [are] sixteen sockets, two sockets under the one board, and two sockets under another board.

26:26 `And thou hast made bars of shittim wood: five for the boards of the one side of the
tabernacle,
26:27 and five bars for the boards of the second side of the tabernacle, and five bars for the boards
of the side of the tabernacle at the two sides, westward;
26:28 and one hath caused the middle bar in the midst of the boards to reach from end unto end;
26:29 and the boards thou dost overlay [with] gold, and their rings thou dost make of gold places
for bars, and hast overlaid their bars with gold;
26:30 and thou hast raised up the tabernacle according to its fashion which thou hast been shewn
in the mount.
26:31 `And thou hast made a vail of blue, and purple, and scarlet, and twined linen, work of a
designer; he maketh it [with] cherubs;
26:32 and thou hast put it on four pillars of shittim wood, overlaid [with] gold, their pegs [are] of
gold, on four sockets of silver.
26:33 `And thou hast put the vail under the hooks, and hast brought in thither within the vail the ark
of the testimony; and the vail hath made a separation for you between the holy and the holy of
holies.
26:34 `And thou hast put the mercy-seat on the ark of the testimony, in the holy of holies.
26:35 `And thou hast set the table at the outside of the vail, and the candlestick over-against the
table on the side of the tabernacle southward, and the table thou dost put on the north side.
26:36 `And thou hast made a covering for the opening of the tent, blue, and purple, and scarlet,
and twined linen, work of an embroiderer;
26:37 and thou hast made for the covering five pillars of shittim [wood], and hast overlaid them
[with] gold, their pegs [are] of gold, and thou hast cast for them five sockets of brass.
27:1 `And thou hast made the altar of shittim wood, five cubits the length, and five cubits the
breadth -- the altar is square -- and three cubits its height.
27:2 And thou hast made its horns on its four corners, its horns are of the same, and thou hast
overlaid it [with] brass.
27:3 And thou hast made its pots to remove its ashes, and its shovels, and its bowls, and its forks,
and its fire-pans, even all its vessels thou dost make of brass.
27:4 `And thou hast made for it a grate of net-work of brass, and hast made on the net four rings of
brass on its four extremities,
27:5 and hast put it under the compass of the altar beneath, and the net hath been unto the middle
of the altar.
27:6 `And thou hast made staves for the altar, staves of shittim wood, and hast overlaid them [with]

brass.
27:7 And the staves have been brought into the rings, and the staves have been on the two sides of the altar in bearing it.
27:8 Hollow with boards thou dost make it, as it hath been shewed thee in the mount, so do they make [it].
27:9 `And thou hast made the court of the tabernacle: for the south side southward, hangings for the court of twined linen, a hundred by the cubit [is] the length for the one side,
27:10 and its twenty pillars and their twenty sockets [are] of brass, the pegs of the pillars and their fillets [are] of silver;
27:11 and so for the north side in length, hangings of a hundred [cubits] in length, and its twenty pillars and their twenty sockets [are] of brass, the pegs of the pillars and their fillets [are] of silver.
27:12 `And [for] the breadth of the court at the west side [are] hangings of fifty cubits, their pillars ten, and their sockets ten.
27:13 And [for] the breadth of the court at the east side, eastward, [are] fifty cubits.
27:14 And the hangings at the side [are] fifteen cubits, their pillars three, and their sockets three.
27:15 And at the second side [are] hangings fifteen [cubits], their pillars three, and their sockets three.
27:16 `And for the gate of the court a covering of twenty cubits, blue, and purple, and scarlet, and twined linen, work of an embroiderer; their pillars four, their sockets four.
27:17 All the pillars of the court round about [are] filleted [with] silver, their pegs [are] silver, and their sockets brass.
27:18 `The length of the court [is] a hundred by the cubit, and the breadth fifty by fifty, and the height five cubits, of twined linen, and their sockets [are] brass,
27:19 even all the vessels of the tabernacle, in all its service, and all its pins, and all the pins of the court, [are] brass.
27:20 `And thou -- thou dost command the sons of Israel, and they bring unto thee pure beaten olive oil for the light, to cause the lamp to go up continually;
27:21 in the tent of meeting, at the outside of the vail, which [is] over the testimony, doth Aaron -- his sons also -- arrange it from evening till morning before Jehovah -- a statute age-during to their generations, from the sons of Israel.
28:1 `And thou, bring thou near unto thee Aaron thy brother, and his sons with him, from the midst of the sons of Israel, for his being priest to Me, [even] Aaron, Nadab, and Abihu, Eleazar and Ithamar, sons of Aaron;
28:2 and thou hast made holy garments for Aaron thy brother, for honour and for beauty;

28:3 and thou -- thou dost speak unto all the wise of heart, whom I have filled [with] a spirit of wisdom, and they have made the garments of Aaron to sanctify him for his being priest to Me.
28:4 `And these [are] the garments which they make: a breastplate, and an ephod, and an upper robe, and an embroidered coat, a mitre, and a girdle; yea, they have made holy garments for Aaron thy brother, and for his sons, for his being priest to Me.
28:5 `And they take the gold, and the blue, and the purple, and the scarlet, and the linen,
28:6 and have made the ephod of gold, blue, and purple, and scarlet, and twined linen, work of a designer;
28:7 it hath two shoulders joining at its two ends, and it is joined.
28:8 `And the girdle of his ephod which [is] on him, according to its work, is of the same, of gold, blue, and purple, and scarlet, and twined linen.
28:9 `And thou hast taken the two shoham stones, and hast opened on them the names of the sons of Israel;
28:10 six of their names on the one stone, and the names of the remaining six on the second stone, according to their births;
28:11 the work of an engraver in stone, openings of a signet, thou dost open the two stones by the names of the sons of Israel; turned round, embroidered [with] gold, thou dost make them.
28:12 `And thou hast set the two stones on the shoulders of the ephod -- stones of memorial to the sons of Israel -- and Aaron hath borne their names before Jehovah, on his two shoulders, for a memorial.
28:13 `And thou hast made embroidered things of gold,
28:14 and two chains of pure gold, wreathed work thou dost make them, work of thick bands, and thou hast put the thick chains on the embroidered things.
28:15 `And thou hast made a breastplate of judgment, work of a designer; according to the work of the ephod thou dost make it; of gold, blue, and purple, and scarlet, and twined linen thou dost make it;
28:16 it is square, doubled, a span its length, and a span its breadth.
28:17 `And thou hast set in it settings of stone, four rows of stone; a row of sardius, topaz, and carbuncle [is] the first row;
28:18 and the second row [is] emerald, sapphire, and diamond;
28:19 and the third row [is] opal, agate, and amethyst;
28:20 and the fourth row [is] beryl, and onyx, and jasper; embroidered with gold are they in their settings,
28:21 and the stones are according to the names of the sons of Israel, twelve, according to their

names, openings of a signet, each by his name are they for the twelve tribes.
28:22 `And thou hast made on the breastplate wreathed chains, work of thick bands, of pure gold;
28:23 and thou hast made on the breastplate two rings of gold, and hast put the two rings on the two ends of the breastplate;
28:24 and thou hast put the two thick bands of gold on the two rings at the ends of the breastplate;
28:25 and the two ends of the two thick bands thou dost put on the two embroidered things, and thou hast put [them] on the shoulders of the ephod over-against its face.
28:26 `And thou hast made two rings of gold, and hast set them on the two ends of the breastplate, on its border, which [is] over-against the ephod within;
28:27 and thou hast made two rings of gold, and hast put them on the two shoulders of the ephod, beneath, over-against its front, over-against its joining, above the girdle of the ephod,
28:28 and they bind the breastplate by its rings unto the rings of the ephod with a ribbon of blue, to be above the girdle of the ephod, and the breastplate is not loosed from the ephod.
28:29 `And Aaron hath borne the names of the sons of Israel in the breastplate of judgment, on his heart, in his going in unto the sanctuary, for a memorial before Jehovah continually.
28:30 `And thou hast put unto the breastplate of judgment the Lights and the Perfections, and they have been on the heart of Aaron, in his going in before Jehovah, and Aaron hath borne the judgment of the sons of Israel on his heart before Jehovah continually.
28:31 `And thou hast made the upper robe of the ephod completely of blue,
28:32 and the opening for its head hath been in its midst, a border is to its opening round about, work of a weaver, as the opening of a habergeon there is to it; it is not rent.
28:33 `And thou hast made on its hem pomegranates of blue, and purple, and scarlet, on its hem round about, and bells of gold in their midst round about;
28:34 a bell of gold and a pomegranate, a bell of gold and a pomegranate [are] on the hems of the upper robe round about.
28:35 `And it hath been on Aaron to minister in, and its sound hath been heard in his coming in unto the sanctuary before Jehovah, and in his going out, and he doth not die.
28:36 `And thou hast made a flower of pure gold, and hast opened on it -- openings of a signet -- `Holy to Jehovah;'
28:37 and thou hast put it on a blue ribbon, and it hath been on the mitre -- over-against the front of the mitre it is;
28:38 and it hath been on the forehead of Aaron, and Aaron hath borne the iniquity of the holy things which the sons of Israel do hallow, even all their holy gifts; and it hath been on his forehead continually for a pleasing thing for them before Jehovah.

28:39 `And thou hast embroidered the coat of linen, and hast made a mitre of linen, and a girdle
thou dost make -- work of an embroiderer.
28:40 `And for the sons of Aaron thou dost make coats, and thou hast made for them girdles, yea,
bonnets thou dost make for them, for honour and for beauty;
28:41 and thou hast clothed Aaron thy brother with them, and his sons with him, and hast anointed
them, and hast consecrated their hand, and hast sanctified them, and they have been priests to
Me.
28:42 `And make thou for them linen trousers to cover the naked flesh: they are from the loins even
unto the thighs;
28:43 and they have been on Aaron and on his sons, in their going in unto the tent of meeting, or in
their drawing nigh unto the altar to minister in the sanctuary, and they do not bear iniquity nor have
they died; a statute age-during to him, and to his seed after him.
29:1 `And this [is] the thing which thou dost to them, to hallow them, for being priests to Me: Take
one bullock, a son of the herd, and two rams, perfect ones,
29:2 and bread unleavened, and cakes unleavened anointed with oil, of fine wheaten flour thou
dost make them,
29:3 and thou hast put them on one basket, and hast brought them near in the basket, also the
bullock and the two rams.
29:4 `And Aaron and his sons thou dost bring near unto the opening of the tent of meeting, and
hast bathed them with water;
29:5 and thou hast taken the garments, and hast clothed Aaron with the coat, and the upper robe of
the ephod, and the ephod, and the breastplate, and hast girded him with the girdle of the ephod,
29:6 and hast set the mitre on his head, and hast put the holy crown on the mitre,
29:7 and hast taken the anointing oil, and hast poured [it] on his head, and hast anointed him.
29:8 `And his sons thou dost bring near, and hast clothed them [with] coats,
29:9 and hast girded them [with] a girdle (Aaron and his sons), and hast bound on them bonnets;
and the priesthood hath been theirs by a statute age-during, and thou hast consecrated the hand of
Aaron, and the hand of his sons,
29:10 and hast brought near the bullock before the tent of meeting, and Aaron hath laid -- his sons
also -- their hands on the head of the bullock.
29:11 `And thou hast slaughtered the bullock before Jehovah, at the opening of the tent of meeting,
29:12 and hast taken of the blood of the bullock, and hast put [it] on the horns of the altar with thy
finger, and all the blood thou dost pour out at the foundation of the altar;
29:13 and thou hast taken all the fat which is covering the inwards, and the redundance on the

liver, and the two kidneys, and the fat which [is] on them, and hast made perfume on the altar;
29:14 and the flesh of the bullock, and his skin, and his dung, thou dost burn with fire at the outside of the camp; it [is] a sin-offering.
29:15 `And the one ram thou dost take, and Aaron and his sons have laid their hands on the head of the ram,
29:16 and thou hast slaughtered the ram, and hast taken its blood, and hast sprinkled [it] on the altar round about,
29:17 and the ram thou dost cut into its pieces, and hast washed its inwards, and its legs, and hast put [them] on its pieces, and on its head;
29:18 and thou hast made perfume with the whole ram on the altar. It [is] a burnt-offering to Jehovah, a sweet fragrance; a fire-offering it [is] to Jehovah.
29:19 `And thou hast taken the second ram, and Aaron hath laid -- his sons also -- their hands on the head of the ram,
29:20 and thou hast slaughtered the ram, and hast taken of its blood, and hast put on the tip of the right ear of Aaron, and on the tip of the right ear of his sons, and on the thumb of their right hand, and on the great toe of their right foot, and hast sprinkled the blood on the altar round about;
29:21 and thou hast taken of the blood which [is] on the altar, and of the anointing oil, and hast sprinkled on Aaron, and on his garments, and on his sons, and on the garments of his sons with him, and he hath been hallowed, he, and his garments, and his sons, and the garments of his sons with him.
29:22 `And thou hast taken from the ram the fat, and the fat tail, and the fat which is covering the inwards, and the redundance on the liver, and the two kidneys, and the fat which [is] on them, and the right leg, for it [is] a ram of consecration,
29:23 and one round cake of bread, and one cake of oiled bread, and one thin cake out of the basket of the unleavened things which [is] before Jehovah.
29:24 `And thou hast set the whole on the hands of Aaron, and on the hands of his sons, and hast waved them -- a wave-offering before Jehovah;
29:25 and thou hast taken them out of their hand, and hast made perfume on the altar beside the burnt-offering, for sweet fragrance before Jehovah; a fire-offering it [is] to Jehovah.
29:26 `And thou hast taken the breast from the ram of the consecration which [is] for Aaron, and hast waved it -- a wave-offering before Jehovah, and it hath become thy portion;
29:27 and thou hast sanctified the breast of the wave-offering, and the leg of the heave-offering, which hath been waved, and which hath been lifted up from the ram of the consecration, of that which [is] for Aaron, and of that which [is] for his sons;

29:28 and it hath been for Aaron and for his sons, by a statute age-during from the sons of Israel, for it [is] a heave-offering; and it is a heave offering from the sons of Israel, from the sacrifices of their peace-offerings -- their heave-offering to Jehovah.
29:29 `And the holy garments which are Aaron's, are for his sons after him, to be anointed in them, and to consecrate in them their hand;
29:30 seven days doth the priest in his stead (of his sons) put them on, when he goeth in unto the tent of meeting, to minister in the sanctuary.
29:31 `And the ram of the consecration thou dost take, and hast boiled its flesh in the holy place;
29:32 and Aaron hath eaten -- his sons also -- the flesh of the ram, and the bread which [is] in the basket, at the opening of the tent of meeting;
29:33 and they have eaten those things by which there is atonement to consecrate their hand, to sanctify them; and a stranger doth not eat -- for they [are] holy;
29:34 and if there be left of the flesh of the consecration or of the bread till the morning, then thou hast burned that which is left with fire; it is not eaten, for it [is] holy.
29:35 `And thou hast done thus to Aaron and to his sons, according to all that I have commanded thee; seven days thou dost consecrate their hand;
29:36 and a bullock, a sin-offering, thou dost prepare daily for the atonements, and thou hast atoned for the altar, in thy making atonement on it, and hast anointed it to sanctify it;
29:37 seven days thou dost make atonement for the altar, and hast sanctified it, and the altar hath been most holy; all that is coming against the altar is holy.
29:38 `And this [is] that which thou dost prepare on the altar; two lambs, sons of a year, daily continually;
29:39 the one lamb thou dost prepare in the morning, and the second lamb thou dost prepare between the evenings;
29:40 and a tenth [deal] of fine flour, mixed with beaten oil, a fourth part of a hin, and a libation, a fourth part of a hin, of wine, [is] for the one lamb.
29:41 `And the second lamb thou dost prepare between the evenings; according to the present of the morning, and according to its libation, thou dost prepare for it, for sweet fragrance, a fire-offering, to Jehovah: --
29:42 a continual burnt-offering for your generations, at the opening of the tent of meeting, before Jehovah, whither I am met with you, to speak unto thee there,
29:43 and I have met there with the sons of Israel, and it hath been sanctified by My honour.
29:44 `And I have sanctified the tent of meeting, and the altar, and Aaron and his sons I sanctify for being priests to Me,

29:45 and I have tabernacled in the midst of the sons of Israel, and have become their God,
29:46 and they have known that I [am] Jehovah their God, who hath brought them out of the land of Egypt, that I may tabernacle in their midst; I [am] Jehovah their God.
30:1 `And thou hast made an altar [for] making perfume; [of] shittim wood thou dost make it;
30:2 a cubit its length, and a cubit its breadth, (it is square), and two cubits its height; its horns [are] of the same.
30:3 `And thou hast overlaid it with pure gold, its top, and its sides round about, and its horns; and thou hast made to it a crown of gold round about;
30:4 and two rings of gold thou dost make to it under its crown; on its two ribs thou dost make [them], on its two sides, and they have become places for staves, to bear it with them.
30:5 `And thou hast made the staves of shittim wood, and hast overlaid them with gold;
30:6 and thou hast put it before the vail, which [is] by the ark of the testimony, before the mercy-seat which [is] over the testimony, whither I am met with thee.
30:7 `And Aaron hath made perfume on it, perfume of spices, morning by morning; in his making the lamps right he doth perfume it,
30:8 and in Aaron's causing the lamps to go up between the evenings, he doth perfume it; a continual perfume before Jehovah to your generations.
30:9 `Ye do not cause strange perfume to go up upon it, and burnt-offering, and present, and libation ye do not pour out on it;
30:10 and Aaron hath made atonement on its horns, once in a year, by the blood of the sin-offering of atonements; once in a year doth he make atonement for it, to your generations; it [is] most holy to Jehovah.'
30:11 And Jehovah speaketh unto Moses, saying,
30:12 `When thou takest up the sum of the sons of Israel for their numbers, then they have given each an atonement [for] his soul to Jehovah in their being numbered, and there is no plague among them in their being numbered.
30:13 `This they do give, every one passing over unto those numbered, half a shekel, by the shekel of the sanctuary (the shekel [is] twenty gerahs); half a shekel [is] the heave-offering to Jehovah;
30:14 every one passing over unto those numbered, from a son of twenty years and upwards, doth give the heave-offering of Jehovah;
30:15 the rich doth not multiply, and the poor doth not diminish from the half-shekel, to give the heave-offering of Jehovah, to make atonement for your souls.
30:16 `And thou hast taken the atonement-money from the sons of Israel, and hast given it for the service of the tent of meeting; and it hath been to the sons of Israel for a memorial before Jehovah,

to make atonement for your souls.'
30:17 And Jehovah speaketh unto Moses, saying,
30:18 `And thou hast made a laver of brass (and its base of brass), for washing; and thou hast put
it between the tent of meeting and the altar, and hast put water there;
30:19 and Aaron and his sons have washed at it their hands and their feet,
30:20 in their going in unto the tent of meeting they wash [with] water, and die not; or in their
drawing nigh unto the altar to minister, to perfume a fire-offering to Jehovah,
30:21 then they have washed their hands and their feet, and they die not, and it hath been to them
a statute age-during, to him and to his seed to their generations.'
30:22 And Jehovah speaketh unto Moses, saying,
30:23 `And thou, take to thyself principal spices, wild honey five hundred [shekels]; and spice-
cinnamon, the half of that, two hundred and fifty; and spice-cane two hundred and fifty;
30:24 and cassia five hundred, by the shekel of the sanctuary, and olive oil a hin;
30:25 and thou hast made it a holy anointing oil, a compound mixture, work of a compounder; it is a
holy anointing oil.
30:26 `And thou hast anointed with it the tent of meeting, and the ark of the testimony,
30:27 and the table and all its vessels, and the candlestick and its vessels, and the altar of
perfume,
30:28 and the altar of burnt-offering and all its vessels, and the laver and its base;
30:29 and thou hast sanctified them, and they have been most holy; all that is coming against them
is holy;
30:30 and Aaron and his sons thou dost anoint, and hast sanctified them for being priests to Me.
30:31 `And unto the sons of Israel thou dost speak, saying, A holy anointing oil is this to Me, to your
generations;
30:32 on flesh of man it is not poured, and with its proper proportion ye make none like it; it [is]
holy; it is holy to you;
30:33 a man who compoundeth [any] like it, or who putteth of it on a stranger -- hath even been cut
off from his people.'
30:34 And Jehovah saith unto Moses, `Take to thee spices, stacte, and onycha, and galbanum,
spices and pure frankincense; they are part for part;
30:35 and thou hast made it a perfume, a compound, work of a compounder, salted, pure, holy;
30:36 and thou hast beaten [some] of it small, and hast put of it before the testimony, in the tent of
meeting, whither I am met with thee; most holy it is to you.
30:37 `As to the perfume which thou makest, with its proper proportion ye do not make to

yourselves, holy it is to thee to Jehovah;
30:38 a man who maketh [any] like it -- to be refreshed by it -- hath even been cut off from his people.'
31:1 And Jehovah speaketh unto Moses, saying,
31:2 `See, I have called by name Bezaleel, son of Uri, son of Hur, of the tribe of Judah,
31:3 and I fill him [with] the Spirit of God, in wisdom, and in understanding, and in knowledge, and in all work,
31:4 to devise devices to work in gold, and in silver, and in brass,
31:5 and in graving of stone for settings, and in graving of wood to work in all work.
31:6 `And I, lo, I have given with him Aholiab, son of Ahisamach, of the tribe of Dan, and in the heart of every wise-hearted one I have given wisdom, and they have made all that which I have commanded thee.
31:7 `The tent of meeting, and the ark of testimony, and the mercy-seat which [is] on it, and all the vessels of the tent,
31:8 and the table and its vessels, and the pure candlestick and all its vessels, and the altar of the perfume,
31:9 and the altar of the burnt-offering and all its vessels, and the laver and its base,
31:10 and the coloured garments, and the holy garments for Aaron the priest, and the garments of his sons, for acting as priests in;
31:11 and the anointing oil, and the perfume of the spices for the sanctuary; according to all that I have commanded thee -- they do.'
31:12 And Jehovah speaketh unto Moses, saying,
31:13 `And thou, speak unto the sons of Israel, saying, Only, My sabbaths ye do keep, for it [is] a sign between Me and you, to your generations, to know that I, Jehovah, am sanctifying you;
31:14 and ye have kept the sabbath, for it [is] holy to you, he who is polluting it is certainly put to death -- for any who doeth work in it -- that person hath even been cut off from the midst of his people.
31:15 `Six days is work done, and in the seventh day [is] a sabbath of holy rest to Jehovah; any who doeth work in the sabbath-day is certainly put to death,
31:16 and the sons of Israel have observed the sabbath; to keep the sabbath to their generations [is] a covenant age-during,
31:17 between Me and the sons of Israel it [is] a sign -- to the age; for six days Jehovah made the heavens and the earth, and in the seventh day He hath ceased, and is refreshed.'
31:18 And He giveth unto Moses, when He finisheth speaking with him in mount Sinai, two tables

of the testimony, tables of stone, written by the finger of God.

32:1 And the people see that Moses is delaying to come down from the mount, and the people assemble against Aaron, and say unto him, `Rise, make for us gods who go before us, for this Moses -- the man who brought us up out of the land of Egypt -- we have not known what hath happened to him.'

32:2 And Aaron saith unto them, `Break off the rings of gold which [are] in the ears of your wives, your sons, and your daughters, and bring in unto me;'

32:3 and all the people themselves break off the rings of gold which [are] in their ears, and bring in unto Aaron,

32:4 and he receiveth from their hand, and doth fashion it with a graving tool, and doth make it a molten calf, and they say, `These thy gods, O Israel, who brought thee up out of the land of Egypt.'

32:5 And Aaron seeth, and buildeth an altar before it, and Aaron calleth, and saith, `A festival to Jehovah -- to-morrow;'

32:6 and they rise early on the morrow, and cause burnt-offerings to ascend, and bring nigh peace-offerings; and the people sit down to eat and to drink, and rise up to play.

32:7 And Jehovah saith unto Moses, `Go, descend, for thy people whom thou hast brought up out of the land of Egypt hath done corruptly,

32:8 they have turned aside hastily from the way that I have commanded them; they have made for themselves a molten calf, and bow themselves to it, and sacrifice to it, and say, These thy gods, O Israel, who brought thee up out of the land of Egypt.'

32:9 And Jehovah saith unto Moses, `I have seen this people, and lo, it [is] a stiff-necked people;

32:10 and now, let Me alone, and My anger doth burn against them, and I consume them, and I make thee become a great nation.'

32:11 And Moses appeaseth the face of Jehovah his God, and saith, `Why, O Jehovah, doth Thine anger burn against Thy people, whom Thou hast brought forth out of the land of Egypt with great power and with a strong hand?

32:12 why do the Egyptians speak, saying, For evil He brought them out to slay them among mountains, and to consume them from off the face of the ground? turn back from the heat of Thine anger, and repent of the evil against Thy people.

32:13 `Be mindful of Abraham, of Isaac, and of Israel, Thy servants, to whom Thou hast sworn by Thyself, and unto whom Thou speakest: I multiply your seed as stars of the heavens, and all this land, as I have said, I give to your seed, and they have inherited to the age;'

32:14 and Jehovah repenteth of the evil which He hath spoken of doing to His people.

32:15 And Moses turneth, and goeth down from the mount, and the two tables of the testimony

[are] in his hand, tables written on both their sides, on this and on that [are] they written;
32:16 and the tables are the work of God, and the writing is the writing of God, graven on the
tables.
32:17 And Joshua heareth the voice of the people in their shouting, and saith unto Moses, `A noise
of battle in the camp!'
32:18 and he saith, `It is not the voice of the crying of might, nor is it the voice of the crying of
weakness -- a voice of singing I am hearing.'
32:19 And it cometh to pass, when he hath drawn near unto the camp, that he seeth the calf, and
the dancing, and the anger of Moses burneth, and he casteth out of his hands the tables, and
breaketh them under the mount;
32:20 and he taketh the calf which they have made, and burneth [it] with fire, and grindeth until [it
is] small, and scattereth on the face of the waters, and causeth the sons of Israel to drink.
32:21 And Moses saith unto Aaron, `What hath this people done to thee, that thou hast brought in
upon it a great sin?'
32:22 and Aaron saith, `Let not the anger of my lord burn; thou -- thou hast known the people that it
[is] in evil;
32:23 and they say to me, Make for us gods, who go before us, for this Moses -- the man who
brought us up out of the land of Egypt -- we have not known what hath happened to him;
32:24 and I say to them, Whoso hath gold, let them break [it] off, and they give to me, and I cast it
into the fire, and this calf cometh out.'
32:25 And Moses seeth the people that it [is] unbridled, for Aaron hath made it unbridled for
contempt among its withstanders,
32:26 and Moses standeth in the gate of the camp, and saith, `Who [is] for Jehovah? -- unto me!'
and all the sons of Levi are gathered unto him;
32:27 and he saith to them, `Thus said Jehovah, God of Israel, Put each his sword by his thigh,
pass over and turn back from gate to gate through the camp, and slay each his brother, and each
his friend, and each his relation.'
32:28 And the sons of Levi do according to the word of Moses, and there fall of the people on that
day about three thousand men,
32:29 and Moses saith, `Consecrate your hand to-day to Jehovah, for a man [is] against his son,
and against his brother, so as to bring on you to-day a blessing.'
32:30 And it cometh to pass, on the morrow, that Moses saith unto the people, `Ye -- ye have
sinned a great sin, and now I go up unto Jehovah, if so be I atone for your sin.'
32:31 And Moses turneth back unto Jehovah, and saith, `Oh this people hath sinned a great sin,

that they make to themselves a god of gold;
32:32 and now, if Thou takest away their sin -- and if not -- blot me, I pray thee, out of Thy book which Thou hast written.'
32:33 And Jehovah saith unto Moses, `Whoso hath sinned against Me -- I blot him out of My book;
32:34 and now, go, lead the people whithersoever I have spoken to thee of; lo, My messenger goeth before thee, and in the day of my charging -- then I have charged upon them their sin.'
32:35 And Jehovah plagueth the people, because they made the calf which Aaron made.
33:1 And Jehovah speaketh unto Moses, `Go, ascend from this [place], thou and the people, whom thou hast brought up out of the land of Egypt, unto the land which I have sworn to Abraham, to Isaac, and to Jacob, saying, To thy seed I give it,'
33:2 (and I have sent before thee a messenger, and have cast out the Canaanite, the Amorite, and the Hittite, and the Perizzite, the Hivite, and the Jebusite,)
33:3 unto a land flowing with milk and honey, for I do not go up in thy midst, for thou [art] a stiff-necked people -- lest I consume thee in the way.'
33:4 And the people hear this sad thing, and mourn; and none put his ornaments on him.
33:5 And Jehovah saith unto Moses, `Say unto the sons of Israel, Ye [are] a stiff-necked people; one moment -- I come up into thy midst, and have consumed thee; and now, put down thine ornaments from off thee, and I know what I do to thee;'
33:6 and the sons of Israel take off their ornaments at mount Horeb.
33:7 And Moses taketh the tent, and hath stretched it out at the outside of the camp, afar off from the camp, and hath called it, `Tent of Meeting;' and it hath come to pass, every one seeking Jehovah goeth out unto the tent of meeting, which [is] at the outside of the camp.
33:8 And it hath come to pass, at the going out of Moses unto the tent, all the people rise, and have stood, each at the opening of his tent, and have looked expectingly after Moses, until his going into the tent.
33:9 And it hath come to pass, at the going in of Moses to the tent, the pillar of the cloud cometh down, and hath stood at the opening of the tent, and He hath spoken with Moses;
33:10 and all the people have seen the pillar of the cloud standing at the opening of the tent, and all the people have risen and bowed themselves, each at the opening of his tent.
33:11 And Jehovah hath spoken unto Moses face unto face, as a man speaketh unto his friend; and he hath turned back unto the camp, and his minister Joshua, son of Nun, a youth, departeth not out of the tent.
33:12 And Moses saith unto Jehovah, `See, Thou art saying unto me, Bring up this people, and Thou hast not caused me to know whom Thou dost send with me; and Thou hast said, I have

known thee by name, and also thou hast found grace in Mine eyes.
33:13 `And now, if, I pray Thee, I have found grace in Thine eyes, cause me to know, I pray Thee, Thy way, and I know Thee, so that I find grace in Thine eyes, and consider that this nation [is] Thy people;'
33:14 and He saith, `My presence doth go, and I have given rest to thee.'
33:15 And he saith unto Him, `If Thy presence is not going -- take us not up from this [place];
33:16 and in what is it known now, that I have found grace in Thine eyes -- I and Thy people -- is it not in Thy going with us? and we have been distinguished -- I and Thy people -- from all the people who [are] on the face of the ground.'
33:17 And Jehovah saith unto Moses, `Even this thing which thou hast spoken I do; for thou hast found grace in Mine eyes, and I know thee by name.'
33:18 And he saith, `Shew me, I pray Thee, Thine honour;'
33:19 and He saith, `I cause all My goodness to pass before thy face, and have called concerning the Name of Jehovah before thee, and favoured him whom I favour, and loved him whom I love.'
33:20 He saith also, `Thou art unable to see My face, for man doth not see Me, and live;'
33:21 Jehovah also saith, `Lo, a place [is] by Me, and thou hast stood on the rock,
33:22 and it hath come to pass, in the passing by of Mine honour, that I have set thee in a cleft of the rock, and spread out My hands over thee, until My passing by,
33:23 and I have turned aside My hands, and thou hast seen My back parts, and My face is not seen.'
34:1 And Jehovah saith unto Moses, `Hew for thyself two tables of stone like the first, and I have written on the tables the words which were on the first tables which thou hast broken;
34:2 and be prepared at morning, and thou hast come up in the morning unto mount Sinai, and hast stood before Me there, on the top of the mount,
34:3 and no man cometh up with thee, and also no man is seen in all the mount, also the flock and the herd do not feed over-against that mount.'
34:4 And he heweth two tables of stone like the first, and Moses riseth early in the morning, and goeth up unto mount Sinai, as Jehovah commanded him, and he taketh in his hand two tables of stone.
34:5 And Jehovah cometh down in a cloud, and stationeth Himself with him there, and calleth in the Name of Jehovah,
34:6 and Jehovah passeth over before his face, and calleth: `Jehovah, Jehovah God, merciful and gracious, slow to anger, and abundant in kindness and truth,
34:7 keeping kindness for thousands, taking away iniquity, and transgression, and sin, and not

entirely acquitting, charging iniquity of fathers on children, and on children's children, on a third [generation], and on a fourth.'
34:8 And Moses hasteth, and boweth to the earth, and doth obeisance,
34:9 and saith, `If, I pray Thee, I have found grace in Thine eyes, O my Lord, let my Lord, I pray Thee, go in our midst (for it [is] a stiff-necked people), and thou hast forgiven our iniquity and our sin, and hast inherited us.'
34:10 And He saith, `Lo, I am making a covenant: before all thy people I do wonders, which have not been done in all the earth, or in any nation, and all the people in whose midst thou [art] have seen the work of Jehovah, for it [is] fearful that which I am doing with thee.
34:11 `Observe for thyself that which I am commanding thee to-day: lo, I am casting out from before thee the Amorite, and the Canaanite, and the Hittite, and the Perizzite, and the Hivite, and the Jebusite;
34:12 take heed to thyself, lest thou make a covenant with the inhabitant of the land into which thou art going, lest it become a snare in thy midst;
34:13 for their altars ye break down, and their standing pillars ye shiver, and its shrines ye cut down;
34:14 for ye do not bow yourselves to another god -- for Jehovah, whose name [is] Zealous, is a zealous God.
34:15 `Lest thou make a covenant with the inhabitant of the land, and they have gone a-whoring after their gods, and have sacrificed to their gods, and [one] hath called to thee, and thou hast eaten of his sacrifice,
34:16 and thou hast taken of their daughters to thy sons, and their daughters have gone a-whoring after their gods, and have caused thy sons to go a-whoring after their gods;
34:17 a molten god thou dost not make to thyself.
34:18 `The feast of unleavened things thou dost keep; seven days thou dost eat unleavened things, as I have commanded thee, at an appointed time, the month of Abib: for in the month of Abib thou didst come out from Egypt.
34:19 `All opening a womb [are] Mine, and every firstling of thy cattle born a male, ox or sheep;
34:20 and the firstling of an ass thou dost ransom with a lamb; and if thou dost not ransom, then thou hast beheaded it; every first-born of thy sons thou dost ransom, and they do not appear before Me empty.
34:21 `Six days thou dost work, and on the seventh day thou dost rest; in ploughing-time and in harvest thou dost rest.
34:22 `And a feast of weeks thou dost observe for thyself; first-fruits of wheat-harvest; and the feast

of in-gathering, at the revolution of the year.
34:23 `Three times in a year do all thy males appear before the Lord Jehovah, God of Israel;
34:24 for I dispossess nations from before thee, and have enlarged thy border, and no man doth desire thy land in thy going up to appear before Jehovah thy God three times in a year.
34:25 `Thou dost not slaughter with a fermented thing the blood of My sacrifice; and the sacrifice of the feast of the passover doth not remain till morning:
34:26 the first of the first-fruits of the land thou dost bring into the house of Jehovah thy God; thou dost not boil a kid in its mother's milk.'
34:27 And Jehovah saith unto Moses, `Write for thyself these words, for, according to the tenor of these words I have made with thee a covenant, and with Israel.'
34:28 And he is there with Jehovah forty days and forty nights; bread he hath not eaten, and water he hath not drunk; and he writeth on the tables the matters of the covenant -- the ten matters.
34:29 And it cometh to pass, when Moses is coming down from mount Sinai (and the two tables of the testimony [are] in the hand of Moses in his coming down from the mount), that Moses hath not known that the skin of his face hath shone in His speaking with him,
34:30 and Aaron seeth -- all the sons of Israel also -- Moses, and lo, the skin of his face hath shone, and they are afraid of coming nigh unto him.
34:31 And Moses calleth unto them, and Aaron and all the princes in the company return unto him, and Moses speaketh unto them;
34:32 and afterwards have all the sons of Israel come nigh, and he chargeth them with all that Jehovah hath spoken with him in mount Sinai.
34:33 And Moses finisheth speaking with them, and putteth on his face a vail;
34:34 and in the going in of Moses before Jehovah to speak with Him, he turneth aside the vail until his coming out; and he hath come out and hath spoken unto the sons of Israel that which he is commanded;
34:35 and the sons of Israel have seen the face of Moses that the skin of the face of Moses hath shone, and Moses hath put back the vail on his face until his going in to speak with Him.
35:1 And Moses assembleth all the company of the sons of Israel, and saith unto them, `These [are] the things which Jehovah hath commanded -- to do them:
35:2 Six days is work done, and on the seventh day there is to you a holy [day], a sabbath of rest to Jehovah; any who doeth work in it is put to death;
35:3 ye do not burn a fire in any of your dwellings on the sabbath-day.'
35:4 And Moses speaketh unto all the company of the sons of Israel, saying, `This [is] the thing which Jehovah hath commanded, saying,

35:5 Take ye from among you a heave-offering to Jehovah; every one whose heart [is] willing doth bring it, -- the heave-offering of Jehovah, -- gold, and silver, and brass,
35:6 and blue, and purple, and scarlet, and linen, and goats' [hair],
35:7 and rams' skins made red, and badgers' skins, and shittim wood,
35:8 and oil for the light, and spices for the anointing oil, and for the spice perfume,
35:9 and shoham stones, and stones for settings, for an ephod, and for a breastplate.
35:10 `And all the wise-hearted among you come in, and make all that Jehovah hath commanded:
35:11 `The tabernacle, its tent, and its covering, its hooks, and its boards, its bars, its pillars, and its sockets,
35:12 `The ark and its staves, the mercy-seat, and the vail of the covering,
35:13 `The table and its staves, and all its vessels, and the bread of the presence,
35:14 `And the candlestick for the light, and its vessels, and its lamps, and the oil for the light,
35:15 `And the altar of perfume, and its staves, and the anointing oil, and the spice perfume, and the covering of the opening at the opening of the tabernacle,
35:16 `The altar of burnt-offering and the brazen grate which it hath, its staves, and all its vessels, the laver and its base,
35:17 `The hangings of the court, its pillars, and their sockets, and the covering of the gate of the court,
35:18 `The pins of the tabernacle, and the pins of the court, and their cords,
35:19 `The coloured garments, to do service in the sanctuary, the holy garments for Aaron the priest, and the garments of his sons to act as priest in.'
35:20 And all the company of the sons of Israel go out from the presence of Moses,
35:21 and they come in -- every man whom his heart hath lifted up, and every one whom his spirit hath made willing -- they have brought in the heave-offering of Jehovah for the work of the tent of meeting, and for all its service, and for the holy garments.
35:22 And they come in -- the men with the women -- every willing-hearted one -- they have brought in nose-ring, and ear-ring, and seal-ring, and necklace, all golden goods, even every one who hath waved a wave-offering of gold to Jehovah.
35:23 And every man with whom hath been found blue, and purple, and scarlet, and linen, and goats' [hair], and rams' skins made red, and badgers' skins, have brought [them] in;
35:24 every one lifting up a heave-offering of silver and brass have brought in the heave-offering of Jehovah; and every one with whom hath been found shittim wood for any work of the service brought [it] in.
35:25 And every wise-hearted woman hath spun with her hands, and they bring in yarn, the blue,

and the purple, the scarlet, and the linen;
35:26 and all the women whose heart hath lifted them up in wisdom, have spun the goats' [hair].
35:27 And the princes have brought in the shoham stones, and the stones for settings, for the ephod, and for the breastplate,
35:28 and the spices, and the oil for the light, and for the anointing oil, and for the spice perfume;
35:29 every man and woman (whom their heart hath made willing to bring in for all the work which Jehovah commanded to be done by the hand of Moses) [of] the sons of Israel brought in a willing-offering to Jehovah.
35:30 And Moses saith unto the sons of Israel, `See, Jehovah hath called by name Bezaleel, son of Uri, son of Hur, of the tribe of Judah,
35:31 and He doth fill him [with] the Spirit of God, in wisdom, in understanding, and in knowledge, and in all work,
35:32 even to devise devices to work in gold, and in silver, and in brass,
35:33 and in graving of stones for settings, and in graving of wood to work in any work of design.
35:34 `And to direct He hath put in his heart, he and Aholiab, son of Ahisamach, of the tribe of Dan;
35:35 He hath filled them with wisdom of heart to do every work, of engraver, and designer, and embroiderer (in blue, and in purple, in scarlet, and in linen), and weaver, who do any work, and of designers of designs.
36:1 And Bezaleel, and Aholiab, and every wise-hearted man, in whom Jehovah hath given wisdom and understanding to know to do every work of the service of the sanctuary, have done according to all that Jehovah commanded.
36:2 And Moses calleth unto Bezaleel, and unto Aholiab, and unto every wise-hearted man in whose heart Jehovah hath given wisdom, every one whom his heart lifted up, to come near unto the work to do it.
36:3 And they take from before Moses all the heave-offering which the sons of Israel have brought in for the work of the service of the sanctuary to do it; and still they have brought in unto him a willing-offering morning by morning.
36:4 And all the wise men, who are doing all the work of the sanctuary, come each from his work which they are doing,
36:5 and speak unto Moses, saying, `The people are multiplying to bring in more than sufficient for the service of the work which Jehovah commanded to make.'
36:6 And Moses commandeth, and they cause a voice to pass over through the camp, saying, `Let not man or woman make any more work for the heave-offering of the sanctuary;' and the people are restrained from bringing,

36:7 and the work hath been sufficient for them, for all the work, to do it, and to leave.
36:8 And all the wise-hearted ones among the doers of the work make the tabernacle; ten curtains of twined linen, and blue, and purple, and scarlet, [with] cherubs, work of a designer, he hath made them.
36:9 The length of the one curtain [is] eight and twenty by the cubit, and the breadth of the one curtain four by the cubit; one measure [is] to all the curtains.
36:10 And he joineth the five curtains one unto another, and the [other] five curtains he hath joined one unto another;
36:11 and he maketh loops of blue on the edge of the one curtain, at the end, in the joining; so he hath made in the edge of the outmost curtain, in the joining of the second;
36:12 fifty loops he hath made in the one curtain, and fifty loops hath he made in the end of the curtain which [is] in the joining of the second; the loops are taking hold one on another.
36:13 And he maketh fifty hooks of gold, and joineth the curtains one unto another by the hooks, and the tabernacle is one.
36:14 And he maketh curtains of goats' [hair] for a tent over the tabernacle; eleven curtains he hath made them;
36:15 the length of the one curtain [is] thirty by the cubit, and the breadth of the one curtain [is] four cubits; one measure [is] to the eleven curtains;
36:16 and he joineth the five curtains apart, and the six curtains apart.
36:17 And he maketh fifty loops on the outer edge of the curtain, in the joining; and fifty loops he hath made on the edge of the curtain which is joining the second;
36:18 and he maketh fifty hooks of brass to join the tent -- to be one;
36:19 and he maketh a covering for the tent of rams' skins made red, and a covering of badgers' skins above.
36:20 And he maketh the boards for the tabernacle of shittim wood, standing up;
36:21 ten cubits [is] the length of the [one] board, and a cubit and a half the breadth of the [one] board;
36:22 two handles [are] to the one board, joined one unto another; so he hath made for all the boards of the tabernacle.
36:23 And he maketh the boards for the tabernacle; twenty boards for the south side southward;
36:24 and forty sockets of silver he hath made under the twenty boards, two sockets under the one board for its two handles, and two sockets under the other board for its two handles.
36:25 And for the second side of the tabernacle, for the north side, he hath made twenty boards,
36:26 and their forty sockets of silver, two sockets under the one board, and two sockets under the

other board;
36:27 and for the sides of the tabernacle, westward, hath he made six boards;
36:28 and two boards hath he made for the corners of the tabernacle, in the two sides;
36:29 and they have been twins below, and together they are twins at its head, at the one ring; so he hath done to both of them at the two corners;
36:30 and there have been eight boards; and their sockets of silver [are] sixteen sockets, two sockets under the one board.
36:31 And he maketh bars of shittim wood, five for the boards of the one side of the tabernacle,
36:32 and five bars for the boards of the second side of the tabernacle, and five bars for the boards of the tabernacle, for the sides westward;
36:33 and he maketh the middle bar to enter into the midst of the boards from end to end;
36:34 and the boards he hath overlaid with gold, and their rings he hath made of gold, places for bars, and he overlayeth the bars with gold.
36:35 And he maketh the vail of blue, and purple, and scarlet, and twined linen, work of a designer he hath made it, [with] cherubs;
36:36 and he maketh for it four pillars of shittim [wood], and overlayeth them with gold; their pegs [are] of gold; and he casteth for them four sockets of silver.
36:37 And he maketh a covering for the opening of the tent, of blue, and purple, and scarlet, and twined linen, work of an embroiderer,
36:38 also its five pillars, and their pegs; and he overlaid their tops and their fillets [with] gold, and their five sockets [are] brass.
37:1 And Bezaleel maketh the ark of shittim wood, two cubits and a half its length, and a cubit and a half its breadth, and a cubit and a half its height;
37:2 and he overlayeth it with pure gold within and without, and maketh for it a wreath of gold round about;
37:3 and he casteth for it four rings of gold, on its four feet, even two rings on its one side, and two rings on its second side;
37:4 and he maketh staves of shittim wood, and overlayeth them with gold,
37:5 and he bringeth in the staves into the rings, by the sides of the ark, to bear the ark.
37:6 And he maketh a mercy-seat of pure gold, two cubits and a half its length, and a cubit and a half its breadth;
37:7 and he maketh two cherubs of gold, of beaten work he hath made them, at the two ends of the mercy-seat;
37:8 one cherub at the end on this [side], and one cherub at the end on that, out of the mercy-seat

he hath made the cherubs, at its two ends;
37:9 and the cherubs are spreading out wings on high, covering over the mercy-seat with their wings, and their faces [are] one towards another; towards the mercy-seat have the faces of the cherubs been.
37:10 And he maketh the table of shittim wood; two cubits its length, and a cubit its breadth, and a cubit and a half its height,
37:11 and overlayeth it with pure gold, and maketh for it a wreath of gold round about.
37:12 And he maketh for it a border of a handbreadth round about, and maketh a wreath of gold for its border round about;
37:13 and he casteth for it four rings of gold, and putteth the rings on the four corners which [are] to its four feet;
37:14 over-against the border have the rings been, places for staves to bear the table.
37:15 And he maketh the staves of shittim wood, and overlayeth them with gold, to bear the table;
37:16 and he maketh the vessels which [are] upon the table, its dishes, and its bowls, and its cups, and the cups by which they pour out, of pure gold.
37:17 And he maketh the candlestick of pure gold; of beaten work he hath made the candlestick, its base, and its branch, its calyxes, its knops, and its flowers, have been of the same;
37:18 and six branches are coming out of its sides, three branches of the candlestick out of its one side, and three branches of the candlestick out of its second side;
37:19 three calyxes, made like almonds, in the one branch, a knop and a flower; and three calyxes, made like almonds, in another branch, a knop and a flower; so to the six branches which are coming out of the candlestick.
37:20 And in the candlestick [are] four calyxes, made like almonds, its knops, and its flowers,
37:21 and a knop under the two branches of the same, and a knop under the two branches of the same, and a knop under the two branches of the same, [are] to the six branches which are coming out of it;
37:22 their knops and their branches have been of the same; all of it one beaten work of pure gold.
37:23 And he maketh its seven lamps, and its snuffers, and its snuff-dishes, of pure gold;
37:24 of a talent of pure gold he hath made it, and all its vessels.
37:25 And he maketh the perfume-altar of shittim wood; a cubit its length, and a cubit its breadth (square), and two cubits its height; its horns have been of the same;
37:26 and he overlayeth it with pure gold, its top and its sides round about, and its horns; and he maketh for it a wreath of gold round about;
37:27 and two rings of gold he hath made for it under its wreath, at its two corners, at its two sides,

for places for staves to bear it with them.
37:28 And he maketh the staves of shittim wood, and overlayeth them with gold;
37:29 and he maketh the holy anointing oil, and the pure spice-perfume -- work of a compounder.
38:1 And he maketh the altar of burnt-offering of shittim wood, five cubits its length, and five cubits its breadth (square), and three cubits its height;
38:2 and he maketh its horns on its four corners; its horns have been of the same; and he overlayeth it with brass;
38:3 and he maketh all the vessels of the altar, the pots, and the shovels, and the sprinkling-pans, the forks, and the fire-pans; all its vessels he hath made of brass.
38:4 And he maketh for the altar a brazen grate of net-work, under its border beneath, unto its midst;
38:5 and he casteth four rings for the four ends of the brazen grate -- places for bars;
38:6 and he maketh the staves of shittim wood, and overlayeth them with brass;
38:7 and he bringeth in the staves into the rings on the sides of the altar, to bear it with them; hollow [with] boards he made it.
38:8 And he maketh the laver of brass, and its base of brass, with the looking-glasses of the women assembling, who have assembled at the opening of the tent of meeting.
38:9 And he maketh the court; at the south side southward, the hangings of the court of twined linen, a hundred by the cubit,
38:10 their pillars [are] twenty, and their brazen sockets twenty, the pegs of the pillars and their fillets [are] silver;
38:11 and at the north side, a hundred by the cubit, their pillars [are] twenty, and their sockets of brass twenty; the pegs of the pillars and their fillets [are] silver;
38:12 and at the west side [are] hangings, fifty by the cubit; their pillars [are] ten, and their sockets ten; the pegs of the pillars and their fillets [are] silver;
38:13 and at the east side eastward fifty cubits.
38:14 The hangings on the side [are] fifteen cubits, their pillars three, and their sockets three,
38:15 and at the second side at the gate of the court, on this and on that, [are] hangings, fifteen cubits, their pillars three, and their sockets three;
38:16 all the hangings of the court round about [are] of twined linen,
38:17 and the sockets for the pillars of brass, the pegs of the pillars and their fillets of silver, and the overlaying of their tops of silver, and all the pillars of the court are filleted with silver.
38:18 And the covering of the gate of the court [is] the work of an embroiderer, of blue, and purple, and scarlet, and twined linen; and twenty cubits [is] the length, and the height with the breadth five

cubits, over-against the hangings of the court;
38:19 and their pillars [are] four, and their sockets of brass four, their pegs [are] of silver, and the overlaying of their tops and their fillets [are] of silver;
38:20 and all the pins for the tabernacle, and for the court round about, [are] of brass.
38:21 These are the numberings of the tabernacle (the tabernacle of testimony), which hath been numbered by the command of Moses, the service of the Levites, by the hand of Ithamar son of Aaron the priest.
38:22 And Bezaleel son of Uri, son of Hur, of the tribe of Judah, hath made all that Jehovah commanded Moses;
38:23 and with him [is] Aholiab son of Ahisamach, of the tribe of Dan, an engraver, and designer, and embroiderer in blue, and in purple, and in scarlet, and in linen.
38:24 All the gold which is prepared for the work in all the work of the sanctuary (and it is the gold of the wave-offering) [is] twenty and nine talents, and seven hundred and thirty shekels, by the shekel of the sanctuary.
38:25 And the silver of those numbered of the company [is] a hundred talents, and a thousand and seven hundred and five and seventy shekels, by the shekel of the sanctuary;
38:26 a bekah for a poll (half a shekel, by the shekel of the sanctuary,) for every one who is passing over unto those numbered, from a son of twenty years and upwards, for six hundred thousand, and three thousand, and five hundred and fifty.
38:27 And a hundred talents of silver are to cast the sockets of the sanctuary, and the sockets of the vail; a hundred sockets for the hundred talents, a talent for a socket;
38:28 and the thousand and seven hundred and five and seventy he hath made pegs for the pillars, and overlaid their tops, and filleted them.
38:29 And the brass of the wave-offering [is] seventy talents, and two thousand and four hundred shekels;
38:30 and he maketh with it the sockets of the opening of the tent of meeting, and the brazen altar, and the brazen grate which it hath, and all the vessels of the altar,
38:31 and the sockets of the court round about, and the sockets of the gate of the court, and all the pins of the tabernacle, and all the pins of the court round about.
39:1 And of the blue, and the purple, and the scarlet, they made coloured garments, to minister in the sanctuary; and they make the holy garments which [are] for Aaron, as Jehovah hath commanded Moses.
39:2 And he maketh the ephod, of gold, blue, and purple, and scarlet, and twined linen,
39:3 and they expand the plates of gold, and have cut off wires to work in the midst of the blue, and

in the midst of the purple, and in the midst of the scarlet, and in the midst of the linen -- work of a designer;

39:4 shoulder-pieces they have made for it, joining; at its two ends it is joined.

39:5 And the girdle of his ephod which [is] on it is of the same, according to its work, of gold, blue, and purple, and scarlet, and twined linen, as Jehovah hath commanded Moses.

39:6 And they prepare the shoham stones, set, embroidered [with] gold, opened with openings of a signet, by the names of the sons of Israel;

39:7 and he setteth them on the shoulders of the ephod -- stones of memorial for the sons of Israel, as Jehovah hath commanded Moses.

39:8 And he maketh the breastplate, work of a designer, like the work of the ephod, of gold, blue, and purple, and scarlet, and twined linen;

39:9 it hath been square; double they have made the breastplate, a span its length, and a span its breadth, doubled.

39:10 And they fill in it four rows of stones; a row of a sardius, a topaz, and a carbuncle [is] the one row;

39:11 and the second row an emerald, a sapphire, and a diamond;

39:12 and the third row an opal, an agate, and an amethyst;

39:13 and the fourth row a beryl, an onyx, and a jasper -- set, embroidered [with] gold, in their settings.

39:14 And the stones, according to the names of the sons of Israel, are twelve, according to their names, openings of a signet, each according to his name, for the twelve tribes.

39:15 And they make on the breastplate wreathed chains, work of thick bands, of pure gold;

39:16 and they make two embroidered things of gold, and two rings of gold, and put the two rings on the two ends of the breastplate,

39:17 and they put the two thick bands of gold on the two rings on the ends of the breastplate;

39:18 and the two ends of the two thick bands they have put on the two embroidered things, and they put them on the shoulders of the ephod, over-against its front.

39:19 And they make two rings of gold, and set [them] on the two ends of the breastplate, on its border, which [is] on the side of the ephod within;

39:20 and they make two rings of gold, and put them on the two shoulders of the ephod below, over-against its front, over-against its joining, above the girdle of the ephod;

39:21 and they bind the breastplate by its rings unto the rings of the ephod, with a ribbon of blue, to be above the girdle of the ephod, and the breastplate is not loosed from off the ephod, as Jehovah hath commanded Moses.

39:22 And he maketh the upper robe of the ephod, work of a weaver, completely of blue;
39:23 and the opening of the upper robe [is] in its midst, as the opening of a habergeon, a border [is] to its opening round about, it is not rent;
39:24 and they make on the hems of the upper robe pomegranates of blue, and purple, and scarlet, twined.
39:25 And they make bells of pure gold, and put the bells in the midst of the pomegranates, on the hems of the upper robe, round about, in the midst of the pomegranates;
39:26 a bell and a pomegranate, a bell and a pomegranate, [are] on the hems of the upper robe, round about, to minister in, as Jehovah hath commanded Moses.
39:27 And they make the coats of linen, work of a weaver, for Aaron and for his sons,
39:28 and the mitre of linen, and the beautiful bonnets of linen, and the linen trousers, of twined linen,
39:29 and the girdle of twined linen, and blue, and purple, and scarlet, work of an embroiderer, as Jehovah hath commanded Moses.
39:30 And they make the flower of the holy crown of pure gold, and write on it a writing, openings of a signet, `Holy to Jehovah;'
39:31 and they put on it a ribbon of blue, to put [it] on the mitre above, as Jehovah hath commanded Moses.
39:32 And all the service of the tabernacle of the tent of meeting is completed; and the sons of Israel do according to all that Jehovah hath commanded Moses; so they have done.
39:33 And they bring in the tabernacle unto Moses, the tent, and all its vessels, its hooks, its boards, its bars, and its pillars, and its sockets;
39:34 and the covering of rams' skins, which are made red, and the covering of badgers' skins, and the vail of the covering;
39:35 the ark of the testimony and its staves, and the mercy-seat;
39:36 the table, all its vessels, and the bread of the presence;
39:37 the pure candlestick, its lamps, the lamps of arrangement, and all its vessels, and the oil for the light.
39:38 And the golden altar, and the anointing oil, and the spice-perfume, and the covering of the opening of the tent;
39:39 the brazen altar and the brazen grate which it hath, its staves, and all its vessels, the laver and its base.
39:40 The hangings of the court, its pillars, and its sockets; and the covering for the gate of the court, its cords, and its pins; and all the vessels of the service of the tabernacle, for the tent of

meeting;
39:41 the coloured clothes to minister in the sanctuary, the holy garments for Aaron the priest, and the garments of his sons, to act as priest in.
39:42 According to all that Jehovah hath commanded Moses, so have the sons of Israel done all the service;
39:43 and Moses seeth all the work, and lo, they have done it as Jehovah hath commanded; so they have done. And Moses doth bless them.
40:1 And Jehovah speaketh unto Moses, saying,
40:2 `On the first day of the month, in the first month, thou dost raise up the tabernacle of the tent of meeting,
40:3 and hast set there the ark of the testimony, and hast covered over the ark with the vail,
40:4 and hast brought in the table, and set its arrangement in order, and hast brought in the candlestick, and caused its lamps to go up.
40:5 `And thou hast put the golden altar for perfume before the ark of the testimony, and hast put the covering of the opening to the tabernacle,
40:6 and hast put the altar of the burnt-offering before the opening of the tabernacle of the tent of meeting,
40:7 and hast put the laver between the tent of meeting and the altar, and hast put water there.
40:8 `And thou hast set the court round about, and hast placed the covering of the gate of the court,
40:9 and hast taken the anointing oil, and anointed the tabernacle, and all that [is] in it, and hallowed it, and all its vessels, and it hath been holy;
40:10 and thou hast anointed the altar of the burnt-offering, and all its vessels, and sanctified the altar, and the altar hath been most holy;
40:11 and thou hast anointed the laver and its base, and sanctified it.
40:12 `And thou hast brought near Aaron and his sons unto the opening of the tent of meeting, and hast bathed them with water;
40:13 and thou hast clothed Aaron with the holy garments, and anointed him, and sanctified him, and he hath acted as priest to Me.
40:14 `And his sons thou dost bring near, and hast clothed them with coats,
40:15 and anointed them as thou hast anointed their father, and they have acted as priests to Me, and their anointing hath been to be to them for a priesthood age-during, to their generations.'
40:16 And Moses doth according to all that Jehovah hath commanded him; so he hath done.
40:17 And it cometh to pass, in the first month, in the second year, in the first of the month, the

tabernacle hath been raised up;
40:18 and Moses raiseth up the tabernacle, and setteth its sockets, and placeth its boards, and placeth its bars, and raiseth its pillars,
40:19 and spreadeth the tent over the tabernacle, and putteth the covering of the tent upon it above, as Jehovah hath commanded Moses.
40:20 And he taketh and putteth the testimony unto the ark, and setteth the staves on the ark, and putteth the mercy-seat on the ark above;
40:21 and bringeth in the ark unto the tabernacle, and placeth the vail of the covering, and covereth over the ark of the testimony, as Jehovah hath commanded Moses.
40:22 And he putteth the table in the tent of meeting, on the side of the tabernacle northward, at the outside of the vail,
40:23 and setteth in order upon it the arrangement of bread, before Jehovah, as Jehovah hath commanded Moses.
40:24 And he putteth the candlestick in the tent of meeting, over-against the table, on the side of the tabernacle southward,
40:25 and causeth the lamps to go up before Jehovah, as Jehovah hath commanded Moses.
40:26 And he setteth the golden altar in the tent of meeting, before the vail,
40:27 and maketh perfume on it -- spice-perfume -- as Jehovah hath commanded Moses.
40:28 And he setteth the covering of the opening to the tabernacle,
40:29 and the altar of the burnt-offering he hath set at the opening of the tabernacle of the tent of meeting, and causeth the burnt-offering to go up upon it, and the present, as Jehovah hath commanded Moses.
40:30 And he putteth the laver between the tent of meeting and the altar, and putteth water there for washing,
40:31 and Moses and Aaron and his sons have washed their hands and their feet at the same;
40:32 in their going in unto the tent of meeting, and in their drawing near unto the altar, they wash, as Jehovah hath commanded Moses.
40:33 And he raiseth up the court round about the tabernacle, and about the altar, and placeth the covering of the gate of the court; and Moses completeth the work.
40:34 And the cloud covereth the tent of meeting, and the honour of Jehovah hath filled the tabernacle;
40:35 and Moses hath not been able to go in unto the tent of meeting, for the cloud hath tabernacled on it, and the honour of Jehovah hath filled the tabernacle.
40:36 And in the going up of the cloud from off the tabernacle the sons of Israel journey in all their

journeys;
40:37 and if the cloud go not up then they journey not, until the day of its going up:
40:38 for the cloud of Jehovah [is] on the tabernacle by day, and fire is in it by night, before the
eyes of all the house of Israel in all their journeys.

Leviticus

1:1 And Jehovah calleth unto Moses, and speaketh unto him out of the tent of meeting, saying,
1:2 `Speak unto the sons of Israel, and thou hast said unto them, Any man of you when he doth
bring near an offering to Jehovah, out of the cattle -- out of the herd, or out of the flock -- ye do
bring near your offering.
1:3 `If his offering [is] a burnt-offering out of the herd -- a male, a perfect one, he doth bring near,
unto the opening of the tent of meeting he doth bring it near, at his pleasure, before Jehovah;
1:4 and he hath laid his hand on the head of the burnt-offering, and it hath been accepted for him to
make atonement for him;
1:5 and he hath slaughtered the son of the herd before Jehovah; and sons of Aaron, the priests,
have brought the blood near, and sprinkled the blood on the altar round about, which [is] at the
opening of the tent of meeting.
1:6 `And he hath stripped the burnt-offering, and hath cut it into its pieces;
1:7 and the sons of Aaron the priest have put fire on the altar, and arranged wood on the fire;
1:8 and sons of Aaron, the priests, have arranged the pieces, with the head and the fat, on the
wood, which [is] on the fire, which [is] on the altar;
1:9 and its inwards and its legs he doth wash with water; and the priest hath made perfume with
the whole on the altar, a burnt-offering, a fire-offering of sweet fragrance to Jehovah.
1:10 `And if his offering [is] out of the flock -- out of the sheep or out of the goats -- for a burnt-
offering, a male, a perfect one, he doth bring near,
1:11 and he hath slaughtered it by the side of the altar northward, before Jehovah; and sons of
Aaron, the priests, have sprinkled its blood on the altar round about;
1:12 and he hath cut it into its pieces, and its head and its fat, and the priest hath arranged them on
the wood, which [is] on the fire, which [is] on the altar;
1:13 and the inwards and the legs he doth wash with water, and the priest hath brought the whole
near, and hath made perfume on the altar; it [is] a burnt-offering, a fire-offering of sweet fragrance
to Jehovah.
1:14 `And if his offering [is] a burnt-offering out of the fowl to Jehovah, than he hath brought near
his offering out of the turtle-doves or out of the young pigeons,
1:15 and the priest hath brought it near unto the altar, and hath wrung off its head, and hath made
perfume on the altar, and its blood hath been wrung out by the side of the altar;
1:16 and he hath turned aside its crop with its feathers, and hath cast it near the altar, eastward,
unto the place of ashes;

1:17 and he hath cleaved it with its wings (he doth not separate [it]), and the priest hath made it a perfume on the altar, on the wood, which [is] on the fire; it [is] a burnt-offering, a fire-offering of sweet fragrance to Jehovah.
2:1 `And when a person bringeth near an offering, a present to Jehovah, of flour is his offering, and he hath poured on it oil, and hath put on it frankincense;
2:2 and he hath brought it in unto the sons of Aaron, the priests, and he hath taken from thence the fulness of his hand of its flour and of its oil, besides all its frankincense, and the priest hath made perfume with its memorial on the altar, a fire-offering of sweet fragrance to Jehovah;
2:3 and the remnant of the present [is] for Aaron and for his sons, most holy, of the fire-offerings of Jehovah.
2:4 `And when thou bringest near an offering, a present baked in an oven, [it is of] unleavened cakes of flour mixed with oil, or thin unleavened cakes anointed with oil.
2:5 `And if thine offering [is] a present [made] on the girdel, it is of flour, mixed with oil, unleavened;
2:6 divide thou it into parts, and thou hast poured on it oil; it [is] a present.
2:7 `And if thine offering [is] a present [made] on the frying-pan, of flour with oil it is made,
2:8 and thou hast brought in the present which is made of these to Jehovah, and [one] hath brought it near unto the priest, and he hath brought it nigh unto the altar,
2:9 and the priest hath lifted up from the present its memorial, and hath made perfume on the altar, a fire-offering of sweet fragrance to Jehovah;
2:10 and the remnant of the present [is] for Aaron and for his sons, most holy, of the fire-offerings of Jehovah.
2:11 No present which ye bring near to Jehovah is made fermented, for with any leaven or any honey ye perfume no fire-offering to Jehovah.
2:12 `An offering of first-[fruits] -- ye bring them near to Jehovah, but on the altar they go not up, for sweet fragrance.
2:13 And every offering -- thy present -- with salt thou dost season, and thou dost not let the salt of the covenant of thy God cease from thy present; with all thine offerings thou dost bring near salt.
2:14 `And if thou bring near a present of first-ripe [fruits] to Jehovah, -- of green ears, roasted with fire, beaten out [corn] of a fruitful field thou dost bring near the present of thy first-ripe [fruits],
2:15 and thou hast put on it oil, and laid on it frankincense, it [is] a present;
2:16 and the priest hath made perfume with its memorial from its beaten out [corn], and from its oil, besides all its frankincense -- a fire-offering to Jehovah.
3:1 `And if his offering [is] a sacrifice of peace-offerings, if out of the herd he is bringing near, whether male or female, a perfect one he doth bring near before Jehovah,

3:2 and he hath laid his hand on the head of his offering, and hath slaughtered it at the opening of the tent of meeting, and sons of Aaron, the priests, have sprinkled the blood on the altar round about.

3:3 `And he hath brought near from the sacrifice of the peace-offerings a fire-offering to Jehovah, the fat which is covering the inwards, and all the fat which [is] on the inwards,

3:4 and the two kidneys, and the fat which [is] on them, which [is] on the flanks, and the redundance above the liver, (beside the kidneys he doth turn it aside),

3:5 and sons of Aaron have made it a perfume on the altar, on the burnt-offering which [is] on the wood, which [is] on the fire -- a fire-offering of sweet fragrance to Jehovah.

3:6 `And if his offering [is] out of the flock for a sacrifice of peace-offerings to Jehovah, male or female, a perfect one he doth bring near;

3:7 if a sheep he is bringing near [for] his offering, then he hath brought it near before Jehovah,

3:8 and hath laid his hand on the head of his offering, and hath slaughtered it before the tent of meeting, and sons of Aaron have sprinkled its blood on the altar round about.

3:9 `And he hath brought near from the sacrifice of the peace-offerings a fire-offering to Jehovah, its fat, the whole fat tail (over-against the bone he doth turn it aside), and the fat which is covering the inwards, and all the fat which [is] on the inwards,

3:10 and the two kidneys, and the fat which [is] on them, which [is] on the flanks, and the redundance above the liver, (beside the kidneys he doth turn it aside),

3:11 and the priest hath made it a perfume on the altar -- bread of a fire-offering to Jehovah.

3:12 `And if his offering [is] a goat, then he hath brought it near before Jehovah,

3:13 and hath laid his hand on its head, and hath slaughtered it before the tent of meeting, and sons of Aaron have sprinkled its blood on the altar round about;

3:14 and he hath brought near from it his offering, a fire-offering to Jehovah, the fat which is covering the inwards, and all the fat which [is] on the inwards,

3:15 and the two kidneys, and the fat which [is] upon them, which [is] on the flanks, and the redundance above the liver, (beside the kidneys he doth turn it aside),

3:16 and the priest hath made them a perfume on the altar -- bread of a fire-offering, for sweet fragrance; all the fat [is] Jehovah's.

3:17 `A statute age-during to your generations in all your dwellings: any fat or any blood ye do not eat.'

4:1 And Jehovah speaketh unto Moses, saying,

4:2 `Speak unto the sons of Israel, saying, When a person doth sin through ignorance against any of the commands of Jehovah [regarding things] which are not to be done, and hath done

[something] against one of these --
4:3 `If the priest who is anointed doth sin according to the guilt of the people, then he hath brought near for his sin which he hath sinned a bullock, a son of the herd, a perfect one, to Jehovah, for a sin-offering,
4:4 and he hath brought in the bullock unto the opening of the tent of meeting before Jehovah, and hath laid his hand on the head of the bullock, and hath slaughtered the bullock before Jehovah.
4:5 `And the priest who is anointed hath taken of the blood of the bullock, and hath brought it in unto the tent of meeting,
4:6 and the priest hath dipped his finger in the blood, and sprinkled of the blood seven times before Jehovah, at the front of the vail of the sanctuary;
4:7 and the priest hath put of the blood on the horns of the altar of spice-perfume before Jehovah, which [is] in the tent of meeting, and all the blood of the bullock he doth pour out at the foundation of the altar of the burnt-offering, which [is] at the opening of the tent of meeting.
4:8 `And all the fat of the bullock of the sin-offering he doth lift up from it, the fat which is covering over the inwards, and all the fat which [is] on the inwards,
4:9 and the two kidneys, and the fat which [is] on them, which [is] on the flanks, and the redundance above the liver, (beside the kidneys he doth turn it aside),
4:10 as it is lifted up from the ox of the sacrifice of the peace-offerings; and the priest hath made them a perfume on the altar of the burnt-offering.
4:11 `And the skin of the bullock, and all its flesh, besides its head, and besides its legs, and its inwards, and its dung --
4:12 he hath even brought out the whole bullock unto the outside of the camp, unto a clean place, unto the place of the pouring out of the ashes, and he hath burnt it on the wood with fire; beside the place of the pouring out of the ashes it is burnt.
4:13 `And if the whole company of Israel err ignorantly, and the thing hath been hidden from the eyes of the assembly, and they have done [something against] one of all the commands of Jehovah [concerning things] which are not to be done, and have been guilty;
4:14 when the sin which they have sinned concerning it hath been known, then have the assembly brought near a bullock, a son of the herd, for a sin-offering, and they have brought it in before the tent of meeting;
4:15 and the elders of the company have laid their hands on the head of the bullock, before Jehovah, and [one] hath slaughtered the bullock before Jehovah.
4:16 `And the priest who is anointed hath brought in of the blood of the bullock unto the tent of meeting,

4:17 and the priest hath dipped his finger in the blood, and hath sprinkled seven times before
Jehovah at the front of the vail,
4:18 and [some] of the blood he doth put on the horns of the altar which [is] before Jehovah, which
[is] in the tent of meeting; and all the blood he doth pour out at the foundation of the altar of the
burnt-offering, which [is] at the opening of the tent of meeting;
4:19 and all its fat he doth lift up from it, and hath made perfume on the altar.
4:20 `And he hath done to the bullock as he hath done to the bullock of the sin-offering, so he doth
to it; and the priest hath made atonement for them, and it hath been forgiven them;
4:21 and he hath brought out the bullock unto the outside of the camp, and hath burned it as he
hath burned the first bullock; it [is] a sin-offering of the assembly.
4:22 `When a prince doth sin, and hath done [something against] one of all the commands of
Jehovah his God [regarding things] which are not to be done, through ignorance, and hath been
guilty --
4:23 or his sin wherein he hath sinned hath been made known unto him, then he hath brought in
his offering, a kid of the goats, a male, a perfect one,
4:24 and he hath laid his hand on the head of the goat, and hath slaughtered it in the place where
he doth slaughter the burnt-offering before Jehovah; it [is] a sin-offering.
4:25 `And the priest hath taken of the blood of the sin-offering with his finger, and hath put on the
horns of the altar of the burnt-offering, and its blood he doth pour out at the foundation of the altar
of the burnt-offering,
4:26 and with all its fat he doth make perfume on the altar, as the fat of the sacrifice of the peace-
offerings; and the priest hath made atonement for him because of his sin, and it hath been forgiven
him.
4:27 `And if any person of the people of the land sin through ignorance, by his doing [something
against] one of the commands of Jehovah [regarding things] which are not to be done, and hath
been guilty --
4:28 or his sin which he hath sinned hath been made known unto him, then he hath brought in his
offering, a kid of the goats, a perfect one, a female, for his sin which he hath sinned,
4:29 and he hath laid his hand on the head of the sin-offering, and hath slaughtered the sin-offering
in the place of the burnt-offering.
4:30 `And the priest hath taken of its blood with his finger, and hath put on the horns of the altar of
the burnt-offering, and all its blood he doth pour out at the foundation of the altar,
4:31 and all its fat he doth turn aside, as the fat hath been turned aside from off the sacrifice of the
peace-offerings, and the priest hath made perfume on the altar, for sweet fragrance to Jehovah;

and the priest hath made atonement for him, and it hath been forgiven him.
4:32 `And if he bring in a sheep [for] his offering, for a sin-offering, a female, a perfect one, he doth bring in,
4:33 and he hath laid his hand on the head of the sin-offering, and hath slaughtered it for a sin-offering in the place where he slaughtereth the burnt-offering.
4:34 `And the priest hath taken of the blood of the sin-offering with his finger, and hath put on the horns of the altar of the burnt-offering, and all its blood he poureth out at the foundation of the altar,
4:35 and all its fat he turneth aside, as the fat of the sheep is turned aside from the sacrifice of the peace-offerings, and the priest hath made them a perfume on the altar, according to the fire-offerings of Jehovah, and the priest hath made atonement for him, for his sin which he hath sinned, and it hath been forgiven him.
5:1 `And when a person doth sin, and hath heard the voice of an oath, and he [is] witness, or hath seen, or hath known -- if he declare not, then he hath borne his iniquity:
5:2 `Or when a person cometh against any thing unclean, or against a carcase of an unclean beast, or against a carcase of unclean cattle, or against a carcase of an unclean teeming creature, and it hath been hidden from him, and he unclean, and guilty;
5:3 `Or when he cometh against uncleanness of man, even any of his uncleanness whereby he is unclean, and it hath been hidden from him, and he hath known, and hath been guilty:
5:4 `Or when a person sweareth, speaking wrongfully with the lips to do evil, or to do good, even anything which man speaketh wrongfully with an oath, and it hath been hid from him; -- when he hath known then he hath been guilty of one of these;
5:5 `And it hath been when he is guilty of one of these, that he hath confessed concerning that which he hath sinned,
5:6 and hath brought in his guilt-offering to Jehovah for his sin which he hath sinned, a female out of the flock, a lamb, or a kid of the goats, for a sin-offering, and the priest hath made atonement for him, because of his sin.
5:7 `And if his hand reach not to the sufficiency of a lamb, then he hath brought in his guilt-offering -- he who hath sinned -- two turtle-doves or two young pigeons to Jehovah, one for a sin-offering, and one for a burnt-offering;
5:8 and he hath brought them in unto the priest, and hath brought near that which [is] for a sin-offering first, and hath wrung off its head from its neck, and doth not separate [it],
5:9 and he hath sprinkled of the blood of the sin-offering on the side of the altar, and that which is left of the blood is wrung out at the foundation of the altar; it [is] a sin-offering.
5:10 `And the second he maketh a burnt-offering, according to the ordinance, and the priest hath

made atonement for him, because of his sin which he hath sinned, and it hath been forgiven him.
5:11 `And if his hand reach not to two turtle-doves, or to two young pigeons, then he hath brought in his offering -- he who hath sinned -- a tenth of an ephah of flour for a sin-offering; he putteth no oil on it, nor doth he put on it frankincense, for it [is] a sin-offering,
5:12 and he hath brought it in unto the priest, and the priest hath taken a handful from it -- the fulness of his hand -- its memorial -- and hath made perfume on the altar, according to the fire-offerings of Jehovah; it [is] a sin-offering.
5:13 `And the priest hath made atonement for him, for his sin which he hath sinned against one of these, and it hath been forgiven him, and [the remnant] hath been to the priest, like the present.'
5:14 And Jehovah speaketh unto Moses, saying,
5:15 `When a person committeth a trespass, and hath sinned through ignorance against the holy things of Jehovah, then he hath brought in his guilt-offering to Jehovah, a ram, a perfect one, out of the flock, at thy valuation [in] silver -- shekels by the shekel of the sanctuary -- for a guilt-offering.
5:16 `And that which he hath sinned against the holy thing he repayeth, and its fifth is adding to it, and hath given it to the priest, and the priest maketh atonement for him with the ram of the guilt-offering, and it hath been forgiven him.
5:17 `And when any person sinneth, and hath done [something against] one of all the commands of Jehovah [regarding things] which are not to be done, and hath not known, and he hath been guilty, and hath borne his iniquity,
5:18 `Then he hath brought in a ram, a perfect one, out of the flock, at thy valuation, for a guilt-offering, unto the priest; and the priest hath made atonement for him, for his ignorance in which he hath erred and he hath not known, and it hath been forgiven him;
5:19 it [is] a guilt-offering; he hath been certainly guilty before Jehovah.'
6:1 And Jehovah speaketh unto Moses, saying,
6:2 `When any person doth sin, and hath committed a trespass against Jehovah, and hath lied to his fellow concerning a deposit, or concerning fellowship, or concerning violent robbery, or hath oppressed his fellow;
6:3 or hath found a lost thing, and hath lied concerning it, and hath sworn to a falsehood, concerning one of all [these] which man doth, sinning in them:
6:4 `Then it hath been, when he sinneth, and hath been guilty, that he hath returned the plunder which he hath taken violently away, or the thing which he hath got by oppression, or the deposit which hath been deposited with him, or the lost thing which he hath found;
6:5 or all that concerning which he sweareth falsely, he hath even repaid it in its principal, and its fifth he is adding to it; to him whose it [is] he giveth it in the day of his guilt-offering.

6:6 `And his guilt-offering he bringeth in to Jehovah, a ram, a perfect one, out of the flock, at thy estimation, for a guilt-offering, unto the priest,
6:7 and the priest hath made atonement for him before Jehovah, and it hath been forgiven him, concerning one thing of all that he doth, by being guilty therein.'
6:8 And Jehovah speaketh unto Moses, saying,
6:9 `Command Aaron and his sons, saying, This [is] a law of the burnt-offering (it [is] the burnt-offering, because of the burning on the altar all the night unto the morning, and the fire of the altar is burning on it,)
6:10 that the priest hath put on his long robe of fine linen, and his fine linen trousers he doth put on his flesh, and hath lifted up the ashes which the fire consumeth with the burnt-offering on the altar, and hath put them near the altar;
6:11 and he hath stripped off his garments, and hath put on other garments, and hath brought out the ashes unto the outside of the camp, unto a clean place.
6:12 `And the fire on the altar is burning on it, it is not quenched, and the priest hath burned on it wood morning by morning, and hath arranged on it the burnt-offering, and hath made perfume on it [with] the fat of the peace-offerings;
6:13 fire is continually burning on the altar, it is not quenched.
6:14 `And this [is] a law of the present: sons of Aaron have brought it near before Jehovah unto the front of the altar,
6:15 and [one] hath lifted up of it with his hand from the flour of the present, and from its oil, and all the frankincense which [is] on the present, and hath made perfume on the altar, sweet fragrance -- its memorial to Jehovah.
6:16 `And the remnant of it do Aaron and his sons eat; [with] unleavened things it is eaten, in the holy place, in the court of the tent of meeting they do eat it.
6:17 It is not baken [with] any thing fermented, their portion I have given it, out of My fire-offerings; it [is] most holy, like the sin-offering, and like the guilt-offering.
6:18 Every male among the sons of Aaron doth eat it -- a statute age-during to your generations, out of the fire-offerings of Jehovah: all that cometh against them is holy.'
6:19 And Jehovah speaketh unto Moses, saying,
6:20 `This [is] an offering of Aaron and of his sons, which they bring near to Jehovah in the day of his being anointed; a tenth of the ephah of flour [for] a continual present, half of it in the morning, and half of it in the evening;
6:21 on a girdel with oil it is made -- fried thou dost bring it in; baked pieces of the present thou dost bring near, a sweet fragrance to Jehovah.

6:22 `And the priest who is anointed in his stead, from among his sons, doth make it, -- a statute
age-during of Jehovah: it is completely perfumed;
6:23 and every present of a priest is a whole burnt-offering; it is not eaten.'
6:24 And Jehovah speaketh unto Moses, saying,
6:25 `Speak unto Aaron and unto his sons, saying, This [is] a law of the sin-offering: in the place
where the burnt-offering is slaughtered is the sin-offering slaughtered before Jehovah; it [is] most
holy.
6:26 `The priest who is making atonement with it doth eat it, in the holy place it is eaten, in the
court of the tent of meeting;
6:27 all that cometh against its flesh is holy, and when [any] of its blood is sprinkled on the
garment, that on which it is sprinkled thou dost wash in the holy place;
6:28 and an earthen vessel in which it is boiled is broken, and if in a brass vessel it is boiled, then it
is scoured and rinsed with water.
6:29 `Every male among the priests doth eat it -- it [is] most holy;
6:30 and no sin-offering, [any] of whose blood is brought in unto the tent of meeting to make
atonement in the sanctuary is eaten; with fire it is burnt.
7:1 `And this [is] a law of the guilt-offering: it [is] most holy;
7:2 in the place where they slaughter the burnt-offering they do slaughter the guilt-offering, and its
blood [one] doth sprinkle on the altar round about,
7:3 and all its fat he bringeth near out of it, the fat tail, and the fat which is covering the inwards,
7:4 and the two kidneys, and the fat which [is] on them, which [is] on the flanks, and the
redundance above the liver (beside the kidneys he doth turn it aside);
7:5 and the priest hath made them a perfume on the altar, a fire-offering to Jehovah; it [is] a guilt-
offering.
7:6 `Every male among the priests doth eat it; in the holy place it is eaten -- it [is] most holy;
7:7 as [is] a sin-offering, so [is] a guilt-offering; one law [is] for them; the priest who maketh
atonement by it -- it is his.
7:8 `And the priest who is bringing near any man's burnt-offering, the skin of the burnt-offering
which he hath brought near, it is the priest's, his own;
7:9 and every present which is baked in an oven, and every one done in a frying-pan, and on a
girdel, [is] the priest's who is bringing it near; it is his;
7:10 and every present, mixed with oil or dry, is for all the sons of Aaron -- one as another.
7:11 `And this [is] a law of the sacrifice of the peace-offerings which [one] bringeth near to Jehovah:
7:12 if for a thank-offering he bring it near, then he hath brought near with the sacrifice of thank-

offering unleavened cakes mixed with oil, and thin unleavened cakes anointed with oil, and of fried
flour cakes mixed with oil;
7:13 besides the cakes, fermented bread he doth bring near [with] his offering, besides the sacrifice
of thank-offering of his peace-offerings;
7:14 and he hath brought near out of it one of the whole offering -- a heave-offering to Jehovah; to
the priest who is sprinkling the blood of the peace-offerings -- it is his;
7:15 as to the flesh of the sacrifice of the thank-offering of his peace-offerings, in the day of his
offering it is eaten; he doth not leave of it till morning.
7:16 `And if the sacrifice of his offering [is] a vow or free-will offering, in the day of his bringing near
his sacrifice it is eaten; and on the morrow also the remnant of it is eaten;
7:17 and the remnant of the flesh of the sacrifice on the third day with fire is burnt;
7:18 and if any of the flesh of the sacrifice of his peace-offerings be really eaten on the third day, it
is not pleasing; for him who is bringing it near it is not reckoned; it is an abominable thing, and the
person who is eating of it his iniquity doth bear.
7:19 `And the flesh which cometh against any unclean thing is not eaten; with fire it is burnt; as to
the flesh, every clean one doth eat of the flesh;
7:20 and the person who eateth of the flesh of the sacrifice of the peace-offerings which [are]
Jehovah's, and his uncleanness upon him, even that person hath been cut off from his people.
7:21 `And when a person cometh against any thing unclean, of the uncleanness of man, or of the
uncleanness of beasts, or of any unclean teeming creature, and hath eaten of the flesh of the
sacrifice of the peace-offerings which [are] Jehovah's, even that person hath been cut off from his
people.'
7:22 And Jehovah speaketh unto Moses, saying,
7:23 `Speak unto the sons of Israel, saying, Any fat of ox and sheep and goat ye do not eat;
7:24 and the fat of a carcase, and the fat of a torn thing is prepared for any work, but ye do
certainly not eat it;
7:25 for whoever eateth the fat of the beast, of which [one] bringeth near a fire-offering to Jehovah,
even the person who eateth hath been cut off from his people.
7:26 `And any blood ye do not eat in all your dwellings, of fowl, or of beast;
7:27 any person who eateth any blood, even that person hath been cut off from his people.'
7:28 And Jehovah speaketh unto Moses, saying,
7:29 `Speak unto the sons of Israel, saying, He who is bringing near the sacrifice of his peace-
offerings to Jehovah doth bring in his offering to Jehovah from the sacrifice of his peace-offerings;
7:30 his own hands do bring in the fire-offerings of Jehovah, the fat beside the breast, it he doth

bring in with the breast, to wave it -- a wave-offering before Jehovah.
7:31 `And the priest hath made perfume with the fat on the altar, and the breast hath been Aaron's and his sons;
7:32 and the right leg ye do make a heave-offering to the priest of the sacrifices of your peace-offerings;
7:33 he of the sons of Aaron who is bringing near the blood of the peace-offerings, and the fat, his is the right leg for a portion.
7:34 `For the breast of the wave-offering, and the leg of the heave-offering, I have taken from the sons of Israel, from the sacrifices of their peace-offerings, and I give them to Aaron the priest, and to his sons, by a statute age-during, from the sons of Israel.'
7:35 This [is] the anointing of Aaron, and the anointing of his sons out of the fire-offerings of Jehovah, in the day he hath brought them near to act as priest to Jehovah,
7:36 which Jehovah hath commanded to give to them in the day of His anointing them, from the sons of Israel -- a statute age-during to their generations.
7:37 This [is] the law for burnt-offering, for present, and for sin-offering, and for guilt-offering, and for consecrations, and for a sacrifice of the peace-offerings,
7:38 which Jehovah hath commanded Moses in Mount Sinai, in the day of his commanding the sons of Israel to bring near their offerings to Jehovah, in the wilderness of Sinai.
8:1 And Jehovah speaketh unto Moses, saying,
8:2 `Take Aaron and his sons with him, and the garments, and the anointing oil, and the bullock of the sin-offering, and the two rams, and the basket of unleavened things,
8:3 and all the company assemble thou unto the opening of the tent of meeting.'
8:4 And Moses doth as Jehovah hath commanded him, and the company is assembled unto the opening of the tent of meeting,
8:5 and Moses saith unto the company, `This [is] the thing which Jehovah hath commanded to do.'
8:6 And Moses bringeth near Aaron and his sons, and doth bathe them with water,
8:7 and doth put on him the coat, and doth gird him with the girdle, and doth clothe him with the upper robe, and doth put on him the ephod, and doth gird him with the girdle of the ephod, and doth bind [it] to him with it,
8:8 and doth put on him the breastplate, and doth put unto the breastplate the Lights and the Perfections,
8:9 and doth put the mitre on his head, and doth put on the mitre, over-against its front, the golden flower of the holy crown, as Jehovah hath commanded Moses.
8:10 And Moses taketh the anointing oil, and anointeth the tabernacle, and all that [is] in it, and

sanctifieth them;
8:11 and he sprinkleth of it on the altar seven times, and anointeth the altar, and all its vessels, and
the laver, and its base, to sanctify them;
8:12 and he poureth of the anointing oil on the head of Aaron, and anointeth him to sanctify him.
8:13 And Moses bringeth near the sons of Aaron, and doth clothe them [with] coats, and girdeth
them [with] girdles, and bindeth for them turbans, as Jehovah hath commanded Moses.
8:14 And he bringeth nigh the bullock of the sin-offering, and Aaron layeth -- his sons also -- their
hands on the head of the bullock of the sin-offering,
8:15 and [one] slaughtereth, and Moses taketh the blood, and putteth on the horns of the altar
round about with his finger, and cleanseth the altar, and the blood he hath poured out at the
foundation of the altar, and sanctifieth it, to make atonement upon it.
8:16 And he taketh all the fat that [is] on the inwards, and the redundance above the liver, and the
two kidneys, and their fat, and Moses maketh Perfume on the altar,
8:17 and the bullock, and its skin, and its flesh, and its dung, he hath burnt with fire, at the outside
of the camp, as Jehovah hath commanded Moses.
8:18 And he bringeth near the ram of the burnt-offering, and Aaron and his sons lay their hands on
the head of the ram,
8:19 and [one] slaughtereth, and Moses sprinkleth the blood on the altar round about;
8:20 and the ram he hath cut into its pieces, and Moses maketh perfume with the head, and the
pieces, and the fat,
8:21 and the inwards and the legs he hath washed with water, and Moses maketh perfume with the
whole ram on the altar; it [is] a burnt-offering, for sweet fragrance; it [is] a fire-offering to Jehovah,
as Jehovah hath commanded Moses.
8:22 And he bringeth near the second ram, a ram of the consecrations, and Aaron and his sons lay
their hands on the head of the ram,
8:23 and [one] slaughtereth, and Moses taketh of its blood, and putteth on the tip of the right ear of
Aaron, and on the thumb of his right hand, and on the great toe of his right foot;
8:24 and he bringeth near the sons of Aaron, and Moses putteth of the blood on the tip of their right
ear, and on the thumb of their right hand, and on the great toe of their right foot. And Moses
sprinkleth the blood on the altar round about,
8:25 and taketh the fat, and the fat tail, and all the fat that [is] on the inwards, and the redundance
above the liver, and the two kidneys, and their fat, and the right leg;
8:26 and out of the basket of unleavened things, which [is] before Jehovah, he hath taken one
unleavened cake, and one cake of oiled bread, and one thin cake, and putteth [them] on the fat,

and on the right leg;
8:27 and putteth the whole on the hands of Aaron, and on the hands of his sons, and waveth them
-- a wave-offering before Jehovah.
8:28 And Moses taketh them from off their hands, and maketh perfume on the altar, on the burnt-
offering, they [are] consecrations for sweet fragrance; it [is] a fire-offering to Jehovah;
8:29 and Moses taketh the breast, and waveth it -- a wave-offering before Jehovah; of the ram of
the consecrations it hath been to Moses for a portion, as Jehovah hath commanded Moses.
8:30 And Moses taketh of the anointing oil, and of the blood which [is] on the altar, and sprinkleth
on Aaron, on his garments, and on his sons, and on the garments of his sons with him, and he
sanctifieth Aaron, his garments, and his sons, and the garments of his sons with him.
8:31 And Moses saith unto Aaron, and unto his sons, `Boil ye the flesh at the opening of the tent of
meeting, and there ye do eat it and the bread which [is] in the basket of the consecrations, as I
have commanded, saying, Aaron and his sons do eat it.
8:32 `And the remnant of the flesh and of the bread with fire ye burn;
8:33 and from the opening of the tent of meeting ye go not out seven days, till the day of the
fulness, the days of your consecration -- for seven days he doth consecrate your hand;
8:34 as he hath done on this day, Jehovah hath commanded to do, to make atonement for you;
8:35 and at the opening of the tent of meeting ye abide, by day and by night seven days, and ye
have kept the charge of Jehovah, and die not, for so I have been commanded.'
8:36 And Aaron doth -- his sons also -- all the things which Jehovah hath commanded by the hand
of Moses.
9:1 And it cometh to pass on the eighth day, Moses hath called for Aaron and for his sons, and for
the elders of Israel,
9:2 and he saith unto Aaron, `Take to thyself a calf, a son of the herd, for a sin-offering, and a ram
for a burnt-offering, perfect ones, and bring near before Jehovah.
9:3 `And unto the sons of Israel thou dost speak, saying, Take ye a kid of the goats for a sin-
offering, and a calf, and a lamb, sons of a year, perfect ones, for a burnt-offering,
9:4 and a bullock and a ram for peace-offerings, to sacrifice before Jehovah, and a present mixed
with oil; for to-day Jehovah hath appeared unto you.'
9:5 And they take that which Moses hath commanded unto the front of the tent of meeting, and all
the company draw near and stand before Jehovah;
9:6 and Moses saith, `This [is] the thing which Jehovah hath commanded; do [it], and the honour of
Jehovah doth appear unto you.'
9:7 And Moses saith unto Aaron, `Draw near unto the altar, and make thy sin-offering, and thy

burnt-offering, and make atonement for thyself, and for the people, and make the offering of the people, and make atonement for them, as Jehovah hath commanded.'

9:8 And Aaron draweth near unto the altar, and slaughtereth the calf of the sin-offering, which [is] for himself;

9:9 and the sons of Aaron bring the blood near unto him, and he dippeth his finger in the blood, and putteth [it] on the horns of the altar, and the blood he hath poured out at the foundation of the altar;

9:10 and the fat, and the kidneys, and the redundance of the liver, of the sin-offering, he hath made a perfume on the altar, as Jehovah hath commanded Moses;

9:11 and the flesh and the skin he hath burnt with fire, at the outside of the camp.

9:12 And he slaughtereth the burnt-offering, and the sons of Aaron have presented unto him the blood, and he sprinkleth it on the altar round about;

9:13 and the burnt-offering they have presented unto him, by its pieces, and the head, and he maketh perfume on the altar;

9:14 and he washeth the inwards and the legs, and maketh perfume for the burnt-offering on the altar.

9:15 And he bringeth near the offering of the people, and taketh the goat of the sin-offering which [is] for the people, and slaughtered it, and maketh it a sin-offering, like the first;

9:16 and he bringeth near the burnt-offering, and maketh it, according to the ordinance;

9:17 and he bringeth near the present, and filleth his palm with it, and maketh perfume on the altar, apart from the burnt-offering of the morning.

9:18 And he slaughtereth the bullock and the ram, a sacrifice of the peace-offerings, which [are] for the people, and sons of Aaron present the blood unto him (and he sprinkleth it on the altar round about),

9:19 and the fat of the bullock, and of the ram, the fat tail, and the covering [of the inwards], and the kidneys, and the redundance above the liver,

9:20 and they set the fat on the breasts, and he maketh perfume with the fat on the altar;

9:21 and the breasts, and the right leg hath Aaron waved -- a wave-offering before Jehovah, as He hath commanded Moses.

9:22 And Aaron lifteth up his hand towards the people, and blesseth them, and cometh down from making the sin-offering, and the burnt-offering, and the peace-offerings.

9:23 And Moses goeth in -- Aaron also -- unto the tent of meeting, and they come out, and bless the people, and the honour of Jehovah appeareth unto all the people;

9:24 and fire cometh out from before Jehovah, and consumeth on the altar the burnt-offering, and the fat; and all the people see, and cry aloud, and fall on their faces.

10:1 And the sons of Aaron, Nadab and Abihu, take each his censer, and put in them fire, and put on it perfume, and bring near before Jehovah strange fire, which He hath not commanded them;
10:2 and fire goeth out from before Jehovah, and consumeth them, and they die before Jehovah.
10:3 And Moses saith unto Aaron, `It [is] that which Jehovah hath spoken, saying, By those drawing near to Me I am sanctified, and in the face of all the people I am honoured;' and Aaron is silent.
10:4 And Moses calleth unto Mishael and unto Elzaphan, sons of Uzziel, uncle of Aaron, and saith unto them, `Come near, bear your brethren from the front of the sanctuary unto the outside of the camp;'
10:5 and they come near, and bear them in their coats unto the outside of the camp, as Moses hath spoken.
10:6 And Moses saith unto Aaron, and to Eleazar, and to Ithamar his sons, `Your heads ye do not uncover, and your garments ye do not rend, that ye die not, and on all the company He be wroth; as to your brethren, the whole house of Israel, they bewail the burning which Jehovah hath kindled;
10:7 and from the opening of the tent of meeting ye do not go out, lest ye die, for the anointing oil of Jehovah [is] upon you;' and they do according to the word of Moses.
10:8 And Jehovah speaketh unto Aaron, saying,
10:9 `Wine and strong drink thou dost not drink, thou, and thy sons with thee, in your going in unto the tent of meeting, and ye die not -- a statute age-during to your generations;
10:10 so as to make a separation between the holy and the common, and between the unclean and the pure;
10:11 and to teach the sons of Israel all the statutes which Jehovah hath spoken unto them by the hand of Moses.'
10:12 And Moses speaketh unto Aaron, and unto Eleazar, and unto Ithamar his sons, who are left, `Take ye the present that is left from the fire-offerings of Jehovah, and eat it unleavened near the altar, for it [is] most holy,
10:13 and ye have eaten it in the holy place, for it [is] thy portion, and the portion of thy sons, from the fire-offerings of Jehovah; for so I have been commanded.
10:14 `And the breast of the wave-offering, and the leg of the heave-offering, ye do eat in a clean place, thou, and thy sons, and thy daughters with thee; for thy portion and the portion of thy sons they have been given, out of the sacrifices of peace-offerings of the sons of Israel;
10:15 the leg of the heave-offering, and breast of the wave-offering, besides fire-offerings of the fat, they do bring in to wave a wave-offering before Jehovah, and it hath been to thee, and to thy sons with thee, by a statute age-during, as Jehovah hath commanded.'

10:16 And the goat of the sin-offering hath Moses diligently sought, and lo, it is burnt, and he is wroth against Eleazar, and against Ithamar, sons of Aaron, who are left, saying,
10:17 `Wherefore have ye not eaten the sin-offering in the holy place, for it [is] most holy -- and it He hath given to you to take away the iniquity of the company, to make atonement for them before Jehovah?
10:18 lo, its blood hath not been brought in unto the holy place within; eating ye do eat it in the holy place, as I have commanded.'
10:19 And Aaron speaketh unto Moses, `Lo, to-day they have brought near their sin-offering and their burnt-offering before Jehovah; and [things] like these meet me, yet I have eaten a sin-offering to-day; is it good in the eyes of Jehovah?'
10:20 And Moses hearkeneth, and it is good in his eyes.
11:1 And Jehovah speaketh unto Moses and unto Aaron, saying unto them,
11:2 `Speak unto the sons of Israel, saying, This [is] the beast which ye do eat out of all the beasts which [are] on the earth:
11:3 any dividing a hoof, and cleaving the cleft of the hoofs, bringing up the cud, among the beasts, it ye do eat.
11:4 `Only, this ye do not eat -- of those bringing up the cud, and of those dividing the hoof -- the camel, though it is bringing up the cud, yet the hoof not dividing -- it [is] unclean to you;
11:5 and the rabbit, though it is bringing up the cud, yet the hoof it divideth not -- unclean it [is] to you;
11:6 and the hare, though it is bringing up the cud, yet the hoof hath not divided -- unclean it [is] to you;
11:7 and the sow, though it is dividing the hoof, and cleaving the cleft of the hoof, yet the cud it bringeth not up -- unclean it [is] to you.
11:8 `Of their flesh ye do not eat, and against their carcase ye do not come -- unclean they [are] to you.
11:9 `This ye do eat of all which [are] in the waters; any one that hath fins and scales in the waters, in the seas, and in the brooks, them ye do eat;
11:10 and any one that hath not fins and scales in the seas, and in the brooks, of any teeming creature of the waters, and of any creature which liveth, which [is] in the waters -- an abomination they [are] to you;
11:11 yea, an abomination they are to you; of their flesh ye do not eat, and their carcase ye abominate.
11:12 `Any one that hath not fins and scales in the waters -- an abomination it [is] to you.

11:13 `And these ye do abominate of the fowl; they are not eaten, an abomination they [are]: the
eagle, and the ossifrage, and the ospray,
11:14 and the vulture, and the kite after its kind,
11:15 every raven after its kind,
11:16 and the owl, and the night-hawk, and the cuckoo, and the hawk after its kind,
11:17 and the little owl, and the cormorant, and the great owl,
11:18 and the swan, and the pelican, and the gier eagle,
11:19 and the stork, the heron after its kind, and the lapwing, and the bat.
11:20 `Every teeming creature which is flying, which is going on four -- an abomination it [is] to you.
11:21 `Only -- this ye do eat of any teeming thing which is flying, which is going on four, which hath
legs above its feet, to move with them on the earth;
11:22 these of them ye do eat: the locust after its kind, and the bald locust after its kind, and the
beetle after its kind, and the grasshopper after its kind;
11:23 and every teeming thing which is flying, which hath four feet -- an abomination it [is] to you.
11:24 `And by these ye are made unclean, any one who is coming against their carcase is unclean
till the evening;
11:25 and anyone who is lifting up [aught] of their carcase doth wash his garments, and hath been
unclean till the evening: --
11:26 even every beast which is dividing the hoof, and is not cloven-footed, and the cud is not
bringing up -- unclean they [are] to you; any one who is coming against them is unclean.
11:27 `And any one going on its paws, among all the beasts which are going on four -- unclean
they [are] to you; any one who is coming against their carcase is unclean until the evening;
11:28 and he who is lifting up their carcase doth wash his garments, and hath been unclean until
the evening -- unclean they [are] to you.
11:29 `And this [is] to you the unclean among the teeming things which are teeming on the earth:
the weasel, and the mouse, and the tortoise after its kind,
11:30 and the ferret, and the chameleon, and the lizard, and the snail, and the mole;
11:31 these [are] the unclean to you among all which are teeming; any one who is coming against
them in their death is unclean till the evening.
11:32 `And anything on which any one of them falleth, in their death, is unclean, of any vessel of
wood or garment or skin or sack, any vessel in which work is done is brought into water, and hath
been unclean till the evening, then it hath been clean;
11:33 and any earthen vessel, into the midst of which [any] one of them falleth, all that [is] in its
midst is unclean, and it ye do break.

11:34 `Of all the food which is eaten, that on which cometh [such] water, is unclean, and all drink which is drunk in any [such] vessel is unclean;
11:35 and anything on which [any] of their carcase falleth is unclean (oven or double pots), it is broken down, unclean they [are], yea, unclean they are to you.
11:36 `Only -- a fountain or pit, a collection of water, is clean, but that which is coming against their carcase is unclean;
11:37 and when [any] of their carcase falleth on any sown seed which is sown -- it [is] clean;
11:38 and when water is put on the seed, and [any] of its carcase hath fallen on it -- unclean it [is] to you.
11:39 `And when any of the beasts which are to you for food dieth, he who is coming against its carcase is unclean till the evening;
11:40 and he who is eating of its carcase doth wash his garments, and hath been unclean till the evening; and he who is lifting up its carcase doth wash his garments, and hath been unclean till the evening.
11:41 `And every teeming thing which is teeming on the earth is an abomination, it is not eaten;
11:42 any thing going on the belly, and any going on four, unto every multiplier of feet, to every teeming thing which is teeming on the earth -- ye do not eat them, for they [are] an abomination;
11:43 ye do not make yourselves abominable with any teeming thing which is teeming, nor do ye make yourselves unclean with them, so that ye have been unclean thereby.
11:44 `For I [am] Jehovah your God, and ye have sanctified yourselves, and ye have been holy, for I [am] holy; and ye do not defile your persons with any teeming thing which is creeping on the earth;
11:45 for I [am] Jehovah who am bringing you up out of the land of Egypt to become your God; and ye have been holy, for I [am] holy.
11:46 `This [is] a law of the beasts, and of the fowl, and of every living creature which is moving in the waters, and of every creature which is teeming on the earth,
11:47 to make separation between the unclean and the pure, and between the beast that is eaten, and the beast that is not eaten.'
12:1 And Jehovah speaketh unto Moses, saying,
12:2 `Speak unto the sons of Israel, saying, A woman when she giveth seed, and hath born a male, then she hath been unclean seven days, according to the days of separation for her sickness she is unclean;
12:3 and in the eighth day is the flesh of his foreskin circumcised;
12:4 and thirty and three days she doth abide in the blood of her cleansing; against any holy thing

she doth not come, and unto the sanctuary she doth not go in, till the fulness of the days of her cleansing.

12:5 `And if a female she bear, then she hath been unclean two weeks, as in her separation; and sixty and six days she doth abide for the blood of her cleansing.

12:6 `And in the fulness of the days of her cleansing for son or for daughter she doth bring in a lamb, a son of a year, for a burnt-offering, and a young pigeon or a turtle-dove for a sin-offering, unto the opening of the tent of meeting, unto the priest;

12:7 and he hath brought it near before Jehovah, and hath made atonement for her, and she hath been cleansed from the fountain of her blood; this [is] the law of her who is bearing, in regard to a male or to a female.

12:8 `And if her hand find not the sufficiency of a sheep, then she hath taken two turtle-doves, or two young pigeons, one for a burnt-offering, and one for a sin-offering, and the priest hath made atonement for her, and she hath been cleansed.'

13:1 And Jehovah speaketh unto Moses, and unto Aaron, saying,

13:2 `When a man hath in the skin of his flesh a rising, or scab, or bright spot, and it hath become in the skin of his flesh a leprous plague, then he hath been brought in unto Aaron the priest, or unto one of his sons the priests;

13:3 and the priest hath seen the plague in the skin of the flesh, and the hair in the plague hath turned white, and the appearance of the plague [is] deeper than the skin of his flesh -- it [is] a plague of leprosy, and the priest hath seen him, and hath pronounced him unclean.

13:4 `And if the bright spot is white in the skin of his flesh, and its appearance is not deeper than the skin, and its hair hath not turned white, then hath the priest shut up [him who hath] the plague seven days.

13:5 `And the priest hath seen him on the seventh day, and lo, the plague hath stood in his eyes, the plague hath not spread in the skin, and the priest hath shut him up a second seven days.

13:6 `And the priest hath seen him on the second seventh day, and lo, the plague is become weak, and the plague hath not spread in the skin -- and the priest hath pronounced him clean, it [is] a scab, and he hath washed his garments, and hath been clean.

13:7 `And if the scab spread greatly in the skin, after his being seen by the priest for his cleansing, then he hath been seen a second time by the priest;

13:8 and the priest hath seen, and lo, the scab hath spread in the skin, and the priest hath pronounced him unclean; it [is] leprosy.

13:9 `When a plague of leprosy is in a man, then he hath been brought in unto the priest,

13:10 and the priest hath seen, and lo, a white rising in the skin, and it hath turned the hair white,

and a quickening of raw flesh [is] in the rising, --
13:11 an old leprosy it [is] in the skin of his flesh, and the priest hath pronounced him unclean; he doth not shut him up, for he [is] unclean.
13:12 `And if the leprosy break out greatly in the skin, and the leprosy hath covered all the skin of [him who hath] the plague, from his head even unto his feet, to all that appeareth to the eyes of the priest,
13:13 then hath the priest seen, and lo, the leprosy hath covered all his flesh, and he hath pronounced [him who hath] the plague clean; it hath all turned white; he [is] clean.
13:14 `And in the day of raw flesh being seen in him he is unclean;
13:15 and the priest hath seen the raw flesh, and hath pronounced him unclean; the raw flesh is unclean, it [is] leprosy.
13:16 Or when the raw flesh turneth back, and hath been turned to white, then he hath come in unto the priest,
13:17 and the priest hath seen him, and lo, the plague hath been turned to white, and the priest hath pronounced clean [him who hath] the plague; he [is] clean.
13:18 `And when flesh hath in it, in its skin, an ulcer, and it hath been healed,
13:19 and there hath been in the place of the ulcer a white rising, or a bright white spot, very red, then it hath been seen by the priest,
13:20 and the priest hath seen, and lo, its appearance [is] lower than the skin, and its hair hath turned white, and the priest hath pronounced him unclean; it [is] a plague of leprosy -- in an ulcer it hath broken out.
13:21 `And if the priest see it, and lo, there is no white hair in it, and it is not lower than the skin, and is become weak, then hath the priest shut him up seven days;
13:22 and if it spread greatly in the skin, then hath the priest pronounced him unclean, it [is] a plague;
13:23 and if in its place the bright spot stay -- it hath not spread -- it [is] an inflammation of the ulcer; and the priest hath pronounced him clean.
13:24 `Or when flesh hath in its skin a fiery burning, and the quickening of the burning, the bright white spot, hath been very red or white,
13:25 and the priest hath seen it, and lo, the hair hath turned white in the bright spot, and its appearance [is] deeper than the skin; leprosy it [is], in the burning it hath broken out, and the priest hath pronounced him unclean; it [is] a plague of leprosy.
13:26 `And if the priest see it, and lo, there is no white hair on the bright spot, and it is not lower than the skin, and it is become weak, then the priest hath shut him up seven days;

13:27 and the priest hath seen him on the seventh day, if it spread greatly in the skin, then the priest hath pronounced him unclean; a plague of leprosy it [is].
13:28 `And if the bright spot stay in its place, it hath not spread in the skin, and is become weak; a rising of the burning it [is], and the priest hath pronounced him clean; for it [is] inflammation of the burning.
13:29 `And when a man (or a woman) hath in him a plague in the head or in the beard,
13:30 then hath the priest seen the plague, and lo, its appearance is deeper than the skin, and in it a thin shining hair, and the priest hath pronounced him unclean; it [is] a scall -- it [is] a leprosy of the head or of the beard.
13:31 `And when the priest seeth the plague of the scall, and lo, its appearance is not deeper than the skin, and there is no black hair in it, then hath the priest shut up [him who hath] the plague of the scall seven days.
13:32 `And the priest hath seen the plague on the seventh day, and lo, the scall hath not spread, and a shining hair hath not been in it, and the appearance of the scall is not deeper than the skin,
13:33 then he hath shaved himself, but the scall he doth not shave; and the priest hath shut up [him who hath] the scall a second seven days.
13:34 And the priest hath seen the scall on the seventh day, and lo, the scall hath not spread in the skin, and its appearance is not deeper than the skin, and the priest hath pronounced him clean, and he hath washed his garments, and hath been clean.
13:35 `And if the scall spread greatly in the skin after his cleansing,
13:36 and the priest hath seen him, and lo, the scall hath spread in the skin, the priest seeketh not for the shining hair, he is unclean;
13:37 and if in his eyes the scall hath stayed, and black hair hath sprung up in it, the scall hath been healed -- he [is] clean -- and the priest hath pronounced him clean.
13:38 `And when a man or woman hath in the skin of their flesh bright spots, white bright spots,
13:39 and the priest hath seen, and lo, in the skin of their flesh white weak bright spots, it [is] a freckled spot broken out in the skin; he [is] clean.
13:40 `And when a man's head [is] polished, he [is] bald, he [is] clean;
13:41 and if from the corner of his face his head is polished, he [is] bald of the forehead; he [is] clean.
13:42 `And when there is in the bald back of the head, or in the bald forehead, a very red white plague, it [is] a leprosy breaking out in the bald back of the head, or in the bald forehead;
13:43 and the priest hath seen him, and lo, the rising of the very red white plague in the bald back of the head, or in the bald forehead, [is] as the appearance of leprosy, in the skin of the flesh,

13:44 he [is] a leprous man, he [is] unclean; the priest doth pronounce him utterly unclean; his plague [is] in his head.
13:45 `As to the leper in whom [is] the plague, his garments are rent, and his head is uncovered, and he covereth over the upper lip, and `Unclean! unclean!' he calleth;
13:46 all the days that the plague [is] in him he is unclean; he [is] unclean, alone he doth dwell, at the outside of the camp [is] his dwelling.
13:47 `And when there is in any garment a plague of leprosy, -- in a garment of wool, or in a garment of linen,
13:48 or in the warp, or in the woof, of linen or of wool, or in a skin, or in any work of skin,
13:49 and the plague hath been very green or very red in the garment, or in the skin, or in the warp, or in the woof, or in any vessel of skin, it [is] a plague of leprosy, and it hath been shewn the priest.
13:50 `And the priest hath seen the plague, and hath shut up [that which hath] the plague, seven days;
13:51 and he hath seen the plague on the seventh day, and the plague hath spread in the garment, or in the warp, or in the woof, or in the skin, of all that is made of skin for work; the plague [is] a fretting leprosy, it [is] unclean.
13:52 `And he hath burnt the garment, or the warp, or the woof, in wool or in linen, or any vessel of skin in which the plague is; for it [is] a fretting leprosy; with fire it is burnt.
13:53 `And if the priest see, and lo, the plague hath not spread in the garment, or in the warp, or in the woof, or in any vessel of skin,
13:54 then hath the priest commanded, and they have washed that in which the plague [is], and he hath shut it up a second seven days.
13:55 And the priest hath seen [that which hath] the plague after it hath been washed, and lo, the plague hath not changed its aspect, and the plague hath not spread, -- it [is] unclean; with fire thou dost burn it; it [is] a fretting in its back-part or in its front-part.
13:56 `And if the priest hath seen, and lo, the plague [is] become weak after it hath been washed, then he hath rent it out of the garment, or out of the skin, or out of the warp, or out of the woof;
13:57 and if it still be seen in the garment, or in the warp, or in the woof, or in any vessel of skin, it [is] a fretting; with fire thou dost burn it -- that in which the plague [is].
13:58 `And the garment, or the warp, or the woof, or any vessel of skin which thou dost wash when the plague hath turned aside from them, then it hath been washed a second time, and hath been clean.
13:59 `This [is] the law of a plague of leprosy [in] a garment of wool or of linen, or of the warp or of

the woof, or of any vessel of skin, to pronounce it clean or to pronounce it unclean.'

14:1 And Jehovah speaketh unto Moses, saying,

14:2 `This is a law of the leper, in the day of his cleansing, that he hath been brought in unto the priest,

14:3 and the priest hath gone out unto the outside of the camp, and the priest hath seen, and lo, the plague of leprosy hath ceased from the leper,

14:4 and the priest hath commanded, and he hath taken for him who is to be cleansed, two clean living birds, and cedar wood, and scarlet, and hyssop.

14:5 `And the priest hath commanded, and he hath slaughtered the one bird upon an earthen vessel, over running water;

14:6 [as to] the living bird, he taketh it, and the cedar wood, and the scarlet, and the hyssop, and hath dipped them and the living bird in the blood of the slaughtered bird, over the running water,

14:7 and he hath sprinkled on him who is to be cleansed from the leprosy seven times, and hath pronounced him clean, and hath sent out the living bird on the face of the field.

14:8 `And he who is to be cleansed hath washed his garments, and hath shaved all his hair, and hath bathed with water, and hath been clean, and afterwards he doth come in unto the camp, and hath dwelt at the outside of his tent seven days.

14:9 `And it hath been, on the seventh day -- he shaveth all his hair, his head, and his beard, and his eyebrows, even all his hair he doth shave, and he hath washed his garments, and hath bathed his flesh with water, and hath been clean.

14:10 `And on the eighth day he taketh two lambs, perfect ones, and one ewe-lamb, daughter of a year, a perfect one, and three tenth deals of flour [for] a present, mixed with oil, and one log of oil.

14:11 `And the priest who is cleansing hath caused the man who is to be cleansed to stand with them before Jehovah, at the opening of the tent of meeting,

14:12 and the priest hath taken the one he-lamb, and hath brought it near for a guilt-offering, also the log of oil, and hath waved them -- a wave offering before Jehovah.

14:13 `And he hath slaughtered the lamb in the place where he slaughtereth the sin-offering and the burnt-offering, in the holy place; for like the sin-offering the guilt-offering is to the priest; it [is] most holy.

14:14 `And the priest hath taken of the blood of the guilt-offering, and the priest hath put on the tip of the right ear of him who is to be cleansed, and on the thumb of his right hand, and on the great toe of his right foot;

14:15 and the priest hath taken of the log of oil, and hath poured on the left palm of the priest,

14:16 and the priest hath dipped his right finger in the oil which [is] on his left palm, and hath

sprinkled of the oil with his finger seven times before Jehovah.
14:17 `And of the residue of the oil which [is] on his palm, the priest putteth on the tip of the right ear of him who is to be cleansed, and on the thumb of his right hand, and on the great toe of his right foot, on the blood of the guilt-offering;
14:18 and the remnant of the oil which [is] on the palm of the priest, he putteth on the head of him who is to be cleansed, and the priest hath made atonement for him before Jehovah.
14:19 `And the priest hath made the sin-offering, and hath made atonement for him who is to be cleansed from his uncleanness, and afterwards he doth slaughter the burnt-offering;
14:20 and the priest hath caused the burnt-offering to ascend, also the present, on the altar, and the priest hath made atonement for him, and he hath been clean.
14:21 `And if he [is] poor, and his hand is not reaching [these things], then he hath taken one lamb -- a guilt-offering, for a wave-offering, to make atonement for him, and one-tenth deal of flour mixed with oil for a present, and a log of oil,
14:22 and two turtle-doves, or two young pigeons, which his hand reacheth to, and one hath been a sin-offering, and the one a burnt-offering;
14:23 and he hath brought them in on the eighth day for his cleansing unto the priest, unto the opening of the tent of meeting, before Jehovah.
14:24 `And the priest hath taken the lamb of the guilt-offering, and the log of oil, and the priest hath waved them -- a wave-offering before Jehovah;
14:25 and he hath slaughtered the lamb of the guilt-offering, and the priest hath taken of the blood of the guilt-offering, and hath put on the tip of the right ear of him who is to be cleansed, and on the thumb of his right hand, and on the great toe of his right foot;
14:26 and the priest doth pour of the oil on the left palm of the priest;
14:27 and the priest hath sprinkled with his right finger of the oil which [is] on his left palm, seven times before Jehovah.
14:28 `And the priest hath put of the oil which [is] on his palm, on the tip of the right ear of him who is to be cleansed, and on the thumb of his right hand, and on the great toe of his right foot, on the place of the blood of the guilt-offering;
14:29 and the remnant of the oil which [is] on the palm of the priest he doth put on the head of him who is to be cleansed, to make atonement for him, before Jehovah.
14:30 `And he hath made the one of the turtle-doves, or of the young pigeons (from that which his hand reacheth to,
14:31 [even] that which his hand reacheth to), the one a sin-offering, and the one a burnt offering, besides the present, and the priest hath made atonement for him who is to be cleansed before

Jehovah.
14:32 This [is] a law of him in whom [is] a plague of leprosy, whose hand reacheth not to his cleansing.'
14:33 And Jehovah speaketh unto Moses, and unto Aaron, saying,
14:34 `When ye come in unto the land of Canaan, which I am giving to you for a possession, and I have put a plague of leprosy in a house [in] the land of your possession;
14:35 then hath he whose the house [is] come in and declared to the priest, saying, As a plague hath appeared to me in the house;
14:36 and the priest hath commanded, and they have prepared the house before the priest cometh in to see the plague (that all which [is] in the house be not unclean), and afterwards doth the priest come in to see the house;
14:37 and he hath seen the plague, and lo, the plague [is] in the walls of the house, hollow strakes, very green or very red, and their appearance [is] lower than the wall,
14:38 and the priest hath gone out of the house unto the opening of the house, and hath shut up the house seven days.
14:39 `And the priest hath turned back on the seventh day, and hath seen, and lo, the plague hath spread in the walls of the house,
14:40 and the priest hath commanded, and they have drawn out the stones in which the plague [is], and have cast them unto the outside of the city, unto an unclean place;
14:41 and the house he doth cause to be scraped within round about, and they have poured out the clay which they have scraped off, at the outside of the city, at an unclean place;
14:42 and they have taken other stones, and brought [them] in unto the place of the stones, and other clay he taketh and hath daubed the house.
14:43 `And if the plague return, and hath broken out in the house, after he hath drawn out the stones, and after the scraping of the house, and after the daubing;
14:44 then hath the priest come in and seen, and lo, the plague hath spread in the house; it [is] a fretting leprosy in the house; it [is] unclean.
14:45 `And he hath broken down the house, its stones, and its wood, and all the clay of the house, and he hath brought [them] forth unto the outside of the city, unto an unclean place.
14:46 `And he who is going in unto the house all the days he hath shut it up, is unclean till the evening;
14:47 and he who is lying in the house doth wash his garments; and he who is eating in the house doth wash his garments.
14:48 `And if the priest certainly come in, and hath seen, and lo, the plague hath not spread in the

house after the daubing of the house, then hath the priest pronounced the house clean, for the plague hath been healed.

14:49 `And he hath taken for the cleansing of the house two birds, and cedar wood, and scarlet, and hyssop;

14:50 and he hath slaughtered the one bird upon an earthen vessel, over running water;

14:51 and he hath taken the cedar wood, and the hyssop, and the scarlet, and the living bird, and hath dipped them in the blood of the slaughtered bird, and in the running water, and hath sprinkled upon the house seven times.

14:52 `And he hath cleansed the house with the blood of the bird, and with the running water, and with the living bird, and with the cedar wood, and with the hyssop, and with the scarlet;

14:53 and he hath sent away the living bird unto the outside of the city unto the face of the field, and hath made atonement for the house, and it hath been clean.

14:54 `This [is] the law for every plague of the leprosy and for scall,

14:55 and for leprosy of a garment, and of a house,

14:56 and for a rising, and for a scab, and for a bright spot, --

14:57 to direct in the day of being unclean, and in the day of being clean; this [is] the law of the leprosy.'

15:1 And Jehovah speaketh unto Moses, and unto Aaron, saying,

15:2 `Speak unto the sons of Israel, and ye have said unto them, When there is an issue out of the flesh of any man, [for] his issue he [is] unclean;

15:3 and this is his uncleanness in his issue -- his flesh hath run with his issue, or his flesh hath stopped from his issue; it [is] his uncleanness.

15:4 `All the bed on which he lieth who hath the issue is unclean, and all the vessel on which he sitteth is unclean;

15:5 and any one who cometh against his bed doth wash his garments, and hath bathed with water, and been unclean till the evening.

15:6 `And he who is sitting on the vessel on which he sitteth who hath the issue, doth wash his garments, and hath bathed with water, and been unclean till the evening.

15:7 `And he who is coming against the flesh of him who hath the issue, doth wash his garments, and hath bathed with water, and hath been unclean till the evening.

15:8 `And when he who hath the issue spitteth on him who is clean, then he hath washed his garments, and hath bathed with water, and been unclean till the evening.

15:9 `And all the saddle on which he rideth who hath the issue is unclean;

15:10 and any one who is coming against anything which is under him is unclean till the evening, and he who is bearing them doth wash his garments, and hath bathed with water, and been unclean till the evening.

15:11 `And anyone against whom he cometh who hath the issue (and his hands hath not rinsed with water) hath even washed his garments, and bathed with water, and been unclean till the evening.

15:12 `And the earthen vessel which he who hath the issue cometh against is broken; and every wooden vessel is rinsed with water.

15:13 `And when he who hath the issue is clean from his issue, then he hath numbered to himself seven days for his cleansing, and hath washed his garments, and hath bathed his flesh with running water, and been clean.

15:14 `And on the eighth day he taketh to himself two turtle-doves, or two young pigeons, and hath come in before Jehovah unto the opening of the tent of meeting, and hath given them unto the priest;

15:15 and the priest hath made them, one a sin-offering, and the one a burnt-offering; and the priest hath made atonement for him before Jehovah, because of his issue.

15:16 `And when a man's seed of copulation goeth out from him, then he hath bathed with water all his flesh, and been unclean till the evening.

15:17 `And any garment, or any skin on which there is seed of copulation, hath also been washed with water, and been unclean till the evening.

15:18 `And a woman with whom a man lieth with seed of copulation, they also have bathed with water, and been unclean till the evening.

15:19 `And when a woman hath an issue -- blood is her issue in her flesh -- seven days she is in her separation, and any one who is coming against her is unclean till the evening.

15:20 `And anything on which she lieth in her separation is unclean, and anything on which she sitteth is unclean;

15:21 and any one who is coming against her bed doth wash his garments, and hath bathed with water, and been unclean till the evening.

15:22 `And any one who is coming against any vessel on which she sitteth doth wash his garments, and hath washed with water, and been unclean till the evening.

15:23 `And if it [is] on the bed, or on the vessel on which she is sitting, in his coming against it, he is unclean till the evening.

15:24 `And if a man really lie with her, and her separation is on him, then he hath been unclean seven days, and all the bed on which he lieth is unclean.

15:25 `And when a woman's issue of blood floweth many days within the time of her separation, or when it floweth over her separation -- all the days of the issue of her uncleanness are as the days of her separation; she [is] unclean.

15:26 `All the bed on which she lieth all the days of her issue is as the bed of her separation to her, and all the vessel on which she sitteth is unclean as the uncleanness of her separation;

15:27 and any one who is coming against them is unclean, and hath washed his garments, and hath bathed with water, and been unclean till the evening.

15:28 `And if she hath been clean from her issue, then she hath numbered to herself seven days, and afterwards she is clean;

15:29 and on the eighth day she taketh to herself two turtle-doves, or two young pigeons, and hath brought them in unto the priest, unto the opening of the tent of meeting;

15:30 and the priest hath made the one a sin-offering, and the one a burnt-offering, and the priest hath made atonement for her before Jehovah, because of the issue of her uncleanness.

15:31 `And ye have separated the sons of Israel from their uncleanness, and they die not in their uncleanness, in their defiling My tabernacle which [is] in their midst.

15:32 `This [is] the law of him who hath an issue, and of him whose seed of copulation goeth out from him, for uncleanness thereby,

15:33 and of her who is sick in her separation, and of him who hath an issue, the issue of a male or of a female, and of a man who lieth with an unclean woman.'

16:1 And Jehovah speaketh unto Moses, after the death of the two sons of Aaron, in their drawing near before Jehovah, and they die;

16:2 yea, Jehovah saith unto Moses, `Speak unto Aaron thy brother, and he cometh not in at all times unto the sanctuary within the vail, unto the front of the mercy-seat, which [is] upon the ark, and he dieth not, for in a cloud I am seen upon the mercy-seat.

16:3 `With this doth Aaron come in unto the sanctuary; with a bullock, a son of the herd, for a sin-offering, and a ram for a burnt-offering;

16:4 a holy linen coat he putteth on, and linen trousers are on his flesh, and with a linen girdle he girdeth himself, and with a linen mitre he wrappeth himself up; they [are] holy garments; and he hath bathed with water his flesh, and hath put them on.

16:5 `And from the company of the sons of Israel he taketh two kids of the goats for a sin-offering, and one ram for a burnt-offering;

16:6 and Aaron hath brought near the bullock of the sin-offering which is his own, and hath made atonement for himself, and for his house;

16:7 and he hath taken the two goats, and hath caused them to stand before Jehovah, at the opening of the tent of meeting.

16:8 `And Aaron hath given lots over the two goats, one lot for Jehovah, and one lot for a goat of departure;
16:9 and Aaron hath brought near the goat on which the lot for Jehovah hath gone up, and hath made it a sin-offering.
16:10 `And the goat on which the lot for a goat of departure hath gone up is caused to stand living before Jehovah to make atonement by it, to send it away for a goat of departure into the wilderness.
16:11 `And Aaron hath brought near the bullock of the sin-offering which is his own, and hath made atonement for himself, and for his house, and hath slaughtered the bullock of the sin-offering which [is] his own,
16:12 and hath taken the fulness of the censer of burning coals of fire from off the altar, from before Jehovah, and the fulness of his hands of thin spice-perfume, and hath brought [it] within the vail;
16:13 and he hath put the perfume on the fire before Jehovah, and the cloud of the perfume hath covered the mercy-seat which [is] on the testimony, and he dieth not.
16:14 `And he hath taken of the blood of the bullock, and hath sprinkled with his finger on the front of the mercy-seat eastward; even at the front of the mercy-seat he doth sprinkle seven times of the blood with his finger.
16:15 `And he hath slaughtered the goat of the sin-offering which [is] the people's, and hath brought in its blood unto the inside of the vail, and hath done with its blood as he hath done with the blood of the bullock, and hath sprinkled it on the mercy-seat, and at the front of the mercy-seat,
16:16 and he hath made atonement for the sanctuary because of the uncleanness of the sons of Israel, and because of their transgressions in all their sins; and so he doth for the tent of meeting which is tabernacling with them in the midst of their uncleannesses.
16:17 `And no man is in the tent of meeting in his going in to make atonement in the sanctuary, till his coming out; and he hath made atonement for himself, and for his house, and for all the assembly of Israel.
16:18 `And he hath gone out unto the altar which [is] before Jehovah, and hath made atonement for it; and he hath taken of the blood of the bullock, and of the blood of the goat, and hath put on the horns of the altar round about;
16:19 and he hath sprinkled on it of the blood with his finger seven times, and hath cleansed it, and hath hallowed it from the uncleannesses of the sons of Israel.
16:20 `And he hath ceased from making atonement [for] the sanctuary, and the tent of meeting, and the altar, and hath brought near the living goat;
16:21 and Aaron hath laid his two hands on the head of the living goat, and hath confessed over it

all the iniquities of the sons of Israel, and all their transgressions in all their sins, and hath put them on the head of the goat, and hath sent [it] away by the hand of a fit man into the wilderness;
16:22 and the goat hath borne on him all their iniquities unto a land of separation. `And he hath sent the goat away into the wilderness,
16:23 and Aaron hath come in unto the tent of meeting, and hath stripped off the linen garments which he had put on in his going in unto the sanctuary, and hath placed them there;
16:24 and he hath bathed his flesh with water in the holy place, and hath put on his garments, and hath come out, and hath made his burnt-offering, and the burnt-offering of the people, and hath made atonement for himself and for the people;
16:25 and with the fat of the sin-offering he doth make perfume on the altar.
16:26 `And he who is sending away the goat for a goat of departure doth wash his garments, and hath bathed his flesh with water, and afterwards he cometh in unto the camp.
16:27 `And the bullock of the sin-offering, and the goat of the sin-offering, whose blood hath been brought in to make atonement in the sanctuary, doth [one] bring out unto the outside of the camp, and they have burnt with fire their skins, and their flesh, and their dung;
16:28 and he who is burning them doth wash his garments, and hath bathed his flesh with water, and afterwards he cometh in unto the camp.
16:29 `And it hath been to you for a statute age-during, in the seventh month, in the tenth of the month, ye humble yourselves, and do no work -- the native, and the sojourner who is sojourning in your midst;
16:30 for on this day he maketh atonement for you, to cleanse you; from all your sins before Jehovah ye are clean;
16:31 it [is] to you a sabbath of rest, and ye have humbled yourselves -- a statute age-during.
16:32 `And the priest whom he doth anoint, and whose hand he doth consecrate to act as priest instead of his father, hath made atonement, and hath put on the linen garments, the holy garments;
16:33 and he hath made atonement [for] the holy sanctuary; and [for] the tent of meeting, even [for] the altar he doth make atonement; yea, for the priests, and for all the people of the assembly he maketh atonement.
16:34 `And this hath been to you for a statute age-during, to make atonement for the sons of Israel, because of all their sins, once in a year;' and he doth as Jehovah hath commanded Moses.
17:1 And Jehovah speaketh unto Moses, saying,
17:2 `Speak unto Aaron, and unto his sons, and unto all the sons of Israel; and thou hast said unto them, This [is] the thing which Jehovah hath commanded, saying,
17:3 Any man of the house of Israel who slaughtereth ox, or lamb, or goat, in the camp, or who

slaughtereth at the outside of the camp,
17:4 and unto the opening of the tent of meeting hath not brought it in to bring near an offering to
Jehovah before the tabernacle of Jehovah, blood is reckoned to that man -- blood he hath shed --
and that man hath been cut off from the midst of his people;
17:5 so that the sons of Israel do bring in their sacrifices which they are sacrificing on the face of
the field, yea, they have brought them in to Jehovah, unto the opening of the tent of meeting, unto
the priest, and they have sacrificed sacrifices of peace-offerings to Jehovah with them.
17:6 `And the priest hath sprinkled the blood upon the altar of Jehovah, at the opening of the tent of
meeting, and hath made perfume with the fat for sweet fragrance to Jehovah;
17:7 and they sacrifice not any more their sacrifices to goats after which they are going a-whoring;
a statute age-during is this to them, to their generations.
17:8 `And unto them thou sayest: Any man of the house of Israel, or of the sojourners, who
sojourneth in your midst, who causeth burnt-offering or sacrifice to ascend,
17:9 and unto the opening of the tent of meeting doth not bring it in to make it to Jehovah -- that
man hath been cut off from his people.
17:10 `And any man of the house of Israel, or of the sojourners, who is sojourning in your midst,
who eateth any blood, I have even set My face against the person who is eating the blood, and
have cut him off from the midst of his people;
17:11 for the life of the flesh is in the blood, and I have given it to you on the altar, to make
atonement for your souls; for it [is] the blood which maketh atonement for the soul.
17:12 `Therefore I have said to the sons of Israel, No person among you doth eat blood, and the
sojourner who is sojourning in your midst doth not eat blood;
17:13 and any man of the sons of Israel, or of the sojourners, who is sojourning in your midst, who
hunteth venison, beast or fowl, which is eaten -- hath even poured out its blood, and hath covered it
with dust;
17:14 for [it is] the life of all flesh, its blood is for its life; and I say to the sons of Israel, Blood of any
flesh ye do not eat, for the life of all flesh is its blood; any one eating it is cut off.
17:15 `And any person who eateth a carcase or torn thing, among natives or among sojourners --
hath both washed his garments, and hath bathed with water, and hath been unclean until the
evening -- then he hath been clean;
17:16 and if he wash not, and his flesh bathe not -- then he hath borne his iniquity.'
18:1 And Jehovah speaketh unto Moses, saying,
18:2 `Speak unto the sons of Israel, and thou hast said unto them, I [am] Jehovah your God;
18:3 according to the work of the land of Egypt in which ye have dwelt ye do not, and according to

the work of the land of Canaan whither I am bringing you in, ye do not, and in their statutes ye walk not.
18:4 `My judgments ye do, and My statutes ye keep, to walk in them; I [am] Jehovah your God;
18:5 and ye have kept My statutes and My judgments which man doth and liveth in them; I [am] Jehovah.
18:6 `None of you unto any relation of his flesh doth draw near to uncover nakedness; I [am] Jehovah.
18:7 `The nakedness of thy father and the nakedness of thy mother thou dost not uncover, she [is] thy mother; thou dost not uncover her nakedness.
18:8 `The nakedness of the wife of thy father thou dost not uncover; it [is] the nakedness of thy father.
18:9 `The nakedness of thy sister, daughter of thy father, or daughter of thy mother, born at home or born without; thou dost not uncover their nakedness.
18:10 `The nakedness of thy son's daughter, or of thy daughter's daughter: thou dost not uncover their nakedness; for theirs [is] thy nakedness.
18:11 `The nakedness of a daughter of thy father's wife, begotten of thy father, she [is] thy sister; thou dost not uncover her nakedness.
18:12 `The nakedness of a sister of thy father thou dost not uncover; she [is] a relation of thy father.
18:13 `The nakedness of thy mother's sister thou dost not uncover; for she [is] thy mother's relation.
18:14 `The nakedness of thy father's brother thou dost not uncover; unto his wife thou dost not draw near; she [is] thine aunt.
18:15 `The nakedness of thy daughter-in-law thou dost not uncover; she [is] thy son's wife; thou dost not uncover her nakedness.
18:16 `The nakedness of thy brother's wife thou dost not uncover; it [is] thy brother's nakedness.
18:17 `The nakedness of a woman and her daughter thou dost not uncover; her son's daughter, and her daughter's daughter thou dost not take to uncover her nakedness; they [are] her relations; it [is] wickedness.
18:18 `And a woman unto another thou dost not take, to be an adversary, to uncover her nakedness beside her, in her life.
18:19 `And unto a woman in the separation of her uncleanness thou dost not draw near to uncover her nakedness.
18:20 `And unto the wife of thy fellow thou dost not give thy seed of copulation, for uncleanness with her.

18:21 `And of thy seed thou dost not give to pass over to the Molech; nor dost thou pollute the name of thy God; I [am] Jehovah.
18:22 `And with a male thou dost not lie as one lieth with a woman; abomination it [is].
18:23 `And with any beast thou dost not give thy copulation, for uncleanness with it; and a woman doth not stand before a beast to lie down with it; confusion it [is].
18:24 `Ye are not defiled with all these, for with all these have the nations been defiled which I am sending away from before you;
18:25 and the land is defiled, and I charge its iniquity upon it, and the land vomiteth out its inhabitants:
18:26 and ye -- ye have kept My statutes and My judgments, and do not [any] of all these abominations, the native and the sojourner who is sojourning in your midst,
18:27 (for all these abominations have the men of the land done who [are] before you, and the land is defiled),
18:28 and the land doth not vomit you out in your defiling it, as it hath vomited out the nation which [is] before you;
18:29 for any one who doth [any] of all these abominations -- even the persons who are doing [so], have been cut off from the midst of their people;
18:30 and ye have kept My charge, so as not to do [any] of the abominable statutes which have been done before you, and ye do not defile yourselves with them; I [am] Jehovah your God.'
19:1 And Jehovah speaketh unto Moses, saying,
19:2 `Speak unto all the company of the sons of Israel, and thou hast said unto them, Ye are holy, for holy [am] I, Jehovah, your God.
19:3 `Each his mother and his father ye do fear, and My sabbaths ye do keep; I [am] Jehovah your God.
19:4 `Ye do not turn unto the idols, and a molten god ye do not make to yourselves; I [am] Jehovah your God.
19:5 `And when ye sacrifice a sacrifice of peace-offerings to Jehovah, at your pleasure ye do sacrifice it;
19:6 in the day of your sacrificing it is eaten, and on the morrow, and that which is left unto the third day with fire is burnt,
19:7 and if it be really eaten on the third day, it [is] an abomination, it is not pleasing,
19:8 and he who is eating it his iniquity doth bear, for the holy thing of Jehovah he hath polluted, and that person hath been cut off from his people.
19:9 `And in your reaping the harvest of your land ye do not completely reap the corner of thy field,

and the gleaning of thy harvest thou dost not gather,
19:10 and thy vineyard thou dost not glean, even the omitted part of thy vineyard thou dost not gather, to the poor and to the sojourner thou dost leave them; I [am] Jehovah your God.
19:11 `Ye do not steal, nor feign, nor lie one against his fellow.
19:12 `And ye do not swear by My name to falsehood, or thou hast polluted the name of thy God; I [am] Jehovah.
19:13 `Thou dost not oppress thy neighbour, nor take plunder; the wages of the hireling doth not remain with thee till morning.
19:14 `Thou dost not revile the deaf; and before the blind thou dost not put a stumbling block; and thou hast been afraid of thy God; I [am] Jehovah.
19:15 `Ye do not do perversity in judgment; thou dost not lift up the face of the poor, nor honour the face of the great; in righteousness thou dost judge thy fellow.
19:16 `Thou dost not go slandering among thy people; thou dost not stand against the blood of thy neighbour; I [am] Jehovah.
19:17 `Thou dost not hate thy brother in thy heart; thou dost certainly reprove thy fellow, and not suffer sin on him.
19:18 `Thou dost not take vengeance, nor watch the sons of thy people; and thou hast had love to thy neighbour as thyself; I [am] Jehovah.
19:19 `My statutes ye do keep: thy cattle thou dost not cause to gender [with] diverse kinds; thy field thou dost not sow with diverse kinds, and a garment of diverse kinds, shaatnez, doth not go up upon thee.
19:20 `And when a man lieth with a woman with seed of copulation, and she a maid-servant, betrothed to a man, and not really ransomed, or freedom hath not been given to her, an investigation there is; they are not put to death, for she [is] not free.
19:21 `And he hath brought in his guilt-offering to Jehovah, unto the opening of the tent of meeting, a ram [for] a guilt-offering,
19:22 and the priest hath made atonement for him with the ram of the guilt-offering before Jehovah, for his sin which he hath sinned, and it hath been forgiven him because of his sin which he hath sinned.
19:23 `And when ye come in unto the land, and have planted all [kinds] of trees [for] food, then ye have reckoned as uncircumcised its fruit, three years it is to you uncircumcised, it is not eaten,
19:24 and in the fourth year all its fruit is holy -- praises for Jehovah.
19:25 And in the fifth year ye do eat its fruit -- to add to you its increase; I [am] Jehovah your God.
19:26 `Ye do not eat with the blood; ye do not enchant, nor observe clouds.

19:27 `Ye do not round the corner of your head, nor destroy the corner of thy beard.
19:28 `And a cutting for the soul ye do not put in your flesh; and a writing, a cross-mark, ye do not put on you; I [am] Jehovah.
19:29 `Thou dost not pollute thy daughter to cause her to go a-whoring, that the land go not a-whoring, and the land hath been full of wickedness.
19:30 `My sabbaths ye do keep, and My sanctuary ye do reverence; I [am] Jehovah.
19:31 `Ye do not turn unto those having familiar spirits; and unto wizards ye do not seek, for uncleanness by them; I [am] Jehovah your God.
19:32 `At the presence of grey hairs thou dost rise up, and thou hast honoured the presence of an old man, and hast been afraid of thy God; I [am] Jehovah.
19:33 `And when a sojourner sojourneth with thee in your land, thou dost not oppress him;
19:34 as a native among you is the sojourner to you who is sojourning with you, and thou hast had love to him as to thyself, for sojourners ye have been in the land of Egypt; I [am] Jehovah your God.
19:35 `Ye do not do perversity in judgment, in mete-yard, in weight, or in liquid measure;
19:36 righteous balances, righteous weights, a righteous ephah, and a righteous hin ye have; I [am] Jehovah your God, who hath brought you out from the land of Egypt;
19:37 and ye have observed all my statutes, and all my judgments, and have done them; I [am] Jehovah.'
20:1 And Jehovah speaketh unto Moses, saying,
20:2 `And unto the sons of Israel thou dost say, Any man of the sons of Israel, and of the sojourners who is sojourning in Israel, who giveth of his seed to the Molech, is certainly put to death; the people of the land do stone him with stones;
20:3 and I -- I set My face against that man, and have cut him off from the midst of his people, for of his seed he hath given to the Molech, so as to defile My sanctuary, and to pollute My holy name.
20:4 `And if the people of the land really hide their eyes from that man, in his giving of his seed to the Molech, so as not to put him to death,
20:5 then I have set My face against that man, and against his family, and have cut him off, and all who are going a-whoring after him, even going a-whoring after the Molech, from the midst of their people.
20:6 `And the person who turneth unto those having familiar spirits, and unto the wizards, to go a-whoring after them, I have even set My face against that person, and cut him off from the midst of his people.
20:7 `And ye have sanctified yourselves, and ye have been holy, for I [am] Jehovah your God;

20:8 and ye have kept My statutes and have done them; I [am] Jehovah, sanctifying you.
20:9 `For any man who revileth his father and his mother is certainly put to death; his father and his mother he hath reviled: his blood [is] on him.
20:10 `And a man who committeth adultery with a man's wife -- who committeth adultery with the wife of his neighbour -- the adulterer and the adulteress are surely put to death.
20:11 `And a man who lieth with his father's wife -- the nakedness of his father he hath uncovered -- both of them are certainly put to death; their blood [is] on them.
20:12 `And a man who lieth with his daughter-in-law -- both of them are certainly put to death; confusion they have made; their blood [is] on them.
20:13 `And a man who lieth with a male as one lieth with a woman; abomination both of them have done; they are certainly put to death; their blood [is] on them.
20:14 `And a man who taketh the woman and her mother -- it [is] wickedness; with fire they burn him and them, and there is no wickedness in your midst.
20:15 `And a man who giveth his lying with a beast is certainly put to death, and the beast ye do slay.
20:16 `And a woman who draweth near unto any beast to lie with it -- thou hast even slain the woman and the beast; they are certainly put to death; their blood [is] on them.
20:17 `And a man who taketh his sister, a daughter of his father or daughter of his mother, and he hath seen her nakedness, and she seeth his nakedness: it is a shame; and they have been cut off before the eyes of the sons of their people; the nakedness of his sister he hath uncovered; his iniquity he beareth.
20:18 `And a man who lieth with a sick woman, and hath uncovered her nakedness, her fountain he hath made bare, and she hath uncovered the fountain of her blood, -- even both of them have been cut off from the midst of their people.
20:19 `And the nakedness of thy mother's sister, and of thy father's sister, thou dost not uncover; because his relation he hath made bare; their iniquity they bear.
20:20 `And a man who lieth with his aunt, the nakedness of his uncle he hath uncovered; their sin they bear; childless they die.
20:21 `And a man who taketh his brother's wife -- it [is] impurity; the nakedness of his brother he hath uncovered; childless they are.
20:22 `And ye have kept all My statutes, and all My judgments, and have done them, and the land vomiteth you not out whither I am bringing you in to dwell in it;
20:23 and ye walk not in the statutes of the nation which I am sending away from before you, for all these they have done, and I am wearied with them;

20:24 and I say to you, Ye -- ye do possess their ground, and I -- I give it to you to possess it, a land flowing with milk and honey; I [am] Jehovah your God, who hath separated you from the peoples.
20:25 `And ye have made separation between the pure beasts and the unclean, and between the unclean fowl and the pure, and ye do not make yourselves abominable by beast or by fowl, or by anything which creepeth [on] the ground which I have separated to you for unclean;
20:26 and ye have been holy to Me; for holy [am] I, Jehovah; and I separate you from the peoples to become Mine.
20:27 `And a man or woman -- when there is in them a familiar spirit, or who [are] wizards -- are certainly put to death; with stones they stone them; their blood [is] on them.'
21:1 And Jehovah saith unto Moses, `Speak unto the priests, sons of Aaron, and thou hast said unto them, For [any] person [a priest] is not defiled among his people,
21:2 except for his relation who [is] near unto him -- for his mother, and for his father, and for his son, and for his daughter, and for his brother.
21:3 and for his sister, the virgin, who is near unto him, who hath not been to a man; for her he is defiled.
21:4 `A master [priest] doth not defile himself among his people -- to pollute himself;
21:5 they do not make baldness on their head, and the corner of their beard they do not shave, and in their flesh they do not make a cutting;
21:6 they are holy to their God, and they pollute not the name of their God, for the fire-offerings of Jehovah, bread of their God, they are bringing near, and have been holy.
21:7 `A woman, a harlot, or polluted, they do not take, and a woman cast out from her husband they do not take, for he [is] holy to his God;
21:8 and thou hast sanctified him, for the bread of thy God he is bringing near; he is holy to thee; for holy [am] I, Jehovah, sanctifying you.
21:9 `And a daughter of any priest when she polluteth herself by going a-whoring -- her father she is polluting; with fire she is burnt.
21:10 `And the high priest of his brethren, on whose head is poured the anointing oil, and hath consecrated his hand to put on the garments, his head doth not uncover, nor rend his garments,
21:11 nor beside any dead person doth he come; for his father and for his mother he doth not defile himself;
21:12 nor from the sanctuary doth he go out, nor doth he pollute the sanctuary of his God, for the separation of the anointing oil of his God [is] on him; I [am] Jehovah.
21:13 `And he taketh a wife in her virginity;

21:14 widow, or cast out, or polluted one -- a harlot -- these he doth not take, but a virgin of his own people he doth take [for] a wife,
21:15 and he doth not pollute his seed among his people; for I [am] Jehovah, sanctifying him.'
21:16 And Jehovah speaketh unto Moses, saying,
21:17 `Speak unto Aaron, saying, No man of thy seed to their generations in whom there is blemish doth draw near to bring near the bread of his God,
21:18 for no man in whom [is] blemish doth draw near -- a man blind, or lame or dwarfed, or enlarged,
21:19 or a man in whom there is a breach in the foot, or a breach in the hand,
21:20 or hump-backed, or a dwarf, or with a mixture in his eye, or a scurvy person, or scabbed, or broken-testicled.
21:21 `No man in whom is blemish (of the seed of Aaron the priest) doth come nigh to bring near the fire-offerings of Jehovah; blemish [is] in him; the bread of his God he doth not come nigh to bring near.
21:22 `Bread of his God -- of the most holy things, and of the holy things -- he doth eat;
21:23 only, unto the vail he doth not enter, and unto the altar he doth not draw nigh; for blemish [is] in him; and he doth not pollute My sanctuaries; for I [am] Jehovah, sanctifying them.'
21:24 And Moses speaketh unto Aaron, and unto his sons, and unto all the sons of Israel.
22:1 And Jehovah speaketh unto Moses, saying,
22:2 `Speak unto Aaron, and unto his sons, and they are separated from the holy things of the sons of Israel, and they pollute not My holy name in what they are hallowing to Me; I [am] Jehovah.
22:3 `Say unto them, To your generations, any man who draweth near, out of all your seed, unto the holy things which the sons of Israel do sanctify to Jehovah, and his uncleanness on him -- even that person hath been cut off from before Me; I [am] Jehovah.
22:4 `Any man of the seed of Aaron, and is leprous or hath an issue -- of the holy things he doth not eat till that he is clean; and he who is coming against any uncleanness of a person, or a man whose seed of copulation goeth out from him,
22:5 or a man who cometh against any teeming thing which is unclean to him, or against a man who is unclean to him, even any of his uncleanness --
22:6 the person who cometh against it -- hath even been unclean till the evening, and doth not eat of the holy things, but hath bathed his flesh with water,
22:7 and the sun hath gone in, and he hath been clean, and afterwards he doth eat of the holy things, for it [is] his food;
22:8 a carcase or torn thing he doth not eat, for uncleanness thereby; I [am] Jehovah.

22:9 `And they have kept My charge, and bear no sin for it, that they have died for it when they pollute it; I [am] Jehovah sanctifying them.
22:10 `And no stranger doth eat of the holy thing; a settler of a priest and an hireling doth not eat of the holy thing;
22:11 and when a priest buyeth a person, the purchase of his money, he doth eat of it, also one born in his house; they do eat of his bread.
22:12 `And a priest's daughter, when she is a strange man's, -- she, of the heave-offering of the holy things doth not eat;
22:13 and a priest's daughter, when she is a widow, or cast out, and hath no seed, and hath turned back unto the house of her father, as [in] her youth, of her father's bread she doth eat; but no stranger doth eat of it.
22:14 `And when a man doth eat of a holy thing through ignorance, then he hath added its fifth part to it, and hath given [it] to the priest, with the holy thing;
22:15 and they do not pollute the holy things of the sons of Israel -- that which they lift up to Jehovah,
22:16 nor have caused them to bear the iniquity of the guilt-offering in their eating their holy things; for I [am] Jehovah, sanctifying them.'
22:17 And Jehovah speaketh unto Moses, saying,
22:18 `Speak unto Aaron, and unto his sons, and unto all the sons of Israel, and thou hast said unto them, Any man of the house of Israel, or of the sojourners in Israel, who bringeth near his offering, of all his vows, or of all his willing offerings which they bring near to Jehovah for a burnt-offering;
22:19 at your pleasure a perfect one, a male of the herd, of the sheep or of the goats;
22:20 nothing in which [is] blemish do ye bring near, for it is not for a pleasing thing for you.
22:21 `And when a man bringeth near a sacrifice of peace-offerings to Jehovah, to complete a vow, or for a willing-offering, of the herd or of the flock, it is perfect for a pleasing thing: no blemish is in it;
22:22 blind, or broken, or maimed, or having a wen, or scurvy, or scabbed -- ye do not bring these near to Jehovah, and a fire-offering ye do not make of them on the altar to Jehovah.
22:23 `As to an ox or a sheep enlarged or dwarfed -- a willing-offering ye do make it, but for a vow it is not pleasing.
22:24 As to a bruised, or beaten, or enlarged, or cut thing -- ye do not bring [it] near to Jehovah; even in your land ye do not do it.
22:25 And from the hand of a son of a stranger ye do not bring near the bread of your God, of any

of these, for their corruption [is] in them; blemish [is] in them; they are not pleasing for you.'
22:26 And Jehovah speaketh unto Moses, saying,
22:27 `When ox or lamb or goat is born, and it hath been seven days under its dam, then from the eighth day and henceforth, it is pleasing for an offering, a fire-offering to Jehovah;
22:28 but an ox or sheep -- it and its young one, ye do not slaughter in one day.
22:29 `And when ye sacrifice a sacrifice of thanksgiving to Jehovah, at your pleasure ye do sacrifice,
22:30 on that day it is eaten, ye do not leave of it till morning; I [am] Jehovah;
22:31 and ye have kept my commands, and have done them; I [am] Jehovah;
22:32 and ye do not pollute My holy name, and I have been hallowed in the midst of the sons of Israel; I [am] Jehovah, sanctifying you,
22:33 who am bringing you up out of the land of Egypt, to become your God; I [am] Jehovah.'
23:1 And Jehovah speaketh unto Moses, saying,
23:2 `Speak unto the sons of Israel, and thou hast said unto them, Appointed seasons of Jehovah, which ye proclaim, holy convocations, [are] these: they [are] My appointed seasons:
23:3 six days is work done, and in the seventh day [is] a sabbath of rest, a holy convocation; ye do no work; it [is] a sabbath to Jehovah in all your dwellings.
23:4 `These [are] appointed seasons of Jehovah, holy convocations, which ye proclaim in their appointed seasons:
23:5 in the first month, on the fourteenth of the month, between the evenings, [is] the passover to Jehovah;
23:6 and on the fifteenth day of this month [is] the feast of unleavened things to Jehovah; seven days unleavened things ye do eat;
23:7 on the first day ye have a holy convocation, ye do no servile work;
23:8 and ye have brought near a fire-offering to Jehovah seven days; in the seventh day [is] a holy convocation; ye do no servile work.'
23:9 And Jehovah speaketh unto Moses, saying,
23:10 `Speak unto the sons of Israel, and thou hast said unto them, When ye come in unto the land which I am giving to you, and have reaped its harvest, and have brought in the sheaf, the beginning of your harvest unto the priest,
23:11 then he hath waved the sheaf before Jehovah for your acceptance; on the morrow of the sabbath doth the priest wave it.
23:12 `And ye have prepared in the day of your waving the sheaf a lamb, a perfect one, a son of a year, for a burnt-offering to Jehovah,

23:13 and its present two tenth deals of flour mixed with oil, a fire-offering to Jehovah, a sweet fragrance, and its drink-offering, wine, a fourth of the hin.
23:14 `And bread and roasted corn and full ears ye do not eat until this self-same day, until your bringing in the offering of your God -- a statute age-during to your generations, in all your dwellings.
23:15 `And ye have numbered to you from the morrow of the sabbath, from the day of your bringing in the sheaf of the wave-offering: they are seven perfect sabbaths;
23:16 unto the morrow of the seventh sabbath ye do number fifty days, and ye have brought near a new present to Jehovah;
23:17 out of your dwellings ye bring in bread of a wave-offering, two [loaves], of two tenth deals of flour they are, [with] yeast they are baken, first-[fruits] to Jehovah.
23:18 `And ye have brought near, besides the bread, seven lambs, perfect ones, sons of a year, and one bullock, a son of the herd, and two rams; they are a burnt-offering to Jehovah, with their present and their libations, a fire-offering of sweet fragrance to Jehovah.
23:19 `And ye have prepared one kid of the goats for a sin-offering, and two lambs, sons of a year, for a sacrifice of peace-offerings,
23:20 and the priest hath waved them, besides the bread of the first-[fruits] -- a wave-offering before Jehovah, besides the two lambs; they are holy to Jehovah for the priest;
23:21 and ye have proclaimed on this self-same day: a holy convocation is to you, ye do no servile work -- a statute age-during in all your dwellings, to your generations.
23:22 `And in your reaping the harvest of your land thou dost not complete the corner of thy field in thy reaping, and the gleaning of thy harvest thou dost not gather, to the poor and to the sojourner thou dost leave them; I Jehovah [am] your God.'
23:23 And Jehovah speaketh unto Moses, saying,
23:24 `Speak unto the sons of Israel, saying, In the seventh month, on the first of the month, ye have a sabbath, a memorial of shouting, a holy convocation;
23:25 ye do no servile work, and ye have brought near a fire-offering to Jehovah.'
23:26 And Jehovah speaketh unto Moses, saying,
23:27 `Only -- on the tenth of this seventh month is a day of atonements; ye have a holy convocation, and ye have humbled yourselves, and have brought near a fire-offering to Jehovah;
23:28 and ye do no work in this self-same day, for it is a day of atonements, to make atonement for you, before Jehovah your God.
23:29 `For any person who is not humbled in this self-same day hath even been cut off from his people;
23:30 and any person who doth any work in this self-same day I have even destroyed that person

from the midst of his people;
23:31 ye do no work -- a statute age-during to your generations in all your dwellings.
23:32 It [is] a sabbath of rest to you, and ye have humbled yourselves in the ninth of the month at even; from evening till evening ye do keep your sabbath.'
23:33 And Jehovah speaketh unto Moses, saying,
23:34 `Speak unto the sons of Israel, saying, In the fifteenth day of this seventh month [is] a feast of booths seven days to Jehovah;
23:35 on the first day [is] a holy convocation, ye do no servile work,
23:36 seven days ye bring near a fire-offering to Jehovah, on the eighth day ye have a holy convocation, and ye have brought near a fire-offering to Jehovah; it [is] a restraint, ye do no servile work.
23:37 `These [are] appointed seasons of Jehovah, which ye proclaim holy convocations, to bring near a fire-offering to Jehovah, a burnt-offering, and a present, a sacrifice, and libations, a thing of a day in its day,
23:38 apart from the sabbaths of Jehovah, and apart from your gifts, and apart from all your vows, and apart from all your willing-offerings, which ye give to Jehovah.
23:39 `Only -- in the fifteenth day of the seventh month, in your gathering the increase of the land, ye do keep the feast of Jehovah seven days; on the first day [is] a sabbath, and on the eighth day a sabbath;
23:40 and ye have taken to yourselves on the first day the fruit of beautiful trees, branches of palms, and boughs of thick trees, and willows of a brook, and have rejoiced before Jehovah your God seven days.
23:41 `And ye have kept it a feast to Jehovah, seven days in a year -- a statute age-during to your generations; in the seventh month ye keep it a feast.
23:42 `In booths ye dwell seven days; all who are natives in Israel dwell in booths,
23:43 so that your generations do know that in booths I caused the sons of Israel to dwell; in my bringing them out of the land of Egypt; I, Jehovah, [am] your God.'
23:44 And Moses speaketh [concerning] the appointed seasons of Jehovah unto the sons of Israel.
24:1 And Jehovah speaketh unto Moses, saying,
24:2 `Command the sons of Israel, and they bring unto thee pure olive oil, beaten, for the lamp, to cause a light to go up continually;
24:3 at the outside of the vail of the testimony in the tent of meeting doth Aaron arrange it from evening till morning before Jehovah continually -- a statute age-during to your generations;
24:4 by the pure candlestick he doth arrange the lights before Jehovah continually.

24:5 `And thou hast taken flour, and hast baked twelve cakes with it, two tenth deals are in the one cake,
24:6 and thou hast set them two ranks (six in the rank) on the pure table before Jehovah,
24:7 and thou hast put on the rank pure frankincense, and it hath been to the bread for a memorial, a fire-offering to Jehovah.
24:8 `On each sabbath-day he arrangeth it before Jehovah continually, from the sons of Israel -- a covenant age-during;
24:9 and it hath been to Aaron, and to his sons, and they have eaten it in the holy place, for it [is] most holy to him, from the fire-offerings of Jehovah -- a statute age-during.'
24:10 And a son of an Israelitish woman goeth out (and he [is] son of an Egyptian man), in the midst of the sons of Israel, and strive in the camp do the son of the Israelitish woman and a man of Israel,
24:11 and the son of the Israelitish woman execrateth the Name, and revileth; and they bring him in unto Moses; and his mother's name [is] Shelomith daughter of Dibri, of the tribe of Dan;
24:12 and he causeth him to rest in charge -- to explain to them by the mouth of Jehovah.
24:13 And Jehovah speaketh unto Moses, saying,
24:14 `Bring out the reviler unto the outside of the camp; and all those hearing have laid their hands on his head, and all the company have stoned him.
24:15 `And unto the sons of Israel thou dost speak, saying, When any man revileth his God -- then he hath borne his sin;
24:16 and he who is execrating the name of Jehovah is certainly put to death; all the company do certainly cast stones at him; as a sojourner so a native, in his execrating the Name, is put to death.
24:17 `And when a man smiteth any soul of man, he is certainly put to death.
24:18 `And he who smiteth a beast repayeth it, body for body.
24:19 `And when a man putteth a blemish in his fellow, as he hath done so it is done to him;
24:20 breach for breach, eye for eye, tooth for tooth; as he putteth a blemish in a man so it is done in him.
24:21 `And he who smiteth a beast repayeth it, and he who smiteth [the life of] man is put to death;
24:22 one judgment is to you; as a sojourner so is a native; for I [am] Jehovah your God.'
24:23 And Moses speaketh unto the sons of Israel, and they bring out the reviler unto the outside of the camp, and stone him with stones; and the sons of Israel have done as Jehovah hath commanded Moses.
25:1 And Jehovah speaketh unto Moses, in mount Sinai, saying,
25:2 `Speak unto the sons of Israel, and thou hast said unto them, When ye come in unto the land

which I am giving to you, then hath the land kept a sabbath to Jehovah.
25:3 `Six years thou dost sow thy field, and six years thou dost prune thy vineyard, and hast gathered its increase,
25:4 and in the seventh year a sabbath of rest is to the land, a sabbath to Jehovah; thy field thou dost not sow, and thy vineyard thou dost not prune;
25:5 the spontaneous growth of thy harvest thou dost not reap, and the grapes of thy separated thing thou dost not gather, a year of rest it is to the land.
25:6 `And the sabbath of the land hath been to you for food, to thee, and to thy man-servant, and to thy handmaid, and to thy hireling, and to thy settler, who are sojourning with thee;
25:7 and to thy cattle, and to the beast which [is] in thy land, is all thine increase for food.
25:8 `And thou hast numbered to thee seven sabbaths of years, seven years seven times, and the days of the seven sabbaths of years have been to thee nine and forty years,
25:9 and thou hast caused a trumpet of shouting to pass over in the seventh month, in the tenth of the month; in the day of the atonements ye do cause a trumpet to pass over through all your land;
25:10 and ye have hallowed the year, the fiftieth year; and ye have proclaimed liberty in the land to all its inhabitants; a jubilee it is to you; and ye have turned back each unto his possession; yea, each unto his family ye do turn back.
25:11 `A jubilee it [is], the fiftieth year, a year it is to you; ye sow not, nor reap its spontaneous growth, nor gather its separated things;
25:12 for a jubilee it [is], holy it is to you; out of the field ye eat its increase;
25:13 in the year of this jubilee ye turn back each unto his possession.
25:14 `And when thou sellest anything to thy fellow, or buyest from the hand of thy fellow, ye do not oppress one another;
25:15 by the number of years after the jubilee thou dost buy from thy fellow; by the number of the years of increase he doth sell to thee;
25:16 according to the multitude of the years thou dost multiply its price, and according to the fewness of the years thou dost diminish its price; for a number of increases he is selling to thee;
25:17 and ye do not oppress one another, and thou hast been afraid of thy God; for I [am] Jehovah your God.
25:18 `And ye have done My statutes, and My judgments ye keep, and have done them, and ye have dwelt on the land confidently,
25:19 and the land hath given its fruit, and ye have eaten to satiety, and have dwelt confidently on it.
25:20 `And when ye say, What do we eat in the seventh year, lo, we do not sow, nor gather our

increase?
25:21 then I have commanded My blessing on you in the sixth year, and it hath made the increase for three years;
25:22 and ye have sown the eighth year, and have eaten of the old increase; until the ninth year, until the coming in of its increase, ye do eat the old.
25:23 `And the land is not sold -- to extinction, for the land [is] Mine, for sojourners and settlers [are] ye with Me;
25:24 and in all the land of your possession a redemption ye do give to the land.
25:25 `When thy brother becometh poor, and hath sold his possession, then hath his redeemer who is near unto him come, and he hath redeemed the sold thing of his brother;
25:26 and when a man hath no redeemer, and his own hand hath attained, and he hath found as sufficient [for] its redemption,
25:27 then he hath reckoned the years of its sale, and hath given back that which is over to the man to whom he sold [it], and he hath returned to his possession.
25:28 `And if his hand hath not found sufficiency to give back to him, then hath his sold thing been in the hand of him who buyeth it till the year of jubilee; and it hath gone out in the jubilee, and he hath returned to his possession.
25:29 `And when a man selleth a dwelling-house [in] a walled city, then hath his right of redemption been until the completion of a year from its selling; days -- is his right of redemption;
25:30 and if it is not redeemed until the fulness to him of a perfect year, then hath the house which [is] in a walled city been established to extinction to the buyer of it, to his generations; it goeth not out in the jubilee;
25:31 and a house of the villages which have no wall round about, on the field of the country is reckoned; redemption is to it, and in the jubilee it goeth out.
25:32 `As to cities of the Levites -- houses of the cities of their possession -- redemption age-during is to the Levites;
25:33 as to him who redeemeth from the Levites, both the sale of a house and the city of his possession have gone out in the jubilee, for the houses of the cities of the Levites are their possession in the midst of the sons of Israel.
25:34 And a field, a suburb of their cities, is not sold; for a possession age-during it [is] to them.
25:35 `And when thy brother is become poor, and his hand hath failed with thee, then thou hast kept hold on him, sojourner and settler, and he hath lived with thee;
25:36 thou takest no usury from him, or increase; and thou hast been afraid of thy God; and thy brother hath lived with thee;

25:37 thy money thou givest not to him in usury, and for increase thou givest not thy food;
25:38 I [am] Jehovah your God, who hath brought you out of the land of Egypt, to give to you the land of Canaan, to become your God.
25:39 `And when thy brother becometh poor with thee, and he hath been sold to thee, thou dost not lay on him servile service;
25:40 as an hireling, as a settler, he is with thee, till the year of the jubilee he doth serve with thee, --
25:41 then he hath gone out from thee, he and his sons with him, and hath turned back unto his family; even unto the possession of his fathers he doth turn back.
25:42 `For they [are] My servants, whom I have brought out from the land of Egypt: they are not sold [with] the sale of a servant;
25:43 thou rulest not over him with rigour, and thou hast been afraid of thy God.
25:44 `And thy man-servant and thy handmaid whom thou hast [are] of the nations who [are] round about you; of them ye buy man-servant and handmaid,
25:45 and also of the sons of the settlers who are sojourning with you, of them ye buy, and of their families who [are] with you, which they have begotten in your land, and they have been to you for a possession;
25:46 and ye have taken them for inheritance to your sons after you, to occupy [for] a possession; to the age ye lay service upon them, but upon your brethren, the sons of Israel, one with another, thou dost not rule over him with rigour.
25:47 `And when the hand of a sojourner or settler with thee attaineth [riches], and thy brother with him hath become poor, and he hath been sold to a sojourner, a settler with thee, or to the root of the family of a sojourner,
25:48 after he hath been sold, there is a right of redemption to him; one of his brethren doth redeem him,
25:49 or his uncle, or a son of his uncle, doth redeem him, or any of the relations of his flesh, of his family, doth redeem him, or -- his own hand hath attained -- then he hath been redeemed.
25:50 `And he hath reckoned with his buyer from the year of his being sold to him till the year of jubilee, and the money of his sale hath been by the number of years; as the days of an hireling it is with him.
25:51 `If yet many years, according to them he giveth back his redemption [money], from the money of his purchase.
25:52 `And if few are left of the years till the year of jubilee, then he hath reckoned with him, according to his years he doth give back his redemption [money];

25:53 as an hireling, year by year, he is with him, and he doth not rule him with rigour before thine eyes.
25:54 `And if he is not redeemed in these [years], then he hath gone out in the year of jubilee, he and his sons with him.
25:55 For to Me [are] the sons of Israel servants; My servants they [are], whom I have brought out of the land of Egypt; I, Jehovah, [am] your God.
26:1 `Ye do not make to yourselves idols; and graven image or standing image ye do not set up to yourselves; and a stone of imagery ye do not put in your land, to bow yourselves to it; for I [am] Jehovah your God.
26:2 `My sabbaths ye do keep, and My sanctuary ye do reverence; I [am] Jehovah.
26:3 `If in My statutes ye walk, and My commands ye keep, and have done them,
26:4 then I have given your rains in their season, and the land hath given her produce, and the tree of the field doth give its fruit;
26:5 and reached to you hath the threshing, the gathering, and the gathering doth reach the sowing-[time]; and ye have eaten your bread to satiety, and have dwelt confidently in your land.
26:6 `And I have given peace in the land, and ye have lain down, and there is none causing trembling; and I have caused evil beasts to cease out of the land, and the sword doth not pass over into your land.
26:7 `And ye have pursued your enemies, and they have fallen before you by the sword;
26:8 and five of you have pursued a hundred, and a hundred of you do pursue a myriad; and your enemies have fallen before you by the sword.
26:9 `And I have turned unto you, and have made you fruitful, and have multiplied you, and have established My covenant with you;
26:10 and ye have eaten old [store], and the old because of the new ye bring out.
26:11 `And I have given My tabernacle in your midst, and My soul doth not loathe you;
26:12 and I have walked habitually in your midst, and have become your God, and ye -- ye are become My people;
26:13 I [am] Jehovah your God, who have brought you out of the land of the Egyptians, from being their servants; and I break the bars of your yoke, and cause you to go erect.
26:14 `And if ye do not hearken to Me, and do not all these commands;
26:15 and if at My statutes ye kick, and if My judgments your soul loathe, so as not to do all My commands -- to your breaking My covenant --
26:16 I also do this to you, and I have appointed over you trouble, the consumption, and the burning fever, consuming eyes, and causing pain of soul; and your seed in vain ye have sowed,

and your enemies have eaten it;
26:17 and I have set My face against you, and ye have been smitten before your enemies; and
those hating you have ruled over you, and ye have fled, and there is none pursuing you.
26:18 `And if unto these ye hearken not to Me, -- then I have added to chastise you seven times for
your sins;
26:19 and I have broken the pride of your strength, and have made your heavens as iron, and your
earth as brass;
26:20 and consumed hath been your strength in vain, and your land doth not give her produce, and
the tree of the land doth not give its fruit.
26:21 `And if ye walk with Me [in] opposition, and are not willing to hearken to Me, then I have
added to you a plague seven times, according to your sins,
26:22 and sent against you the beast of the field, and it hath bereaved you; and I have cut off your
cattle, and have made you few, and your ways have been desolate.
26:23 `And if by these ye are not instructed by Me, and have walked with Me [in] opposition,
26:24 then I have walked -- I also -- with you in opposition, and have smitten you, even I, seven
times for your sins;
26:25 and I have brought in on you a sword, executing the vengeance of a covenant; and ye have
been gathered unto your cities, and I have sent pestilence into your midst, and ye have been given
into the hand of an enemy.
26:26 `In My breaking to you the staff of bread, then ten women have baked your bread in one
oven, and have given back your bread by weight; and ye have eaten, and are not satisfied.
26:27 `And if for this ye hearken not to Me, and have walked with Me in opposition,
26:28 then I have walked with you in the fury of opposition, and have chastised you, even I, seven
times for your sins.
26:29 `And ye have eaten the flesh of your sons; even flesh of your daughters ye do eat.
26:30 And I have destroyed your high places, and cut down your images, and have put your
carcases on the carcases of your idols, and My soul hath loathed you;
26:31 and I have made your cities a waste, and have made desolate your sanctuaries, and I smell
not at your sweet fragrances;
26:32 and I have made desolate the land, and your enemies, who are dwelling in it, have been
astonished at it.
26:33 And you I scatter among nations, and have drawn out after you a sword, and your land hath
been a desolation, and your cities are a waste.
26:34 `Then doth the land enjoy its sabbaths -- all the days of the desolation, and ye in the land of

your enemies -- then doth the land rest, and hath enjoyed its sabbaths;
26:35 all the days of the desolation it resteth that which it hath not rested in your sabbaths in your dwelling on it.
26:36 `And those who are left of you -- I have also brought a faintness into their heart in the lands of their enemies, and the sound of a leaf driven away hath pursued them, and they have fled -- flight from a sword -- and they have fallen, and there is none pursuing.
26:37 And they have stumbled one on another, as from the face of a sword, and there is none pursuing, and ye have no standing before your enemies,
26:38 and ye have perished among the nations, and the land of your enemies hath consumed you.
26:39 `And those who are left of you -- they consume away in their iniquity, in the lands of your enemies; and also in the iniquities of their fathers, with them they consume away.
26:40 `And -- they have confessed their iniquity, and the iniquity of their fathers, in their trespass which they have trespassed against Me, and also, that they have walked with Me, in opposition,
26:41 also I walk to them in opposition, and have brought them into the land of their enemies -- or then their uncircumcised heart is humbled, and then they accept the punishment of their iniquity, --
26:42 then I have remembered My covenant [with] Jacob, and also My covenant [with] Isaac, and also My covenant [with] Abraham I remember, and the land I remember.
26:43 `And -- the land is left of them, and doth enjoy its sabbaths, in the desolation without them, and they accept the punishment of their iniquity, because, even because, against My judgments they have kicked, and My statutes hath their soul loathed,
26:44 and also even this, in their being in the land of their enemies, I have not rejected them, nor have I loathed them, to consume them, to break My covenant with them; for I [am] Jehovah their God; --
26:45 then I have remembered for them the covenant of the ancestors, whom I brought forth out of the land of Egypt before the eyes of the nations to become their God; I [am] Jehovah.'
26:46 These [are] the statutes, and the judgments, and the laws, which Jehovah hath given between Him and the sons of Israel, in mount Sinai, by the hand of Moses.
27:1 And Jehovah speaketh unto Moses, saying,
27:2 `Speak unto the sons of Israel, and thou hast said unto them, When a man maketh a wonderful vow, by thy valuation the persons [are] Jehovah's.
27:3 When thy valuation hath been of the male from a son of twenty years even unto a son of sixty years, then hath been thy valuation fifty shekels of silver by the shekel of the sanctuary.
27:4 And if it [is] a female -- then hath thy valuation been thirty shekels;
27:5 and if from a son of five years even unto a son of twenty years -- then hath thy valuation been

of the male twenty shekels, and for the female, ten shekels;
27:6 and if from a son of a month even unto a son of five years -- then hath thy valuation been of the male five shekels of silver, and for the female thy valuation [is] three shekels of silver;
27:7 and if from a son of sixty years and above -- if a male, then hath thy valuation been fifteen shekels, and for a female, ten shekels.
27:8 `And if he is poorer than thy valuation, then he hath presented himself before the priest, and the priest hath valued him; according to that which the hand of him who is vowing doth reach doth the priest value him.
27:9 `And if [it is] a beast of which they bring near an offering to Jehovah, all that [one] giveth of it to Jehovah is holy;
27:10 he doth not change it nor exchange it, a good for a bad, or a bad for a good; and if he really change beast for beast, -- then it hath been -- it and its exchange is holy.
27:11 `And if [it is] any unclean beast of which they do not bring near an offering to Jehovah, then he hath presented the beast before the priest,
27:12 and the priest hath valued it; whether good or bad, according to thy valuation, O priest, so it is;
27:13 and if he really redeem it, then he hath added its fifth to thy valuation.
27:14 `And when a man sanctifieth his house, a holy thing to Jehovah, then hath the priest valued it, whether good or bad; as the priest doth value it so it standeth;
27:15 and if he who is sanctifying doth redeem his house, then he hath added a fifth of the money of thy valuation to it, and it hath become his.
27:16 `And if of the field of his possession a man sanctify to Jehovah, then hath thy valuation been according to its seed; a homer of barley-seed at fifty shekels of silver;
27:17 if from the year of the jubilee he sanctify his field, according to thy valuation it standeth;
27:18 and if after the jubilee he sanctify his field, then hath the priest reckoned to him the money according to the years which are left, unto the year of the jubilee, and it hath been abated from thy valuation.
27:19 `And if he really redeem the field -- he who is sanctifying it -- then he hath added a fifth of the money of thy valuation to it, and it hath been established to him;
27:20 and if he do not redeem the field, or if he hath sold the field to another man, it is not redeemed any more;
27:21 and the field hath been, in its going out in the jubilee, holy to Jehovah as a field which is devoted; to the priest is its possession.
27:22 `And if the field of his purchase (which [is] not of the fields of his possession) [one] sanctify to

Jehovah --

27:23 then hath the priest reckoned to him the amount of thy valuation unto the year of jubilee, and he hath given thy valuation in that day -- a holy thing to Jehovah;

27:24 in the year of the jubilee the field returneth to him from whom he bought it, to him whose [is] the possession of the land.

27:25 And all thy valuation is by the shekel of the sanctuary: twenty gerahs is the shekel.

27:26 `Only, a firstling which is Jehovah's firstling among beasts -- no man doth sanctify it, whether ox or sheep; it [is] Jehovah's.

27:27 And if among the unclean beasts, then he hath ransomed [it] at thy valuation, and he hath added its fifth to it; and if it is not redeemed, then it hath been sold at thy valuation.

27:28 `Only, no devoted thing which a man devoteth to Jehovah, of all that he hath, of man, and beast, and of the field of his possession, is sold or redeemed; every devoted thing is most holy to Jehovah.

27:29 `No devoted thing, which is devoted of man, is ransomed, it is surely put to death.

27:30 And all tithe of the land, of the seed of the land, of the fruit of the tree, is Jehovah's -- holy to Jehovah.

27:31 `And if a man really redeem [any] of his tithe, its fifth he addeth to it.

27:32 `And all the tithe of the herd and of the flock -- all that passeth by under the rod -- the tenth is holy to Jehovah;

27:33 he enquireth not between good and bad, nor doth he change it; and if he really change it -- then it hath been -- it and its exchange is holy; it is not redeemed.'

27:34 These [are] the commands which Jehovah hath commanded Moses for the sons of Israel, in mount Sinai.

Numbers

1:1 And Jehovah speaketh unto Moses in the wilderness of Sinai, in the tent of meeting, on the first of the second month, in the second year of their going out of the land of Egypt, saying:
1:2 `Take ye up the sum of all the company of the sons of Israel by their families, by the house of their fathers, in the number of names -- every male by their polls;
1:3 from a son of twenty years and upward, every one going out to the host in Israel, ye do number them by their hosts, thou and Aaron;
1:4 and with you there is a man for a tribe, each is a head to the house of his fathers.
1:5 `And these [are] the names of the men who stand with you: `For Reuben -- Elizur son of Shedeur.
1:6 `For Simeon -- Shelumiel son of Zurishaddai.
1:7 `For Judah -- Nahshon son of Amminadab.
1:8 `For Issachar -- Nathaneel son of Zuar.
1:9 `For Zebulun -- Eliab son of Helon.
1:10 `For the sons of Joseph -- for Ephraim: Elishama son of Ammihud: for Manasseh -- Gamaliel son of Pedahzur.
1:11 `For Benjamin -- Abidan son of Gideoni.
1:12 `For Dan -- Ahiezer son of Ammishaddai.
1:13 `For Asher -- Pagiel son of Ocran.
1:14 `For Gad -- Eliasaph son of Deuel.
1:15 `For Naphtali -- Ahira son of Enan.'
1:16 These [are] those called of the company, princes of the tribes of their fathers; they [are] heads of the thousands of Israel.
1:17 And Moses taketh -- Aaron also -- these men, who were defined by name,
1:18 and all the company they assembled on the first of the second month, and they declare their births, by their families, by the house of their fathers, in the number of names from a son of twenty years and upward, by their polls,
1:19 as Jehovah hath commanded Moses; and he numbereth them in the wilderness of Sinai.
1:20 And the sons of Reuben, Israel's first-born -- their births, by their families, by the house of their fathers, in the number of names, by their polls, every male from a son of twenty years and upward, every one going out to the host --
1:21 their numbered ones, for the tribe of Reuben, are six and forty thousand and five hundred.
1:22 Of the sons of Simeon -- their births, by their families, by the house of their fathers, its

numbered ones in the number of names, by their polls, every male from a son of twenty years and
upward, every one going out to the host --
1:23 their numbered ones, for the tribe of Simeon, [are] nine and fifty thousand and three hundred.
1:24 Of the sons of Gad -- their births, by their families, by the house of their fathers, in the number
of names, from a son of twenty years and upward, every one going out to the host --
1:25 their numbered ones, for the tribe of Gad, [are] five and forty thousand and six hundred and
fifty.
1:26 Of the sons of Judah -- their births, by their families, by the house of their fathers, in the
number of names, from a son of twenty years and upward, every one going out to the host --
1:27 their numbered ones, for the tribe of Judah, [are] four and seventy thousand and six hundred.
1:28 Of the sons of Issachar -- their births, by their families, by the house of their fathers, in the
number of names, from a son of twenty years and upward, every one going out to the host --
1:29 their numbered ones, for the tribe of Issachar, [are] four and fifty thousand and four hundred.
1:30 Of the sons of Zebulun -- their births, by their families, by the house of their fathers, in the
number of names, from a son of twenty years and upward, every one going out to the host --
1:31 their numbered ones, for the tribe of Zebulun, [are] seven and fifty thousand and four hundred.
1:32 Of the sons of Joseph -- of the sons of Ephraim -- their births, by their families, by the house
of their fathers, in the number of names, from a son of twenty years and upward, every one going
out to the host --
1:33 their numbered ones, for the tribe of Ephraim, [are] forty thousand and five hundred.
1:34 Of the sons of Manasseh -- their births, by their families, by the house of their fathers, in the
number of names, from a son of twenty years and upward, every one going out to the host --
1:35 their numbered ones, for the tribe of Manasseh, [are] two and thirty thousand and two
hundred.
1:36 Of the sons of Benjamin -- their births, by their families, by the house of their fathers, in the
number of names, from a son of twenty years and upward, every one going out to the host --
1:37 their numbered ones, for the tribe of Benjamin, [are] five and thirty thousand and four hundred.
1:38 Of the sons of Dan -- their births, by their families, by the house of their fathers, in the number
of names, from a son of twenty years and upward, every one going out to the host --
1:39 their numbered ones, for the tribe of Dan, [are] two and sixty thousand and seven hundred.
1:40 Of the sons of Asher -- their births, by their families, by the house of their fathers, in the
number of names, from a son of twenty years and upward, every one going out to the host --
1:41 their numbered ones, for the tribe of Asher, [are] one and forty thousand and five hundred.
1:42 [Of] the sons of Naphtali -- their births, by their families, by the house of their fathers, in the

number of names, from a son of twenty years and upward, every one going out to the host --
1:43 their numbered ones, for the tribe of Naphtali, [are] three and fifty thousand and four hundred.
1:44 These [are] those numbered, whom Moses numbered -- Aaron also, and the princes of Israel, twelve men -- each for the house of his fathers, they have been.
1:45 And they are, all those numbered of the sons of Israel, by the house of their fathers, from a son of twenty years and upward, every one going out to the host in Israel,
1:46 yea, all those numbered are six hundred thousand, and three thousand, and five hundred and fifty.
1:47 And the Levites, for the tribe of their fathers, have not numbered themselves in their midst,
1:48 seeing Jehovah speaketh unto Moses, saying,
1:49 `Only, the tribe of Levi thou dost not number, and their sum thou dost not take up in the midst of the sons of Israel;
1:50 and thou, appoint the Levites over the tabernacle of the testimony, and over all its vessels, and over all that it hath; they bear the tabernacle, and all its vessels, and they serve it; and round about the tabernacle they encamp.
1:51 `And in the journeying of the tabernacle, the Levites take it down, and in the encamping of the tabernacle, the Levites raise it up; and the stranger who is coming near is put to death.'
1:52 And the sons of Israel have encamped, each by his camp, and each by his standard, by their hosts;
1:53 and the Levites encamp round about the tabernacle of the testimony; and there is no wrath on the company of the sons of Israel, and the Levites have kept the charge of the tabernacle of the testimony.
1:54 And the sons of Israel do according to all that Jehovah hath commanded Moses; so they have done.
2:1 And Jehovah speaketh unto Moses, and unto Aaron, saying,
2:2 `Each by his standard, with ensigns of the house of their fathers, do the sons of Israel encamp; over-against round about the tent of meeting they encamp.'
2:3 And those encamping eastward towards the sun-rising, [are of] the standard of the camp of Judah, by their hosts; and the prince of the sons of Judah [is] Nahshon, son of Amminadab;
2:4 and his host, and their numbered ones, [are] four and seventy thousand and six hundred.
2:5 And those encamping by him [are of] the tribe of Issachar; and the prince of the sons of Issachar [is] Nethaneel son of Zuar;
2:6 and his host, and its numbered ones, [are] four and fifty thousand and four hundred.
2:7 The tribe of Zebulun; and the prince of the sons of Zebulun [is] Eliab son of Helon;

2:8 and his host, and its numbered ones, [are] seven and fifty thousand and four hundred;
2:9 all those numbered of the camp of Judah [are] a hundred thousand, and eighty thousand, and six thousand, and four hundred, by their hosts; they journey first.
2:10 The standard of the camp of Reuben [is] southward, by their hosts; and the prince of the sons of Reuben [is] Elizur son of Shedeur;
2:11 and his host, and its numbered ones, [are] six and forty thousand and five hundred.
2:12 And those encamping by him [are of] the tribe of Simeon; and the prince of the sons of Simeon [is] Shelumiel son of Zurishaddai;
2:13 and his host, and their numbered ones, [are] nine and fifty thousand and three hundred.
2:14 And the tribe of Gad; and the prince of the sons of Gad [is] Eliasaph son of Reuel;
2:15 and his host, and their numbered ones, [are] five and forty thousand and six hundred and fifty.
2:16 All those numbered of the camp of Reuben [are] a hundred thousand, and one and fifty thousand, and four hundred and fifty, by their hosts; and they journey second.
2:17 And the tent of meeting -- the camp of the Levites -- hath journeyed in the midst of the camps; as they encamp so they journey, each at his station by their standards.
2:18 The standard of the camp of Ephraim, by their hosts, [is] westward; and the prince of the sons of Ephraim [is] Elishama son of Ammihud;
2:19 and his host, and their numbered ones, [are] forty thousand and five hundred.
2:20 And by him [is] the tribe of Manasseh; and the prince of the sons of Manasseh [is] Gamaliel son of Pedahzur;
2:21 and his host, and their numbered ones, [are] two and thirty thousand, and two hundred.
2:22 And the tribe of Benjamin; and the prince of the sons of Benjamin [is] Abidan son of Gideoni;
2:23 and his host, and their numbered ones, [are] five and thirty thousand and four hundred.
2:24 All those numbered of the camp of Ephraim [are] a hundred thousand, and eight thousand, and a hundred, by their hosts; and they journey third.
2:25 The standard of the camp of Dan [is] northward, by their hosts; and the prince of the sons of Dan [is] Ahiezer son of Ammishaddai;
2:26 and his host, and their numbered ones, [are] two and sixty thousand and seven hundred.
2:27 And those encamping by him [are of] the tribe of Asher; and the prince of the sons of Asher [is] Pagiel son of Ocran;
2:28 and his host, and their numbered ones, [are] one and forty thousand and five hundred.
2:29 And the tribe of Naphtali; and the prince of the sons of Naphtali [is] Ahira son of Enan;
2:30 and his host, and their numbered ones, [are] three and fifty thousand and four hundred.
2:31 All those numbered of the camp of Dan [are] a hundred thousand, and seven and fifty

thousand, and six hundred; at the rear they journey, by their standards.
2:32 These [are] those numbered of the sons of Israel by the house of their fathers; all those numbered of the camps by their hosts [are] six hundred thousand, and three thousand, and five hundred and fifty.
2:33 And the Levites have not numbered themselves in the midst of the sons of Israel, as Jehovah hath commanded Moses.
2:34 And the sons of Israel do according to all that Jehovah hath commanded Moses; so they have encamped by their standards, and so they have journeyed; each by his families, by the house of his fathers.
3:1 And these [are] births of Aaron and Moses, in the day of Jehovah's speaking with Moses in mount Sinai.
3:2 And these [are] the names of the sons of Aaron: the first-born Nadab, and Abihu, Eleazar, and Ithamar;
3:3 these [are] the names of the sons of Aaron, the anointed priests, whose hand he hath consecrated for acting as priest.
3:4 And Nadab dieth -- Abihu also -- before Jehovah, in their bringing near strange fire before Jehovah, in the wilderness of Sinai, and sons they had not; and Eleazar -- Ithamar also -- acteth as priest in the presence of Aaron their father.
3:5 And Jehovah speaketh unto Moses, saying,
3:6 `Bring near the tribe of Levi, and thou hast caused it to stand before Aaron the priest, and they have served him,
3:7 and kept his charge, and the charge of all the company before the tent of meeting, to do the service of the tabernacle;
3:8 and they have kept all the vessels of the tent of meeting, and the charge of the sons of Israel, to do the service of the tabernacle;
3:9 and thou hast given the Levites to Aaron and to his sons; they are surely given to him out of the sons of Israel.
3:10 `And Aaron and his sons thou dost appoint, and they have kept their priesthood, and the stranger who cometh near is put to death.'
3:11 And Jehovah speaketh unto Moses, saying,
3:12 `And I, lo, I have taken the Levites from the midst of the sons of Israel instead of every first-born opening a womb among the sons of Israel, and the Levites have been Mine;
3:13 for Mine [is] every first-born, in the day of My smiting every first-born in the land of Egypt I have sanctified to Myself every first-born in Israel, from man unto beast; Mine they are; I [am]

Jehovah.'

3:14 And Jehovah speaketh unto Moses in the wilderness of Sinai, saying,

3:15 `Number the sons of Levi by the house of their fathers, by their families; every male from a son of a month and upward thou dost number them.'

3:16 And Moses numbereth them according to the command of Jehovah, as he hath been commanded.

3:17 And these are sons of Levi by their names: Gershon, and Kohath, and Merari.

3:18 And these [are] the names of the sons of Gershon by their families: Libni and Shimei.

3:19 And the sons of Kohath, by their families, [are] Amram and Izhar, Hebron and Uzziel.

3:20 And the sons of Merari by their families [are] Mahli and Mushi; these are the families of the Levites, by the house of their fathers.

3:21 Of Gershon [is] the family of the Libnite, and the family of the Shimite; these are the families of the Gershonite.

3:22 Their numbered ones, in number, every male from a son of a month and upward, their numbered ones [are] seven thousand and five hundred.

3:23 The families of the Gershonite, behind the tabernacle, do encamp westward.

3:24 And the prince of a father's house for the Gershonite [is] Eliasaph son of Lael.

3:25 And the charge of the sons of Gershon in the tent of meeting [is] the tabernacle, and the tent, its covering, and the vail at the opening of the tent of meeting,

3:26 and the hangings of the court, and the vail at the opening of the court, which [is] by the tabernacle and by the altar round about, and its cords, to all its service.

3:27 And of Kohath [is] the family of the Amramite, and the family of the Izharite, and the family of the Hebronite, and the family of the Uzzielite; these are families of the Kohathite.

3:28 In number, all the males, from a son of a month and upward, [are] eight thousand and six hundred, keeping the charge of the sanctuary.

3:29 The families of the sons of Kohath encamp by the side of the tabernacle southward.

3:30 And the prince of a father's house for the families of the Kohathite [is] Elizaphan son of Uzziel.

3:31 And their charge [is] the ark, and the table, and the candlestick, and the altars, and the vessels of the sanctuary with which they serve, and the vail, and all its service.

3:32 And [to] the prince of the princes of the Levites, Eleazar son of Aaron the priest, [is] the oversight of the keepers of the charge of the sanctuary.

3:33 Of Merari [is] the family of the Mahlite, and the family of the Mushite; these [are] the families of Merari.

3:34 And their numbered ones, in number, all the males from a son of a month and upward, [are]

six thousand and two hundred.
3:35 And the prince of a father's house for the families of Merari [is] Zuriel son of Abihail; by the side of the tabernacle they encamp northward.
3:36 And the oversight -- the charge of the sons of Merari -- [is] the boards of the tabernacle, and its bars, and its pillars, and its sockets, and all its vessels, and all its service,
3:37 and the pillars of the court round about, and their sockets, and their pins, and their cords.
3:38 And those encamping before the tabernacle eastward, before the tent of meeting, at the east, [are] Moses and Aaron, and his sons, keeping the charge of the sanctuary for the charge of the sons of Israel, and the stranger who cometh near is put to death.
3:39 All those numbered of the Levites whom Moses numbered -- Aaron also -- by the command of Jehovah, by their families, every male from a son of a month and upward, [are] two and twenty thousand.
3:40 And Jehovah saith unto Moses, `Number every first-born male of the sons of Israel from a son of a month and upward, and take up the number of their names;
3:41 and thou hast taken the Levites for Me (I [am] Jehovah), instead of every first-born among the sons of Israel, and the cattle of the Levites instead of every firstling among the cattle of the sons of Israel.'
3:42 And Moses numbereth, as Jehovah hath commanded him, all the first-born among the sons of Israel.
3:43 And all the first-born -- male -- by the number of names, from a son of a month and upward, of their numbered ones, are two and twenty thousand two hundred and seventy and three.
3:44 And Jehovah speaketh unto Moses, saying,
3:45 `Take the Levites instead of every first-born among the sons of Israel, and the cattle of the Levites instead of their cattle; and the Levites have been Mine; I [am] Jehovah.
3:46 `And [from] those ransomed of the two hundred and seventy and three (who are more than the Levites) of the first-born of the sons of Israel,
3:47 thou hast even taken five shekels a-piece by the poll -- by the shekel of the sanctuary thou takest; twenty gerahs the shekel [is];
3:48 and thou hast given the money to Aaron, and to his sons, whereby those over and above are ransomed.'
3:49 And Moses taketh the ransom money from those over and above those ransomed by the Levites;
3:50 from the first-born of the sons of Israel he hath taken the money, a thousand and three hundred and sixty and five -- by the shekel of the sanctuary;

3:51 and Moses giveth the money of those ransomed to Aaron, and to his sons, according to the command of Jehovah, as Jehovah hath commanded Moses.
4:1 And Jehovah speaketh unto Moses, and unto Aaron, saying,
4:2 `Take up the sum of the sons of Kohath from the midst of the sons of Levi, by their families, by the house of their fathers;
4:3 from a son of thirty years and upward, even till a son of fifty years, every one going in to the host, to do work in the tent of meeting.
4:4 `This [is] the service of the sons of Kohath in the tent of meeting, the holy of holies:
4:5 that Aaron and his sons have come in, in the journeying of the camp, and have taken down the vail of the hanging, and have covered with it the ark of the testimony;
4:6 and have put on it a covering of badger skin, and have spread a garment completely of blue above, and have placed its staves.
4:7 `And on the table of the presence they spread a garment of blue, and have put on it the dishes, and the spoons, and the bowls, and the cups of the libation, and the bread of continuity is on it,
4:8 and they have spread over them a garment of scarlet, and have covered it with a covering of badger skin, and have placed its staves,
4:9 and have taken a garment of blue, and have covered the candlestick of the lamp, and its lights, and its snuffers, and its snuff-dishes, and all its oil vessels wherewith they minister to it;
4:10 and they have put it and all its vessels unto a covering of badger skin, and have put [it] on the bar.
4:11 `And on the golden altar they spread a garment of blue, and have covered it with a covering of badger skin, and have placed its staves;
4:12 and have taken all the vessels of ministry wherewith they minister in the sanctuary, and have put [them] unto a garment of blue, and have covered them with a covering of badger skin, and have put [them] on the bar,
4:13 and have removed the ashes of the altar, and have spread over it a garment of purple;
4:14 and have put on it all its vessels wherewith they minister about it, the censers, the hooks, and the shovels, and the bowls, all the vessels of the altar, and have spread on it a covering of badger skin, and have placed its staves:
4:15 `And Aaron hath finished -- his sons also -- covering the sanctuary, and all the vessels of the sanctuary, in the journeying of the camp, and afterwards do the sons of Kohath come in to bear [it], and they do not come unto the holy thing, that they have died; these [things are] the burden of the sons of Kohath in the tent of meeting.
4:16 `And the oversight of Eleazar, son of Aaron the priest, [is] the oil of the lamp, and the spice-

perfume, and the present of continuity, and the anointing oil, the oversight of all the tabernacle, and of all that [is] in it, in the sanctuary, and in its vessels.'
4:17 And Jehovah speaketh unto Moses and unto Aaron, saying,
4:18 `Ye do not cut off the tribe of the families of the Kohathite from the midst of the Levites;
4:19 but this do to them, and they have lived, and do not die in their drawing nigh the holy of holies: -- Aaron and his sons go in, and have set them, each man to his service, and unto his burden,
4:20 and they go not in to see when the holy thing is swallowed, that they have died.'
4:21 And Jehovah speaketh unto Moses, saying,
4:22 `Take up the sum of the sons of Gershon also by the house of their fathers, by their families;
4:23 from a son of thirty years and upward, till a son of fifty years thou dost number them, every one who is going in to serve the host, to do the service in the tent of meeting.
4:24 `This [is] the service of the families of the Gershonite, to serve -- and for burden,
4:25 and they have borne the curtains of the tabernacle, and the tent of meeting, its covering, and the covering of the badger [skin] which [is] on it above, and the vail at the opening of the tent of meeting,
4:26 and the hangings of the court, and the vail at the opening of the gate of the court which [is] by the tabernacle, and by the altar round about, and their cords, and all the vessels of their service, and all that is made for them -- and they have served.
4:27 `By the command of Aaron and his sons is all the service of the sons of the Gershonite in all their burden, and in all their service; and ye have laid a charge on them concerning the charge of all their burden.
4:28 This [is] the service of the families of the sons of the Gershonite in the tent of meeting; and their charge [is] under the hand of Ithamar son of Aaron the priest.
4:29 `The sons of Merari, by their families, by the house of their fathers, thou dost number them;
4:30 from a son of thirty years and upward even unto a son of fifty years thou dost number them, every one who is going in to the host, to do the service of the tent of meeting.
4:31 `And this [is] the charge of their burden, of all their service in the tent of meeting; the boards of the tabernacle, and its bars, and its pillars, and its sockets,
4:32 and the pillars of the court round about, and their sockets, and their pins, and their cords, of all their vessels, and of all their service; and by name ye do number the vessels of the charge of their burden.
4:33 `This [is] the service of the families of the sons of Merari, for all their service, in the tent of meeting, by the hand of Ithamar son of Aaron the priest.'
4:34 And Moses numbereth -- Aaron also, and the princes of the company -- the sons of the

Kohathite, by their families, and by the house of their fathers,
4:35 from a son of thirty years and upward even unto a son of fifty years, every one who is going in to the host, for service in the tent of meeting,
4:36 and their numbered ones, by their families, are two thousand seven hundred and fifty.
4:37 These [are] those numbered of the families of the Kohathite, every one who is serving in the tent of meeting, whom Moses and Aaron numbered, by the command of Jehovah, by the hand of Moses.
4:38 And those numbered of the sons of Gershon, by their families, and by the house of their fathers,
4:39 from a son of thirty years and upward even unto a son of fifty years, every one who is going in to the host, for service in the tent of meeting,
4:40 even their numbered ones, by their families, by the house of their fathers, are two thousand and six hundred and thirty.
4:41 These [are] those numbered of the families of the sons of Gershon, every one who is serving in the tent of meeting, whom Moses and Aaron numbered by the command of Jehovah.
4:42 And those numbered of the families of the sons of Merari, by their families, by the house of their fathers,
4:43 from a son of thirty years and upward even unto a son of fifty years, every one who is going in to the host, for service in the tent of meeting,
4:44 even their numbered ones, by their families, are three thousand and two hundred.
4:45 These [are] those numbered of the families of the sons of Merari, whom Moses and Aaron numbered, by the command of Jehovah, by the hand of Moses.
4:46 All those numbered, whom Moses numbered -- Aaron also, and the princes of Israel -- of the Levites, by their families, and by the house of their fathers,
4:47 from a son of thirty years and upward even unto a son of fifty years, every one who is going in to do the work of the service, even the service of burden in the tent of meeting,
4:48 even their numbered ones are eight thousand and five hundred and eighty;
4:49 by the command of Jehovah hath [one] numbered them, by the hand of Moses, each man by his service, and by his burden, with his numbered ones, as Jehovah hath commanded Moses.
5:1 And Jehovah speaketh unto Moses, saying,
5:2 `Command the sons of Israel, and they send out of the camp every leper, and every one with an issue, and every one defiled by a body;
5:3 from male unto female ye do send out; unto the outside of the camp ye do send them; and they defile not their camps in the midst of which I do tabernacle.'

5:4 And the sons of Israel do so, and they send them out unto the outside of the camp; as Jehovah hath spoken unto Moses so have the sons of Israel done.
5:5 And Jehovah speaketh unto Moses, saying,
5:6 `Speak unto the sons of Israel, Man or woman, when they do any of the sins of man, by committing a trespass against Jehovah, and that person [is] guilty,
5:7 and they have confessed their sin which they have done, then he hath restored his guilt in its principal, and its fifth is adding to it, and hath given [it] to him in reference to whom he hath been guilty.
5:8 `And if the man have no redeemer to restore the guilt to, the guilt which is restored [is] Jehovah's, the priest's, apart from the ram of the atonements, whereby he maketh atonement for him.
5:9 `And every heave-offering of all the holy things of the sons of Israel, which they bring near to the priest, becometh his;
5:10 and any man's hallowed things become his; that which any man giveth to the priest becometh his.'
5:11 And Jehovah speaketh unto Moses, saying,
5:12 `Speak unto the sons of Israel, and thou hast said unto them, When any man's wife turneth aside, and hath committed against him a trespass,
5:13 and a man hath lain with her [with] the seed of copulation, and it hath been hid from the eyes of her husband, and concealed, and she hath been defiled, and there is no witness against her, and she hath not been caught,
5:14 and a spirit of jealousy hath passed over him, and he hath been jealous of his wife, and she hath been defiled; -- or, a spirit of jealousy hath passed over him, and he hath been jealous of his wife, and she hath not been defiled --
5:15 `Then hath the man brought in his wife unto the priest, and he hath brought in her offering for her, a tenth of the ephah of barley meal, he doth not pour on it oil, nor doth he put on it frankincense, for it [is] a present of jealousy, a present of memorial, causing remembrance of iniquity.
5:16 `And the priest hath brought her near, and hath caused her to stand before Jehovah,
5:17 and the priest hath taken holy water in an earthen vessel, and of the dust which is on the floor of the tabernacle doth the priest take, and hath put [it] into the water,
5:18 and the priest hath caused the woman to stand before Jehovah, and hath uncovered the woman's head, and hath given into her hands the present of the memorial, it [is] a present of jealousy, and in the hand of the priest are the bitter waters which cause the curse.

5:19 `And the priest hath caused her to swear, and hath said unto the woman, If no man hath lain with thee, and if thou hast not turned aside [to] uncleanness under thy husband, be free from these bitter waters which cause the curse;
5:20 and thou, if thou hast turned aside under thy husband, and if thou hast been defiled, and any man doth give his copulation to thee besides thy husband --
5:21 (then the priest hath caused the woman to swear with an oath of execration, and the priest hath said to the woman) -- Jehovah doth give thee for an execration, and for a curse, in the midst of thy people, in Jehovah's giving thy thigh to fall, and thy belly to swell,
5:22 and these waters which cause the curse have gone into thy bowels, to cause the belly to swell, and the thigh to fall; and the woman hath said, Amen, Amen.
5:23 `And the priest hath written these execrations in a book, and hath blotted [them] out with the bitter waters,
5:24 and hath caused the woman to drink the bitter waters which cause the curse, and the waters which cause the curse have entered into her for bitter things.
5:25 `And the priest hath taken out of the hand of the woman the present of jealousy, and hath waved the present before Jehovah, and hath brought it near unto the altar;
5:26 and the priest hath taken a handful of the present, its memorial, and hath made perfume on the altar, and afterwards doth cause the woman to drink the water:
5:27 yea, he hath caused her to drink the water, and it hath come to pass, if she hath been defiled, and doth commit a trespass against her husband, that the waters which cause the curse have gone into her for bitter things, and her belly hath swelled, and her thigh hath fallen, and the woman hath become an execration in the midst of her people.
5:28 `And if the woman hath not been defiled, and is clean, then she hath been acquitted, and hath been sown [with] seed.
5:29 `This [is] the law of jealousies, when a wife turneth aside under her husband, and hath been defiled,
5:30 or when a spirit of jealousy passeth over a man, and he hath been jealous of his wife, then he hath caused the woman to stand before Jehovah, and the priest hath done to her all this law,
5:31 and the man hath been acquitted from iniquity, and that woman doth bear her iniquity.'
6:1 And Jehovah speaketh unto Moses, saying,
6:2 `Speak unto the sons of Israel, and thou hast said unto them, When a man or woman doeth singularly, by vowing a vow of a Nazarite, to be separate to Jehovah;
6:3 from wine and strong drink he doth keep separate; vinegar of wine, and vinegar of strong drink he doth not drink, and any juice of grapes he doth not drink, and grapes moist or dry he doth not

eat;
6:4 all days of his separation, of anything which is made of the wine-vine, from kernels even unto husk, he doth not eat.
6:5 `All days of the vow of his separation a razor doth not pass over his head; till the fulness of the days which he doth separate to Jehovah he is holy; grown up hath the upper part of the hair of his head.
6:6 `All days of his keeping separate to Jehovah, near a dead person he doth not go;
6:7 for his father, or for his mother, for his brother, or for his sister -- he is not unclean for them at their death, for the separation of his God [is] on his head;
6:8 all days of his separation he [is] holy to Jehovah.
6:9 `And when the dead dieth beside him in an instant, suddenly, and he hath defiled the head of his separation, then he hath shaved his head in the day of his cleansing; on the seventh day he doth shave it,
6:10 and on the eighth day he bringeth in two turtle-doves or two young pigeons unto the priest, unto the opening of the tent of meeting,
6:11 and the priest hath prepared one for a sin-offering, and one for a burnt-offering, and hath made atonement for him, because of that which he hath sinned by the body, and he hath hallowed his head on that day;
6:12 and he hath separated to Jehovah the days of his separation, and he hath brought in a lamb, a son of a year, for a guilt-offering, and the former days are fallen, for his separation hath been defiled.
6:13 `And this [is] the law of the Nazarite; in the day of the fulness of the days of his separation doth [one] bring him in unto the opening of the tent of meeting,
6:14 and he hath brought near his offering to Jehovah, one he-lamb, a son of a year, a perfect one, for a burnt-offering, and one she-lamb, a daughter of a year, a perfect one, for a sin-offering, and one ram, a perfect one, for peace-offerings,
6:15 and a basket of unleavened things of flour, cakes mixed with oil, and thin cakes of unleavened things anointed with oil, and their present, and their libations.
6:16 `And the priest hath brought [them] near before Jehovah, and hath made his sin-offering and his burnt-offering;
6:17 and the ram he maketh a sacrifice of peace-offerings to Jehovah, besides the basket of unleavened things; and the priest hath made its present and its libation.
6:18 `And the Nazarite hath shaved (at the opening of the tent of meeting) the head of his separation, and hath taken the hair of the head of his separation, and hath put [it] on the fire which

[is] under the sacrifice of the peace-offerings.
6:19 `And the priest hath taken the boiled shoulder from the ram, and one unleavened cake out of the basket, and one thin unleavened cake, and hath put on the palms of the Nazarite after his shaving his separation;
6:20 and the priest hath waved them, a wave-offering before Jehovah; it [is] holy to the priest, besides the breast of the wave-offering, and besides the leg of the heave-offering; and afterwards doth the Nazarite drink wine.
6:21 `This [is] the law of the Nazarite, who voweth his offering to Jehovah for his separation, apart from that which his hand attaineth; according to his vow which he voweth so he doth by the law of his separation.'
6:22 And Jehovah speaketh unto Moses, saying,
6:23 `Speak unto Aaron, and unto his sons, saying, Thus ye do bless the sons of Israel, saying to them,
6:24 `Jehovah bless thee and keep thee;
6:25 `Jehovah cause His face to shine upon thee, and favour thee;
6:26 `Jehovah lift up His countenance upon thee, and appoint for thee -- peace.
6:27 `And they have put My name upon the sons of Israel, and I -- I do bless them.'
7:1 And it cometh to pass on the day of Moses' finishing setting up the tabernacle, that he anointeth it, and sanctifieth it, and all its vessels, and the altar, and all its vessels, and he anointeth them, and sanctifieth them,
7:2 and the princes of Israel (heads of the house of their fathers, they [are] princes of the tribes, they who are standing over those numbered) bring near,
7:3 yea, they bring their offering before Jehovah, six waggons covered, and twelve oxen -- a waggon for two of the princes, and an ox for one -- and they bring them near before the tabernacle.
7:4 And Jehovah speaketh unto Moses, saying,
7:5 `Receive from them, and they have been to do the service of the tent of meeting, and thou hast given them unto the Levites, each according to his service.'
7:6 And Moses taketh the waggons and the oxen, and giveth them unto the Levites.
7:7 The two of the waggons and the four of the oxen he hath given to the sons of Gershon, according to their service,
7:8 and the four of the waggons and the eight of the oxen he hath given to the sons of Merari, according to their service, by the hand of Ithamar son of Aaron the priest;
7:9 and to the sons of Kohath he hath not given, for the service of the sanctuary [is] on them: on the shoulder they bear.

7:10 And the princes bring near the dedication of the altar in the day of its being anointed; yea, the princes bring near their offering before the altar.
7:11 And Jehovah saith unto Moses, `One prince a day -- one prince a day -- do they bring near their offering for the dedication of the altar.'
7:12 And he who is bringing near on the first day his offering is Nahshon son of Amminadab, of the tribe of Judah.
7:13 And his offering [is] one silver dish, its weight a hundred and thirty [shekels]; one silver bowl of seventy shekels, by the shekel of the sanctuary; both of them full of flour mixed with oil, for a present;
7:14 one golden spoon of ten [shekels], full of perfume;
7:15 one bullock, a son of the herd, one ram, one lamb, a son of a year, for a burnt-offering;
7:16 one kid of the goats for a sin-offering;
7:17 and for a sacrifice of the peace-offerings two oxen, five rams, five he-goats, five lambs, sons of a year; this [is] the offering of Nahshon son of Amminadab.
7:18 On the second day hath Nethaneel son of Zuar, prince of Issachar, brought near.
7:19 He hath brought near his offering, one silver dish, its weight a hundred and thirty [shekels]; one silver bowl of seventy shekels, by the shekel of the sanctuary, both of them full of flour mixed with oil, for a present;
7:20 one golden spoon of ten [shekels], full of perfume;
7:21 one bullock, a son of the herd, one ram, one lamb, a son of a year, for a burnt-offering;
7:22 one kid of the goats for a sin-offering;
7:23 and for a sacrifice of the peace-offerings two oxen, five rams, five he-goats, five lambs, sons of a year; this [is] the offering of Nethaneel son of Zuar.
7:24 On the third day, the prince of the sons of Zebulun, Eliab son of Helon; --
7:25 his offering [is] one silver dish, its weight a hundred and thirty [shekels]; one silver bowl of seventy shekels, by the shekel of the sanctuary, both of them full of flour mixed with oil, for a present;
7:26 one golden spoon of ten [shekels], full of perfume;
7:27 one bullock, a son of the herd, one ram, one lamb, a son of a year, for a burnt-offering;
7:28 one kid of the goats for a sin-offering;
7:29 and for a sacrifice of the peace-offerings two oxen, five rams, five he-goats, five lambs, sons of a year; this [is] the offering of Eliab son of Helon.
7:30 On the fourth day, Elizur, son of Shedeur, prince of the sons of Reuben; --
7:31 his offering is one silver dish, its weight a hundred and thirty [shekels]; one silver bowl of

seventy shekels, by the shekel of the sanctuary, both of them full of flour mixed with oil, for a present;
7:32 one golden spoon of ten [shekels], full of perfume;
7:33 one bullock, a son of the herd, one ram, one lamb, a son of a year, for a burnt-offering;
7:34 one kid of the goats for a sin-offering;
7:35 and for a sacrifice of the peace-offerings two oxen, five rams, five he-goats, five lambs, sons of a year; this [is] the offering of Elizur son of Shedeur.
7:36 On the fifth day, the prince of the sons of Simeon, Shelumiel son of Zurishaddai; --
7:37 his offering [is] one silver dish, its weight a hundred and thirty [shekels]; one silver bowl of seventy shekels, by the shekel of the sanctuary, both of them full of flour mixed with oil, for a present;
7:38 one golden spoon of ten [shekels], full of perfume;
7:39 one bullock, a son of the herd, one ram, one lamb, a son of a year, for a burnt-offering;
7:40 one kid of the goats for a sin-offering;
7:41 and for a sacrifice of the peace-offerings two oxen, five rams, five he-goats, five lambs, sons of a year; this [is] the offering of Shelumiel son of Zurishaddai.
7:42 On the sixth day, the prince of the sons of Gad, Eliasaph son of Deuel; --
7:43 his offering [is] one silver dish, its weight a hundred and thirty [shekels]; one silver bowl of seventy shekels, by the shekel of the sanctuary, both of them full of flour mixed with oil, for a present;
7:44 one golden spoon of ten [shekels], full of perfume;
7:45 one bullock, a son of the herd, one ram, one lamb, a son of a year, for a burnt-offering;
7:46 one kid of the goats for a sin-offering;
7:47 and for a sacrifice of the peace-offerings two oxen, five rams, five he-goats, five lambs, sons of a year; this [is] the offering of Eliasaph son of Deuel.
7:48 On the seventh day, the prince of the sons of Ephraim, Elishama son of Ammihud; --
7:49 his offering [is] one silver dish, its weight a hundred and thirty [shekels]; one silver bowl of seventy shekels, by the shekel of the sanctuary, both of them full of flour mixed with oil, for a present;
7:50 one golden spoon of ten [shekels], full of perfume;
7:51 one bullock, a son of the herd, one ram, one lamb, a son of a year, for a burnt-offering;
7:52 one kid of the goats for a sin-offering;
7:53 and for a sacrifice of the peace-offerings two oxen, five rams, five he-goats, five lambs, sons of a year; this [is] the offering of Elishama son of Ammihud.

7:54 On the eighth day, the prince of the sons of Manasseh, Gamaliel son of Pedahzur; --
7:55 his offering [is] one silver dish, its weight a hundred and thirty [shekels]; one silver bowl of seventy shekels, by the shekel of the sanctuary, both of them full of flour mixed with oil, for a present;
7:56 one golden spoon of ten [shekels], full of perfume;
7:57 one bullock, a son of the herd, one ram, one lamb, a son of a year, for a burnt-offering;
7:58 one kid of the goats for a sin-offering;
7:59 and for a sacrifice of the peace-offerings two oxen, five rams, five he-goats, five lambs, sons of a year; this [is] the offering of Gamaliel son of Pedahzur.
7:60 On the ninth day, the prince of the sons of Benjamin, Abidan son of Gideoni; --
7:61 his offering [is] one silver dish, its weight a hundred and thirty [shekels]; one silver bowl of seventy shekels, by the shekel of the sanctuary, both of them full of flour mixed with oil, for a present;
7:62 one golden spoon of ten [shekels], full of perfume;
7:63 one bullock, a son of the herd, one ram, one lamb, a son of a year, for a burnt-offering;
7:64 one kid of the goats for a sin-offering:
7:65 and for a sacrifice of the peace-offerings two oxen, five rams, five he-goats, five lambs, sons of a year; this [is] the offering of Abidan son of Gideoni.
7:66 On the tenth day, the prince of the sons of Dan, Ahiezer son of Ammishaddai; --
7:67 his offering [is] one silver dish, its weight a hundred and thirty [shekels]; one silver bowl of seventy shekels, by the shekel of the sanctuary, both of them full of flour mixed with oil, for a present;
7:68 one golden spoon of ten [shekels], full of perfume;
7:69 one bullock, a son of the herd, one ram, one lamb, a son of a year, for a burnt-offering;
7:70 one kid of the goats for a sin-offering;
7:71 and for a sacrifice of the peace-offerings two oxen, five rams, five he-goats, five lambs, sons of a year; this [is] the offering of Ahiezer son of Ammishaddai.
7:72 On the eleventh day, the prince of the sons of Asher, Pagiel son of Ocran; --
7:73 his offering [is] one silver dish, its weight a hundred and thirty [shekels]; one silver bowl of seventy shekels, by the shekel of the sanctuary, both of them full of flour mixed with oil, for a present;
7:74 one golden spoon of ten [shekels], full of perfume;
7:75 one bullock, a son of the herd, one ram, one lamb, a son of a year, for a burnt-offering;
7:76 one kid of the goats for a sin-offering;

7:77 and for a sacrifice of the peace-offerings two oxen, five rams, five he-goats, five lambs, sons of a year; this [is] the offering of Pagiel son of Ocran.
7:78 On the twelfth day, the prince of the sons of Naphtali, Ahira son of Enan; --
7:79 his offering [is] one silver dish, its weight a hundred and thirty [shekels]; one silver bowl of seventy shekels, by the shekel of the sanctuary, both of them full of flour mixed with oil, for a present;
7:80 one golden spoon of ten [shekels], full of perfume;
7:81 one bullock, a son of the herd, one ram, one lamb, a son of a year, for a burnt-offering;
7:82 one kid of the goats for a sin-offering;
7:83 and for a sacrifice of the peace-offerings two oxen, five rams, five he-goats, five lambs, sons of a year; this [is] the offering of Ahira son of Enan.
7:84 This [is] the dedication of the altar, in the day of its being anointed, by the princes of Israel: twelve silver dishes, twelve silver bowls, twelve golden spoons;
7:85 a hundred and thirty [shekels] each silver dish, and each bowl seventy; all the silver of the vessels [is] two thousand and four hundred [shekels], by the shekel of the sanctuary.
7:86 Golden spoons [are] twelve, full of perfume; ten [shekels] each spoon, by the shekel of the sanctuary; all the gold of the spoons [is] a hundred and twenty [shekels];
7:87 all the oxen for burnt-offering [are] twelve bullocks, rams twelve, lambs, sons of a year twelve, and their present; and kids of the goats twelve, for sin-offering;
7:88 and all the oxen for the sacrifice of the peace-offerings [are] twenty and four bullocks, rams sixty, he-goats sixty, lambs, sons of a year, sixty; this is the dedication of the altar, in the day of its being anointed.
7:89 And in the going in of Moses unto the tent of meeting to speak with Him -- he doth even hear the voice speaking unto him from off the mercy-seat which [is] upon the ark of the testimony, from between the two cherubs; and He speaketh unto him.
8:1 And Jehovah speaketh unto Moses, saying,
8:2 `Speak unto Aaron, and thou hast said unto him, In thy causing the lights to go up, over-against the face of the candlestick do the seven lights give light.'
8:3 And Aaron doth so; over-against the face of the candlestick he hath caused its lights to go up, as Jehovah hath commanded Moses.
8:4 And this [is] the work of the candlestick: beaten work of gold; unto its thigh, unto its flower it [is] beaten work; as the appearance which Jehovah shewed Moses, so he hath made the candlestick.
8:5 And Jehovah speaketh unto Moses, saying,
8:6 `Take the Levites from the midst of the sons of Israel, and thou hast cleansed them.

8:7 `And thus thou dost to them to cleanse them: sprinkle upon them waters of atonement, and they have caused a razor to pass over all their flesh, and have washed their garments, and cleansed themselves,
8:8 and have taken a bullock, a son of the herd, and its present, flour mixed with oil, -- and a second bullock a son of the herd thou dost take for a sin-offering,
8:9 and thou hast brought near the Levites before the tent of meeting, and thou hast assembled the whole company of the sons of Israel,
8:10 and thou hast brought near the Levites before Jehovah, and the sons of Israel have laid their hands on the Levites,
8:11 and Aaron hath waved the Levites -- a wave-offering before Jehovah, from the sons of Israel, and they have been -- for doing the service of Jehovah.
8:12 `And the Levites lay their hands on the head of the bullocks, and make thou the one a sin-offering, and the one a burnt-offering to Jehovah, to atone for the Levites,
8:13 and thou hast caused the Levites to stand before Aaron, and before his sons, and hast waved them -- a wave-offering to Jehovah;
8:14 and thou hast separated the Levites from the midst of the sons of Israel, and the Levites have become Mine;
8:15 and afterwards do the Levites come in to serve the tent of meeting, and thou hast cleansed them, and hast waved them -- a wave-offering.
8:16 `For they are certainly given to Me out of the midst of the sons of Israel, instead of him who openeth any womb -- the first-born of all -- from the sons of Israel I have taken them to Myself;
8:17 for Mine [is] every first-born among the sons of Israel, among man and among beast; in the day of my smiting every first-born in the land of Egypt I sanctified them for Myself;
8:18 and I take the Levites instead of every first-born among the sons of Israel:
8:19 `And I give the Levites gifts to Aaron and to his sons, from the midst of the sons of Israel, to do the service of the sons of Israel in the tent of meeting, and to make atonement for the sons of Israel, and there is no plague among the sons of Israel in the sons of Israel's drawing nigh unto the sanctuary.'
8:20 And Moses doth -- Aaron also, and all the company of the sons of Israel -- to the Levites according to all that Jehovah hath commanded Moses concerning the Levites; so have the sons of Israel done to them.
8:21 And the Levites cleanse themselves, and wash their garments, and Aaron waveth them a wave-offering before Jehovah, and Aaron maketh atonement for them to cleanse them,
8:22 and afterwards have the Levites gone in to do their service in the tent of meeting, before

Aaron and before his sons; as Jehovah hath commanded Moses concerning the Levites, so they have done to them.
8:23 And Jehovah speaketh unto Moses, saying,
8:24 `This [is] that which [is] the Levites': from a son of five and twenty years and upward he doth go in to serve the host in the service of the tent of meeting,
8:25 and from a son of fifty years he doth return from the host of the service, and doth not serve any more,
8:26 and he hath ministered with his brethren in the tent of meeting, to keep the charge, and doth not do service; thus thou dost to the Levites concerning their charge.'
9:1 And Jehovah speaketh unto Moses, in the wilderness of Sinai, in the second year of their going out of the land of Egypt, in the first month, saying,
9:2 `Also, the sons of Israel prepare the passover in its appointed season;
9:3 in the fourteenth day of this month between the evenings ye prepare it in its appointed season; according to all its statutes, and according to all its ordinances ye prepare it.'
9:4 And Moses speaketh unto the sons of Israel to prepare the passover,
9:5 and they prepare the passover in the first [month], on the fourteenth day of the month, between the evenings, in the wilderness of Sinai; according to all that Jehovah hath commanded Moses, so have the sons of Israel done.
9:6 And there are men who have been defiled by the body of a man, and they have not been able to prepare the passover on that day, and they come near before Moses, and before Aaron, on that day,
9:7 and those men say unto him, `We are defiled by the body of a man; why are we withheld so as not to bring near the offering of Jehovah in its appointed season, in the midst of the sons of Israel?'
9:8 And Moses saith unto them, `Stand ye, and I hear what Jehovah hath commanded concerning you.'
9:9 And Jehovah speaketh unto Moses, saying,
9:10 `Speak unto the sons of Israel, saying, Though any man is unclean by a body or in a distant journey (of you or of your generations), yet he hath prepared a passover to Jehovah;
9:11 in the second month, on the fourteenth day, between the evenings they prepare it; with unleavened and bitter things they eat it;
9:12 they do not leave of till morning; and a bone they do not break in it: according to all the statute of the passover they prepare it.
9:13 `And the man who is clean, and hath not been on a journey, and hath ceased to prepare the passover, even that person hath been cut off from his people; because the offering of Jehovah he

hath not brought near, in its appointed season, that man doth bear his sin.
9:14 `And when a sojourner sojourneth with you, then he hath prepared a passover to Jehovah, according to the statute of the passover, and according to its ordinance, so he doth; one statute is to you, even to a sojourner, and to a native of the land.'
9:15 And in the day of the raising up of the tabernacle hath the cloud covered the tabernacle, even the tent of the testimony; and in the evening there is on the tabernacle as an appearance of fire till morning;
9:16 so it is continually; the cloud covereth it, also the appearance of fire by night.
9:17 And according to the going up of the cloud from off the tent and afterwards do the sons of Israel journey; and in the place where the cloud doth tabernacle, there do the sons of Israel encamp;
9:18 by the command of Jehovah the sons of Israel journey, and by the command of Jehovah they encamp; all the days that the cloud doth tabernacle over the tabernacle they encamp.
9:19 And in the cloud prolonging itself over the tabernacle many days, then have the sons of Israel kept the charge of Jehovah, and journey not,
9:20 and so when the cloud is a number of days over the tabernacle; by the command of Jehovah they encamp, and by the command of Jehovah they journey.
9:21 And so when the cloud is from evening till morning, when the cloud hath gone up in the morning, then they have journeyed; whether by day or by night, when the cloud hath gone up, then they have journeyed.
9:22 Whether two days, or a month, or days, in the cloud prolonging itself over the tabernacle, to tabernacle over it, the sons of Israel encamp, and journey not; and in its being lifted up they journey;
9:23 by the command of Jehovah they encamp, and by the command of Jehovah they journey; the charge of Jehovah they have kept, by the command of Jehovah in the hand of Moses.
10:1 And Jehovah speaketh unto Moses, saying,
10:2 `Make to thee two trumpets of silver; beaten work thou dost make them, and they have been to thee for the convocation of the company, and for the journeying of the camps;
10:3 and they have blown with them, and all the company have met together unto thee, unto the opening of the tent of meeting.
10:4 And if with one they blow, then have the princes, heads of the thousands of Israel, met together unto thee;
10:5 `And ye have blown -- a shout, and the camps which are encamping eastward have journeyed.

10:6 `And ye have blown -- a second shout, and the camps which are encamping southward have journeyed; a shout they blow for their journeys.
10:7 `And in the assembling of the assembly ye blow, and do not shout;
10:8 and sons of Aaron, the priests, blow with the trumpets; and they have been to you for a statute age-during to your generations.
10:9 `And when ye go into battle in your land against the adversary who is distressing you, then ye have shouted with the trumpets, and ye have been remembered before Jehovah your God, and ye have been saved from your enemies.
10:10 `And in the day of your gladness, and in your appointed seasons, and in the beginnings of your months, ye have blown also with the trumpets over your burnt-offerings, and over the sacrifices of your peace-offerings, and they have been to you for a memorial before your God; I, Jehovah, [am] your God.'
10:11 And it cometh to pass -- in the second year, in the second month, in the twentieth of the month -- the cloud hath gone up from off the tabernacle of the testimony,
10:12 and the sons of Israel journey in their journeyings from the wilderness of Sinai, and the cloud doth tabernacle in the wilderness of Paran;
10:13 and they journey at first, by the command of Jehovah, in the hand of Moses.
10:14 And the standard of the camp of the sons of Judah journeyeth in the first [place], by their hosts, and over its host [is] Nahshon son of Amminadab.
10:15 And over the host of the tribe of the sons of Issachar [is] Nathaneel son of Zuar.
10:16 And over the host of the tribe of the sons of Zebulun [is] Eliab son of Helon;
10:17 And the tabernacle hath been taken down, and the sons of Gershon and the sons of Merari have journeyed, bearing the tabernacle.
10:18 And the standard of the camp of Reuben hath journeyed, by their hosts, and over its host [is] Elizur son of Shedeur.
10:19 And over the host of the tribe of the sons of Simeon [is] Shelumiel son of Zurishaddai.
10:20 And over the host of the tribe of the sons of Gad [is] Eliasaph son of Deuel;
10:21 And the Kohathites have journeyed, bearing the tabernacle, and the [others] have raised up the tabernacle until their coming in.
10:22 And the standard of the camp of the sons of Ephraim hath journeyed, by their hosts, and over its host [is] Elishama son of Ammihud.
10:23 And over the host of the tribe of the sons of Manasseh [is] Gamalial son of Pedahzur.
10:24 And over the host of the tribe of the sons of Benjamin [is] Abidan son of Gideoni.
10:25 And the standard of the camp of the sons of Dan hath journeyed (rearward to all the camps),

by their hosts, and over its host [is] Ahiezer son of Ammishaddai.
10:26 And over the host of the tribe of the sons of Asher [is] Pagiel son of Ocran.
10:27 And over the host of the tribe of the sons of Naphtali [is] Ahira son of Enan.
10:28 These [are] journeyings of the sons of Israel by their hosts -- and they journey.
10:29 And Moses saith to Hobab son of Raguel the Midianite, father-in-law of Moses, `We are journeying unto the place of which Jehovah hath said, I give it to you; go with us, and we have done good to thee; for Jehovah hath spoken good concerning Israel.'
10:30 And he saith unto him, `I do not go; but unto my land and unto my kindred do I go.'
10:31 And he saith, `I pray thee, forsake us not, because thou hast known our encamping in the wilderness, and thou hast been to us for eyes;
10:32 and it hath come to pass when thou goest with us, yea, it hath come to pass -- that good which Jehovah doth kindly with us -- it we have done kindly to thee.'
10:33 And they journey from the mount of Jehovah a journey of three days; and the ark of the covenant of Jehovah is journeying before them the journey of three days, to spy out for them a resting-place;
10:34 and the cloud of Jehovah [is] on them by day, in their journeying from the camp.
10:35 And it cometh to pass in the journeying of the ark, that Moses saith, `Rise, O Jehovah, and Thine enemies are scattered, and those hating Thee flee from Thy presence.'
10:36 And in its resting he saith, `Return, O Jehovah, [to] the myriads, the thousands of Israel.'
11:1 And the people is evil, as those sighing habitually in the ears of Jehovah, and Jehovah heareth, and His anger burneth, and the fire of Jehovah burneth among them, and consumeth in the extremity of the camp.
11:2 And the people cry unto Moses, and Moses prayeth unto Jehovah, and the fire is quenched;
11:3 and he calleth the name of that place Taberah, for the fire of Jehovah hath `burned' among them.
11:4 And the rabble who [are] in its midst have lusted greatly, and the sons of Israel also turn back and weep, and say, `Who doth give us flesh?
11:5 We have remembered the fish which we do eat in Egypt for nought, the cucumbers, and the melons, and the leeks, and the onions, and the garlick;
11:6 and now our soul [is] dry, there is not anything, save the manna, before our eyes.'
11:7 And the manna is as coriander seed, and its aspect as the aspect of bdolach;
11:8 the people have turned aside and gathered [it], and ground [it] with millstones, or beat [it] in a mortar, and boiled [it] in a pan, and made it cakes, and its taste hath been as the taste of the moisture of oil.

11:9 And in the descending of the dew on the camp by night, the manna descendeth upon it.
11:10 And Moses heareth the people weeping by its families, each at the opening of his tent, and the anger of Jehovah burneth exceedingly, and in the eyes of Moses [it is] evil.
11:11 And Moses saith unto Jehovah, `Why hast Thou done evil to Thy servant? and why have I not found grace in Thine eyes -- to put the burden of all this people upon me?
11:12 I -- have I conceived all this people? I -- have I begotten it, that Thou sayest unto me, Carry it in thy bosom as the nursing father beareth the suckling, unto the ground which Thou hast sworn to its fathers?
11:13 Whence have I flesh to give to all this people? for they weep unto me, saying, Give to us flesh, and we eat.
11:14 I am not able -- I alone -- to bear all this people, for [it is] too heavy for me;
11:15 and if thus Thou art doing to me -- slay me, I pray Thee; slay, if I have found grace in thine eyes, and let me not look on mine affliction.'
11:16 And Jehovah saith unto Moses, `Gather to Me seventy men of the elders of Israel, whom thou hast known that they are elders of the people, and its authorities; and thou hast taken them unto the tent of meeting, and they have stationed themselves there with thee,
11:17 and I have come down and spoken with thee there, and have kept back of the Spirit which [is] upon thee, and have put on them, and they have borne with thee some of the burden of the people, and thou dost not bear [it] thyself alone.
11:18 `And unto the people thou dost say, Sanctify yourselves for to-morrow, and ye have eaten flesh (for ye have wept in the ears of Jehovah, saying, Who doth give us flesh? for we [had] good in Egypt) -- and Jehovah hath given to you flesh, and ye have eaten.
11:19 Ye do not eat one day, nor two days, nor five days, nor ten days, nor twenty days; --
11:20 unto a month of days, till that it come out from your nostrils, and it hath become to you an abomination; because that ye have loathed Jehovah, who [is] in your midst, and weep before Him, saying, Why is this? -- we have come out of Egypt!'
11:21 And Moses saith, `Six hundred thousand footmen [are] the people in whose midst I [am]; and Thou, Thou hast said, Flesh I give to them, and they have eaten, a month of days!
11:22 Is flock and herd slaughtered for them, that one hath found for them? -- are all the fishes of the sea gathered for them -- that one hath found for them?'
11:23 And Jehovah saith unto Moses, `Is the hand of Jehovah become short? now thou dost see whether My word meeteth thee or not.'
11:24 And Moses goeth out, and speaketh unto the people the words of Jehovah, and gathereth seventy men of the elders of the people, and causeth them to stand round about the tent,

11:25 and Jehovah cometh down in the cloud, and speaketh unto him, and keepeth back of the Spirit which [is] on him, and putteth on the seventy men of the elders; and it cometh to pass at the resting of the Spirit on them, that they prophesy, and do not cease.
11:26 And two of the men are left in the camp, the name of the one [is] Eldad, and the name of the second Medad, and the spirit resteth upon them, (and they are among those written, and have not gone out to the tent), and they prophesy in the camp;
11:27 and the young man runneth, and declareth to Moses, and saith, `Eldad and Medad are prophesying in the camp.'
11:28 And Joshua son of Nun, minister of Moses, [one] of his young men, answereth and saith, `My lord Moses, restrain them.'
11:29 And Moses saith to him, `Art thou zealous for me? O that all Jehovah's people were prophets! that Jehovah would put His Spirit upon them!'
11:30 And Moses is gathered unto the camp, he and the elders of Israel.
11:31 And a spirit hath journeyed from Jehovah, and cutteth off quails from the sea, and leaveth by the camp, as a day's journey here, and as a day's journey there, round about the camp, and about two cubits, on the face of the land.
11:32 And the people rise all that day, and all the night, and all the day after, and gather the quails -- he who hath least hath gathered ten homers -- and they spread them out for themselves round about the camp.
11:33 The flesh is yet between their teeth -- it is not yet cut off -- and the anger of Jehovah hath burned among the people, and Jehovah smiteth among the people -- a very great smiting;
11:34 and [one] calleth the name of that place Kibroth-Hattaavah, for there they have buried the people who lust.
11:35 From Kibroth-Hattaavah have the people journeyed to Hazeroth, and they are in Hazeroth.
12:1 And Miriam speaketh -- Aaron also -- against Moses concerning the circumstance of the Cushite woman whom he had taken: for a Cushite woman he had taken;
12:2 and they say, `Only by Moses hath Jehovah spoken? also by us hath he not spoken?' and Jehovah heareth.
12:3 And the man Moses [is] very humble, more than any of the men who [are] on the face of the ground.
12:4 And Jehovah saith suddenly unto Moses, and unto Aaron, and unto Miriam, `Come out ye three unto the tent of meeting;' and they three come out.
12:5 And Jehovah cometh down in the pillar of the cloud, and standeth at the opening of the tent, and calleth Aaron and Miriam, and they come out both of them.

12:6 And He saith, `Hear, I pray you, My words: If your prophet is of Jehovah -- in an appearance
unto him I make Myself known; in a dream I speak with him;
12:7 not so My servant Moses; in all My house he [is] stedfast;
12:8 mouth unto mouth I speak with him, and [by] an appearance, and not in riddles; and the form
of Jehovah he beholdeth attentively; and wherefore have ye not been afraid to speak against My
servant -- against Moses?'
12:9 And the anger of Jehovah burneth against them, and He goeth on,
12:10 and the cloud hath turned aside from off the tent, and lo, Miriam [is] leprous as snow; and
Aaron turneth unto Miriam, and lo, leprous!
12:11 And Aaron saith unto Moses, `O, my lord, I pray thee, lay not upon us sin [in] which we have
been foolish, and [in] which we have sinned;
12:12 let her not, I pray thee, be as [one] dead, when in his coming out from the womb of his
mother -- the half of his flesh is consumed.'
12:13 And Moses crieth unto Jehovah, saying, `O God, I pray Thee, give, I pray Thee, healing to
her.'
12:14 And Jehovah saith unto Moses, `And her father had but spat in her face -- is she not
ashamed seven days? she is shut out seven days at the outside of the camp, and afterwards she is
gathered.'
12:15 And Miriam is shut out at the outside of the camp seven days, and the people hath not
journeyed till Miriam is gathered;
12:16 and afterwards have the people journeyed from Hazeroth, and they encamp in the
wilderness of Paran.
13:1 And Jehovah speaketh unto Moses, saying,
13:2 `Send for thee men, and they spy the land of Canaan, which I am giving to the sons of Israel;
one man, one man for the tribe of his fathers ye do send, every one a prince among them.'
13:3 And Moses sendeth them from the wilderness of Paran by the command of Jehovah; all of
them [are] men, heads of the sons of Israel they are,
13:4 and these their names: For the tribe of Reuben, Shammua son of Zaccur.
13:5 For the tribe of Simeon, Shaphat son of Hori.
13:6 For the tribe of Judah, Caleb son of Jephunneh.
13:7 For the tribe of Issachar, Igal son of Joseph.
13:8 For the tribe of Ephraim, Oshea, son of Nun.
13:9 For the tribe of Benjamin, Palti son of Raphu.
13:10 For the tribe of Zebulun, Gaddiel son of Sodi.

13:11 For the tribe of Joseph, (for the tribe of Manasseh,) Gaddi son of Susi.
13:12 For the tribe of Dan, Ammiel son of Gemalli.
13:13 For the tribe of Asher, Sethur son of Michael.
13:14 For the tribe of Naphtali, Nahbi son of Vopshi.
13:15 For the tribe of Gad, Geuel son of Machi.
13:16 These [are] the names of the men whom Moses hath sent to spy the land; and Moses calleth Hoshea son of Nun, Jehoshua.
13:17 And Moses sendeth them to spy the land of Canaan, and saith unto them, `Go ye up this [way] into the south, and ye have gone up the mountain,
13:18 and have seen the land what it [is], and the people which is dwelling on it, whether it [is] strong or feeble; whether it [is] few or many;
13:19 and what the land [is] in which it is dwelling, whether it [is] good or bad; and what [are] the cities in which it is dwelling, whether in camps or in fortresses;
13:20 And what the land [is], whether it [is] fat or lean; whether there is wood in it or not; and ye have strengthened yourselves, and have taken of the fruit of the land;' and the days [are] days of the first-fruits of grapes.
13:21 And they go up and spy the land, from the wilderness of Zin unto Rehob at the going in to Hamath;
13:22 and they go up by the south, and come in unto Hebron, and there [are] Ahiman, Sheshai, and Talmai, children of Anak (and Hebron was built seven years before Zoan in Egypt),
13:23 and they come in unto the brook of Eshcol, and cut down thence a branch and one cluster of grapes, and they bear it on a staff by two, also [some] of the pomegranates, and of the figs.
13:24 That place hath [one] called Brook of Eshcol, because of the cluster which the sons of Israel cut from thence.
13:25 And they turn back from spying the land at the end of forty days.
13:26 And they go and come in unto Moses, and unto Aaron, and unto all the company of the sons of Israel, unto the wilderness of Paran, to Kadesh; and they bring them and all the company back word, and shew them the fruit of the land.
13:27 And they recount to him, and say, `We came in unto the land whither thou hast sent us, and also it [is] flowing with milk and honey -- and this [is] its fruit;
13:28 only, surely the people which is dwelling in the land [is] strong; and the cities are fenced, very great; and also children of Anak we have seen there.
13:29 Amalek is dwelling in the land of the south, and the Hittite, and the Jebusite, and the Amorite is dwelling in the hill country, and the Canaanite is dwelling by the sea, and by the side of the

Jordan.'
13:30 And Caleb stilleth the people concerning Moses, and saith, `Let us certainly go up -- and we have possessed it; for we are thoroughly able for it.'
13:31 And the men who have gone up with him said, `We are not able to go up against the people, for it [is] stronger than we;'
13:32 and they bring out an evil account of the land which they have spied unto the sons of Israel, saying, `The land into which we passed over to spy it, is a land eating up its inhabitants; and all the people whom we saw in its midst [are] men of stature;
13:33 and there we saw the Nephilim, sons of Anak, of the Nephilim; and we are in our own eyes as grasshoppers; and so we were in their eyes.'
14:1 And all the company lifteth up and give forth their voice, and the people weep during that night;
14:2 and all the sons of Israel murmur against Moses, and against Aaron, and all the company say unto them, `O that we had died in the land of Egypt, or in this wilderness, O that we had died!
14:3 and why is Jehovah bringing us in unto this land to fall by the sword? our wives and our infants are become a prey; is it not good for us to turn back to Egypt?'
14:4 And they say one unto another, `Let us appoint a head, and turn back to Egypt.'
14:5 And Moses falleth -- Aaron also -- on their faces, before all the assembly of the company of the sons of Israel.
14:6 And Joshua son of Nun, and Caleb son of Jephunneh, of those spying the land, have rent their garments,
14:7 and they speak unto all the company of the sons of Israel, saying, `The land into which we have passed over to spy it, [is] a very very good land;
14:8 if Jehovah hath delighted in us, then He hath brought us in unto this land, and hath given it to us, a land which is flowing with milk and honey;
14:9 only, against Jehovah rebel not ye: and ye, fear not ye the people of the land, for our bread they [are]; their defence hath turned aside from off them, and Jehovah [is] with us; fear them not.'
14:10 And all the company say to stone them with stones, and the honour of Jehovah hath appeared in the tent of meeting unto all the sons of Israel.
14:11 And Jehovah saith unto Moses, `Until when doth this people despise Me? and until when do they not believe in Me, for all the signs which I have done in its midst?
14:12 I smite it with pestilence, and dispossess it, and make thee become a nation greater and mightier than it.'
14:13 And Moses saith unto Jehovah, `Then have the Egyptians heard! for Thou hast brought up

with Thy power this people out of their midst,
14:14 and they have said [it] unto the inhabitant of this land, they have heard that Thou, Jehovah,
[art] in the midst of this people, that eye to eye Thou art seen -- O Jehovah, and Thy cloud is
standing over them, -- and in a pillar of cloud Thou art going before them by day, and in a pillar of
fire by night.
14:15 `And Thou hast put to death this people as one man, and the nations who have heard Thy
fame have spoken, saying,
14:16 From Jehovah's want of ability to bring in this people unto the land which He hath sworn to
them -- He doth slaughter them in the wilderness.
14:17 `And now, let, I pray Thee, the power of my Lord be great, as Thou hast spoken, saying:
14:18 Jehovah [is] slow to anger, and of great kindness; bearing away iniquity and transgression,
and not entirely acquitting, charging iniquity of fathers on sons, on a third [generation], and on a
fourth; --
14:19 forgive, I pray Thee, the iniquity of this people, according to the greatness of Thy kindness,
and as Thou hast borne with this people from Egypt, even until now.'
14:20 And Jehovah saith, `I have forgiven, according to thy word;
14:21 and yet, I live -- and it is filled -- the whole earth -- [with] the honour of Jehovah;
14:22 for all the men who are seeing My honour, and My signs, which I have done in Egypt, and in
the wilderness, and try Me these ten times, and have not hearkened to My voice --
14:23 they see not the land which I have sworn to their fathers, yea, none of those despising Me
see it;
14:24 and My servant Caleb, because there hath been another spirit with him, and he is fully after
Me -- I have brought him in unto the land whither he hath entered, and his seed doth possess it.
14:25 `And the Amalekite and the Canaanite are dwelling in the valley; to-morrow turn ye and
journey for yourselves into the wilderness -- the way of the Red Sea.'
14:26 And Jehovah speaketh unto Moses, and unto Aaron, saying,
14:27 `Until when hath this evil company that which they are murmuring against Me? the
murmurings of the sons of Israel, which they are murmuring against Me, I have heard;
14:28 say unto them, I live -- an affirmation of Jehovah -- if, as ye have spoken in Mine ears -- so I
do not to you;
14:29 in this wilderness do your carcases fall, even all your numbered ones, to all your number,
from a son of twenty years and upward, who have murmured against Me;
14:30 ye -- ye come not in unto the land which I have lifted up My hand to cause you to tabernacle
in it, except Caleb son of Jephunneh, and Joshua son of Nun.

14:31 `As to your infants -- of whom ye have said, A spoil they are become -- I have even brought them in, and they have known the land which ye have kicked against;
14:32 as to you -- your carcases do fall in this wilderness,
14:33 and your sons are evil in the wilderness forty years, and have borne your whoredoms till your carcases are consumed in the wilderness;
14:34 by the number of the days [in] which ye spied the land, forty days, -- a day for a year, a day for a year -- ye do bear your iniquities, forty years, and ye have known my breaking off;
14:35 I [am] Jehovah, I have spoken; if I do not this to all this evil company who are meeting against me; -- in this wilderness they are consumed, and there they die.'
14:36 And the men whom Moses hath sent to spy the land, and they turn back and cause all the company to murmur against him, by bringing out an evil account concerning the land,
14:37 even the men bringing out an evil account of the land die by the plague before Jehovah;
14:38 and Joshua son of Nun, and Caleb son of Jephunneh, have lived of those men who go to spy out the land.
14:39 And Moses speaketh these words unto all the sons of Israel, and the people mourn exceedingly,
14:40 and they rise early in the morning, and go up unto the top of the mountain, saying, `Here we [are], and we have come up unto the place which Jehovah hath spoken of, for we have sinned.'
14:41 And Moses saith, `Why [is] this? -- ye are transgressing the command of Jehovah, and it doth not prosper;
14:42 go not up, for Jehovah is not in your midst, and ye are not smitten before your enemies;
14:43 for the Amalekite and the Canaanite [are] there before you, and ye have fallen by the sword, because that ye have turned back from after Jehovah, and Jehovah is not with you.'
14:44 And they presume to go up unto the top of the mountain, and the ark of the covenant of Jehovah and Moses have not departed out of the midst of the camp.
14:45 And the Amalekite and the Canaanite who are dwelling in that mountain come down and smite them, and beat them down -- unto Hormah.
15:1 And Jehovah speaketh unto Moses, saying,
15:2 `Speak unto the sons of Israel, and thou hast said unto them, When ye come in unto the land of your dwellings, which I am giving to you,
15:3 then ye have prepared a fire-offering to Jehovah, a burnt-offering, or a sacrifice, at separating a vow or free-will-offering, or in your appointed things, to make a sweet fragrance to Jehovah, out of the herd, or out of the flock.
15:4 `And he who is bringing near his offering to Jehovah hath brought near a present of flour, a

tenth deal, mixed with a fourth of the hin of oil;
15:5 and wine for a libation, a fourth of the hin thou dost prepare for the burnt-offering or for a sacrifice, for the one lamb;
15:6 or for a ram thou dost prepare a present of flour, two-tenth deals, mixed with oil, a third of the hin;
15:7 and wine for a libation, a third part of the hin, thou dost bring near -- a sweet fragrance to Jehovah.
15:8 `And when thou makest a son of the herd a burnt-offering or a sacrifice, at separating a vow or peace-offerings to Jehovah,
15:9 then he hath brought near for the son of the herd a present of flour, three-tenth deals, mixed with oil, a half of the hin;
15:10 and wine thou bringest near for a libation, a half of the hin -- a fire-offering of sweet fragrance to Jehovah;
15:11 thus it is done for the one ox, or for the one ram, or for a lamb of the sheep or of the goats.
15:12 `According to the number that ye prepare, so ye do to each, according to their number;
15:13 every native doth thus with these, at bringing near a fire-offering of sweet fragrance to Jehovah;
15:14 and when a sojourner sojourneth with you, or whoso [is] in your midst to your generations, and he hath made a fire-offering of sweet fragrance to Jehovah, as ye do so he doth.
15:15 `One statute is for you of the congregation and for the sojourner who is sojourning, a statute age-during to your generations: as ye [are] so is the sojourner before Jehovah;
15:16 one law and one ordinance is to you and to the sojourner who is sojourning with you.'
15:17 And Jehovah speaketh unto Moses, saying,
15:18 `Speak unto the sons of Israel, and thou hast said unto them, In your coming in unto the land whither I am bringing you in,
15:19 then it hath been, in your eating of the bread of the land, ye heave up a heave-offering to Jehovah;
15:20 the beginning of your dough a cake ye heave up -- a heave-offering; as the heave-offering of a threshing-floor, so ye do heave it.
15:21 Of the beginning of your dough ye do give to Jehovah a heave-offering -- to your generations.
15:22 `And when ye err, and do not all these commands which Jehovah hath spoken unto Moses,
15:23 the whole that Jehovah hath charged upon you by the hand of Moses, from the day that Jehovah hath commanded, and henceforth, to your generations,

15:24 then it hath been, if from the eyes of the company it hath been done in ignorance, that all the company have prepared one bullock, a son of the herd, for a burnt-offering, for sweet fragrance to Jehovah, and its present, and its libation, according to the ordinance, and one kid of the goats for a sin-offering.
15:25 `And the priest hath made atonement for all the company of the sons of Israel, and it hath been forgiven them, for it [is] ignorance, and they -- they have brought in their offering, a fire-offering to Jehovah, even their sin-offering before Jehovah for their ignorance;
15:26 and it hath been forgiven to all the company of the sons of Israel, and to the sojourner who is sojourning in their midst; for to all the company [it is done] in ignorance.
15:27 `And if one person sin in ignorance, then he hath brought near a she-goat, daughter of a year, for a sin-offering;
15:28 and the priest hath made atonement for the person who is erring, in his sinning in ignorance before Jehovah, by making atonement for him, and it hath been forgiven him;
15:29 for the native among the sons of Israel, and for the sojourner who is sojourning in their midst -- one law is to you, for him who is doing [anything] through ignorance.
15:30 `And the person who doth [aught] with a high hand -- of the native or of the sojourner -- Jehovah he is reviling, and that person hath been cut off from the midst of his people;
15:31 because the word of Jehovah he despised, and His command hath broken -- that person is certainly cut off; his iniquity [is] on him.'
15:32 And the sons of Israel are in the wilderness, and they find a man gathering wood on the sabbath-day,
15:33 and those finding him gathering wood bring him near unto Moses, and unto Aaron, and unto all the company,
15:34 and they place him in ward, for it [is] not explained what is [to be] done to him.
15:35 And Jehovah saith unto Moses, `The man is certainly put to death, all the company stoning him with stones, at the outside of the camp.'
15:36 And all the company bring him out unto the outside of the camp, and stone him with stones, and he dieth, as Jehovah hath commanded Moses.
15:37 And Jehovah speaketh unto Moses, saying,
15:38 `Speak unto the sons of Israel, and thou hast said unto them, and they have made for themselves fringes on the skirts of their garments, to their generations, and they have put on the fringe of the skirt a ribbon of blue,
15:39 and it hath been to you for a fringe, and ye have seen it, and have remembered all the commands of Jehovah, and have done them, and ye search not after your heart, and after your

eyes, after which ye are going a-whoring;
15:40 so that ye remember and have done all My commands, and ye have been holy to your God;
15:41 I [am] Jehovah your God, who hath brought you out from the land of Egypt to become your God; I, Jehovah, [am] your God.'
16:1 And Korah, son of Izhar, son of Kohath, son of Levi, taketh both Dathan and Abiram sons of Eliab, and On son of Peleth, sons of Reuben,
16:2 and they rise up before Moses, with men of the sons of Israel, two hundred and fifty, princes of the company, called of the convention, men of name,
16:3 and they are assembled against Moses and against Aaron, and say unto them, `Enough of you! for all the company -- all of them [are] holy, and in their midst [is] Jehovah; and wherefore do ye lift yourselves up above the assembly of Jehovah?'
16:4 And Moses heareth, and falleth on his face,
16:5 and he speaketh unto Korah, and unto all his company, saying, `Morning! -- and Jehovah is knowing those who are his, and him who is holy, and hath brought near unto Him; even him whom He doth fix on He bringeth near unto Him.
16:6 This do: take to yourselves censers, Korah, and all his company,
16:7 and put in them fire, and put on them perfume, before Jehovah to-morrow, and it hath been, the man whom Jehovah chooseth, he [is] the holy one; -- enough of you, sons of Levi.'
16:8 And Moses saith unto Korah, `Hear ye, I pray you, sons of Levi;
16:9 is it little to you that the God of Israel hath separated you from the company of Israel to bring you near unto Himself, to do the service of the tabernacle of Jehovah, and to stand before the company to serve them? --
16:10 yea, He doth bring thee near, and all thy brethren the sons of Levi with thee -- and ye have sought also the priesthood!
16:11 Therefore, thou and all thy company who are met [are] against Jehovah; and Aaron, what [is] he, that ye murmur against him?'
16:12 And Moses sendeth to call for Dathan and for Abiram sons of Eliab, and they say, `We do not come up;
16:13 is it little that thou hast brought us up out of a land flowing with milk and honey to put us to death in a wilderness that thou also certainly makest thyself prince over us?
16:14 Yea, unto a land flowing with milk and honey thou hast not brought us in, nor dost thou give to us an inheritance of field and vineyard; the eyes of these men dost thou pick out? we do not come up.'
16:15 And it is very displeasing to Moses, and he saith unto Jehovah, `Turn not Thou unto their

present; not one ass from them have I taken, nor have I afflicted one of them.'
16:16 And Moses saith unto Korah, `Thou and all thy company, be ye before Jehovah, thou, and they, and Aaron, to-morrow;
16:17 and take ye each his censer, and ye have put on them perfume, and brought near before Jehovah, each his censer, two hundred and fifty censers; and thou and Aaron, each his censer.'
16:18 And they take each his censer, and put on them fire, and lay on them perfume, and they stand at the opening of the tent of meeting, with Moses and Aaron.
16:19 And Korah assembleth against them all the company unto the opening of the tent of meeting, and the honour of Jehovah is seen by all the company.
16:20 And Jehovah speaketh unto Moses and unto Aaron, saying,
16:21 `Be ye separated from the midst of this company, and I consume them in a moment;'
16:22 and they fall on their faces, and say, `God, God of the spirits of all flesh -- the one man sinneth, and against all the company Thou art wroth!'
16:23 And Jehovah speaketh unto Moses, saying,
16:24 `Speak unto the company, saying, Go ye up from round about the tabernacle of Korah, Dathan, and Abiram.'
16:25 And Moses riseth, and goeth unto Dathan and Abiram, and the elders of Israel go after him,
16:26 and he speaketh unto the company, saying, `Turn aside, I pray you, from the tents of these wicked men, and come not against anything that they have, lest ye be consumed in all their sins.'
16:27 And they go up from the tabernacle of Korah, Dathan and Abiram, from round about, and Dathan, and Abiram have come out, standing at the opening of their tents, and their wives, and their sons, and their infants.
16:28 And Moses saith, `By this ye do know that Jehovah hath sent me to do all these works, that [they are] not from my own heart;
16:29 if according to the death of all men these die -- or the charge of all men is charged upon them -- Jehovah hath not sent me;
16:30 and if a strange thing Jehovah do, and the ground hath opened her mouth and swallowed them, and all that they have, and they have gone down alive to Sheol -- then ye have known that these men have despised Jehovah.'
16:31 And it cometh to pass at his finishing speaking all these words, that the ground which [is] under them cleaveth,
16:32 and the earth openeth her mouth, and swalloweth them, and their houses, and all the men who [are] for Korah, and all the goods,
16:33 and they go down, they, and all that they have, alive to Sheol, and the earth closeth over

them, and they perish from the midst of the assembly;
16:34 and all Israel who [are] round about them have fled at their voice, for they said, `Lest the earth swallow us;'
16:35 and fire hath come out from Jehovah, and consumeth the two hundred and fifty men bringing near the perfume.
16:36 And Jehovah speaketh unto Moses, saying,
16:37 `Say unto Eleazar son of Aaron the priest, and he lifteth up the censers from the midst of the burning, and the fire scatter thou yonder, for they have been hallowed,
16:38 [even] the censers of these sinners against their own souls; and they have made them spread-out plates, a covering for the altar, for they have brought them near before Jehovah, and they are hallowed; and they are become a sign to the sons of Israel.'
16:39 And Eleazar the priest taketh the brazen censers which they who are burnt had brought near, and they spread them out, a covering for the altar --
16:40 a memorial to the sons of Israel, so that a stranger who is not of the seed of Aaron doth not draw near to make a perfume before Jehovah, and is not as Korah, and as his company, -- as Jehovah hath spoken by the hand of Moses to him.
16:41 And all the company of the sons of Israel murmur, on the morrow, against Moses and against Aaron, saying, `Ye -- ye have put to death the people of Jehovah.'
16:42 And it cometh to pass, in the company being assembled against Moses and against Aaron, that they turn towards the tent of meeting, and lo, the cloud hath covered it, and the honour of Jehovah is seen;
16:43 and Moses cometh -- Aaron also -- unto the front of the tent of meeting.
16:44 And Jehovah speaketh unto Moses, saying,
16:45 `Get you up from the midst of this company, and I consume them in a moment;' and they fall on their faces,
16:46 and Moses saith unto Aaron, `Take the censer, and put on it fire from off the altar, and place perfume, and go, hasten unto the company, and make atonement for them, for the wrath hath gone out from the presence of Jehovah -- the plague hath begun.'
16:47 And Aaron taketh as Moses hath spoken, and runneth unto the midst of the assembly, and lo, the plague hath begun among the people; and he giveth the perfume, and maketh atonement for the people,
16:48 and standeth between the dead and the living, and the plague is restrained;
16:49 and those who die by the plague are fourteen thousand and seven hundred, apart from those who die for the matter of Korah;

16:50 and Aaron turneth back unto Moses, unto the opening of the tent of meeting, and the plague hath been restrained.
17:1 And Jehovah speaketh unto Moses, saying,
17:2 `Speak unto the sons of Israel, and take from them each a rod, for a father's house, from all their princes, for the house of their fathers, twelve rods; the name of each thou dost write on his rod,
17:3 and Aaron's name thou dost write on the tribe of Levi; for one rod [is] for the head of their fathers' house:
17:4 and thou hast placed them in the tent of meeting, before the testimony, where I meet with you.
17:5 `And it hath come to pass, the man's rod on whom I fix doth flourish, and I have caused to cease from off me the murmurings of the sons of Israel, which they are murmuring against you.'
17:6 And Moses speaketh unto the sons of Israel, and all their princes give unto him one rod for a prince, one rod for a prince, for their fathers' house, twelve rods, and the rod of Aaron [is] in the midst of their rods;
17:7 and Moses placeth the rods before Jehovah, in the tent of the testimony.
17:8 And it cometh to pass, on the morrow, that Moses goeth in unto the tent of the testimony, and lo, the rod of Aaron hath flourished for the house of Levi, and is bringing out flourishing, and doth blossom blossoms, and doth produce almonds;
17:9 and Moses bringeth out all the rods from before Jehovah, unto all the sons of Israel, and they look, and take each his rod.
17:10 And Jehovah saith unto Moses, `Put back the rod of Aaron, before the testimony, for a charge, for a sign to the sons of rebellion, and thou dost remove their murmurings from off me, and they do not die;'
17:11 and Moses doth as Jehovah hath commanded him; so he hath done.
17:12 And the sons of Israel speak unto Moses, saying, `Lo, we have expired; we have perished; we have all of us perished;
17:13 any who is at all drawing near unto the tabernacle of Jehovah dieth; have we not been consumed -- to expire?'
18:1 And Jehovah saith unto Aaron, `Thou, and thy sons, and the house of thy father with thee, do bear the iniquity of the sanctuary; and thou, and thy sons with thee, do bear the iniquity of your priesthood;
18:2 and also thy brethren, the tribe of Levi, the tribe of thy father, bring near with thee, and they are joined unto thee, and serve thee, even thou and thy sons with thee, before the tent of the testimony.

18:3 `And they have kept thy charge, and the charge of all the tent; only, unto the vessels of the sanctuary and unto the altar they do not come near, and they die not, either they or you;
18:4 and they have been joined unto thee, and have kept the charge of the tent of meeting, for all the service of the tent; and a stranger doth not come near unto you;
18:5 and ye have kept the charge of the sanctuary, and the charge of the altar, and there is no more wrath against the sons of Israel.
18:6 `And I, lo, I have taken your brethren the Levites from the midst of the sons of Israel; to you a gift they are given by Jehovah, to do the service of the tent of meeting;
18:7 and thou, and thy sons with thee, do keep your priesthood, for everything of the altar, and within the vail, and ye have served; a service of gift I make your priesthood; and the stranger who is coming near is put to death.'
18:8 And Jehovah speaketh unto Aaron: `And I, lo, I have given to thee the charge of My heave-offerings, of all the hallowed things of the sons of Israel -- to thee I have given them for the anointing, and to thy sons, by a statute age-during.
18:9 This is thine of the most holy things, from the fire: all their offering, to all their present, and to all their sin-offering, and to all their guilt-offering, which they give back to Me, is most holy to thee, and to thy sons;
18:10 in the holy of holies thou dost eat it; every male doth eat it; holy it is to thee.
18:11 `And this [is] thine: the heave-offering of their gift, to all the wave-offerings of the sons of Israel, to thee I have given them, and to thy sons, and to thy daughters with thee, by a statute age-during; every clean one in thy house doth eat it;
18:12 all the best of the oil, and all the best of the new wine, and wheat -- their first-[fruits] which they give to Jehovah -- to thee I have given them.
18:13 `The first-fruits of all that [is] in their land, which they bring in to Jehovah, are thine; every clean one in thy house doth eat it;
18:14 every devoted thing in Israel is thine,
18:15 every one opening a womb of all flesh which they bring near to Jehovah, among man and among beast, is thine; only, thou dost certainly ransom the first-born of man, and the firstling of the unclean beast thou dost ransom.
18:16 `And their ransomed ones from a son of a month, thou dost ransom with thy valuation, of silver, five shekels, by the shekel of the sanctuary, twenty gerahs it [is].
18:17 `Only, the firstling of a cow, or the firstling of a sheep, or the firstling of a goat, thou dost not ransom, holy they [are]: their blood thou dost sprinkle on the altar, and of their fat thou makest perfume, a fire-offering of sweet fragrance to Jehovah,

18:18 and their flesh is thine, as the breast of the wave-offering, and as the right leg, it is thine;
18:19 all the heave-offerings of the holy things which the sons of Israel lift up to Jehovah I have given to thee and to thy sons, and to thy daughters with thee, by a statute age-during, a covenant of salt, age-during it [is] before Jehovah, to thee and to thy seed with thee.'
18:20 And Jehovah saith unto Aaron, `In their land thou dost not inherit, and a portion thou hast not in their midst: I [am] thy portion, and thine inheritance in the midst of the sons of Israel;
18:21 and to the sons of Levi, lo, I have given all the tenth in Israel for inheritance in exchange for their service which they are serving -- the service of the tent of meeting.
18:22 `And the sons of Israel come no more near unto the tent of meeting, to bear sin, to die,
18:23 and the Levites have done the service of the tent of meeting, and they -- they bear their iniquity; a statute age-during to your generations, that in the midst of the sons of Israel they have no inheritance;
18:24 but the tithe of the sons of Israel which they lift up to Jehovah, a heave-offering, I have given to the Levites for inheritance; therefore I have said of them, In the midst of the sons of Israel they have no inheritance.'
18:25 And Jehovah speaketh unto Moses, saying,
18:26 `And unto the Levites thou dost speak; and thou hast said unto them, When ye take from the sons of Israel the tithe which I have given to you from them, for your inheritance, then ye have lifted up from it the heave-offering of Jehovah, a tithe of the tithe;
18:27 and your heave-offering hath been reckoned to you as corn from the threshing-floor, and as fulness from the wine-vat;
18:28 so ye do lift up -- ye also -- the heave-offering of Jehovah from all your tithes which ye receive from the sons of Israel; and ye have given from it the heave-offering of Jehovah to Aaron the priest;
18:29 out of all your gifts ye do lift up the whole heave-offering of Jehovah; out of all its fat, -- its hallowed part -- out of it.
18:30 `And thou hast said unto them, In your lifting up its fat out of it, then it hath been reckoned to the Levites, as increase of a threshing-floor, and as increase of a wine-vat;
18:31 and ye have eaten it in every place, ye and your households, for it [is] your hire in exchange for your service in the tent of meeting;
18:32 and ye bear no sin for it, in your lifting up its fat out of it, and the holy things of the sons of Israel ye do not pollute, and ye die not.'
19:1 And Jehovah speaketh unto Moses, and unto Aaron, saying,
19:2 `This [is] a statute of the law which Jehovah hath commanded, saying, Speak unto the sons of

Israel, and they bring unto thee a red cow, a perfect one, in which there is no blemish, on which no yoke hath gone up;
19:3 and ye have given it unto Eleazar the priest, and he hath brought it out unto the outside of the camp, and hath slaughtered it before him.
19:4 `And Eleazar the priest hath taken of its blood with his finger, and hath sprinkled over-against the front of the tent of meeting of her blood seven times;
19:5 and [one] hath burnt the cow before his eyes; her skin, and her flesh, and her blood, besides her dung, he doth burn;
19:6 and the priest hath taken cedar wood, and hyssop, and scarlet, and hath cast unto the midst of the burning of the cow;
19:7 and the priest hath washed his garments, and hath bathed his flesh with water, and afterwards doth come in unto the camp, and the priest is unclean till the evening;
19:8 and he who is burning it doth wash his garments with water, and hath bathed his flesh with water, and is unclean till the evening.
19:9 `And a clean man hath gathered the ashes of the cow, and hath placed at the outside of the camp, in a clean place, and it hath become to the company of the sons of Israel a charge for waters of separation -- it [is] a [cleansing];
19:10 and he who is gathering the ashes of the heifer hath washed his garments, and is unclean till the evening; and it hath been to the sons of Israel, and to the sojourner who is sojourning in their midst, for a statute age-during.
19:11 `He who is coming against the dead body of any man -- is unclean seven days;
19:12 he doth cleanse himself for it on the third day, and on the seventh day he is clean; and if he cleanse not himself on the third day, then on the seventh day he is not clean.
19:13 Any one who is coming against the dead, against the body of man who dieth, and cleanseth not himself -- the tabernacle of Jehovah he hath defiled, and that person hath been cut off from Israel, for water of separation is not sprinkled upon him; he is unclean; his uncleanness [is] still upon him.
19:14 `This [is] the law, when a man dieth in a tent: every one who is coming in unto the tent, and all that [is] in the tent, is unclean seven days;
19:15 and every open vessel which hath no covering of thread upon it is unclean.
19:16 `And every one who cometh, on the face of the field, against the pierced of a sword, or against the dead, or against a bone of man, or against a grave, is unclean seven days;
19:17 and they have taken for the unclean person of the ashes of the burning of the [cleansing], and he hath put upon it running water unto a vessel;

19:18 and a clean person hath taken hyssop, and hath dipped [it] in water, and hath sprinkled on the tent, and on all the vessels, and on the persons who have been there, and on him who is coming against a bone, or against one pierced, or against the dead, or against a grave.
19:19 `And the clean hath sprinkled [it] on the unclean on the third day, and on the seventh day, and hath cleansed him on the seventh day, and he hath washed his garments, and hath bathed with water, and hath been clean in the evening.
19:20 `And the man who is unclean, and doth not cleanse himself, even that person hath been cut off from the midst of the assembly; for the sanctuary of Jehovah he hath defiled; water of separation is not sprinkled upon him; he [is] unclean.
19:21 `And it hath been to them for a statute age-during, that he who is sprinkling the water of separation doth wash his garments, and he who is coming against the water of separation is unclean till the evening,
19:22 and all against which the unclean person cometh is unclean, and the person who is coming against [it] is unclean till the evening.'
20:1 And the sons of Israel come in, -- all the company -- to the wilderness of Zin, in the first month, and the people abide in Kadesh, and Miriam dieth there, and is buried there.
20:2 And there hath been no water for the company, and they are assembled against Moses, and against Aaron,
20:3 and the people strive with Moses, and speak, saying, `And oh that we had expired when our brethren expired before Jehovah!
20:4 and why have ye brought in the assembly of Jehovah unto this wilderness to die there, we and our beasts?
20:5 and why hast thou brought us up out of Egypt to bring us in unto this evil place? no place of seed, and fig, and vine, and pomegranate; and water there is none to drink.
20:6 And Moses and Aaron go in from the presence of the assembly unto the opening of the tent of meeting, and fall on their faces, and the honour of Jehovah is seen by them.
20:7 And Jehovah speaketh unto Moses, saying,
20:8 `Take the rod, and assemble the company, thou and Aaron thy brother; and ye have spoken unto the rock before their eyes, and it hath given its water, and thou hast brought out to them water from the rock, and hast watered the company, and their beasts.'
20:9 And Moses taketh the rod from before Jehovah, as He hath commanded him,
20:10 and Moses and Aaron assemble the assembly unto the front of the rock, and he saith to them, `Hear, I pray you, O rebels, from this rock do we bring out to you water?'
20:11 and Moses lifteth up his hand, and smiteth the rock with his rod twice; and much water

cometh out, and the company drink, also their beasts.
20:12 And Jehovah saith unto Moses, and unto Aaron, `Because ye have not believed in Me to sanctify Me before the eyes of the sons of Israel, therefore ye do not bring in this assembly unto the land which I have given to them.'
20:13 These [are] waters of Meribah, because the sons of Israel have `striven' with Jehovah, and He is sanctified upon them.
20:14 And Moses sendeth messengers from Kadesh unto the king of Edom, `Thus said thy brother Israel, Thou -- thou hast known all the travail which hath found us;
20:15 that our fathers go down to Egypt, and we dwell in Egypt many days, and the Egyptians do evil to us and to our fathers;
20:16 and we cry unto Jehovah, and He heareth our voice, and sendeth a messenger, and is bringing us out of Egypt; and lo, we [are] in Kadesh, a city [in] the extremity of thy border.
20:17 Let us pass over, we pray thee, through thy land; we pass not over through a field, or through a vineyard, nor do we drink waters of a well; the way of the king we go, we turn not aside -- right or left -- till that we pass over thy border.'
20:18 And Edom saith unto him, `Thou dost not pass over through me, lest with sword I come out to meet thee.'
20:19 And the sons of Israel say unto him, `In the highway we go, and if of thy waters we drink -- I and my cattle -- then I have given their price; only (it is nothing) on my feet I pass over.'
20:20 And he saith, `Thou dost not pass over;' and Edom cometh out to meet him with much people, and with a strong hand;
20:21 and Edom refuseth to suffer Israel to pass over through his border, and Israel turneth aside from off him.
20:22 And the sons of Israel, the whole company, journey from Kadesh, and come in unto mount Hor,
20:23 and Jehovah speaketh unto Moses and unto Aaron in mount Hor, on the border of the land of Edom, saying,
20:24 `Aaron is gathered unto his people, for he doth not go in unto the land which I have given to the sons of Israel, because that ye provoked My mouth at the waters of Meribah.
20:25 `Take Aaron and Eleazar his son, and cause them to go up mount Hor,
20:26 and strip Aaron of his garments, and thou hast clothed [with] them Eleazar his son, and Aaron is gathered, and doth die there.'
20:27 And Moses doth as Jehovah hath commanded, and they go up unto mount Hor before the eyes of all the company,

20:28 and Moses strippeth Aaron of his garments, and clotheth with them Eleazar his son, and Aaron dieth there on the top of the mount; and Moses cometh down -- Eleazar also -- from the mount,
20:29 and all the company see that Aaron hath expired, and they bewail Aaron thirty days -- all the house of Israel.
21:1 And the Canaanite -- king Arad -- dwelling in the south, heareth that Israel hath come the way of the Atharim, and he fighteth against Israel, and taketh [some] of them captive.
21:2 And Israel voweth a vow to Jehovah, and saith, `If Thou dost certainly give this people into my hand, then I have devoted their cities;'
21:3 and Jehovah hearkeneth to the voice of Israel, and giveth up the Canaanite, and he devoteth them and their cities, and calleth the name of the place Hormah.
21:4 And they journey from mount Hor, the way of the Red Sea, to compass the land of Edom, and the soul of the people is short in the way,
21:5 and the people speak against God, and against Moses, `Why hast thou brought us up out of Egypt to die in a wilderness? for there is no bread, and there is no water, and our soul hath been weary of this light bread.'
21:6 And Jehovah sendeth among the people the burning serpents, and they bite the people, and much people of Israel die;
21:7 and the people come in unto Moses and say, `We have sinned, for we have spoken against Jehovah, and against thee; pray unto Jehovah, and He doth turn aside from us the serpent;' and Moses prayeth in behalf of the people.
21:8 And Jehovah saith unto Moses, `Make for thee a burning [serpent], and set it on an ensign; and it hath been, every one who is bitten and hath seen it -- he hath lived.
21:9 And Moses maketh a serpent of brass, and setteth it on the ensign, and it hath been, if the serpent hath bitten any man, and he hath looked expectingly unto the serpent of brass -- he hath lived.
21:10 And the sons of Israel journey, and encamp in Oboth.
21:11 And they journey from Oboth, and encamp in Ije-Abarim, in the wilderness that [is] on the front of Moab, at the rising of the sun.
21:12 From thence they have journeyed, and encamp in the valley of Zared.
21:13 From thence they have journeyed, and encamp beyond Arnon, which [is] in the wilderness which is coming out of the border of the Amorite, for Arnon [is] the border of Moab, between Moab and the Amorite;
21:14 therefore it is said in a book, `The wars of Jehovah,' -- `Waheb in Suphah, And the brooks of

Arnon;
21:15 And the spring of the brooks, Which turned aside to the dwelling of Ar, And hath leaned to the border of Moab.'
21:16 And from thence [they journeyed] to Beer; it [is] the well [concerning] which Jehovah said to Moses, `Gather the people, and I give to them -- water.'
21:17 Then singeth Israel this song, concerning the well -- they have answered to it:
21:18 `A well -- digged it have princes, Prepared it have nobles of the people, With the lawgiver, with their staves.' And from the wilderness [they journeyed] to Mattanah,
21:19 and from Mattanah to Nahaliel, and from Nahaliel to Bamoth,
21:20 and from Bamoth in the valley which [is] in the field of Moab [to] the top of Pisgah, which hath looked on the front of the wilderness.
21:21 And Israel sendeth messengers unto Sihon king of the Amorite, saying,
21:22 `Let me pass through thy land, we do not turn aside into a field, or into a vineyard, we do not drink waters of a well; in the king's way we go, till that we pass over thy border.'
21:23 And Sihon hath not suffered Israel to pass through his border, and Sihon gathereth all his people, and cometh out to meet Israel into the wilderness, and cometh in to Jahaz, and fighteth against Israel.
21:24 And Israel smiteth him by the mouth of the sword, and possesseth his land from Arnon unto Jabbok -- unto the sons of Ammon; for the border of the sons of Ammon [is] strong.
21:25 And Israel taketh all these cities, and Israel dwelleth in all the cities of the Amorite, in Heshbon, and in all its villages;
21:26 for Heshbon is a city of Sihon king of the Amorite, and he hath fought against the former king of Moab, and taketh all his land out of his hand, unto Arnon;
21:27 therefore those using similes say -- `Enter ye Heshbon, Let the city of Sihon be built and ready,
21:28 For fire hath gone out from Heshbon, A flame from the city of Sihon, It hath consumed Ar of Moab, Owners of the high places of Arnon.
21:29 Wo to thee, O Moab, Thou hast perished, O people of Chemosh, He hath given his sons who escape -- Also his daughters -- Into captivity, to a king of the Amorite -- Sihon!
21:30 And we shoot them, Perished hath Heshbon unto Dibon, And we make desolate unto Nophah, Which [is] unto Medeba.'
21:31 And Israel dwelleth in the land of the Amorite,
21:32 and Moses sendeth to spy out Jaazer, and they capture its villages, and dispossess the Amorite who [is] there,

21:33 and turn and go up the way of Bashan, and Og king of Bashan cometh out to meet them, he and all his people, to battle, [at] Edrei.
21:34 And Jehovah saith unto Moses, `Fear him not, for into thy hand I have given him, and all his people, and his land, and thou hast done to him as thou hast done to Sihon king of the Amorite, who is dwelling in Heshbon.'
21:35 And they smite him, and his sons, and all his people, until he hath not left to him a remnant, and they possess his land.
22:1 And the sons of Israel journey and encamp in the plains of Moab, beyond the Jordan, [by] Jericho.
22:2 And Balak son of Zippor seeth all that Israel hath done to the Amorite,
22:3 and Moab is exceedingly afraid of the presence of the people, for it [is] numerous; and Moab is vexed by the presence of the sons of Israel,
22:4 and Moab saith unto the elders of Midian, `Now doth the assembly lick up all that is round about us, as the ox licketh up the green thing of the field.' And Balak son of Zippor [is] king of Moab at that time,
22:5 and he sendeth messengers unto Balaam son of Beor, to Pethor, which [is] by the River of the land of the sons of his people, to call for him, saying, `Lo, a people hath come out of Egypt; lo, it hath covered the eye of the land, and it is abiding over-against me;
22:6 and now, come, I pray thee, curse for me this people, for it [is] mightier than I; it may be I prevail -- we smite it -- and I cast it out from the land; for I have known -- that which thou blessest is blessed, and that which thou cursest is cursed.'
22:7 And the elders of Moab and the elders of Midian go, and divinations in their hand, and they come in unto Balaam, and speak unto him the words of Balak,
22:8 and he saith unto them, `Lodge here to-night, and I have brought you back word, as Jehovah speaketh unto me;' and the princes of Moab abide with Balaam.
22:9 And God cometh in unto Balaam, and saith, `Who [are] these men with thee?'
22:10 And Balaam saith unto God, `Balak, son of Zippor, king of Moab, hath sent unto me:
22:11 Lo, the people that is coming out from Egypt and covereth the eye of the land, -- now come, pierce it for me; it may be I am able to fight against it, and have cast it out;'
22:12 and God saith unto Balaam, `Thou dost not go with them; thou dost not curse the people; for it [is] blessed.'
22:13 And Balaam riseth in the morning, and saith unto the princes of Balak, `Go unto your land, for Jehovah is refusing to suffer me to go with you;'
22:14 and the princes of Moab rise, and come in unto Balak, and say, `Balaam is refusing to come

with us.'
22:15 And Balak addeth yet to send princes, more numerous and honoured than these,
22:16 and they come in unto Balaam, and say to him, `Thus said Balak son of Zippor, Be not, I pray thee, withheld from coming unto me,
22:17 for very greatly I honour thee, and all that thou sayest unto me I do; and come, I pray thee, pierce for me this people.'
22:18 And Balaam answereth and saith unto the servants of Balak, `If Balak doth give to me the fulness of his house of silver and gold, I am not able to pass over the command of Jehovah my God, to do a little or a great thing;
22:19 and, now, abide, I pray you, in this [place], you also, to-night; and I know what Jehovah is adding to speak with me.'
22:20 And God cometh in unto Balaam, by night, and saith to him, `If to call for thee the men have come, rise, go with them, and only the thing which I speak unto thee -- it thou dost do.'
22:21 And Balaam riseth in the morning, and saddleth his ass, and goeth with the princes of Moab,
22:22 and the anger of God burneth because he is going, and a messenger of Jehovah stationeth himself in the way for an adversary to him, and he is riding on his ass, and two of his servants [are] with him,
22:23 and the ass seeth the messenger of Jehovah standing in the way, and his drawn sword in his hand, and the ass turneth aside out of the way, and goeth into a field, and Balaam smiteth the ass to turn it aside into the way.
22:24 And the messenger of Jehovah standeth in a narrow path of the vineyards -- a wall on this [side] and a wall on that --
22:25 and the ass seeth the messenger of Jehovah, and is pressed unto the wall, and presseth Balaam's foot unto the wall, and he addeth to smite her;
22:26 and the messenger of Jehovah addeth to pass over, and standeth in a strait place where there is no way to turn aside -- right or left --
22:27 and the ass seeth the messenger of Jehovah, and croucheth under Balaam, and the anger of Balaam burneth, and he smiteth the ass with a staff.
22:28 And Jehovah openeth the mouth of the ass, and she saith to Balaam, `What have I done to thee that thou hast smitten me these three times?'
22:29 and Balaam saith to the ass, `Because thou hast rolled thyself against me; oh that there were a sword in my hand, for now I had slain thee;'
22:30 and the ass saith unto Balaam, `Am not I thine ass, upon which thou hast ridden since [I was] thine unto this day? have I at all been accustomed to do to thee thus?' and he saith, `No.'

22:31 And Jehovah uncovereth the eyes of Balaam, and he seeeth the messenger of Jehovah standing in the way, and his drawn sword in his hand, and he boweth and doth obeisance, to his face;
22:32 and the messenger of Jehovah saith unto him, `Wherefore hast thou smitten thine ass these three times? lo, I -- I have come out for an adversary, for [thy] way hath been perverse before me,
22:33 and the ass seeth me, and turneth aside at my presence these three times; unless she had turned aside from my presence, surely now also, thee I had slain, and her kept alive.'
22:34 And Balaam saith unto the messenger of Jehovah, `I have sinned, for I did not know that thou [art] standing to meet me in the way; and now, if evil in thine eyes -- I turn back by myself.'
22:35 And the messenger of Jehovah saith unto Balaam, `Go with the men; and only the word which I speak unto thee -- it thou dost speak;' and Balaam goeth with the princes of Balak.
22:36 And Balak heareth that Balaam hath come, and goeth out to meet him, unto a city of Moab, which [is] on the border of Arnon, which [is] in the extremity of the border;
22:37 and Balak saith unto Balaam, `Did I not diligently sent unto thee to call for thee? why didst thou not come unto me? am I not truly able to honour thee?'
22:38 And Balaam saith unto Balak, `Lo, I have come unto thee; now -- am I at all able to speak anything? the word which God setteth in my mouth -- it I do speak.'
22:39 And Balaam goeth with Balak, and they come to Kirjath-Huzoth,
22:40 and Balak sacrificeth oxen and sheep, and sendeth to Balaam, and to the princes who [are] with him;
22:41 and it cometh to pass in the morning, that Balak taketh Balaam, and causeth him to go up the high places of Baal, and he seeth from thence the extremity of the people.
23:1 And Balaam saith unto Balak, `Build for me in this [place] seven altars, and make ready for me in this [place] seven bullocks and seven rams.'
23:2 And Balak doth as Balaam hath spoken, and Balak -- Balaam also -- offereth a bullock and a ram on the altar,
23:3 and Balaam saith to Balak, `Station thyself by thy burnt-offering and I go on, it may be Jehovah doth come to meet me, and the thing which He sheweth me -- I have declared to thee;' and he goeth [to] a high place.
23:4 And God cometh unto Balaam, and he saith unto Him, `The seven altars I have arranged, and I offer a bullock and a ram on the altar;'
23:5 and Jehovah putteth a word in the mouth of Balaam, and saith, `Turn back unto Balak, and thus thou dost speak.'
23:6 And he turneth back unto him, and lo, he is standing by his burnt-offering, he and all the

princes of Moab.
23:7 And he taketh up his simile, and saith: `From Aram he doth lead me -- Balak king of Moab; From mountains of the east: Come -- curse for me Jacob, And come -- be indignant [with] Israel.
23:8 What -- do I pierce? -- God hath not pierced! And what -- am I indignant? -- Jehovah hath not been indignant!
23:9 For from the top of rocks I see it, And from heights I behold it; Lo a people! alone it doth tabernacle, And among nations doth not reckon itself.
23:10 Who hath counted the dust of Jacob, And the number of the fourth of Israel? Let me die the death of upright ones, And let my last end be like his!'
23:11 And Balak saith unto Balaam, `What hast thou done to me? to pierce mine enemies I have taken thee -- and lo, thou hast certainly blessed;'
23:12 and he answereth and saith, `That which Jehovah doth put in my mouth -- it do I not take heed to speak?'
23:13 And Balak saith unto him, `Come, I pray thee, with me unto another place, whence thou dost see it, only its extremity thou dost see, and all of it thou dost not see, and pierce it for me thence;'
23:14 and he taketh him [to] the field of Zophim, unto the top of Pisgah, and buildeth seven altars, and offereth a bullock and a ram on the altar.
23:15 And he saith unto Balak, `Station thyself here by thy burnt-offering, and I -- I meet [Him] there;'
23:16 and Jehovah cometh unto Balaam, and setteth a word in his mouth, and saith, `Turn back unto Balak, and thus thou dost speak.'
23:17 And he cometh unto him, and lo, he is standing by his burnt-offering, and the princes of Moab with him, and Balak saith to him: `What hath Jehovah spoken?'
23:18 And he taketh up his simile, and saith: `Rise, Balak, and hear; Give ear unto me, son of Zippor!
23:19 God [is] not a man -- and lieth, And a son of man -- and repenteth! Hath He said -- and doth He not do [it]? And spoken -- and doth He not confirm it?
23:20 Lo, to bless I have received: Yea, He blesseth, and I [can]not reverse it.
23:21 He hath not beheld iniquity in Jacob, Nor hath He seen perverseness in Israel; Jehovah his God [is] with him, And a shout of a king [is] in him.
23:22 God is bringing them out from Egypt, As the swiftness of a Reem is to him;
23:23 For no enchantment [is] against Jacob, Nor divination against Israel, At the time it is said of Jacob and Israel, What hath God wrought!
23:24 Lo, the people as a lioness riseth, And as a lion he lifteth himself up, He lieth not down till he

eateth prey, And blood of pierced ones doth drink.'
23:25 And Balak saith unto Balaam, `Neither pierce it at all, nor bless it at all;'
23:26 and Balaam answereth and saith unto Balak, `Have I not spoken unto thee, saying, All that Jehovah speaketh -- it I do?'
23:27 And Balak saith unto Balaam, `Come, I pray thee, I take thee unto another place; it may be it is right in the eyes of God -- to pierce it for me from thence.'
23:28 And Balak taketh Balaam to the top of Peor, which is looking on the front of the wilderness,
23:29 and Balaam saith unto Balak, `Build for me in this [place] seven altars, and make ready for me in this [place] seven bullocks and seven rams;'
23:30 and Balak doth as Balaam said, and he offereth a bullock and a ram on an altar.
24:1 And Balaam seeth that [it is] good in the eyes of Jehovah to bless Israel, and he hath not gone as time by time to meet enchantments, and he setteth towards the wilderness his face;
24:2 and Balaam lifteth up his eyes, and seeth Israel tabernacling, by its tribes, and the Spirit of God is upon him,
24:3 and he taketh up his simile, and saith: `An affirmation of Balaam son of Beor -- And an affirmation of the man whose eyes are shut --
24:4 An affirmation of him who is hearing sayings of God -- Who a vision of the Almighty seeth, Falling -- and eyes uncovered:
24:5 How good have been thy tents, O Jacob, Thy tabernacles, O Israel;
24:6 As valleys they have been stretched out, As gardens by a river; As aloes Jehovah hath planted, As cedars by waters;
24:7 He maketh water flow from his buckets, And his seed [is] in many waters; And higher than Agag [is] his king, And exalted is his kingdom.
24:8 God is bringing him out of Egypt; As the swiftness of a Reem is to him, He eateth up nations his adversaries, And their bones he breaketh, And [with] his arrows he smiteth,
24:9 He hath bent, he hath lain down as a lion, And as a lioness: who doth raise him up? He who is blessing thee [is] blessed, And he who is cursing thee [is] cursed.'
24:10 And the anger of Balak burneth against Balaam, and he striketh his hands; and Balak saith unto Balaam, `To pierce mine enemies I called thee, and lo, thou hast certainly blessed -- these three times;
24:11 and now, flee for thyself unto thy place; I have said, I do greatly honour thee, and lo, Jehovah hath kept thee back from honour.'
24:12 And Balaam saith unto Balak, `Did I not also unto thy messengers whom thou hast sent unto me, speak, saying,

24:13 If Balak doth give to me the fulness of his house of silver and gold, I am not able to pass over the command of Jehovah, to do good or evil of mine own heart -- that which Jehovah speaketh -- it I speak?
24:14 and, now, lo, I am going to my people; come, I counsel thee [concerning] that which this people doth to thy people, in the latter end of the days.'
24:15 And he taketh up his simile, and saith: `An affirmation of Balaam son of Beor -- And an affirmation of the man whose eyes [are] shut --
24:16 An affirmation of him who is hearing sayings of God -- And knowing knowledge of the Most High; A vision of the Almighty he seeth, Falling -- and eyes uncovered:
24:17 I see it, but not now; I behold it, but not near; A star hath proceeded from Jacob, And a sceptre hath risen from Israel, And hath smitten corners of Moab, And hath destroyed all sons of Sheth.
24:18 And Edom hath been a possession, And Seir hath been a possession, [for] its enemies, And Israel is doing valiantly;
24:19 And [one] doth rule out of Jacob, And hath destroyed a remnant from Ar.'
24:20 And he seeth Amalek, and taketh up his simile, and saith: `A beginning of the Goyim [is] Amalek; And his latter end -- for ever he perisheth.'
24:21 And he seeth the Kenite, and taketh up his simile, and saith: `Enduring [is] thy dwelling, And setting in a rock thy nest,
24:22 But the Kenite is for a burning; Till when doth Asshur keep thee captive?'
24:23 And he taketh up his simile, and saith: `Alas! who doth live when God doth this?
24:24 And -- ships [are] from the side of Chittim, And they have humbled Asshur, And they have humbled Eber, And it also for ever is perishing.'
24:25 And Balaam riseth, and goeth, and turneth back to his place, and Balak also hath gone on his way.
25:1 And Israel dwelleth in Shittim, and the people begin to go a-whoring unto daughters of Moab,
25:2 and they call for the people to the sacrifices of their gods, and the people eat, and bow themselves to their gods,
25:3 and Israel is joined to Baal-Peor, and the anger of Jehovah burneth against Israel.
25:4 And Jehovah saith unto Moses, `Take all the chiefs of the people, and hang them before Jehovah -- over-against the sun; and the fierceness of the anger of Jehovah doth turn back from Israel.'
25:5 And Moses saith unto the judges of Israel, `Slay ye each his men who are joined to Baal-Peor.'

25:6 And lo, a man of the sons of Israel hath come, and bringeth in unto his brethren the Midianitess, before the eyes of Moses, and before the eyes of all the company of the sons of Israel, who are weeping at the opening of the tent of meeting;
25:7 and Phinehas, son of Eleazar, son of Aaron, the priest, seeth, and riseth from the midst of the company, and taketh a javelin in his hand,
25:8 and goeth in after the man of Israel unto the hollow place, and pierceth them both, the man of Israel and the woman -- unto her belly, and the plague is restrained from the sons of Israel;
25:9 and the dead by the plague are four and twenty thousand.
25:10 And Jehovah speaketh unto Moses, saying,
25:11 `Phinehas, son of Eleazar, son of Aaron the priest, hath turned back My fury from the sons of Israel, by his being zealous with My zeal in their midst, and I have not consumed the sons of Israel in My zeal.
25:12 `Therefore say, Lo, I am giving to him My covenant of peace,
25:13 and it hath been to him and to his seed after him a covenant of a priesthood age-during, because that he hath been zealous for his God, and doth make atonement for the sons of Israel.'
25:14 And the name of the man of Israel who is smitten, who hath been smitten with the Midianitess, [is] Zimri son of Salu, prince of the house of a father of the Simeonite;
25:15 and the name of the woman who is smitten, the Midianitess, [is] Cozbi daughter of Zur, head of a people -- of the house of a father in Midian [is] he.
25:16 And Jehovah speaketh unto Moses, saying,
25:17 `Distress the Midianites, and ye have smitten them,
25:18 for they are adversaries to you with their frauds, [with] which they have acted fraudulently to you, concerning the matter of Peor, and concerning the matter of Cozbi, daughter of a prince of Midian, their sister, who is smitten in the day of the plague for the matter of Peor.'
26:1 And it cometh to pass, after the plague, that Jehovah speaketh unto Moses, and unto Eleazar son of Aaron the priest, saying,
26:2 `Take up the sum of all the company of the sons of Israel, from a son of twenty years and upward, by the house of their fathers, every one going out to the host in Israel.'
26:3 And Moses speaketh -- Eleazar the priest also -- with them, in the plains of Moab, by Jordan, [near] Jericho, saying,
26:4 `From a son of twenty years and upward,' as Jehovah hath commanded Moses and the sons of Israel who are coming out from the land of Egypt.
26:5 Reuben, first-born of Israel -- sons of Reuben: [of] Hanoch [is] the family of the Hanochite; of Pallu the family of the Palluite;

26:6 of Hezron the family of the Hezronite; of Carmi the family of the Carmite.
26:7 These [are] families of the Reubenite, and their numbered ones are three and forty thousand and seven hundred and thirty.
26:8 And the son of Pallu [is] Eliab;
26:9 and the sons of Eliab [are] Nemuel and Dathan and Abiram; this [is that] Dathan and Abiram, called ones of the company, who have striven against Moses and against Aaron in the company of Korah, in their striving against Jehovah,
26:10 and the earth openeth her mouth, and swalloweth them and Korah, in the death of the company, in the fire consuming the two hundred and fifty men, and they become a sign;
26:11 and the sons of Korah died not.
26:12 Sons of Simeon by their families: of Nemuel [is] the family of the Nemuelite; of Jamin the family of the Jaminite; of Jachin the family of the Jachinite;
26:13 of Zerah the family of the Zarhite; of Shaul the family of the Shaulite.
26:14 These [are] families of the Simeonite, two and twenty thousand and two hundred.
26:15 Sons of Gad by their families: of Zephon [is] the family of the Zephonite; of Haggi the family of the Haggite; of Shuni the family of the Shunite;
26:16 of Ozni the family of the Oznite; of Eri the family of the Erite:
26:17 of Arod the family of the Arodite; of Areli the family of the Arelite.
26:18 These [are] families of the sons of Gad, by their numbered ones, forty thousand and five hundred.
26:19 Sons of Judah [are] Er and Onan; and Er dieth -- Onan also -- in the land of Canaan.
26:20 And sons of Judah, by their families, are: of Shelah the family of the Shelanite; of Pharez the family of the Pharzite; of Zerah the family of the Zarhite;
26:21 and sons of Pharez are: of Hezron the family of the Hezronite; of Hamul the family of the Hamulite.
26:22 These [are] families of Judah, by their numbered ones, six and seventy thousand and five hundred.
26:23 Sons of Issachar by their families; [of] Tola [is] the family of the Tolaite; of Pua the family of the Punite;
26:24 of Jashub the family of the Jashubite; of Shimron the family of the Shimronite.
26:25 These [are] families of Issachar, by their numbered ones, four and sixty thousand and three hundred.
26:26 Sons of Zebulun by their families: of Sered [is] the family of the Sardite; of Elon the family of the Elonite; of Jahleel the family of the Jahleelite.

26:27 These [are] families of the Zebulunite by their numbered ones, sixty thousand and five hundred.

26:28 Sons of Joseph by their families [are] Manasseh and Ephraim.

26:29 Sons of Manasseh: of Machir [is] the family of the Machirite; and Machir hath begotten Gilead; of Gilead [is] the family of the Gileadite.

26:30 These [are] sons of Gilead: [of] Jeezer [is] the family of the Jeezerite; of Helek the family of the Helekite;

26:31 and [of] Asriel the family of the Asrielite; and [of] Shechem the family of the Shechemite;

26:32 and [of] Shemida the family of the Shemidaite; and [of] Hepher the family of the Hepherite.

26:33 And Zelophehad son of Hepher had no sons but daughters, and the names of the daughters of Zelophehad [are] Mahlah, and Noah, Hoglah, Milcah, and Tirzah.

26:34 These [are] families of Manasseh, and their numbered ones [are] two and fifty thousand and seven hundred.

26:35 These [are] sons of Ephraim by their families: of Shuthelah [is] the family of the Shuthelhite; of Becher the family of the Bachrite; of Tahan the family of the Tahanite.

26:36 And these [are] sons of Shuthelah: of Eran the family of the Eranite.

26:37 These [are] families of the sons of Ephraim, by their numbered ones, two and thirty thousand and five hundred. These [are] sons of Joseph by their families.

26:38 Sons of Benjamin by their families: of Bela [is] the family of the Belaite; of Ashbel the family of the Ashbelite; of Ahiram the family of the Ahiramite;

26:39 of Shupham the family of the Shuphamite; of Hupham the family of the Huphamite.

26:40 And sons of Bela are Ard and Naaman: [of Ard is] the family of the Ardite: of Naaman the family of the Naamite.

26:41 These [are] sons of Benjamin by their families, and their numbered ones [are] five and forty thousand and six hundred.

26:42 These [are] sons of Dan by their families: of Shuham [is] the family of the Shuhamite; these [are] families of Dan by their families;

26:43 all the families of the Shuhamite, by their numbered ones, [are] four and sixty thousand and four hundred.

26:44 Sons of Asher by their families: of Jimna [is] the family of the Jimnite; of Jesui the family of the Jesuite; of Beriah the family of the Beriite.

26:45 Of sons of Beriah: of Heber [is] the family of the Heberite; of Malchiel the family of the Malchielite.

26:46 And the name of the daughter of Asher [is] Sarah.

26:47 These [are] families of the sons of Asher, by their numbered ones, three and fifty thousand
and four hundred.
26:48 Sons of Naphtali by their families: of Jahzeel [is] the family of the Jahzeelite; of Guni the
family of the Gunite;
26:49 of Jezer the family of the Jezerite; of Shillem the family of the Shillemite.
26:50 These [are] families of Naphtali by their families, and their numbered ones [are] five and forty
thousand and four hundred.
26:51 These [are] numbered ones of the sons of Israel, six hundred thousand, and a thousand,
seven hundred and thirty.
26:52 And Jehovah speaketh unto Moses, saying,
26:53 `To these is the land apportioned by inheritance, by the number of names;
26:54 to the many thou dost increase their inheritance, and to the few thou dost diminish their
inheritance; [to] each according to his numbered ones is given his inheritance.
26:55 `Only by lot is the land apportioned, by the names of the tribes of their fathers they inherit;
26:56 according to the lot is their inheritance apportioned between many and few.'
26:57 And these [are] numbered ones of the Levite by their families: of Gershon [is] the family of
the Gershonite; of Kohath the family of the Kohathite; of Merari the family of the Merarite.
26:58 These [are] families of the Levite: the family of the Libnite, the family of the Hebronite, the
family of the Mahlite, the family of the Mushite, the family of the Korathite. And Kohath hath
begotten Amram,
26:59 and the name of Amram's wife is Jochebed, daughter of Levi, whom [one] hath born to Levi
in Egypt; and she beareth to Amram Aaron, and Moses, and Miriam their sister.
26:60 And born to Aaron Nadab and Abihu, Eleazar and Ithamar;
26:61 and Nadab dieth -- Abihu also -- in their bringing near strange fire before Jehovah.
26:62 And their numbered ones are three and twenty thousand, every male from a son of a month
and upwards, for they have not numbered themselves in the midst of the sons of Israel; for an
inheritance hath not been given to them in the midst of the sons of Israel.
26:63 These [are] those numbered by Moses and Eleazar the priest, who have numbered the sons
of Israel in the plains of Moab, by Jordan, [near] Jericho;
26:64 and among these there hath not been a man of those numbered by Moses, and Aaron the
priest, who numbered the sons of Israel in the wilderness of Sinai,
26:65 for Jehovah said of them, `They do certainly die in the wilderness;' and there hath not been
left of them a man save Caleb son of Jephunneh, and Joshua son of Nun.
27:1 And daughters of Zelophehad son of Hepher, son of Gilead, son of Machir, son of Manasseh,

of the families of Manasseh son of Joseph, draw near -- and these [are] the names of his daughters, Mahlah, Noah, and Hoglah, and Milcah, and Tirzah --
27:2 and stand before Moses, and before Eleazar the priest, and before the princes, and all the company, at the opening of the tent of meeting, saying:
27:3 `Our father died in the wilderness, and he -- he was not in the midst of the company who were met together against Jehovah in the company of Korah, but for his own sin he died, and had no sons;
27:4 why is the name of our father withdrawn from the midst of his family because he hath no son? give to us a possession in the midst of the brethren of our father;'
27:5 and Moses bringeth near their cause before Jehovah.
27:6 And Jehovah speaketh unto Moses, saying,
27:7 `Rightly are the daughters of Zelophehad speaking; thou dost certainly give to them a possession of an inheritance in the midst of their father's brethren, and hast caused to pass over the inheritance of their father to them.
27:8 `And unto the sons of Israel thou dost speak, saying, When a man dieth, and hath no son, then ye have caused his inheritance to pass over to his daughter;
27:9 and if he have no daughter, then ye have given his inheritance to his brethren;
27:10 and if he have no brethren, then ye have given his inheritance to his father's brethren;
27:11 and if his father have no brethren, then ye have given his inheritance to his relation who is near unto him of his family, and he hath possessed it;' and it hath been to the sons of Israel for a statute of judgment, as Jehovah hath commanded Moses.
27:12 And Jehovah saith unto Moses, `Go up unto this mount Abarim, and see the land which I have given to the sons of Israel;
27:13 and thou hast seen it, and thou hast been gathered unto thy people, also thou, as Aaron thy brother hath been gathered,
27:14 because ye provoked My mouth in the wilderness of Zin, in the strife of the company -- to sanctify Me at the waters before their eyes;' they [are] waters of Meribah, in Kadesh, in the wilderness of Zin.
27:15 And Moses speaketh unto Jehovah, saying,
27:16 `Jehovah -- God of the spirits of all flesh -- appoint a man over the company,
27:17 who goeth out before them, and who cometh in before them, and who taketh them out, and who bringeth them in, and the company of Jehovah is not as sheep which have no shepherd.'
27:18 And Jehovah saith unto Moses, `Take to thee Joshua son of Nun, a man in whom [is] the Spirit, and thou hast laid thine hand upon him,

27:19 and hast caused him to stand before Eleazar the priest, and before all the company, and
hast charged him before their eyes,
27:20 and hast put of thine honour upon him, so that all the company of the sons of Israel do
hearken.
27:21 `And before Eleazar the priest he standeth, and he hath asked for him by the judgment of the
Lights before Jehovah; at His word they go out, and at His word they come in; he, and all the sons
of Israel with him, even all the company.'
27:22 And Moses doth as Jehovah hath commanded him, and taketh Joshua, and causeth him to
stand before Eleazar the priest, and before all the company,
27:23 and layeth his hands upon him, and chargeth him, as Jehovah hath spoken by the hand of
Moses.
28:1 And Jehovah speaketh unto Moses, saying,
28:2 `Command the sons of Israel, and thou hast said unto them, My offering, My bread for My fire-
offerings, My sweet fragrance, ye take heed to bring near to Me in its appointed season.
28:3 `And thou hast said to them, This [is] the fire-offering which ye bring near to Jehovah: two
lambs, sons of a year, perfect ones, daily, a continual burnt-offering;
28:4 the one lamb thou preparest in the morning, and the second lamb thou preparest between the
evenings;
28:5 and a tenth of the ephah of flour for a present, mixed with beaten oil, a fourth of the hin;
28:6 a continual burnt-offering, which was made in mount Sinai, for sweet fragrance, a fire-offering
to Jehovah;
28:7 and its libation, a fourth of the hin for the one lamb; in the sanctuary cause thou a libation of
strong drink to be poured out to Jehovah.
28:8 `And the second lamb thou dost prepare between the evenings; as the present of the morning,
and as its libation thou preparest -- a fire-offering, a sweet fragrance to Jehovah.
28:9 `And on the sabbath-day, two lambs, sons of a year, perfect ones, and two-tenth deals of flour,
a present, mixed with oil, and its libation;
28:10 the burnt-offering of the sabbath in its sabbath, besides the continual burnt-offering and its
libation.
28:11 `And in the beginnings of your months ye bring near a burnt-offering to Jehovah: two
bullocks, sons of the herd, and one ram, seven lambs, sons of a year, perfect ones;
28:12 and three-tenth deals of flour, a present, mixed with oil, for the one bullock, and two-tenth
deals of flour, a present, mixed with oil, for the one ram;
28:13 and a several tenth deal of flour, a present, mixed with oil, for the one lamb; a burnt-offering,

a sweet fragrance, a fire-offering to Jehovah;
28:14 and their libations are a half of the hin to a bullock, and a third of the hin to a ram, and a fourth of the hin to a lamb, of wine; this [is] the burnt-offering of every month for the months of the year;
28:15 and one kid of the goats for a sin-offering to Jehovah; besides the continual burnt-offering it is prepared, and its libation.
28:16 `And in the first month, in the fourteenth day of the month, [is] the passover to Jehovah;
28:17 and in the fifteenth day of this month [is] a festival, seven days unleavened food is eaten;
28:18 in the first day [is] an holy convocation, ye do no servile work,
28:19 and ye have brought near a fire-offering, a burnt-offering to Jehovah: two bullocks, sons of the herd, and one ram, and seven lambs, sons of a year, perfect ones they are for you;
28:20 and their present, flour mixed with oil, three-tenth deals for a bullock, and two-tenth deals for a ram ye do prepare;
28:21 a several tenth deal thou preparest for the one lamb, for the seven lambs,
28:22 and one goat, a sin-offering, to make atonement for you.
28:23 `Apart from the burnt-offering of the morning, which [is] for the continual burnt-offering, ye prepare these;
28:24 according to these ye prepare daily, seven days, bread of a fire-offering, a sweet fragrance, to Jehovah; besides the continual burnt-offering it is prepared, and its libation;
28:25 and on the seventh day a holy convocation ye have, ye do no servile work.
28:26 `And in the day of the first-fruits, in your bringing near a new present to Jehovah, in your weeks, a holy convocation ye have; ye do no servile work;
28:27 and ye have brought near a burnt-offering for sweet fragrance to Jehovah: two bullocks, sons of the herd, one ram, seven lambs, sons of a year,
28:28 and their present, flour mixed with oil, three-tenth deals to the one bullock, two-tenth deals to the one ram,
28:29 a several tenth deal to the one lamb, for the seven lambs;
28:30 one kid of the goats to make atonement for you;
28:31 apart from the continual burnt-offering and its present ye prepare [them] (perfect ones they are for you) and their libations.
29:1 `And in the seventh month, in the first of the month, a holy convocation ye have, ye do no servile work; a day of shouting it is to you;
29:2 and ye have prepared a burnt-offering, for sweet fragrance to Jehovah: one bullock, a son of the herd, one ram, seven lambs, sons of a year, perfect ones;

29:3 and their present, flour mixed with oil, three-tenth deals for the bullock, two-tenth deals for the ram,
29:4 and one-tenth deal for the one lamb, for the seven lambs;
29:5 and one kid of the goats, a sin-offering, to make atonement for you;
29:6 apart from the burnt-offering of the month, and its present, and the continual burnt-offering, and its present, and their libations, according to their ordinance, for sweet fragrance, a fire-offering to Jehovah.
29:7 `And on the tenth of this seventh month a holy convocation ye have, and ye have humbled your souls; ye do no work;
29:8 and ye have brought near a burnt-offering to Jehovah, a sweet fragrance, one bullock, a son of the herd, one ram, seven lambs, sons of a year, perfect ones they are for you,
29:9 and their present, flour mixed with oil, three-tenth deals for the bullock, two-tenth deals for the one ram,
29:10 a several tenth deal for the one lamb, for the seven lambs,
29:11 one kid of the goats, a sin-offering; apart from the sin-offering of the atonements, and the continual burnt-offering, and its present, and their libations.
29:12 `And on the fifteenth day of the seventh month a holy convocation ye have; ye do no servile work; and ye have celebrated a festival to Jehovah seven days,
29:13 and have brought near a burnt-offering, a fire-offering, a sweet fragrance, to Jehovah; thirteen bullocks, sons of the herd, two rams, fourteen lambs, sons of a year; perfect ones they are;
29:14 and their present, flour mixed with oil, three-tenth deals to the one bullock, for the thirteen bullocks, two-tenth deals to the one ram, for the two rams,
29:15 and a several tenth deal to the one lamb, for the fourteen lambs,
29:16 and one kid of the goats, a sin-offering; apart from the continual burnt-offering, its present, and its libation.
29:17 `And on the second day twelve bullocks, sons of the herd, two rams, fourteen lambs, sons of a year, perfect ones;
29:18 and their present, and their libations, for the bullocks, for the rams, and for the sheep, in their number, according to the ordinance;
29:19 and one kid of the goats, a sin-offering; apart from the continual burnt-offering, and its present, and their libations.
29:20 `And on the third day eleven bullocks, two rams, fourteen lambs, sons of a year, perfect ones;
29:21 and their present, and their libations, for the bullocks, for the rams, and for the lambs, in their

number, according to the ordinance;
29:22 and one goat, a sin-offering; apart from the continual burnt-offering, and its present, and its libation.
29:23 `And on the fourth day ten bullocks, two rams, fourteen lambs, sons of a year, perfect ones;
29:24 their present, and their libations, for the bullocks, for the rams, and for the lambs, in their number, according to the ordinance;
29:25 and one kid of the goats, a sin-offering, apart from the continual burnt-offering, its present, and its libation.
29:26 `And on the fifth day nine bullocks, two rams, fourteen lambs, sons of a year, perfect ones;
29:27 and their present, and their libations, for the bullocks, for the rams, and for the lambs, in their number, according to the ordinance;
29:28 and one goat, a sin-offering; apart from the continual burnt-offering, and its present, and its libation.
29:29 `And on the sixth day eight bullocks, two rams, fourteen lambs, sons of a year, perfect ones;
29:30 and their present, and their libations, for the bullocks, for the rams, and for the lambs, in their number, according to the ordinance;
29:31 and one goat, a sin-offering; apart from the continual burnt-offering, its present, and its libation.
29:32 `And on the seventh day seven bullocks, two rams, fourteen lambs, sons of a year, perfect ones;
29:33 and their present, and their libations, for the bullocks, for the rams, and for the lambs, in their number, according to the ordinance;
29:34 and one goat, a sin-offering; apart from the continual burnt-offering, its present, and its libation.
29:35 `On the eighth day a restraint ye have, ye do no servile work;
29:36 and ye have brought near a burnt-offering, a fire-offering, a sweet fragrance, to Jehovah; one bullock, one ram, seven lambs, sons of a year, perfect ones;
29:37 their present, and their libations, for the bullock, for the ram, and for the lambs, in their number, according to the ordinance;
29:38 and one goat, a sin-offering; apart from the continual burnt-offering, and its present, and its libation.
29:39 `These ye prepare to Jehovah in your appointed seasons, apart from your vows, and your free-will offerings, for your burnt-offerings, and for your presents, and for your libations, and for your peace-offerings.'

29:40 And Moses saith unto the sons of Israel according to all that Jehovah hath commanded Moses.

30:1 And Moses speaketh unto the heads of the tribes of the sons of Israel, saying, `This [is] the thing which Jehovah hath commanded:

30:2 `When a man voweth a vow to Jehovah, or hath sworn an oath to bind a bond on his soul, he doth not pollute his word; according to all that is going out from his mouth he doth.

30:3 `And when a woman voweth a vow to Jehovah, and hath bound a bond in the house of her father in her youth,

30:4 and her father hath heard her vow, and her bond which she hath bound on her soul, and her father hath kept silent at her, then have all her vows been established, and every bond which she hath bound on her soul is established.

30:5 `And if her father hath disallowed her in the day of his hearing, none of her vows and her bonds which she hath bound on her soul is established, and Jehovah is propitious to her, for her father hath disallowed her.

30:6 `And if she be at all to a husband, and her vows [are] on her, or a wrongful utterance [on] her lips, which she hath bound on her soul,

30:7 and her husband hath heard, and in the day of his hearing, he hath kept silent at her, then have her vows been established, and her bonds which she hath bound on her soul are established.

30:8 `And if in the day of her husband's hearing he disalloweth her, then he hath broken her vow which [is] on her, and the wrongful utterance of her lips which she hath bound on her soul, and Jehovah is propitious to her.

30:9 `As to the vow of a widow or cast-out woman, all that she hath bound on her soul is established on her.

30:10 `And if [in] the house of her husband she hath vowed, or hath bound a bond on her soul with an oath,

30:11 and her husband hath heard, and hath kept silent at her -- he hath not disallowed her -- then have all her vows been established, and every bond which she hath bound on her soul is established.

30:12 `And if her husband doth certainly break them in the day of his hearing, none of the outgoing of her lips concerning her vows, or concerning the bond of her soul, is established -- her husband hath broken them -- and Jehovah is propitious to her.

30:13 `Every vow and every oath -- a bond to humble a soul -- her husband doth establish it, or her husband doth break it;

30:14 and if her husband certainly keep silent at her, from day unto day, then he hath established

all her vows, or all her bonds which [are] upon her; he hath established them, for he hath kept silent at her in the day of his hearing;
30:15 and if he doth at all break them after his hearing, then he hath borne her iniquity.'
30:16 These [are] the statutes which Jehovah hath commanded Moses between a man and his wife, between a father and his daughter, in her youth, [in] the house of her father.
31:1 And Jehovah speaketh unto Moses, saying,
31:2 `Execute the vengeance of the sons of Israel against the Midianites -- afterwards thou art gathered unto thy people.'
31:3 And Moses speaketh unto the people, saying, `Be ye armed some of you for the host, and they are against Midian, to put the vengeance of Jehovah on Midian;
31:4 a thousand for a tribe -- a thousand for a tribe, to all the tribes of Israel -- ye do send to the host.'
31:5 And there are given out of the thousands of Israel a thousand for a tribe, twelve thousand armed ones of the host;
31:6 and Moses sendeth them, a thousand for a tribe, to the host, them and Phinehas son of Eleazar the priest, to the host; and the holy vessels, and the trumpets of the shouting, in his hand.
31:7 And they war against Midian, as Jehovah hath commanded Moses, and slay every male;
31:8 and the kings of Midian they have slain, besides their pierced ones, Evi, and Rekem, and Zur, and Hur, and Reba, five kings of Midian; and Balaam son of Beor, they have slain with the sword.
31:9 And the sons of Israel take captive the women of Midian, and their infants; and all their cattle, and all their substance, and all their wealth they have plundered;
31:10 and all their cities, with their habitations, and all their towers, they have burnt with fire.
31:11 And they take all the spoil, and all the prey, among man and among beast;
31:12 and they bring in, unto Moses, and unto Eleazar the priest, and unto the company of the sons of Israel, the captives, and the prey, and the spoil, unto the camp, unto the plains of Moab, which [are] by Jordan, [near] Jericho.
31:13 And Moses, and Eleazar the priest, and all the princes of the company, go out to meet them, unto the outside of the camp,
31:14 and Moses is wroth against the inspectors of the force, chiefs of the thousands, and chiefs of the hundreds, who are coming in from the host of the battle.
31:15 And Moses saith unto them, `Have ye kept alive every female?
31:16 lo, they -- they have been to the sons of Israel, through the word of Balaam, to cause a trespass against Jehovah in the matter of Peor, and the plague is in the company of Jehovah.
31:17 `And now, slay ye every male among the infants, yea, every woman known of man by the

lying of a male ye have slain;
31:18 and all the infants among the women, who have not known the lying of a male, ye have kept alive for yourselves.
31:19 `And ye, encamp ye at the outside of the camp seven days -- any who hath slain a person, and any who hath come against a pierced one, ye cleanse yourselves on the third day, and on the seventh day -- ye and your captives;
31:20 and every garment, and every skin vessel, and every work of goats' [hair], and every wooden vessel, ye yourselves cleanse.'
31:21 And Eleazar the priest saith unto the men of the host who go in to battle, `This [is] the statute of the law which Jehovah hath commanded Moses:
31:22 only, the gold, and the silver, the brass, the iron, the tin, and the lead,
31:23 every thing which may go into fire, ye cause to pass over through fire, and it hath been clean; only, with the water of separation it is cleansed, and all that may not go into fire, ye cause to pass over through water;
31:24 and ye have washed your garments on the seventh day, and have been clean, and afterwards ye come in unto the camp.'
31:25 And Jehovah speaketh unto Moses, saying,
31:26 `Take up the sum of the prey of the captives, among man and among beast, thou, and Eleazar the priest, and the heads of the fathers of the company;
31:27 and thou hast halved the prey between those handling the battle who go out to the host and all the company;
31:28 and thou hast raised a tribute to Jehovah from the men of war, who go out to the host, one body out of five hundred, of man, and of the herd, and of the asses, and of the flock;
31:29 from their half ye do take, and thou hast given to Eleazar the priest -- the heave-offering of Jehovah.
31:30 `And from the sons of Israel's half thou dost take one possession out of fifty, of man, of the herd, of the asses, and of the flock, of all the cattle, and thou hast given them to the Levites keeping the charge of the tabernacle of Jehovah.'
31:31 And Moses doth -- Eleazar the priest also -- as Jehovah hath commanded Moses.
31:32 And the prey, the residue of the spoil which the people of the host have spoiled, is of the flock six hundred thousand, and seventy thousand, and five thousand;
31:33 and of the herd two and seventy thousand;
31:34 and of asses one and sixty thousand;
31:35 and of human beings -- of the women who have not known the lying of a male -- all the

persons [are] two and thirty thousand.
31:36 And the half -- the portion of those who go out into the host -- the number of the flock is three hundred thousand, and thirty thousand, and seven thousand and five hundred.
31:37 And the tribute to Jehovah of the sheep is six hundred five and seventy;
31:38 and the herd [is] six and thirty thousand, and their tribute to Jehovah [is] two and seventy;
31:39 and the asses [are] thirty thousand and five hundred, and their tribute to Jehovah [is] one and sixty;
31:40 and the human beings [are] sixteen thousand, and their tribute to Jehovah [is] two and thirty persons.
31:41 And Moses giveth the tribute -- Jehovah's heave-offering -- to Eleazar the priest, as Jehovah hath commanded Moses.
31:42 And of the sons of Israel's half, which Moses halved from the men who war --
31:43 and the company's half is, of the flock three hundred thousand, and thirty thousand, seven thousand and five hundred;
31:44 and of the herd six and thirty thousand;
31:45 and of asses thirty thousand and five hundred;
31:46 and of human beings sixteen thousand --
31:47 Moses taketh from the sons of Israel's half the one possession from the fifty, of man and of beast, and giveth them to the Levites keeping the charge of the tabernacle of Jehovah, as Jehovah hath commanded Moses.
31:48 And the inspectors whom the thousands of the host hath, (heads of the thousands and heads of the hundreds), draw near unto Moses,
31:49 and they say unto Moses, `Thy servants have taken up the sum of the men of war who [are] with us, and not a man of us hath been missed;
31:50 and we bring near Jehovah's offering, each that which he hath found, vessels of gold -- chain, and bracelet, seal-ring, [ear]-ring, and bead -- to make atonement for ourselves before Jehovah.'
31:51 And Moses receiveth -- Eleazar the priest also -- the gold from them, every made vessel,
31:52 and all the gold of the heave-offering which they have lifted up to Jehovah is sixteen thousand seven hundred and fifty shekels, from heads of the thousands, and from heads of the hundreds;
31:53 (the men of the host have spoiled each for himself);
31:54 and Moses taketh -- Eleazar the priest also -- the gold from the heads of the thousands and of the hundreds, and they bring it in unto the tent of meeting -- a memorial for the sons of Israel

before Jehovah.
32:1 And much cattle hath been to the sons of Reuben and to the sons of Gad, very many; and they see the land of Jazer, and the land of Gilead, and lo, the place [is] a place [for] cattle;
32:2 and the sons of Gad, and the sons of Reuben, come in and speak unto Moses, and unto Eleazar the priest, and unto the princes of the company, saying:
32:3 `Ataroth, and Dibon, and Jazer, and Nimrah, and Heshbon, and Elealeh, and Shebam, and Nebo, and Beon --
32:4 the land which Jehovah hath smitten before the company of Israel, is a land for cattle, and thy servants have cattle.'
32:5 And they say, `If we have found grace in thine eyes, let this land be given to thy servants for a possession; cause us not to pass over the Jordan.'
32:6 And Moses saith to the sons of Gad and to the sons of Reuben, `Do your brethren go in to the battle, and ye -- do ye sit here?
32:7 and why discourage ye the heart of the sons of Israel from passing over unto the land which Jehovah hath given to them?
32:8 `Thus did your fathers in my sending them from Kadesh-Barnea to see the land;
32:9 and they go up unto the valley of Eshcol, and see the land, and discourage the heart of the sons of Israel so as not to go in unto the land which Jehovah hath given to them;
32:10 and the anger of Jehovah burneth in that day, and He sweareth, saying,
32:11 They do not see -- the men who are coming up out of Egypt from a son of twenty years and upward -- the ground which I have sworn to Abraham, to Isaac, and to Jacob, for they have not been fully after Me;
32:12 save Caleb son of Jephunneh the Kenezite, and Joshua son of Nun, for they have been fully after Jehovah;
32:13 and the anger of Jehovah burneth against Israel, and He causeth them to wander in the wilderness forty years, until the consumption of all the generation which is doing the evil thing in the eyes of Jehovah.
32:14 `And lo, ye have risen in the stead of your fathers, an increase of men -- sinners, to add yet to the fury of the anger of Jehovah toward Israel;
32:15 when ye turn back from after Him, then He hath added yet to leave him in the wilderness, and ye have done corruptly to all this people.'
32:16 And they come nigh unto him, and say, `Folds for the flock we build for our cattle here, and cities for our infants;
32:17 and we -- we are armed hasting before the sons of Israel till that we have brought them in

unto their place; and our infants have dwelt in the cities of defence because of the inhabitants of
the land;
32:18 we do not turn back unto our houses till the sons of Israel have inherited each his
inheritance,
32:19 for we do not inherit with them beyond the Jordan and yonder, for our inheritance hath come
unto us beyond the Jordan at the [sun]-rising.'
32:20 And Moses saith unto them, `If ye do this thing: if ye are armed before Jehovah for battle,
32:21 and every armed one of you hath passed over the Jordan before Jehovah, till his
dispossessing His enemies from before Him,
32:22 and the land hath been subdued before Jehovah -- then afterwards ye do turn back, and
have been acquitted by Jehovah, and by Israel; and this land hath been to you for a possession
before Jehovah.
32:23 `And if ye do not so, lo, ye have sinned against Jehovah, and know ye your sin, that it doth
find you;
32:24 build for yourselves cities for your infants, and folds for your flock, and that which is going out
from your mouth do ye.'
32:25 And the sons of Gad and the sons of Reuben speak unto Moses, saying, `Thy servants do
as my lord is commanding;
32:26 our infants, our wives, our cattle, and all our beasts, are there in cities of Gilead,
32:27 and thy servants pass over, every armed one of the host, before Jehovah, to battle, as my
lord is saying.'
32:28 And Moses commandeth concerning them Eleazar the priest, and Joshua son of Nun, and
the heads of the fathers of the tribes of the sons of Israel;
32:29 and Moses saith unto them, `If the sons of Gad and the sons of Reuben pass over with you
the Jordan, every one armed for battle, before Jehovah, and the land hath been subdued before
you, then ye have given to them the land of Gilead for a possession;
32:30 and if they do not pass over armed with you, then they have possessions in your midst in the
land of Canaan.'
32:31 And the sons of Gad and the sons of Reuben answer, saying, `That which Jehovah hath
spoken unto thy servants -- so we do;
32:32 we -- we pass over armed before Jehovah [to] the land of Canaan, and with us [is] the
possession of our inheritance beyond the Jordan.'
32:33 And Moses giveth to them, to the sons of Gad, and to the sons of Reuben, and to the half of
the tribe of Manasseh son of Joseph, the kingdom of Sihon king of the Amorite, and the kingdom of

Og king of Bashan, the land by its cities, in the borders, the cities of the land round about.
32:34 And the sons of Gad build Dihon, and Ataroth, and Aroer,
32:35 and Atroth, Shophan, and Jaazer, and Jogbehah,
32:36 and Beth-Nimrah, and Beth-Haran, cities of defence, and sheepfolds.
32:37 And the sons of Reuben have build Heshbon, and Elealeh, and Kirjathaim,
32:38 and Nebo, and Baal-Meon (changed in name), and Shibmah, and they call by [these] names the names of the cities which they have built.
32:39 And sons of Machir son of Manasseh go to Gilead, and capture it, and dispossess the Amorite, who [is] in it;
32:40 and Moses giveth Gilead to Machir son of Manasseh, and he dwelleth in it.
32:41 And Jair son of Manasseh hath gone and captureth their towns, and calleth them `Towns of Jair;'
32:42 and Nobah hath gone and captureth Kenath, and its villages, and calleth it Nobah, by his own name.
33:1 These [are] journeys of the sons of Israel who have come out of the land of Egypt, by their hosts, by the hand of Moses and Aaron;
33:2 and Moses writeth their outgoings, by their journeys, by the command of Jehovah; and these [are] their journeys, by their outgoings:
33:3 And they journey from Rameses in the first month, on the fifteenth day of the first month, on the morrow of the passover have the sons of Israel gone out with a high hand, before the eyes of all the Egyptians --
33:4 and the Egyptians are burying those whom Jehovah hath smitten among them, every first-born, and on their gods hath Jehovah done judgments --
33:5 and the sons of Israel journey from Rameses, and encamp in Succoth.
33:6 And they journey from Succoth, and encamp in Etham, which [is] in the extremity of the wilderness;
33:7 and they journey from Etham, and turn back on Pi-Hahiroth, which [is] on the front of Baal-Zephon, and they encamp before Migdol.
33:8 And they journey from Pi-Hahiroth, and pass over through the midst of the sea, into the wilderness, and go a journey of three days in the wilderness of Etham, and encamp in Marah.
33:9 And they journey from Marah, and come in to Elim, and in Elim [are] twelve fountains of waters, and seventy palm trees, and they encamp there;
33:10 and they journey from Elim, and encamp by the Red Sea.
33:11 And they journey from the Red Sea, and encamp in the wilderness of Sin;

33:12 and they journey from the wilderness of Sin, and encamp in Dophkah.
33:13 And they journey from Dophkah, and encamp in Alush;
33:14 and they journey from Alush, and encamp in Rephidim; and there was there no water for the people to drink.
33:15 And they journey from Rephidim, and encamp in the wilderness of Sinai;
33:16 and they journey from the wilderness of Sinai, and encamp in Kibroth-Hattaavah.
33:17 And they journey from Kibroth-Hattaavah, and encamp in Hazeroth;
33:18 and they journey from Hazeroth, and encamp in Rithmah.
33:19 And they journey from Rithmah, and encamp in Rimmon-Parez;
33:20 and they journey from Rimmon-Parez, and encamp in Libnah.
33:21 And they journey from Libnah, and encamp in Rissah;
33:22 and they journey from Rissah, and encamp in Kehelathah.
33:23 And they journey from Kehelathah, and encamp in mount Shapher;
33:24 and they journey from mount Shapher, and encamp in Haradah.
33:25 And they journey from Haradah, and encamp in Makheloth;
33:26 and they journey from Makheloth, and encamp in Tahath.
33:27 And they journey from Tahath, and encamp in Tarah;
33:28 and they journey from Tarah, and encamp in Mithcah.
33:29 And they journey from Mithcah, and encamp in Hashmonah;
33:30 and they journey from Hashmonah, and encamp in Moseroth.
33:31 And they journey from Moseroth, and encamp in Bene-Jaakan;
33:32 and they journey from Bene-Jaakan, and encamp at Hor-Hagidgad.
33:33 And they journey from Hor-Hagidgad, and encamp in Jotbathah;
33:34 and they journey from Jotbathah, and encamp in Ebronah.
33:35 And they journey from Ebronah, and encamp in Ezion-Gaber;
33:36 and they journey from Ezion-Gaber, and encamp in the wilderness of Zin, which [is] Kadesh.
33:37 And they journey from Kadesh, and encamp in mount Hor, in the extremity of the land of Edom.
33:38 And Aaron the priest goeth up unto mount Hor, by the command of Jehovah, and dieth there, in the fortieth year of the going out of the sons of Israel from the land of Egypt, in the fifth month, on the first of the month;
33:39 and Aaron [is] a son of a hundred and twenty and three years in his dying in mount Hor.
33:40 And the Canaanite -- king Arad -- who is dwelling in the south, in the land of Canaan, heareth of the coming of the sons of Israel.

33:41 And they journey from mount Hor, and encamp in Zalmonah;
33:42 and they journey from Zalmonah, and encamp in Punon.
33:43 And they journey from Punon, and encamp in Oboth;
33:44 and they journey from Oboth, and encamp in Ije-Abarim, in the border of Moab.
33:45 And they journey from Iim, and encamp in Dibon-Gad;
33:46 and they journey from Dibon-Gad, and encamp in Almon-Diblathaim.
33:47 And they journey from Almon-Diblathaim, and encamp in the mountains of Abarim, before Nebo;
33:48 and they journey from the mountains of Abarim, and encamp in the plains of Moab, by Jordan, [near] Jericho.
33:49 And they encamp by the Jordan from Beth-Jeshimoth, unto Abel-Shittim, in the plains of Moab.
33:50 And Jehovah speaketh unto Moses, in the plains of Moab, by Jordan, [near] Jericho, saying,
33:51 `Speak unto the sons of Israel, and thou hast said unto them, When ye are passing over the Jordan unto the land of Canaan,
33:52 then ye have dispossessed all the inhabitants of the land from before you, and have destroyed all their imagery, yea, all their molten images ye destroy, and all their high places ye lay waste,
33:53 and ye have possessed the land, and dwelt in it, for to you I have given the land -- to possess it.
33:54 `And ye have inherited the land by lot, by your families; to the many ye increase their inheritance, and to the few ye diminish their inheritance; whither the lot goeth out to him, it is his; by the tribes of your fathers ye inherit.
33:55 `And if ye do not dispossess the inhabitants of the land from before you, then it hath been, those whom ye let remain of them, [are] for pricks in your eyes, and for thorns in your sides, and they have distressed you on the land in which ye are dwelling,
33:56 and it hath come to pass, as I thought to do to them -- I do to you.'
34:1 And Jehovah speaketh unto Moses, saying,
34:2 `Command the sons of Israel, and thou hast said unto them, When ye are coming in unto the land of Canaan -- this [is] the land which falleth to you by inheritance, the land of Canaan, by its borders --
34:3 then hath the south quarter been to you from the wilderness of Zin, by the sides of Edom, yea, the south border hath been to you from the extremity of the Salt Sea, eastward;
34:4 and the border hath turned round to you from the south to the ascent of Akrabbim, and hath

passed on to Zin, and its outgoings have been from the south to Kadesh-Barnea, and it hath gone out at Hazar-Addar, and hath passed on to Azmon;

34:5 and the border hath turned round from Azmon to the brook of Egypt, and its outgoings have been at the sea.

34:6 `As to the west border, even the great sea hath been to you a border; this is to you the west border.

34:7 `And this is to you the north border: from the great sea ye mark out for yourselves mount Hor;

34:8 from mount Hor ye mark out to go in to Hamath, and the outgoings of the border have been to Zedad;

34:9 and the border hath gone out to Ziphron, and its outgoings have been at Hazar-Enan; this is to you the north border.

34:10 `And ye have marked out for yourselves for the border eastward, from Hazar-Enan to Shepham;

34:11 and the border hath gone down from Shepham to Riblah, on the east of Ain, and the border hath gone down, and hath smitten against the shoulder of the sea of Chinnereth eastward;

34:12 and the border hath gone down to the Jordan, and its outgoings have been at the Salt Sea; this is for you the land by its borders round about.'

34:13 And Moses commandeth the sons of Israel, saying, `This [is] the land which ye inherit by lot, which Jehovah hath commanded to give to the nine tribes and the half of the tribe;

34:14 for the tribe of the sons of Reuben have received, by the house of their fathers; and the tribe of the children of Gad, by the house of their fathers; and the half of the tribe of Manasseh have received their inheritance;

34:15 the two tribes and the half of the tribe have received their inheritance beyond the Jordan, [near] Jericho, eastward, at the [sun]-rising.'

34:16 And Jehovah speaketh unto Moses, saying,

34:17 `These [are] the names of the men who give to you the inheritance of the land: Eleazar the priest, and Joshua son of Nun,

34:18 and one prince -- one prince -- for a tribe ye do take to give the land by inheritance.

34:19 `And these [are] the names of the men: of the tribe of Judah, Caleb son of Jephunneh;

34:20 and of the tribe of the sons of Simeon, Shemuel son of Aminihud;

34:21 of the tribe of Benjamin, Elidad son of Chislon;

34:22 and of the tribe of the sons of Dan, the prince Bukki son of Jogli;

34:23 of the sons of Joseph, of the tribe of the sons of Manasseh, the prince Hanniel son of Ephod;

34:24 and of the tribe of the sons of Ephraim, the prince Kemuel son of Shiphtan;

34:25 and of the tribe of the sons of Zebulun, the prince Elizaphan son of Parnach;
34:26 and of the tribe of the sons of Issachar, the prince Paltiel son of Azzan;
34:27 and of the tribe of the sons of Asher, the prince Ahihud son of Shelomi;
34:28 and of the tribe of the sons of Naphtali, the prince Pedahel son of Ammihud.'
34:29 These [are] those whom Jehovah hath commanded to give the sons of Israel inheritance in the land of Canaan.
35:1 And Jehovah speaketh unto Moses, in the plains of Moab, by Jordan, [near] Jericho, saying,
35:2 `Command the sons of Israel, and they have given to the Levites of the inheritance of their possession cities to inhabit; also a suburb for the cities round about them ye do give to the Levites.
35:3 And the cities have been to them to inhabit, and their suburbs are for their cattle, and for their goods, and for all their beasts.
35:4 `And the suburbs of the cities which ye give to the Levites [are], from the wall of the city and without, a thousand cubits round about.
35:5 And ye have measured from the outside of the city, the east quarter, two thousand by the cubit, and the south quarter, two thousand by the cubit, and the west quarter, two thousand by the cubit, and the north quarter, two thousand by the cubit; and the city [is] in the midst; this is to them the suburbs of the cities.
35:6 `And the cities which ye give to the Levites [are] the six cities of refuge, which ye give for the fleeing thither of the man-slayer, and besides them ye give forty and two cities;
35:7 all the cities which ye give to the Levites [are] forty and eight cities, them and their suburbs.
35:8 And the cities which ye give [are] of the possession of the sons of Israel, from the many ye multiply, and from the few ye diminish; each, according to his inheritance which they inherit, doth give of his cities to the Levites.'
35:9 And Jehovah speaketh unto Moses, saying,
35:10 `Speak unto the sons of Israel, and thou hast said unto them, When ye are passing over the Jordan to the land of Canaan,
35:11 and have prepared to yourselves cities -- cities of refuge they are to you -- then fled thither hath a man-slayer, smiting a person unawares,
35:12 and the cities have been to you for a refuge from the redeemer, and the man-slayer doth not die till his standing before the company for judgment.
35:13 `As to the cities which ye give -- six [are] cities of refuge to you;
35:14 the three of the cities ye give beyond the Jordan, and the three of the cities ye give in the land of Canaan; cities of refuge they are.
35:15 To sons of Israel, and to a sojourner, and to a settler in their midst, are these six cities for a

refuge, for the fleeing thither of any one smiting a person unawares.
35:16 `And if with an instrument of iron he hath smitten him, and he dieth, he [is] a murderer: the murderer is certainly put to death.
35:17 `And if with a stone [in] the hand, wherewith he dieth, he hath smitten him, and he dieth, he [is] a murderer: the murderer is certainly put to death.
35:18 `Or with a wooden instrument [in] the hand, wherewith he dieth, he hath smitten him, and he dieth, he [is] a murderer: the murderer is certainly put to death.
35:19 `The redeemer of blood himself doth put the murderer to death; in his coming against him he doth put him to death.
35:20 `And if in hatred he thrust him through, or hath cast [anything] at him by lying in wait, and he dieth;
35:21 or in enmity he hath smitten him with his hand, and he dieth; the smiter is certainly put to death; he [is] a murderer; the redeemer of blood doth put the murderer to death in his coming against him.
35:22 `And if, in an instant, without enmity, he hath thrust him through, or hath cast at him any instrument, without lying in wait;
35:23 or with any stone wherewith he dieth, without seeing, and causeth [it] to fall upon him, and he dieth, and he [is] not his enemy, nor seeking his evil;
35:24 then have the company judged between the smiter and the redeemer of blood, by these judgments.
35:25 `And the company have delivered the man-slayer out of the hand of the redeemer of blood, and the company have caused him to turn back unto the city of his refuge, whither he hath fled, and he hath dwelt in it till the death of the chief priest, who hath been anointed with the holy oil.
35:26 `And if the man-slayer at all go out [from] the border of the city of his refuge whither he fleeth,
35:27 and the redeemer of blood hath found him at the outside of the border of the city of his refuge, and the redeemer of blood hath slain the man-slayer, blood is not for him;
35:28 for in the city of his refuge he doth dwell till the death of the chief priest; and after the death of the chief priest doth the man-slayer turn back unto the city of his possession.
35:29 `And these things have been to you for a statute of judgment to your generations, in all your dwellings:
35:30 whoso smiteth a person, by the mouth of witnesses doth [one] slay the murderer; and one witness doth not testify against a person -- to die.
35:31 `And ye take no atonement for the life of a murderer who [is] condemned -- to die, for he is certainly put to death;

35:32 and ye take no atonement for him to flee unto the city of his refuge, to turn back to dwell in the land, until the death of the priest.
35:33 `And ye profane not the land which ye [are] in, for blood profaneth the land; as to the land, it is not pardoned for blood which is shed in it except by the blood of him who sheddeth it;
35:34 and ye defile not the land in which ye are dwelling, in the midst of which I do tabernacle, for I Jehovah do tabernacle in the midst of the sons of Israel.'
36:1 And the heads of the fathers of the families of the sons of Gilead, son of Machir, son of Manasseh, of the families of the sons of Joseph, come near, and speak before Moses, and before the princes, heads of the fathers of the sons of Israel,
36:2 and say, Jehovah commanded my lord to give the land for inheritance by lot to the sons of Israel, and my lord hath been commanded by Jehovah to give the inheritance of Zelophehad our brother to his daughters.
36:3 `And -- they have been to one of the sons of the [other] tribes of the sons of Israel for wives, and their inheritance hath been withdrawn from the inheritance of our fathers, and hath been added to the inheritance of the tribe which is theirs, and from the lot of our inheritance it is withdrawn,
36:4 and if it is the jubilee of the sons of Israel, then hath their inheritance been added to the inheritance of the tribe which is theirs, and from the inheritance of the tribe of our fathers is their inheritance withdrawn.'
36:5 And Moses commandeth the sons of Israel, by the command of Jehovah, saying, `Rightly are the tribe of the sons of Joseph speaking;
36:6 this [is] the thing which Jehovah hath commanded concerning the daughters of Zelophehad, saying, To those good in their eyes let them be for wives; only, to a family of the tribe of their fathers let them be for wives;
36:7 and the inheritance of the sons of Israel doth not turn round from tribe unto tribe; for each to the inheritance of the tribe of his fathers, do the sons of Israel cleave.
36:8 `And every daughter possessing an inheritance, of the tribes of the sons of Israel, is to one of the family of the tribe of her father for a wife, so that the sons of Israel possess each the inheritance of his fathers,
36:9 and the inheritance doth not turn round from [one] tribe to another tribe; for each to his inheritance do they cleave, the tribes of the sons of Israel.'
36:10 As Jehovah hath commanded Moses, so have the daughters of Zelophehad done,
36:11 and Mahlah, Tirzah, and Hoglah, and Milcah, and Noah, daughters of Zelophehad, are to the sons of their fathers' brethren for wives;
36:12 [to men] of the families of the sons of Manasseh, son of Joseph, they have been for wives,

and their inheritance is with the tribe of the family of their father.
36:13 These [are] the commands and the judgments which Jehovah hath commanded, by the hand
of Moses, concerning the sons of Israel, in the plains of Moab, by Jordan, [near] Jericho.

Deuteronomy

1:1 These [are] the words which Moses hath spoken unto all Israel, beyond the Jordan, in the wilderness, in the plain over-against Suph, between Paran and Tophel, and Laban, and Hazeroth, and Di-Zahab;
1:2 eleven days' from Horeb, the way of mount Seir, unto Kadesh-Barnea.
1:3 And it cometh to pass in the fortieth year, in the eleventh month, on the first of the month hath Moses spoken unto the sons of Israel according to all that Jehovah hath commanded him concerning them;
1:4 after his smiting Sihon king of the Amorite who is dwelling in Heshbon, and Og king of Bashan who is dwelling in Ashtaroth in Edrei,
1:5 beyond the Jordan, in the land of Moab, hath Moses begun to explain this law, saying:
1:6 `Jehovah our God hath spoken unto us in Horeb, saying, Enough to you -- of dwelling in this mount;
1:7 turn ye and journey for you, and enter the mount of the Amorite, and unto all its neighbouring places, in the plain, in the hill-country, and in the low country, and in the south, and in the haven of the sea, the land of the Canaanite, and of Lebanon, unto the great river, the river Phrat;
1:8 see, I have set before you the land; go in and possess the land which Jehovah hath sworn to your fathers, to Abraham, to Isaac, and to Jacob, to give to them, and to their seed after them.
1:9 `And I speak unto you at that time, saying, I am not able by myself to bear you;
1:10 Jehovah your God hath multiplied you, and lo, ye [are] to-day as the stars of the heavens for multitude;
1:11 Jehovah, God of your fathers, is adding to you, as ye [are], a thousand times, and doth bless you as He hath spoken to you.
1:12 `How do I bear by myself your pressure, and your burden, and your strife?
1:13 Give for yourselves men, wise and intelligent, and known to your tribes, and I set them for your heads;
1:14 and ye answer me and say, Good [is] the thing which thou hast spoken -- to do.
1:15 `And I take the heads of your tribes, men, wise and known, and I appoint them heads over you, princes of thousands, and princes of hundreds, and princes of fifties, and princes of tens, and authorities, for your tribes.
1:16 And I command your judges at that time, saying, Hearkening between your brethren -- then ye have judged righteousness between a man, and his brother, and his sojourner;
1:17 ye do not discern faces in judgment; as the little so the great ye do hear; ye are not afraid of

the face of any, for the judgment is God's, and the thing which is too hard for you, ye bring near unto me, and I have heard it;
1:18 and I command you, at that time, all the things which ye do.
1:19 `And we journey from Horeb, and go [through] all that great and fearful wilderness which ye have seen -- the way of the hill-country of the Amorite, as Jehovah our God hath commanded us, and we come in unto Kadesh-Barnea.
1:20 `And I say unto you, Ye have come in unto the hill-country of the Amorite, which Jehovah our God is giving to us;
1:21 see, Jehovah thy God hath set before thee the land; go up, possess, as Jehovah, God of thy fathers, hath spoken to thee; fear not, nor be affrighted.
1:22 `And ye come near unto me, all of you, and say, Let us send men before us, and they search for us the land, and they bring us back word [concerning] the way in which we go up into it, and the cities unto which we come in;
1:23 and the thing is good in mine eyes, and I take of you twelve men, one man for a tribe.
1:24 `And they turn and go up to the hill-country, and come in unto the valley of Eshcol, and spy it,
1:25 and they take with their hand of the fruit of the land, and bring down unto us, and bring us back word, and say, Good is the land which Jehovah our God is giving to us.
1:26 `And ye have not been willing to go up, and ye provoke the mouth of Jehovah your God,
1:27 and murmur in your tents, and say, In Jehovah's hating us He hath brought us out of the land of Egypt, to give us into the hand of the Amorite -- to destroy us;
1:28 whither are we going up? our brethren have melted our heart, saying, A people greater and taller than we, cities great and fenced to heaven, and also sons of Anakim -- we have seen there.
1:29 `And I say unto you, Be not terrified, nor be afraid of them;
1:30 Jehovah your God, who is going before you -- He doth fight for you, according to all that He hath done with you in Egypt before your eyes,
1:31 and in the wilderness, where thou hast seen that Jehovah thy God hath borne thee as a man beareth his son, in all the way which ye have gone, till your coming in unto this place.
1:32 `And in this thing ye are not stedfast in Jehovah your God,
1:33 who is going before you in the way to search out to you a place for your encamping, in fire by night, to shew you in the way in which ye go, and in a cloud by day.
1:34 `And Jehovah heareth the voice of your words, and is wroth, and sweareth, saying,
1:35 Not one of these men of this evil generation doth see the good land which I have sworn to give to your fathers,
1:36 save Caleb son of Jephunneh -- he doth see it, and to him I give the land on which he hath

trodden, and to his sons, because that he hath been fully after Jehovah.
1:37 `Also with me hath Jehovah been angry for your sake, saying, Also, thou dost not go in thither;
1:38 Joshua son of Nun, who is standing before thee, he goeth in thither; him strengthen thou; for he doth cause Israel to inherit.
1:39 `And your infants, of whom ye have said, For a prey they are, and your sons who have not known to-day good and evil, they go in thither, and to them I give it, and they possess it;
1:40 and ye, turn for yourselves, and journey toward the wilderness, the way of the Red Sea.
1:41 `And ye answer and say unto me, We have sinned against Jehovah; we -- we go up, and we have fought, according to all that which Jehovah our God hath commanded us; and ye gird on each his weapons of war, and ye are ready to go up into the hill-country;
1:42 and Jehovah saith unto me, Say to them, Ye do not go up, nor fight, for I am not in your midst, and ye are not smitten before your enemies.
1:43 `And I speak unto you, and ye have not hearkened, and provoke the mouth of Jehovah, and act proudly, and go up into the hill-country;
1:44 and the Amorite who is dwelling in that hill-country cometh out to meet you, and they pursue you as the bees do, and smite you in Seir -- unto Hormah.
1:45 `And ye turn back and weep before Jehovah, and Jehovah hath not hearkened to your voice, nor hath he given ear unto you;
1:46 and ye dwell in Kadesh many days, according to the days which ye had dwelt.
2:1 `And we turn, and journey into the wilderness, the way of the Red Sea, as Jehovah hath spoken unto me, and we go round the mount of Seir many days.
2:2 `And Jehovah speaketh unto me, saying,
2:3 Enough to you -- is the going round of this mount; turn for yourselves northward.
2:4 `And the people command thou, saying, Ye are passing over into the border of your brethren, sons of Esau, who are dwelling in Seir, and they are afraid of you; and ye have been very watchful,
2:5 ye do not strive with them, for I do not give to you of their land even the treading of the sole of a foot; for a possession to Esau I have given mount Seir.
2:6 `Food ye buy from them with money, and have eaten; and also water ye buy from them with money, and have drunk,
2:7 for Jehovah thy God hath blessed thee in all the work of thy hands; He hath known thy walking in this great wilderness these forty years; Jehovah thy God [is] with thee; thou hast not lacked anything.
2:8 `And we pass by from our brethren, sons of Esau, who are dwelling in Seir, by the way of the plain, by Elath, and by Ezion-Gaber; and we turn, and pass over the way of the wilderness of

Moab;

2:9 and Jehovah saith unto me, Do not distress Moab, nor stir thyself up against them [in] battle, for I do not give to thee of their land [for] a possession; for to the sons of Lot I have given Ar [for] a possession.'

2:10 `The Emim formerly have dwelt in it, a people great, and numerous, and tall, as the Anakim;

2:11 Rephaim they are reckoned, they also, as the Anakim; and the Moabites call them Emim.

2:12 And in Seir have the Horim dwelt formerly; and the sons of Esau dispossess them, and destroy them from before them, and dwell in their stead, as Israel hath done to the land of his possession, which Jehovah hath given to them;

2:13 now, rise ye, and pass over for yourselves the brook Zered; and we pass over the brook Zered.

2:14 `And the days which we have walked from Kadesh-Barnea until that we have passed over the brook Zered, [are] thirty and eight years, till the consumption of all the generation of the men of battle from the midst of the camp, as Jehovah hath sworn to them;

2:15 and also the hand of Jehovah hath been against them, to destroy them from the midst of the camp, till they are consumed.

2:16 `And it cometh to pass, when all the men of battle have finished dying from the midst of the people,

2:17 that Jehovah speaketh unto me, saying,

2:18 Thou art passing over to-day the border of Moab, even Ar,

2:19 and thou hast come near over-against the sons of Ammon, thou dost not distress them, nor stir up thyself against them, for I do not give [any] of the land of the sons of Ammon to thee [for] a possession; for to the sons of Lot I have given it [for] a possession.

2:20 `A land of Rephaim it is reckoned, even it; Rephaim dwelt in it formerly, and the Ammonites call them Zamzummim;

2:21 a people great, and numerous, and tall, as the Anakim, and Jehovah destroyeth them before them, and they dispossess them, and dwell in their stead,

2:22 as He hath done for the sons of Esau, who are dwelling in Seir, when He destroyed the Horim from before them, and they dispossess them, and dwell in their stead, unto this day.

2:23 `As to the Avim who are dwelling in Hazerim unto Azzah, the Caphtorim -- who are coming out from Caphtor -- have destroyed them, and dwell in their stead.

2:24 `Rise ye, journey and pass over the brook Arnon; see, I have given into thy hand Sihon king of Heshbon, the Amorite, and his land; begin to possess, and stir up thyself against him [in] battle.

2:25 This day I begin to put thy dread and thy fear on the face of the peoples under the whole

heavens, who hear thy fame, and have trembled and been pained because of thee.
2:26 `And I send messengers from the wilderness of Kedemoth, unto Sihon king of Heshbon, -- words of peace -- saying,
2:27 Let me pass over through thy land; in the several ways I go; I turn not aside -- right or left --
2:28 food for money thou dost sell me, and I have eaten; and water for money thou dost give to me, and I have drunk; only, let me pass over on my feet, --
2:29 as the sons of Esau who are dwelling in Seir, and the Moabites who are dwelling in Ar, have done to me -- till that I pass over the Jordan, unto the land which Jehovah our God is giving to us.
2:30 `And Sihon king of Heshbon hath not been willing to let us pass over by him, for Jehovah thy God hath hardened his spirit, and strengthened his heart, so as to give him into thy hand as at this day.
2:31 `And Jehovah saith unto me, See, I have begun to give before thee Sihon and his land; begin to possess -- to possess his land.
2:32 `And Sihon cometh out to meet us, he and all his people, to battle to Jahaz;
2:33 and Jehovah our God giveth him before us, and we smite him, and his sons, and all his people;
2:34 and we capture all his cities at that time, and devote the whole city, men, and the women, and the infants -- we have not left a remnant;
2:35 only, the cattle we have spoiled for ourselves, and the spoil of the cities which we have captured.
2:36 `From Aroer, which [is] by the edge of the brook Arnon, and the city which [is] by the brook, even unto Gilead there hath not been a city which [is] too high for us; the whole hath Jehovah our God given before us.
2:37 `Only, unto the land of the sons of Ammon thou hast not drawn near, any part of the brook Jabbok, and cities of the hill-country, and anything which Jehovah our God hath [not] commanded.
3:1 `And we turn, and go up the way to Bashan, and Og king of Bashan cometh out to meet us, he and all his people, to battle, [to] Edrei.
3:2 `And Jehovah saith unto me, Fear him not, for into thy hand I have given him, and all his people, and his land, and thou hast done to him as thou hast done to Sihon king of the Amorite who is dwelling in Heshbon.
3:3 `And Jehovah our God giveth into our hands also Og king of Bashan, and all his people, and we smite him till there hath not been left to him a remnant;
3:4 and we capture all his cities at that time, there hath not been a city which we have not taken from them, sixty cities, all the region of Argob, the kingdom of Og in Bashan.

3:5 All these [are] cities fenced with high walls, two-leaved doors and bar, apart from cities of villages very many;
3:6 and we devote them, as we have done to Sihon king of Heshbon, devoting every city, men, the women, and the infants;
3:7 and all the cattle, and the spoil of the cities, we have spoiled for ourselves.
3:8 `And we take, at that time, the land out of the hand of the two kings of the Amorite, which is beyond the Jordan, from the brook Arnon unto mount Hermon;
3:9 (Sidonians call Hermon, Sirion; and the Amorites call it Senir,)
3:10 all the cities of the plain, and all Gilead, and all Bashan, unto Salchah and Edrei, cities of the kingdom of Og in Bashan,
3:11 for only Og king of Bashan had been left of the remnant of the Rephaim; lo, his bedstead [is] a bedstead of iron; is it not in Rabbath of the sons of Ammon? nine cubits its length, and four cubits its breadth, by the cubit of a man.
3:12 `And this land we have possessed, at that time; from Aroer, which [is] by the brook Arnon, and the half of mount Gilead, and its cities, I have given to the Reubenite, and to the Gadite;
3:13 and the rest of Gilead and all Bashan, the kingdom of Og, I have given to the half tribe of Manasseh; all the region of Argob, to all that Bashan, called the land of Rephaim.
3:14 `Jair son of Manasseh hath taken all the region of Argob, unto the border of Geshuri, and Maachathi, and calleth them by his own name, Bashan-Havoth-Jair, unto this day.
3:15 And to Machir I have given Gilead.
3:16 `And to the Reubenite and to the Gadite I have given from Gilead even unto the brook Arnon, the middle of the valley and the border, even unto Jabbok the brook, the border of the sons of Ammon,
3:17 and the plain, and the Jordan, and the border, from Chinnereth even unto the sea of the plain, the salt sea, under the springs of Pisgah, at the [sun]-rising.
3:18 `And I command you, at that time, saying, Jehovah your God hath given to you this land to possess it; armed ye pass over before your brethren the sons of Israel, all the sons of might.
3:19 Only, your wives, and your infants, and your cattle -- I have known that ye have much cattle -- do dwell in your cities which I have given to you,
3:20 till that Jehovah give rest to your brethren like yourselves, and they also have possessed the land which Jehovah your God is giving to them beyond the Jordan, then ye have turned back each to his possession, which I have given to you.
3:21 `And Jehoshua I have commanded at that time, saying, Thine eyes are seeing all that which Jehovah your God hath done to these two kings -- so doth Jehovah to all the kingdoms whither

thou are passing over;
3:22 fear them not, for Jehovah your God, He is fighting for you.
3:23 `And I entreat for grace unto Jehovah, at that time, saying,
3:24 Lord Jehovah, Thou -- Thou hast begun to shew Thy servant Thy greatness, and Thy strong hand; for who [is] a God in the heavens or in earth who doth according to Thy works, and according to Thy might?
3:25 Let me pass over, I pray Thee, and see the good land which [is] beyond the Jordan, this good hill-country, and Lebanon.
3:26 `And Jehovah sheweth himself wroth with me, for your sake, and hath not hearkened unto me, and Jehovah saith unto me, Enough for thee; add not to speak unto Me any more about this thing:
3:27 go up [to] the top of Pisgah, and lift up thine eyes westward, and northward, and southward, and eastward, and see with thine eyes -- for thou dost not pass over this Jordan;
3:28 and charge Jehoshua, and strengthen him, and harden him, for he doth pass over before this people, and he doth cause them to inherit the land which thou seest.
3:29 `And we dwell in a valley over-against Beth-Peor.
4:1 `And now, Israel, hearken unto the statutes, and unto the judgments which I am teaching you to do, so that ye live, and have gone in, and possessed the land which Jehovah God of your fathers is giving to you.
4:2 Ye do not add to the word which I am commanding you, nor diminish from it, to keep the commands of Jehovah your God which I am commanding you.
4:3 `Your eyes are seeing that which Jehovah hath done in Baal-Peor, for every man who hath gone after Baal-Peor, Jehovah thy God hath destroyed him from thy midst;
4:4 and ye who are cleaving to Jehovah your God, [are] alive, all of you, to-day.
4:5 `See, I have taught you statutes and judgments, as Jehovah my God hath commanded me -- to do so, in the midst of the land whither ye are going in to possess it;
4:6 and ye have kept and done [them] (for it [is] your wisdom and your understanding) before the eyes of the peoples who hear all these statutes, and they have said, Only, a people wise and understanding [is] this great nation.
4:7 `For which [is] the great nation that hath God near unto it, as Jehovah our God, in all we have called unto him?
4:8 and which [is] the great nation which hath righteous statutes and judgments according to all this law which I am setting before you to-day?
4:9 `Only, take heed to thyself, and watch thy soul exceedingly, lest thou forget the things which thine eyes have seen, and lest they turn aside from thy heart, all days of thy life; and thou hast

made them known to thy sons, and to thy sons' sons.
4:10 `The day when thou hast stood before Jehovah thy God in Horeb -- in Jehovah's saying unto me, Assemble to Me the people, and I cause them to hear My words, so that they learn to fear Me all the days that they are alive on the ground, and their sons they teach; --
4:11 and ye draw near and stand under the mountain, and the mountain is burning with fire unto the heart of the heavens -- darkness, cloud, yea, thick darkness:
4:12 `And Jehovah speaketh unto you out of the midst of the fire; a voice of words ye are hearing and a similitude ye are not seeing, only a voice;
4:13 and He declareth to you His covenant, which He hath commanded you to do, the Ten Matters, and He writeth them upon two tables of stone.
4:14 `And me hath Jehovah commanded at that time to teach you statutes and judgments, for your doing them in the land whither ye are passing over to possess it;
4:15 and ye have been very watchful of your souls, for ye have not seen any similitude in the day of Jehovah's speaking unto you in Horeb out of the midst of the fire,
4:16 lest ye do corruptly, and have made to you a graven image, a similitude of any figure, a form of male or female --
4:17 a form of any beast which [is] in the earth -- a form of any winged bird which flieth in the heavens --
4:18 a form of any creeping thing on the ground -- a form of any fish which [is] in the waters under the earth;
4:19 `And lest thou lift up thine eyes towards the heavens, and hast seen the sun, and the moon, and the stars, all the host of the heavens, and thou hast been forced, and hast bowed thyself to them, and served them, which Jehovah thy God hath apportioned to all the peoples under the whole heavens.
4:20 `And you hath Jehovah taken, and He is bringing you out from the iron furnace, from Egypt, to be to Him for a people -- an inheritance, as [at] this day.
4:21 `And Jehovah hath shewed himself wroth with me because of your words, and sweareth to my not passing over the Jordan, and to my not going in unto the good land which Jehovah thy God is giving to thee -- an inheritance;
4:22 for I am dying in this land; I am not passing over the Jordan, and ye are passing over, and have possessed this good land.
4:23 `Take heed to yourselves, lest ye forget the covenant of Jehovah your God, which He hath made with you, and have made to yourselves a graven image, a similitude of anything [concerning] which Jehovah thy God hath charged thee:

4:24 for Jehovah thy God is a fire consuming -- a zealous God.

4:25 `When thou begettest sons and sons' sons, and ye have become old in the land, and have done corruptly, and have made a graven image, a similitude of anything, and have done the evil thing in the eyes of Jehovah, to provoke Him to anger: --

4:26 I have caused to testify against you this day the heavens and the earth, that ye do perish utterly hastily from off the land whither ye are passing over the Jordan to possess it; ye do not prolong days upon it, but are utterly destroyed;

4:27 and Jehovah hath scattered you among the peoples, and ye have been left few in number among the nations, whither Jehovah leadeth you,

4:28 and ye have served there gods, work of man's hands, wood and stone, which see not, nor hear, nor eat, nor smell.

4:29 `And -- ye have sought from thence Jehovah thy God, and hast found, when thou seekest Him with all thy heart, and with all thy soul,

4:30 in distress [being] to thee, and all these things have found thee, in the latter end of the days, and thou hast turned back unto Jehovah thy God, and hast hearkened to His voice;

4:31 for a merciful God [is] Jehovah thy God; He doth not fail thee, nor destroy thee, nor forget the covenant of thy fathers, which He hath sworn to them.

4:32 `For, ask, I pray thee, at the former days which have been before thee, from the day that God prepared man on the earth, and from the [one] end of the heavens even unto the [other] end of the heavens, whether there hath been as this great thing -- or hath been heard like it?

4:33 Hath a people heard the voice of God speaking out of the midst of the fire, as thou hast heard, thou -- and doth live?

4:34 Or hath God tried to go in to take to Himself, a nation from the midst of a nation, by trials, by signs, and by wonders, and by war, and by a strong hand, and by a stretched-out arm, and by great terrors -- according to all that Jehovah your God hath done to you, in Egypt, before your eyes?

4:35 Thou, thou hast been shewn [it], to know that Jehovah He [is] God; there is none else besides Him.

4:36 `From the heavens He hath caused thee to hear His voice, to instruct thee, and on earth He hath shewed thee His great fire, and His words thou hast heard out of the midst of the fire.

4:37 `And because that He hath loved thy fathers, He doth also fix on their seed after them, and doth bring thee out, in His presence, by His great power, from Egypt:

4:38 to dispossess nations greater and stronger than thou, from thy presence, to bring thee in to give to thee their land -- an inheritance, as [at] this day.

4:39 `And thou hast known to-day, and hast turned [it] back unto thy heart, that Jehovah He [is]

God, in the heavens above, and on the earth beneath -- there is none else;
4:40 and thou hast kept His statutes and His commands which I am commanding thee to-day, so that it is well to thee, and to thy sons after thee, and so that thou prolongest days on the ground which Jehovah thy God is giving to thee -- all the days.'
4:41 Then Moses separateth three cities beyond the Jordan, towards the sun-rising,
4:42 for the fleeing thither of the man-slayer, who slayeth his neighbour unknowingly, and he is not hating him heretofore, and he hath fled unto one of these cities, and he hath lived:
4:43 Bezer, in the wilderness, in the land of the plain, of the Reubenite; and Ramoth, in Gilead, of the Gadite; and Golan, in Bashan, of the Manassahite.
4:44 And this [is] the law which Moses hath set before the sons of Israel;
4:45 these [are] the testimonies, and the statutes, and the judgments, which Moses hath spoken unto the sons of Israel, in their coming out of Egypt,
4:46 beyond the Jordan, in the valley over-against Beth-Peor, in the land of Sihon, king of the Amorite, who is dwelling in Heshbon, whom Moses and the sons of Israel have smitten, in their coming out of Egypt,
4:47 and they possess his land, and the land of Og king of Bashan, two kings of the Amorite who [are] beyond the Jordan, [towards] the sun-rising;
4:48 from Aroer, which [is] by the edge of the brook Arnon, even unto mount Sion, which [is] Hermon --
4:49 and all the plain beyond the Jordan eastward, even unto the sea of the plain, under the springs of Pisgah.
5:1 And Moses calleth unto all Israel, and saith unto them, `Hear, Israel, the statutes and the judgments which I am speaking in your ears to-day, and ye have learned them, and have observed to do them.
5:2 Jehovah our God made with us a covenant in Horeb;
5:3 not with our fathers hath Jehovah made this covenant, but with us; we -- these -- here to-day -- all of us alive.
5:4 Face to face hath Jehovah spoken with you, in the mount, out of the midst of the fire;
5:5 I am standing between Jehovah and you, at that time, to declare to you the word of Jehovah, for ye have been afraid from the presence of the fire, and ye have not gone up into the mount; saying:
5:6 `I Jehovah [am] thy God, who hath brought thee out from the land of Egypt, from a house of servants.
5:7 `Thou hast no other gods in My presence.

5:8 `Thou dost not make to thee a graven image, any similitude which [is] in the heavens above,
and which [is] in the earth beneath, and which [is] in the waters under the earth;
5:9 thou dost not bow thyself to them nor serve them, for I Jehovah thy God [am] a zealous God,
charging iniquity of fathers on children, and on a third [generation], and on a fourth, to those hating
Me;
5:10 and doing kindness to thousands, to those loving Me, and to those keeping My commands.
5:11 `Thou dost not take up the Name of Jehovah thy God for a vain thing, for Jehovah doth not
acquit him who taketh up His Name for a vain thing.
5:12 `Observe the day of the sabbath -- to sanctify it, as Jehovah thy God hath commanded thee;
5:13 six days thou dost labour, and hast done all thy work,
5:14 and the seventh day [is] a sabbath to Jehovah thy God; thou dost not do any work, thou, and
thy son, and thy daughter, and thy man-servant, and thy handmaid, and thine ox, and thine ass,
and all thy cattle, and thy sojourner who [is] within thy gates; so that thy man-servant, and thy
handmaid doth rest like thyself;
5:15 and thou hast remembered that a servant thou hast been in the land of Egypt, and Jehovah
thy God is bringing thee out thence by a strong hand, and by a stretched-out arm; therefore hath
Jehovah thy God commanded thee to keep the day of the sabbath.
5:16 `Honour thy father and thy mother, as Jehovah thy God hath commanded thee, so that thy
days are prolonged, and so that it is well with thee, on the ground which Jehovah thy God is giving
to thee.
5:17 `Thou dost not murder.
5:18 `Thou dost not commit adultery.
5:19 `Thou dost not steal.
5:20 `Thou dost not answer against thy neighbour -- a false testimony.
5:21 `Thou dost not desire thy neighbour's wife; nor dost thou covet thy neighbour's house, his
field, and his man-servant, and his handmaid, his ox, and his ass, and anything which [is] thy
neighbour's.
5:22 `These words hath Jehovah spoken unto all your assembly, in the mount out of the midst of
the fire, of the cloud, and of the thick darkness -- a great voice; and He hath not added, and He
writeth them on two tables of stone, and giveth them unto me.
5:23 `And it cometh to pass as ye hear the voice out of the midst of the darkness, and of the
mountain burning with fire, that ye come near unto me, all the heads of your tribes, and your elders,
5:24 and say, Lo, Jehovah our God hath shewed us His honour, and His greatness; and His voice
we have heard out of the midst of the fire; this day we have seen that God doth speak with man --

and he hath lived.
5:25 `And, now, why do we die? for consume us doth this great fire -- if we add to hear the voice of Jehovah our God any more -- then we have died.
5:26 For who of all flesh [is] he who hath heard the voice of the living God speaking out of the midst of the fire like us -- and doth live?
5:27 Draw near thou, and hear all that which Jehovah our God saith, and thou, thou dost speak unto us all that which Jehovah our God speaketh unto thee, and we have hearkened, and done it.
5:28 `And Jehovah heareth the voice of your words, in your speaking unto me, and Jehovah saith unto me, I have heard the voice of the words of this people which they have spoken unto thee; they have done well [in] all that they have spoken.
5:29 O that their heart had been thus to them, to fear Me, and to keep My commands all the days, that it may be well with them, and with their sons -- to the age!
5:30 `Go, say to them, Turn back for yourselves, to your tents;
5:31 and thou here stand thou with Me, and let Me speak unto thee all the command, and the statutes, and the judgments which thou dost teach them, and they have done in the land which I am giving to them to possess it.
5:32 `And ye have observed to do as Jehovah your God hath commanded you, ye turn not aside -- right or left;
5:33 in all the way which Jehovah your God hath commanded you ye walk, so that ye live, and [it is] well with you, and ye have prolonged days in the land which ye possess.
6:1 `And this [is] the command, the statutes and the judgments which Jehovah your God hath commanded to teach you, to do in the land which ye are passing over thither to possess it,
6:2 so that thou dost fear Jehovah thy God, to keep all His statutes and His commands, which I am commanding thee, thou, and thy son, and thy son's son, all days of thy life, and so that thy days are prolonged.
6:3 `And thou hast heard, O Israel, and observed to do, that it may be well with thee, and that thou mayest multiply exceedingly, as Jehovah, God of thy fathers, hath spoken to thee, [in] the land flowing with milk and honey.
6:4 `Hear, O Israel, Jehovah our God [is] one Jehovah;
6:5 and thou hast loved Jehovah thy God with all thy heart, and with all thy soul, and with all thy might,
6:6 and these words which I am commanding thee to-day have been on thine heart,
6:7 and thou hast repeated them to thy sons, and spoken of them in thy sitting in thine house, and in thy walking in the way, and in thy lying down, and in thy rising up,

6:8 and hast bound them for a sign upon thy hand, and they have been for frontlets between thine eyes,
6:9 and thou hast written them on door-posts of thy house, and on thy gates.
6:10 `And it hath been, when Jehovah thy God doth bring thee in unto the land which He hath sworn to thy fathers, to Abraham, to Isaac, and to Jacob, to give to thee -- cities great and good, which thou hast not built,
6:11 and houses full of all good things which thou hast not filled, and wells digged which thou hast not digged, vineyards and olive-yards which thou hast not planted, and thou hast eaten, and been satisfied;
6:12 `Take heed to thyself lest thou forget Jehovah who hath brought thee out of the land of Egypt, out of a house of servants;
6:13 Jehovah thy God thou dost fear, and Him thou dost serve, and by His name thou dost swear;
6:14 ye do not go after other gods, of the gods of the peoples who [are] round about you;
6:15 for a zealous God [is] Jehovah thy God in thy midst -- lest the anger of Jehovah thy God burn against thee, and He hath destroyed thee from off the face of the ground.
6:16 `Ye do not try Jehovah your God as ye tried in Massah;
6:17 ye do diligently keep the commands of Jehovah your God, and His testimonies, and His statutes which He hath commanded thee,
6:18 and thou hast done that which is right and good in the eyes of Jehovah, so that it is well with thee, and thou hast gone in and possessed the good land which Jehovah hath sworn to thy fathers,
6:19 to drive away all thine enemies from thy presence, as Jehovah hath spoken.
6:20 `When thy son asketh thee hereafter, saying, What [are] the testimonies, and the statutes, and the judgments, which Jehovah our God hath commanded you?
6:21 then thou hast said to thy son, Servants we have been to Pharaoh in Egypt, and Jehovah bringeth us out of Egypt by a high hand;
6:22 and Jehovah giveth signs and wonders, great and sad, on Egypt, on Pharaoh, and on all his house, before our eyes;
6:23 and us He hath brought out thence, in order to bring us in, to give to us the land which He had sworn to our fathers.
6:24 And Jehovah commandeth us to do all these statutes, to fear Jehovah our God, for good to ourselves all the days, to keep us alive, as [at] this day;
6:25 and righteousness it is for us, when we observe to do all this command before Jehovah our God, as He hath commanded us.
7:1 `When Jehovah thy God doth bring thee in unto the land whither thou art going in to possess it,

and He hath cast out many nations from thy presence, the Hittite, and the Girgashite, and the Amorite, and the Canaanite, and the Perizzite, and the Hivite, and the Jebusite, seven nations more numerous and mighty than thou,
7:2 and Jehovah thy God hath given them before thee, and thou hast smitten them -- thou dost utterly devote them -- thou dost not make with them a covenant, nor dost thou favour them.
7:3 `And thou dost not join in marriage with them; thy daughter thou dost not give to his son, and his daughter thou dost not take to thy son,
7:4 for he doth turn aside thy son from after Me, and they have served other gods, and the anger of Jehovah hath burned against you, and hath destroyed thee hastily.
7:5 `But thus thou dost to them: their altars ye break down, and their standing pillars ye shiver, and their shrines ye cut down, and their graven images ye burn with fire;
7:6 for a holy people [art] thou to Jehovah thy God; on thee hath Jehovah thy God fixed, to be to Him for a peculiar people, out of all the peoples who [are] on the face of the ground.
7:7 `Not because of your being more numerous than any of the peoples hath Jehovah delighted in you, and fixeth on you, for ye [are] the least of all the peoples,
7:8 but because of Jehovah's loving you, and because of His keeping the oath which He hath sworn to your fathers, hath Jehovah brought you out by a strong hand, and doth ransom you from a house of servants, from the hand of Pharaoh king of Egypt.
7:9 `And thou hast known that Jehovah thy God He [is] God, the faithful God, keeping the covenant, and the kindness, to those loving Him, and to those keeping His commands -- to a thousand generations,
7:10 and repaying to those hating Him, unto their face, to destroy them; He delayeth not to him who is hating Him -- unto his face, He repayeth to him --
7:11 and thou hast kept the command, and the statutes, and the judgments, which I am commanding thee to-day to do them.
7:12 `And it hath been, because ye hear these judgments, and have kept, and done them, that Jehovah thy God hath kept to thee the covenant and the kindness which He hath sworn to thy fathers,
7:13 and hath loved thee, and blessed thee, and multiplied thee, and hath blessed the fruit of thy womb, and the fruit of thy ground, thy corn, and thy new wine, and thine oil, the increase of thine oxen, and the wealth of thy flock, on the ground which He hath sworn to thy fathers to give to thee.
7:14 `Blessed art thou above all the peoples, there is not in thee a barren man or a barren woman -- nor among your cattle;
7:15 and Jehovah hath turned aside from thee every sickness, and none of the evil diseases of

Egypt (which thou hast known) doth He put on thee, and He hath put them on all hating thee.
7:16 `And thou hast consumed all the peoples whom Jehovah thy God is giving to thee; thine eye hath no pity on them, and thou dost not serve their gods, for a snare it [is] to thee.
7:17 `When thou sayest in thine heart, These nations [are] more numerous than I, how am I able to dispossess them? --
7:18 thou art not afraid of them; thou dost surely remember that which Jehovah thy God hath done to Pharaoh, and to all Egypt,
7:19 the great trials which thine eyes have seen, and the signs, and the wonders, and the strong hand, and the stretched-out arm, with which Jehovah thy God hath brought thee out; so doth Jehovah thy God to all the peoples of whose presence thou art afraid.
7:20 `And also the locust doth Jehovah thy God send among them, till the destruction of those who are left, and of those who are hidden from thy presence;
7:21 thou art not terrified by their presence, for Jehovah thy God [is] in thy midst, a God great and fearful.
7:22 `And Jehovah thy God hath cast out these nations from thy presence little [by] little, (thou art not able to consume them hastily, lest the beast of the field multiply against thee),
7:23 and Jehovah thy God hath given them before thee, and destroyed them -- a great destruction -- till their destruction;
7:24 and He hath given their kings into thy hand, and thou hast destroyed their name from under the heavens; no man doth station himself in thy presence till thou hast destroyed them.
7:25 `The graven images of their gods ye do burn with fire; thou dost not desire the silver and gold on them, nor hast thou taken [it] to thyself, lest thou be snared by it, for the abomination of Jehovah thy God it [is];
7:26 and thou dost not bring in an abomination unto thy house -- or thou hast been devoted like it; -- thou dost utterly detest it, and thou dost utterly abominate it; for it [is] devoted.
8:1 `All the command which I am commanding thee to-day ye observe to do, so that ye live, and have multiplied, and gone in, and possessed the land which Jehovah hath sworn to your fathers;
8:2 and thou hast remembered all the way which Jehovah thy God hath caused thee to go these forty years in the wilderness, in order to humble thee to try thee, to know that which [is] in thy heart, whether thou dost keep His commands or not.
8:3 `And He doth humble thee, and cause thee to hunger and doth cause thee to eat the manna (which thou hast not known, even thy fathers have not known), in order to cause thee to know that not by bread alone doth man live, but by every produce of the mouth of Jehovah man doth live.
8:4 `Thy raiment hath not worn out from off thee, and thy foot hath not swelled these forty years,

8:5 and thou hast known, with thy heart, that as a man chastiseth his son Jehovah thy God is
chastising thee,
8:6 and thou hast kept the commands of Jehovah thy God, to walk in His ways, and to fear Him.
8:7 `For Jehovah thy God is bringing thee in unto a good land, a land of brooks of waters, of
fountains, and of depths coming out in valley and in mountain:
8:8 a land of wheat, and barley, and vine, and fig, and pomegranate; a land of oil olive and honey;
8:9 a land in which without scarcity thou dost eat bread, thou dost not lack anything in it; a land
whose stones [are] iron, and out of its mountains thou dost dig brass;
8:10 and thou hast eaten, and been satisfied, and hast blessed Jehovah thy God, on the good land
which he hath given to thee.
8:11 `Take heed to thyself, lest thou forget Jehovah thy God so as not to keep His commands, and
His judgments, and His statutes which I am commanding thee to-day;
8:12 lest thou eat, and hast been satisfied, and good houses dost build, and hast inhabited;
8:13 and thy herd and thy flock be multiplied, and silver and gold be multiplied to thee; and all that
is thine be multiplied:
8:14 `And thy heart hath been high, and thou hast forgotten Jehovah thy God (who is bringing thee
out of the land of Egypt, out of a house of servants;
8:15 who is causing thee to go in the great and the terrible wilderness -- burning serpent, and
scorpion, and thirst -- where there is no water; who is bringing out to thee waters from the flinty
rock;
8:16 who is causing thee to eat manna in the wilderness, which thy fathers have not known, in
order to humble thee, and in order to try thee, to do thee good in thy latter end),
8:17 and thou hast said in thy heart, My power, and the might of my hand, hath made for me this
wealth:
8:18 `And thou hast remembered Jehovah thy God, for He it [is] who is giving to thee power to
make wealth, in order to establish His covenant which He hath sworn to thy fathers as [at] this day.
8:19 `And it hath been -- if thou really forget Jehovah thy God, and hast gone after other gods, and
served them, and bowed thyself to them, I have testified against you to-day that ye do utterly
perish;
8:20 as the nations whom Jehovah is destroying from your presence, so ye perish; because ye
hearken not to the voice of Jehovah your God.
9:1 `Hear, Israel, thou art passing over to-day the Jordan, to go in to possess nations greater and
mightier than thyself; cities great and fenced in the heavens;
9:2 a people great and tall, sons of Anakim, whom thou -- thou hast known, (and thou -- thou hast

heard: Who doth station himself before sons of Anak?)
9:3 and thou hast known to-day, that Jehovah thy God [is] He who is passing over before thee -- a fire consuming; He doth destroy them, and He doth humble them before thee, and thou hast dispossessed them, and destroyed them hastily, as Jehovah hath spoken to thee.
9:4 `Thou dost not speak in thy heart (in Jehovah thy God's driving them away from before thee), saying, For my righteousness hath Jehovah brought me in to possess this land, seeing for the wickedness of these nations is Jehovah dispossessing them from thy presence;
9:5 not for thy righteousness, and for the uprightness of thy heart, art thou going in to possess their land; but for the wickedness of these nations is Jehovah thy God dispossessing them from before thee; and in order to establish the word which Jehovah hath sworn to thy fathers, to Abraham, to Isaac, and to Jacob;
9:6 and thou hast known, that not for thy righteousness is Jehovah thy God giving to thee this good land to possess it, for a people stiff of neck thou [art].
9:7 `Remember -- do not forget -- that [with] which thou hast made Jehovah thy God wroth in the wilderness; even from the day that thou hast come out of the land of Egypt till your coming in unto this place rebels ye have been with Jehovah;
9:8 even in Horeb ye have made Jehovah wroth, and Jehovah sheweth Himself angry against you -- to destroy you.
9:9 `In my going up into the mount to receive the tables of stone (tables of the covenant which Jehovah hath made with you), and I abide in the mount forty days and forty nights; bread I have not eaten, and water I have not drunk;
9:10 and Jehovah giveth unto me the two tables of stone written with the finger of God, and on them according to all the words which Jehovah hath spoken with you in the mount, out of the midst of the fire, in the day of the assembly.
9:11 `And it cometh to pass, at the end of forty days and forty nights, Jehovah hath given unto me the two tables of stone -- tables of the covenant,
9:12 and Jehovah saith unto me, Rise, go down, hasten from this, for thy people hath done corruptly, whom thou hast brought out of Egypt; they have turned aside hastily out of the way which I have commanded them -- they have made to themselves a molten thing!
9:13 `And Jehovah speaketh unto me, saying, I have seen this people, and lo, a people stiff of neck it [is];
9:14 desist from Me, and I destroy them, and blot out their name from under the heavens, and I make thee become a nation more mighty and numerous than it.
9:15 `And I turn, and come down from the mount, and the mount is burning with fire, and the two

tables of the covenant on my two hands,
9:16 and I see, and lo, ye have sinned against Jehovah your God; ye have made to yourselves a
molten calf; ye have turned aside hastily out of the way which Jehovah hath commanded you.
9:17 `And I lay hold on the two tables, and cast them out of my two hands, and break them before
your eyes,
9:18 and I throw myself before Jehovah, as at first, forty days and forty nights; bread I have not
eaten, and water I have not drunk, because of all your sins which ye have sinned, by doing the evil
thing in the eyes of Jehovah, to make Him angry.
9:19 `For I have been afraid because of the anger and the fury with which Jehovah hath been
wroth against you, to destroy you; and Jehovah doth hearken unto me also at this time.
9:20 `And with Aaron hath Jehovah shewed himself very angry, to destroy him, and I pray also for
Aaron at that time;
9:21 and your sin, which ye have made -- the calf -- I have taken, and I burn it with fire, and beat it,
grinding well till that it [is] small as dust, and I cast its dust unto the brook which is going down out
of the mount.
9:22 `And in Taberah, and in Massah, and in Kibroth-Hattaavah, ye have been making Jehovah
wroth:
9:23 and in Jehovah's sending you from Kadesh-Barnea, saying, Go up, and possess the land
which I have given to you, then ye provoke the mouth of Jehovah your God, and have not given
credence to Him, nor hearkened to His voice;
9:24 rebels ye have been with Jehovah from the day of my knowing you.
9:25 `And I throw myself before Jehovah, the forty days and the forty nights, as I had thrown
myself, for Jehovah hath said -- to destroy you;
9:26 and I pray unto Jehovah, and say, Lord Jehovah, destroy not Thy people, and Thine
inheritance, whom Thou hast ransomed in Thy greatness; whom Thou hast brought out of Egypt
with a strong hand;
9:27 be mindful of Thy servants, of Abraham, of Isaac, and of Jacob, turn not unto the stiffness of
this people, and unto its wickedness, and unto its sin;
9:28 lest the land say from which Thou hast brought us out, Because of Jehovah's want of ability to
bring them in unto the land of which He hath spoken to them, and because of His hating them, He
brought them out to put them to death in the wilderness;
9:29 and they [are] Thy people, and Thine inheritance, whom Thou hast brought out by Thy great
power, and by Thy stretched-out arm!
10:1 `At that time hath Jehovah said unto me, Grave for thee two tables of stone, like the first, and

come up unto Me, into the mount, and thou hast made for thee an ark of wood,
10:2 and I write on the tables the words which were on the first tables, which thou hast broken, and thou hast placed them in the ark;
10:3 and I make an ark of shittim wood, and grave two tables of stone like the first, and go up to the mount, and the two tables in my hand.
10:4 `And He writeth on the tables, according to the first writing, the Ten Matters, which Jehovah hath spoken unto you in the mount, out of the midst of the fire, in the day of the assembly, and Jehovah giveth them unto me,
10:5 and I turn and come down from the mount, and put the tables in the ark which I had made, and they are there, as Jehovah commanded me.
10:6 `And the sons of Israel have journeyed from Beeroth of the sons of Jaakan to Mosera, there Aaron died, and he is buried there, and Eleazar his son doth act as priest in his stead;
10:7 thence they journeyed to Gudgodah, and from Gudgodah to Jotbathah, a land of brooks of water.
10:8 `At that time hath Jehovah separated the tribe of Levi, to bear the ark of the covenant of Jehovah, to stand before Jehovah, to serve Him, and to bless in His name, unto this day,
10:9 therefore there hath not been to Levi a portion and inheritance with his brethren; Jehovah Himself [is] his inheritance, as Jehovah thy God hath spoken to him.
10:10 `And I -- I have stood in the mount, as the former days, forty days and forty nights, and Jehovah hearkeneth unto me also at that time; Jehovah hath not willed to destroy thee.
10:11 `And Jehovah saith unto me, Rise, go to journey before the people, and they go in and possess the land which I have sworn to their fathers to give to them.
10:12 `And now, Israel, what is Jehovah thy God asking from thee, except to fear Jehovah thy God, to walk in all His ways, and to love Him, and to serve Jehovah thy God with all thy heart, and with all thy soul,
10:13 to keep the commands of Jehovah, and His statutes which I am commanding thee to-day, for good to thee?
10:14 `Lo, to Jehovah thy God [are] the heavens and the heavens of the heavens, the earth and all that [is] in it;
10:15 only in thy fathers hath Jehovah delighted -- to love them, and He doth fix on their seed after them -- on you, out of all the peoples as [at] this day;
10:16 and ye have circumcised the foreskin of your heart, and your neck ye do not harden any more;
10:17 for Jehovah your God -- He [is] God of the gods, and Lord of the lords; God, the great, the

mighty, and the fearful; who accepteth not persons, nor taketh a bribe;
10:18 He is doing the judgment of fatherless and widow, and loving the sojourner, to give to him bread and raiment.
10:19 `And ye have loved the sojourner, for sojourners ye were in the land of Egypt.
10:20 `Jehovah thy God thou dost fear, Him thou dost serve, and to Him thou dost cleave, and by His name thou dost swear.
10:21 He [is] thy praise, and He [is] thy God, who hath done with thee these great and fearful [things] which thine eyes have seen:
10:22 with seventy persons did thy fathers go down to Egypt, and now hath Jehovah thy God made thee as stars of the heavens for multitude.
11:1 `And thou hast loved Jehovah thy God, and kept His charge, and His statutes, and His judgments, and His commands, all the days;
11:2 and ye have known to-day -- for it is not your sons who have not known, and who have not seen the chastisement of Jehovah your God, His greatness, His strong hand, and His stretched-out arm,
11:3 and His signs, and His doings, which He hath done in the midst of Egypt, to Pharaoh king of Egypt, and to all his land;
11:4 and that which He hath done to the force of Egypt, to its horses, and to its chariot, when He hath caused the waters of the Red Sea to flow against their faces in their pursuing after them, and Jehovah destroyeth them, unto this day;
11:5 and that which He hath done to you in the wilderness, till your coming in unto this place;
11:6 and that which He hath done to Dathan, and to Abiram, sons of Eliab, sons of Reuben, when the earth hath opened her mouth and swalloweth them, and their houses, and their tents, and all that liveth, which is at their feet, in the midst of all Israel:
11:7 `-- But [it is] your eyes which are seeing all the great work of Jehovah, which He hath done;
11:8 and ye have kept all the command which I am commanding thee to-day, so that ye are strong, and have gone in, and possessed the land whither ye are passing over to possess it,
11:9 and so that ye prolong days on the ground which Jehovah hath sworn to your fathers to give to them and to their seed -- a land flowing with milk and honey.
11:10 `For the land whither thou art going in to possess it, is not as the land of Egypt whence ye have come out, where thou sowest thy seed, and hast watered with thy foot, as a garden of the green herb;
11:11 but the land whither ye are passing over to possess it, [is] a land of hills and valleys; of the rain of the heavens it drinketh water;

11:12 a land which Jehovah thy God is searching; continually [are] the eyes of Jehovah thy God
upon it, from the beginning of the year even unto the latter end of the year.
11:13 `And it hath been -- if thou hearken diligently unto My commands which I am commanding
you to-day, to love Jehovah your God, and to serve Him with all your heart, and with all your soul --
11:14 that I have given the rain of your land in its season -- sprinkling and gathered -- and thou hast
gathered thy corn, and thy new wine, and thine oil,
11:15 and I have given herbs in thy field for thy cattle, and thou hast eaten, and been satisfied.
11:16 `Take heed to yourselves, lest your heart be enticed, and ye have turned aside, and served
other gods, and bowed yourselves to them,
11:17 and the anger of Jehovah hath burned against you, and He hath restrained the heavens, and
there is no rain, and the ground doth not give her increase, and ye have perished hastily from off
the good land which Jehovah is giving to you.
11:18 `And ye have placed these my words on your heart, and on your soul, and have bound them
for a sign on your hand, and they have been for frontlets between your eyes;
11:19 and ye have taught them to your sons, by speaking of them in thy sitting in thy house, and in
thy going in the way, and in thy lying down, and in thy rising up,
11:20 and hast written them on the side-posts of thy house, and on thy gates,
11:21 so that your days are multiplied, and the days of your sons, on the ground which Jehovah
hath sworn to your fathers to give to them, as the days of the heavens on the earth.
11:22 `For, if ye diligently keep all this command which I am commanding you -- to do it, to love
Jehovah your God, to walk in all His ways, and to cleave to Him,
11:23 then hath Jehovah dispossessed all these nations from before you, and ye have possessed
nations, greater and mightier than you;
11:24 every place on which the sole of your foot treadeth is yours; from the wilderness, and
Lebanon, from the river, the river Phrat, even unto the farther sea is your border;
11:25 no man doth station himself in your presence; your dread and your fear doth Jehovah your
God put on the face of all the land on which ye tread, as He hath spoken to you.
11:26 `See, I am setting before you to-day a blessing and a reviling:
11:27 the blessing, when ye hearken unto the commands of Jehovah your God, which I am
commanding you to-day;
11:28 and the reviling, if ye do not hearken unto the commands of Jehovah your God, and have
turned aside out of the way which I am commanding you to-day, to go after other gods which ye
have not known.
11:29 `And it hath been, when Jehovah thy God doth bring thee in unto the land whither thou art

going in to possess it, that thou hast given the blessing on mount Gerizim, and the reviling on mount Ebal;
11:30 are they not beyond the Jordan, behind the way of the going in of the sun, in the land of the Canaanite, who is dwelling in the plain over-against Gilgal, near the oaks of Moreh?
11:31 for ye are passing over the Jordan to go in to possess the land which Jehovah your God is giving to you; and ye have possessed it, and dwelt in it,
11:32 and observed to do all the statutes and the judgments which I am setting before you to day.
12:1 `These [are] the statutes and the judgments which ye observe to do in the land which Jehovah, God of thy fathers, hath given to thee to possess it, all the days that ye are living on the ground:
12:2 ye do utterly destroy all the places where the nations which ye are dispossessing served their gods, on the high mountains, and on the heights, and under every green tree;
12:3 and ye have broken down their altars, and shivered their standing pillars, and their shrines ye burn with fire, and graven images of their gods ye cut down, and have destroyed their name out of that place.
12:4 `Ye do not do so to Jehovah your God;
12:5 but unto the place which Jehovah your God doth choose out of all your tribes to put His name there, to His tabernacle ye seek, and thou hast entered thither,
12:6 and hast brought in thither your burnt-offerings, and your sacrifices, and your tithes, and the heave-offering of your hand, and your vows, and your free-will offerings, and the firstlings of your herd and of your flock;
12:7 and ye have eaten there before Jehovah your God, and have rejoiced in every putting forth of your hand, ye and your households, with which Jehovah thy God hath blessed thee.
12:8 `Ye do not do according to all that we are doing here to-day, each anything that is right in his own eyes,
12:9 for ye have not come in hitherto unto the rest, and unto the inheritance, which Jehovah thy God is giving to thee;
12:10 and ye have passed over the Jordan, and have dwelt in the land which Jehovah your God is causing you to inherit, and He hath given rest to you from all your enemies round about, and ye have dwelt confidently:
12:11 `And it hath been, the place on which Jehovah your God doth fix to cause His name to tabernacle there, thither ye bring in all that which I am commanding you, your burnt-offerings, and your sacrifices, your tithes, and the heave-offering of your hand, and all the choice of your vows which ye vow to Jehovah;

12:12 and ye have rejoiced before Jehovah your God, ye, and your sons, and your daughters, and your men-servants, and your handmaids, and the Levite who [is] within your gates, for he hath no part and inheritance with you.
12:13 `Take heed to thee, lest thou cause thy burnt-offerings to ascend in any place which thou seest,
12:14 except in the place which Jehovah doth choose in one of thy tribes, there thou dost cause thy burnt-offerings to ascend, and there thou dost do all that which I am commanding thee.
12:15 `Only, with all the desire of thy soul thou dost sacrifice, and hast eaten flesh according to the blessing of Jehovah thy God which He hath given to thee, in all thy gates; the unclean and the clean do eat it, as of the roe, and as of the hart.
12:16 `Only, the blood ye do not eat -- on the earth thou dost pour it as water;
12:17 thou art not able to eat within thy gates the tithe of thy corn, and of thy new wine, and thine oil, and the firstlings of thy herd and of thy flock, and any of thy vows which thou vowest, and thy free-will offerings, and heave-offering of thy hand;
12:18 but before Jehovah thy God thou dost eat it, in the place which Jehovah thy God doth fix on, thou, and thy son, and thy daughter, and thy man-servant, and thy handmaid, and the Levite who [is] within thy gates, and thou hast rejoiced before Jehovah thy God in every putting forth of thy hand;
12:19 take heed to thee lest thou forsake the Levite all thy days on thy ground.
12:20 `When Jehovah thy God doth enlarge thy border, as He hath spoken to thee, and thou hast said, Let me eat flesh -- for thy soul desireth to eat flesh -- of all the desire of thy soul thou dost eat flesh.
12:21 `When the place is far from thee which Jehovah thy God doth choose to put His name there, then thou hast sacrificed of thy herd and of thy flock which Jehovah hath given to thee, as I have commanded thee, and hast eaten within thy gates, of all the desire of thy soul;
12:22 only, as the roe and the hart is eaten, so dost thou eat it; the unclean and the clean doth alike eat it.
12:23 `Only, be sure not to eat the blood, for the blood [is] the life, and thou dost not eat the life with the flesh;
12:24 thou dost not eat it, on the earth thou dost pour it as water;
12:25 thou dost not eat it, in order that it may be well with thee, and with thy sons after thee, when thou dost that which [is] right in the eyes of Jehovah.
12:26 `Only, thy holy things which thou hast, and thy vows, thou dost take up, and hast gone in unto the place which Jehovah doth choose,

12:27 and thou hast made thy burnt-offerings -- the flesh and the blood -- on the altar of Jehovah thy God; and the blood of thy sacrifices is poured out by the altar of Jehovah thy God, and the flesh thou dost eat.
12:28 Observe, and thou hast obeyed all these words which I am commanding thee, in order that it may be well with thee and with thy sons after thee -- to the age, when thou dost that which [is] good and right in the eyes of Jehovah thy God.
12:29 `When Jehovah thy God doth cut off the nations -- whither thou art going in to possess them -- from thy presence, and thou hast possessed them, and hast dwelt in their land --
12:30 take heed to thee, lest thou be snared after them, after their being destroyed out of thy presence, and lest thou enquire about their gods, saying, How do these nations serve their gods, and I do so -- even I?
12:31 `Thou dost not do so to Jehovah thy God; for every abomination of Jehovah which He is hating they have done to their gods, for even their sons and their daughters they burn with fire to their gods.
12:32 The whole thing which I am commanding you -- it ye observe to do; thou dost not add unto it, nor diminish from it.
13:1 `When there ariseth in your midst a prophet, or a dreamer of a dream, and he hath given unto thee a sign or wonder,
13:2 and the sign and the wonder hath come which he hath spoken of unto thee, saying, Let us go after other gods (which thou hast not known), and serve them,
13:3 thou dost not hearken unto the words of that prophet, or unto that dreamer of the dream, for Jehovah your God is trying you, to know whether ye are loving Jehovah your God with all your heart, and with all your soul;
13:4 after Jehovah your God ye walk, and Him ye fear, and His commands ye keep, and to His voice ye hearken, and Him ye serve, and to Him ye cleave.
13:5 `And that prophet, or that dreamer of the dream, is put to death, for he hath spoken apostacy against Jehovah your God (who is bringing you out of the land of Egypt, and hath ransomed you out of a house of servants), to drive you out of the way in which Jehovah thy God hath commanded thee to walk, and thou hast put away the evil thing from thy midst.
13:6 `When thy brother -- son of thy mother, or thy son, or thy daughter, or the wife of thy bosom, or thy friend who [is] as thine own soul -- doth move thee, in secret, saying, Let us go and serve other gods -- (which thou hast not known, thou and thy fathers,
13:7 of the gods of the peoples who [are] round about you, who are near unto thee, or who are far off from thee, from the end of the earth even unto the end of the earth) --

13:8 thou dost not consent to him, nor hearken unto him, nor doth thine eye have pity on him, nor dost thou spare, nor dost thou cover him over.
13:9 `But thou dost surely kill him; thy hand is on him, in the first place, to put him to death, and the hand of all the people last;
13:10 and thou hast stoned him with stones, and he hath died, for he hath sought to drive thee away from Jehovah thy God, who is bringing thee out of the land of Egypt, out of a house of servants;
13:11 and all Israel do hear and fear, and add not to do like this evil thing in thy midst.
13:12 `When thou hearest, in one of thy cities which Jehovah thy God is giving to thee to dwell there, [one] saying,
13:13 Men, sons of worthlessness, have gone out of thy midst, and they force away the inhabitants of their city, saying, Let us go and serve other gods, which ye have not known --
13:14 and thou hast enquired, and searched, and asked diligently, and lo, truth; the thing is established; this abomination hath been done in thy midst:
13:15 `Thou dost surely smite the inhabitants of that city by the mouth of the sword; devoting it, and all that [is] in it, even its cattle, by the mouth of the sword;
13:16 and all its spoil thou dost gather unto the midst of its broad place, and hast burned with fire the city and all its spoil completely, before Jehovah thy God, and it hath been a heap age-during, it is not built any more;
13:17 and there doth not cleave to thy hand any of the devoted thing, so that Jehovah doth turn back from the fierceness of His anger, and hath given to thee mercies, and loved thee, and multiplied thee, as He hath sworn to thy fathers,
13:18 when thou dost hearken to the voice of Jehovah thy God, to keep all his commands which I am commanding thee to-day, to do that which [is] right in the eyes of Jehovah thy God.
14:1 `Sons ye [are] to Jehovah your God; ye do not cut yourselves, nor make baldness between your eyes for the dead;
14:2 for a holy people [art] thou to Jehovah thy God, and on thee hath Jehovah fixed to be to Him for a people, a peculiar treasure, out of all the peoples who [are] on the face of the ground.
14:3 `Thou dost not eat any abominable thing;
14:4 `this [is] the beast which ye do eat: ox, lamb of the sheep, or kid of the goats,
14:5 hart, and roe, and fallow deer, and wild goat, and pygarg, and wild ox, and chamois;
14:6 and every beast dividing the hoof, and cleaving the cleft into two hoofs, bringing up the cud, among the beasts -- it ye do eat.
14:7 `Only, this ye do not eat, of those bringing up the cud, and of those dividing the cloven hoof:

the camel, and the hare, and the rabbit, for they are bringing up the cud but the hoof have not divided; unclean they [are] to you;
14:8 and the sow, for it is dividing the hoof, and not [bringing] up the cud, unclean it [is] to you; of their flesh ye do not eat, and against their carcase ye do not come.
14:9 `This ye do eat of all that [are] in the waters; all that hath fins and scales ye do eat;
14:10 and anything which hath not fins and scales ye do not eat; unclean it [is] to you.
14:11 `Any clean bird ye do eat;
14:12 and these [are] they of which ye do not eat: the eagle, and the ossifrage, and the ospray,
14:13 and the glede, and the kite, and the vulture after its kind,
14:14 and every raven after its kind;
14:15 and the owl, and the night-hawk, and the cuckoo, and the hawk after its kind;
14:16 the [little] owl, and the [great] owl, and the swan,
14:17 and the pelican, and the gier-eagle, and the cormorant,
14:18 and the stork, and the heron after its kind, and the lapwing, and the bat;
14:19 and every teeming thing which is flying, unclean it [is] to you; they are not eaten;
14:20 any clean fowl ye do eat.
14:21 `Ye do not eat of any carcase; to the sojourner who [is] within thy gates thou dost give it, and he hath eaten it; or sell [it] to a stranger; for a holy people thou [art] to Jehovah thy God; thou dost not boil a kid in its mother's milk.
14:22 `Thou dost certainly tithe all the increase of thy seed which the field is bringing forth year by year;
14:23 and thou hast eaten before Jehovah thy God, in the place where He doth choose to cause His name to tabernacle, the tithe of thy corn, of thy new wine, and of thine oil, and the firstlings of thy herd, and of thy flock, so that thou dost learn to fear Jehovah thy God all the days.
14:24 `And when the way is too much for thee, that thou art not able to carry it -- when the place is too far off from thee which Jehovah thy God doth choose to put His name there, when Jehovah thy God doth bless thee; --
14:25 then thou hast given [it] in money, and hast bound up the money in thy hand, and gone unto the place on which Jehovah thy God doth fix;
14:26 and thou hast given the money for any thing which thy soul desireth, for oxen, and for sheep, and for wine, and for strong drink, and for any thing which thy soul asketh, and thou hast eaten there before Jehovah thy God, and thou hast rejoiced, thou and thy house.
14:27 As to the Levite who [is] within thy gates, thou dost not forsake him, for he hath no portion and inheritance with thee.

14:28 `At the end of three years thou dost bring out all the tithe of thine increase in that year, and hast placed [it] within thy gates;
14:29 and come in hath the Levite (for he hath no part and inheritance with thee), and the sojourner, and the fatherless, and the widow, who [are] within thy gates, and they have eaten, and been satisfied, so that Jehovah thy God doth bless thee in all the work of thy hand which thou dost.
15:1 `At the end of seven years thou dost make a release,
15:2 and this [is] the matter of the release: Every owner of a loan [is] to release his hand which he doth lift up against his neighbour, he doth not exact of his neighbour and of his brother, but hath proclaimed a release to Jehovah;
15:3 of the stranger thou mayest exact, and that which is thine with thy brother doth thy hand release;
15:4 only when there is no needy one with thee, for Jehovah doth greatly bless thee in the land which Jehovah thy God is giving to thee -- an inheritance to possess it.
15:5 `Only, if thou dost diligently hearken to the voice of Jehovah thy God, to observe to do all this command which I am commanding thee to-day,
15:6 for Jehovah thy God hath blessed thee as He hath spoken to thee; and thou hast lent [to] many nations, and thou hast not borrowed; and thou hast ruled over many nations, and over thee they do not rule.
15:7 `When there is with thee any needy one of one of thy brethren, in one of thy cities, in thy land which Jehovah thy God is giving to thee, thou dost not harden thy heart, nor shut thy hand from thy needy brother;
15:8 for thou dost certainly open thy hand to him, and dost certainly lend him sufficient for his lack which he lacketh.
15:9 `Take heed to thee lest there be a word in thy heart -- worthless, saying, Near [is] the seventh year, the year of release; and thine eye is evil against thy needy brother, and thou dost not give to him, and he hath called concerning thee unto Jehovah, and it hath been in thee sin;
15:10 thou dost certainly give to him, and thy heart is not sad in thy giving to him, for because of this thing doth Jehovah thy God bless thee in all thy works, and in every putting forth of thy hand;
15:11 because the needy one doth not cease out of the land, therefore I am commanding thee, saying, Thou dost certainly open thy hand to thy brother, to thy poor, and to thy needy one, in thy land.
15:12 `When thy brother is sold to thee, a Hebrew or a Hebrewess, and he hath served thee six years -- then in the seventh year thou dost send him away free from thee.
15:13 And when thou dost send him away free from thee, thou dost not send him away empty;

15:14 thou dost certainly encircle him out of thy flock, and out of thy threshing-floor, and out of thy wine-vat; [of] that which Jehovah thy God hath blessed thee thou dost give to him,
15:15 and thou hast remembered that a servant thou hast been in the land of Egypt, and Jehovah thy God doth ransom thee; therefore I am commanding thee this thing to-day.
15:16 `And it hath been, when he saith unto thee, I go not out from thee -- because he hath loved thee, and thy house, because [it is] good for him with thee --
15:17 then thou hast taken the awl, and hast put [it] through his ear, and through the door, and he hath been to thee a servant age-during; and also to thy handmaid thou dost do so.
15:18 `It is not hard in thine eyes, in thy sending him away free from thee; for the double of the hire of an hireling he hath served thee six years, and Jehovah thy God hath blessed thee in all that thou dost.
15:19 `Every firstling that is born in thy herd and in thy flock -- the male thou dost sanctify to Jehovah thy God; thou dost not work with the firstling of thine ox, nor shear the firstling of thy flock;
15:20 before Jehovah thy God thou dost eat it year by year, in the place which Jehovah doth choose, thou and thy house.
15:21 `And when there is in it a blemish, lame, or blind, any evil blemish, thou dost not sacrifice it to Jehovah thy God;
15:22 within thy gates thou dost eat it, the unclean and the clean alike, as the roe, and as the hart.
15:23 Only, its blood thou dost not eat; on the earth thou dost pour it as water.
16:1 `Observe the month of Abib -- and thou hast made a passover to Jehovah thy God, for in the month of Abib hath Jehovah thy God brought thee out of Egypt by night;
16:2 and thou hast sacrificed a passover to Jehovah thy God, of the flock, and of the herd, in the place which Jehovah doth choose to cause His name to tabernacle there.
16:3 `Thou dost not eat with it any fermented thing, seven days thou dost eat with it unleavened things, bread of affliction; for in haste thou hast come out of the land of Egypt; so that thou dost remember the day of thy coming out of the land of Egypt all days of thy life;
16:4 and there is not seen with thee leaven in all thy border seven days, and there doth not remain of the flesh which thou dost sacrifice at evening on the first day till morning.
16:5 `Thou art not able to sacrifice the passover within any of thy gates which Jehovah thy God is giving to thee,
16:6 except at the place which Jehovah thy God doth choose to cause His name to tabernacle -- there thou dost sacrifice the passover in the evening, at the going in of the sun, the season of thy coming out of Egypt;
16:7 and thou hast cooked and eaten in the place on which Jehovah thy God doth fix, and hast

turned in the morning, and gone to thy tents;
16:8 six days thou dost eat unleavened things, and on the seventh day [is] a restraint to Jehovah thy God; thou dost do no work.
16:9 `Seven weeks thou dost number to thee; from the beginning of the sickle among the standing corn thou dost begin to number seven weeks,
16:10 and thou hast made the feast of weeks to Jehovah thy God, a tribute of a free-will offering of thy hand, which thou dost give, as Jehovah thy God doth bless thee.
16:11 And thou hast rejoiced before Jehovah thy God, thou, and thy son, and thy daughter, and thy man-servant, and thy handmaid, and the Levite who [is] within thy gates, and the sojourner, and the fatherless, and the widow, who [are] in thy midst, in the place which Jehovah thy God doth choose to cause His name to tabernacle there,
16:12 and thou hast remembered that a servant thou hast been in Egypt, and hast observed and done these statutes.
16:13 `The feast of booths thou dost make for thee seven days, in thine in-gathering of thy threshing-floor, and of thy wine-vat;
16:14 and thou hast rejoiced in thy feast, thou, and thy son, and thy daughter, and thy man-servant, and thy handmaid, and the Levite, and the sojourner, and the fatherless, and the widow, who [are] within thy gates.
16:15 Seven days thou dost feast before Jehovah thy God, in the place which Jehovah doth choose, for Jehovah thy God doth bless thee in all thine increase, and in every work of thy hands, and thou hast been only rejoicing.
16:16 `Three times in a year doth every one of thy males appear before Jehovah thy God in the place which He doth choose -- in the feast of unleavened things, and in the feast of weeks, and in the feast of booths; and they do not appear before Jehovah empty;
16:17 each according to the gift of his hand, according to the blessing of Jehovah thy God, which He hath given to thee.
16:18 `Judges and authorities thou dost make to thee within all thy gates which Jehovah thy God is giving to thee, for thy tribes; and they have judged the people -- a righteous judgment.
16:19 Thou dost not turn aside judgment; thou dost not discern faces, nor take a bribe, for the bribe blindeth the eyes of the wise, and perverteth the words of the righteous.
16:20 Righteousness -- righteousness thou dost pursue, so that thou livest, and hast possessed the land which Jehovah thy God is giving to thee.
16:21 `Thou dost not plant for thee a shrine of any trees near the altar of Jehovah thy God, which thou makest for thyself,

16:22 and thou dost not raise up to thee any standing image which Jehovah thy God is hating.
17:1 `Thou dost not sacrifice to Jehovah thy God ox or sheep in which there is a blemish -- any evil thing; for it [is] the abomination of Jehovah thy God.
17:2 `When there is found in thy midst, in one of thy cities which Jehovah thy God is giving to thee, a man or a woman who doth the evil thing in the eyes of Jehovah thy God by transgressing His covenant,
17:3 and he doth go and serve other gods, and doth bow himself to them, and to the sun, or to the moon, or to any of the host of the heavens, which I have not commanded --
17:4 and it hath been declared to thee, and thou hast heard, and hast searched diligently, and lo, truth; the thing is established; this abomination hath been done in Israel --
17:5 `Then thou hast brought out that man, or that woman, who hath done this evil thing, unto thy gates -- the man or the woman -- and thou hast stoned them with stones, and they have died.
17:6 By the mouth of two witnesses or of three witnesses is he who is dead put to death; he is not put to death by the mouth of one witness;
17:7 the hand of the witnesses is on him, in the first place, to put him to death, and the hand of all the people last; and thou hast put away the evil thing out of thy midst.
17:8 `When anything is too hard for thee for judgment, between blood and blood, between plea and plea, and between stroke and stroke -- matters of strife within thy gates -- then thou hast risen, and gone up unto the place on which Jehovah thy God doth fix,
17:9 and hast come in unto the priests, the Levites, and unto the judge who is in those days, and hast inquired, and they have declared to thee the word of judgment,
17:10 and thou hast done according to the tenor of the word which they declare to thee ([they] of that place which Jehovah doth choose; and thou hast observed to do according to all that they direct thee.
17:11 `According to the tenor of the law which they direct thee, and according to the judgment which they say to thee thou dost do; thou dost not turn aside from the word which they declare to thee, right or left.
17:12 And the man who acteth with presumption, so as not to hearken unto the priest (who is standing to serve there Jehovah thy God), or unto the judge, even that man hath died, and thou hast put away the evil thing from Israel,
17:13 and all the people do hear and fear, and do not presume any more.
17:14 `When thou comest in unto the land which Jehovah thy God is giving to thee, and hast possessed it, and dwelt in it, and thou hast said, Let me set over me a king like all the nations which [are] round about me, --

17:15 thou dost certainly set over thee a king on whom Jehovah doth fix; from the midst of thy brethren thou dost set over thee a king; thou art not able to set over thee a stranger, who is not thy brother.
17:16 `Only, he doth not multiply to himself horses, nor cause the people to turn back to Egypt, so as to multiply horses, seeing Jehovah hath said to you, Ye do not add to turn back in this way any more.
17:17 And he doth not multiply to himself wives, and his heart doth not turn aside, and silver and gold he doth not multiply to himself -- exceedingly.
17:18 `And it hath been, when he sitteth on the throne of his kingdom, that he hath written for himself the copy of this law, on a book, from [that] before the priests the Levites,
17:19 and it hath been with him, and he hath read in it all days of his life, so that he doth learn to fear Jehovah his God, to keep all the words of this law, and these statutes, to do them;
17:20 so that his heart is not high above his brethren, and so as not to turn aside from the command, right or left, so that he prolongeth days over his kingdom, he and his sons, in the midst of Israel.
18:1 `There is not to the priests the Levites -- all the tribe of Levi -- a portion and inheritance with Israel; fire-offerings of Jehovah, even His inheritance, they eat,
18:2 and he hath no inheritance in the midst of his brethren; Jehovah Himself [is] his inheritance, as He hath spoken to him.
18:3 `And this is the priest's right from the people, from those sacrificing a sacrifice, whether ox or sheep, he hath even given to the priest the leg, and the two cheeks, and the stomach;
18:4 the first of thy corn, of thy new wine, and of thine oil, and the first of the fleece of thy flock, thou dost give to him;
18:5 for on him hath Jehovah thy God fixed, out of all thy tribes, to stand to serve in the name of Jehovah, He and his sons continually.
18:6 `And when the Levite cometh from one of thy cities out of all Israel, where he hath sojourned, and hath come with all the desire of his soul unto the place which Jehovah doth choose,
18:7 then he hath ministered in the name of Jehovah his God, like all his brethren, the Levites, who are standing there before Jehovah,
18:8 portion as portion they do eat, apart from his sold things, with the fathers.
18:9 `When thou art coming in unto the land which Jehovah thy God is giving to thee, thou dost not learn to do according to the abominations of those nations:
18:10 there is not found in thee one causing his son and his daughter to pass over into fire, a user of divinations, an observer of clouds, and an enchanter, and a sorcerer,

18:11 and a charmer, and one asking at a familiar spirit, and a wizard, and one seeking unto the
dead.
18:12 `For the abomination of Jehovah [is] every one doing these, and because of these
abominations is Jehovah thy God dispossessing them from thy presence.
18:13 Perfect thou art with Jehovah thy God,
18:14 for these nations whom thou art possessing, unto observers of clouds, and unto diviners, do
hearken; and thou -- not so hath Jehovah thy God suffered thee.
18:15 `A prophet out of thy midst, out of thy brethren, like to me, doth Jehovah thy God raise up to
thee -- unto him ye hearken;
18:16 according to all that thou didst ask from Jehovah thy God, in Horeb, in the day of the
assembly, saying, Let me not add to hear the voice of Jehovah my God, and this great fire let me
not see any more, and I die not;
18:17 and Jehovah saith unto me, They have done well that they have spoken;
18:18 a prophet I raise up to them, out of the midst of their brethren, like to thee; and I have given
my words in his mouth, and he hath spoken unto them all that which I command him;
18:19 and it hath been -- the man who doth not hearken unto My words which he doth speak in My
name, I require [it] of him.
18:20 `Only, the prophet who presumeth to speak a word in My name -- that which I have not
commanded him to speak -- and who speaketh in the name of other gods -- even that prophet hath
died.
18:21 `And when thou sayest in thy heart, How do we know the word which Jehovah hath not
spoken? --
18:22 that which the prophet speaketh in the name of Jehovah, and the thing is not, and cometh
not -- it [is] the word which Jehovah hath not spoken; in presumption hath the prophet spoken it; --
thou art not afraid of him.
19:1 `When Jehovah thy God doth cut off the nations, whose land Jehovah thy God is giving to
thee, and thou hast succeeded them, and dwelt in their cities, and in their houses,
19:2 three cities thou dost separate for thee in the midst of thy land which Jehovah thy God is
giving to thee to possess it.
19:3 Thou dost prepare for thee the way, and hast divided into three parts the border of thy land
which Jehovah thy God doth cause thee to inherit, and it hath been for the fleeing thither of every
man-slayer.
19:4 `And this [is] the matter of the man-slayer who fleeth thither, and hath lived: He who smiteth
his neighbour unknowingly, and is not hating him heretofore,

19:5 even he who cometh in with his neighbour into a forest to hew wood, and his hand hath driven
with an axe to cut the tree, and the iron hath slipped from the wood, and hath met his neighbour,
and he hath died -- he doth flee unto one of these cities, and hath lived,
19:6 lest the redeemer of blood pursue after the man-slayer when his heart is hot, and hath
overtaken him (because the way is great), and hath smitten him -- the life, and he hath no sentence
of death, for he is not hating him heretofore;
19:7 therefore I am commanding thee, saying, Three cities thou dost separate to thee.
19:8 `And if Jehovah thy God doth enlarge thy border, as He hath sworn to thy fathers, and hath
given to thee all the land which He hath spoken to give to thy fathers --
19:9 when thou keepest all this command to do it, which I am commanding thee to-day, to love
Jehovah thy God, and to walk in His ways all the days -- then thou hast added to thee yet three
cities to these three;
19:10 and innocent blood is not shed in the midst of thy land which Jehovah thy God is giving to
thee -- an inheritance, and there hath been upon thee blood.
19:11 `And when a man is hating his neighbour, and hath lain in wait for him, and risen against him,
and smitten him -- the life, and he hath died, and he hath fled unto one of these cities,
19:12 then the elders of his city have sent and taken him from thence, and given him into the hand
of the redeemer of blood, and he hath died;
19:13 thine eye hath no pity on him, and thou hast put away the innocent blood from Israel, and it is
well with thee.
19:14 `Thou dost not remove a border of thy neighbour, which they of former times have made, in
thine inheritance, which thou dost inherit in the land which Jehovah thy God is giving to thee to
possess it.
19:15 `One witness doth not rise against a man for any iniquity, and for any sin, in any sin which he
sinneth; by the mouth of two witnesses, or by the mouth of three witnesses, is a thing established.
19:16 `When a violent witness doth rise against a man, to testify against him apostacy,
19:17 then have both the men who have the strife stood before Jehovah, before the priests and the
judges who are in those days,
19:18 and the judges have searched diligently, and lo, the witness [is] a false witness, a falsehood
he hath testified against his brother:
19:19 `Then ye have done to him as he devised to do to his brother, and thou hast put away the
evil thing out of thy midst,
19:20 and those who are left do hear and fear, and add not to do any more according to this evil
thing in thy midst;

19:21 and thine eye doth not pity -- life for life, eye for eye, tooth for tooth, hand for hand, foot for foot.
20:1 `When thou goest out to battle against thine enemy, and hast seen horse and chariot -- a people more numerous than thou -- thou art not afraid of them, for Jehovah thy God [is] with thee, who is bringing thee up out of the land of Egypt;
20:2 and it hath been, in your drawing near unto the battle, that the priest hath come nigh, and spoken unto the people,
20:3 and said unto them, Hear, Israel, ye are drawing near to-day to battle against your enemies, let not your hearts be tender, fear not, nor make haste, nor be terrified at their presence,
20:4 for Jehovah your God [is] He who is going with you, to fight for you with your enemies -- to save you.
20:5 `And the authorities have spoken unto the people, saying, Who [is] the man that hath built a new house, and hath not dedicated it? -- let him go and turn back to his house, lest he die in battle, and another man dedicate it.
20:6 `And who [is] the man that hath planted a vineyard, and hath not made it common? -- let him go and turn back to his house, lest he die in battle, and another man make it common.
20:7 `And who [is] the man that hath betrothed a woman, and hath not taken her? -- let him go and turn back to his house, lest he die in battle, and another man take her.
20:8 `And the authorities have added to speak unto the people, and said, Who [is] the man that is afraid and tender of heart? -- let him go and turn back to his house, and the heart of his brethren doth not melt like his heart;
20:9 and it hath come to pass as the authorities finish to speak unto the people, that they have appointed princes of the hosts at the head of the people.
20:10 `When thou drawest near unto a city to fight against it, then thou hast called unto it for Peace,
20:11 and it hath been, if Peace it answer thee, and hath opened to thee, then it hath come to pass -- all the people who are found in it are to thee for tributaries, and have served thee.
20:12 `And if it doth not make peace with thee, and hath made with thee war, then thou hast laid siege against it,
20:13 and Jehovah thy God hath given it into thy hand, and thou hast smitten every male of it by the mouth of the sword.
20:14 Only, the women, and the infants, and the cattle, and all that is in the city, all its spoil, thou dost seize for thyself, and thou hast eaten the spoil of thine enemies which Jehovah thy God hath given to thee.

20:15 So thou dost do to all the cities which are very far off from thee, which are not of the cities of these nations.
20:16 `Only, of the cities of these peoples which Jehovah thy God is giving to thee [for] an inheritance, thou dost not keep alive any breathing;
20:17 for thou dost certainly devote the Hittite, and the Amorite, the Canaanite, and the Perizzite, the Hivite, and the Jebusite, as Jehovah thy God hath commanded thee,
20:18 so that they teach you not to do according to all their abominations which they have done to their gods, and ye have sinned against Jehovah your God.
20:19 `When thou layest siege unto a city many days, to fight against it, to capture it, thou dost not destroy its trees to force an axe against them, for of them thou dost eat, and them thou dost not cut down -- for man's [is] the tree of the field -- to go in at thy presence in the siege.
20:20 Only, the tree, which thou knowest that it [is] not a fruit-tree, it thou dost destroy, and hast cut down, and hast built a bulwark against the city which is making with thee war till thou hast subdued it.
21:1 `When one is found slain on the ground which Jehovah thy God is giving to thee to possess it -- fallen in a field -- it is not known who hath smitten him,
21:2 then have thine elders and thy judges gone out and measured unto the cities which [are] round about the slain one,
21:3 and it hath been, the city which [is] near unto the slain one, even the elders of that city have taken a heifer of the herd, which hath not been wrought with, which hath not drawn in the yoke,
21:4 and the elders of that city have brought down the heifer unto a hard valley, which is not tilled nor sown, and have beheaded there the heifer in the valley.
21:5 `And the priests, sons of Levi, have come nigh -- for on them hath Jehovah thy God fixed to serve Him, and to bless in the name of Jehovah, and by their mouth is every strife, and every stroke --
21:6 and all the elders of that city, who are near unto the slain one, do wash their hands over the heifer which is beheaded in the valley,
21:7 and they have answered and said, Our hands have not shed this blood, and our eyes have not seen --
21:8 receive atonement for Thy people Israel, whom Thou hast ransomed, O Jehovah, and suffer not innocent blood in the midst of Thy people Israel; and the blood hath been pardoned to them,
21:9 and thou dost put away the innocent blood out of thy midst, for thou dost that which [is] right in the eyes of Jehovah.
21:10 `When thou goest out to battle against thine enemies, and Jehovah thy God hath given them

into thy hand, and thou hast taken captive its captivity,
21:11 and hast seen in the captivity a woman of fair form, and hast delighted in her, and hast taken to thee for a wife,
21:12 then thou hast brought her in unto the midst of thy household, and she hath shaved her head, and prepared her nails,
21:13 and turned aside the raiment of her captivity from off her, and hath dwelt in thy house, and bewailed her father and her mother a month of days, and afterwards thou dost go in unto her and hast married her, and she hath been to thee for a wife:
21:14 `And it hath been -- if thou hast not delighted in her, that thou hast sent her away at her desire, and thou dost not at all sell her for money; thou dost not tyrannize over her, because that thou hast humbled her.
21:15 `When a man hath two wives, the one loved and the other hated, and they have borne to him sons (the loved one and the hated one), and the first-born son hath been to the hated one;
21:16 then it hath been, in the day of his causing his sons to inherit that which he hath, he is not able to declare first-born the son of the loved one, in the face of the son of the hated one -- the first-born.
21:17 But the first-born, son of the hated one, he doth acknowledge, to give to him a double portion of all that is found with him, for he [is] the beginning of his strength; to him [is] the right of the first-born.
21:18 `When a man hath a son apostatizing and rebellious -- he is not hearkening to the voice of his father, and to the voice of his mother, and they have chastised him, and he doth not hearken unto them --
21:19 then laid hold on him have his father and his mother, and they have brought him out unto the elders of his city, and unto the gate of his place,
21:20 and have said unto the elders of his city, Our son -- this one -- is apostatizing and rebellious; he is not hearkening to our voice -- a glutton and drunkard;
21:21 and all the men of his city have stoned him with stones, and he hath died, and thou hast put away the evil out of thy midst, and all Israel do hear and fear.
21:22 `And when there is in a man a sin -- a cause of death, and he hath been put to death, and thou hast hanged him on a tree,
21:23 his corpse doth not remain on the tree, for thou dost certainly bury him in that day -- for a thing lightly esteemed of God [is] the hanged one -- and thou dost not defile thy ground which Jehovah thy God is giving to thee -- an inheritance.
22:1 `Thou dost not see the ox of thy brother or his sheep driven away, and hast hidden thyself

from them, thou dost certainly turn them back to thy brother;
22:2 and if thy brother [is] not near unto thee, and thou hast not known him, then thou hast removed it unto the midst of thy house, and it hath been with thee till thy brother seek it, and thou hast given it back to him;
22:3 and so thou dost to his ass, and so thou dost to his garment, and so thou dost to any lost thing of thy brother's, which is lost by him, and thou hast found it; thou art not able to hide thyself.
22:4 `Thou dost not see the ass of thy brother, or his ox, falling in the way, and hast hid thyself from them; thou dost certainly raise [them] up with him.
22:5 `The habiliments of a man are not on a woman, nor doth a man put on the garment of a woman, for the abomination of Jehovah thy God [is] any one doing these.
22:6 `When a bird's nest cometh before thee in the way, in any tree, or on the earth, brood or eggs, and the mother sitting on the brood or on the eggs, thou dost not take the mother with the young ones;
22:7 thou dost certainly send away the mother, and the young ones dost take to thyself, so that it is well with thee, and thou hast prolonged days.
22:8 `When thou buildest a new house, then thou hast made a parapet to thy roof, and thou dost not put blood on thy house when one falleth from it.
22:9 `Thou dost not sow thy vineyard [with] divers things, lest the fulness of the seed which thou dost sow, and the increase of the vineyard, be separated.
22:10 `Thou dost not plow with an ox and with an ass together.
22:11 `Thou dost not put on a mixed cloth, wool and linen together.
22:12 `Fringes thou dost make to thee on the four skirts of thy covering with which thou dost cover [thyself].
22:13 `When a man taketh a wife, and hath gone in unto her, and hated her,
22:14 and laid against her actions of words, and brought out against her an evil name, and said, This woman I have taken, and I draw near unto her, and I have not found in her tokens of virginity:
22:15 `Then hath the father of the damsel -- and her mother -- taken and brought out the tokens of virginity of the damsel unto the elders of the city in the gate,
22:16 and the father of the damsel hath said unto the elders, My daughter I have given to this man for a wife, and he doth hate her;
22:17 and lo, he hath laid actions of words, saying, I have not found to thy daughter tokens of virginity -- and these [are] the tokens of the virginity of my daughter! and they have spread out the garment before the elders of the city.
22:18 `And the elders of that city have taken the man, and chastise him,

22:19 and fined him a hundred silverlings, and given to the father of the damsel, because he hath brought out an evil name on a virgin of Israel, and she is to him for a wife, he is not able to send her away all his days.
22:20 `And if this thing hath been truth -- tokens of virginity have not been found for the damsel --
22:21 then they have brought out the damsel unto the opening of her father's house, and stoned her have the men of her city with stones, and she hath died, for she hath done folly in Israel, to go a-whoring [in] her father's house; and thou hast put away the evil thing out of thy midst.
22:22 `When a man is found lying with a woman, married to a husband, then they have died even both of them, the man who is lying with the woman, also the woman; and thou hast put away the evil thing out of Israel.
22:23 `When there is a damsel, a virgin, betrothed to a man, and a man hath found her in a city, and lain with her;
22:24 then ye have brought them both out unto the gate of that city, and stoned them with stones, and they have died: -- the damsel, because that she hath not cried, [being] in a city; and the man, because that he hath humbled his neighbour's wife; and thou hast put away the evil thing out of thy midst.
22:25 `And if in a field the man find the damsel who is betrothed, and the man hath laid hold on her, and lain with her, then hath the man who hath lain with her died alone;
22:26 and to the damsel thou dost not do anything, the damsel hath no deadly sin; for as a man riseth against his neighbour and hath murdered him -- the life, so [is] this thing;
22:27 for in a field he found her, she hath cried -- the damsel who is betrothed -- and she hath no saviour.
22:28 `When a man findeth a damsel, a virgin who is not betrothed, and hath caught her, and lain with her, and they have been found,
22:29 then hath the man who is lying with her given to the father of the damsel fifty silverlings, and to him she is for a wife; because that he hath humbled her, he is not able to send her away all his days.
22:30 `A man doth not take his father's wife, nor uncover his father's skirt.
23:1 `One wounded, bruised, or cut in the member doth not enter into the assembly of Jehovah;
23:2 a bastard doth not enter into the assembly of Jehovah; even a tenth generation of him doth not enter into the assembly of Jehovah.
23:3 `An Ammonite and a Moabite doth not enter into the assembly of Jehovah; even a tenth generation of them doth not enter into the assembly of Jehovah -- to the age;
23:4 because that they have not come before you with bread and with water in the way, in your

coming out from Egypt, and because he hath hired against thee Balaam son of Beor, of Pethor of Aram-Naharaim, to revile thee;
23:5 and Jehovah thy God hath not been willing to hearken unto Balaam, and Jehovah thy God doth turn for thee the reviling to a blessing, because Jehovah thy God hath loved thee;
23:6 thou dost not seek their peace and their good all thy days -- to the age.
23:7 `Thou dost not abominate an Edomite, for thy brother he [is]; thou dost not abominate an Egyptian, for a sojourner thou hast been in his land;
23:8 sons who are begotten of them, a third generation of them, doth enter into the assembly of Jehovah.
23:9 `When a camp goeth out against thine enemies, then thou hast kept from every evil thing.
23:10 `When there is in thee a man who is not clean, from an accident at night -- then he hath gone out unto the outside of the camp -- he doth not come in unto the midst of the camp --
23:11 and it hath been, at the turning of the evening, he doth bathe with water, and at the going in of the sun he doth come in unto the midst of the camp.
23:12 `And a station thou hast at the outside of the camp, and thou hast gone out thither without,
23:13 and a nail thou hast on thy staff, and it hath been, in thy sitting without, that thou hast digged with it, and turned back, and covered thy filth;
23:14 for Jehovah thy God is walking up and down in the midst of thy camp, to deliver thee, and to give thine enemies before thee, and thy camp hath been holy, and He doth not see in thee the nakedness of anything, and hath turned back from after thee.
23:15 `Thou dost not shut up a servant unto his lord, who is delivered unto thee from his lord;
23:16 with thee he doth dwell, in thy midst, in the place which he chooseth within one of thy gates, where it is pleasing to him; thou dost not oppress him.
23:17 `There is not a whore among the daughters of Israel, nor is there a whoremonger among the sons of Israel;
23:18 thou dost not bring a gift of a whore, or a price of a dog, into the house of Jehovah thy God, for any vow; for the abomination of Jehovah thy God [are] even both of them.
23:19 `Thou dost not lend in usury to thy brother; usury of money, usury of food, usury of anything which is lent on usury.
23:20 To a stranger thou mayest lend in usury, and to thy brother thou dost not lend in usury, so that Jehovah thy God doth bless thee in every putting forth of thy hand on the land whither thou goest in to possess it.
23:21 `When thou vowest a vow to Jehovah thy God, thou dost not delay to complete it; for Jehovah thy God doth certainly require it from thee, and it hath been in thee -- sin.

23:22 `And when thou forbearest to vow, it is not in thee a sin.
23:23 The produce of thy lips thou dost keep, and hast done [it], as thou hast vowed to Jehovah thy God; a free-will-offering, which thou hast spoken with thy mouth.
23:24 `When thou comest in unto the vineyard of thy neighbour, then thou hast eaten grapes, according to thy desire, thy sufficiency; but into thy vessel thou dost not put [any].
23:25 When thou comest in among the standing-corn of thy neighbour, then thou hast plucked the ears with thy hand, but a sickle thou dost not wave over the standing-corn of thy neighbour.
24:1 `When a man doth take a wife, and hath married her, and it hath been, if she doth not find grace in his eyes (for he hath found in her nakedness of anything), and he hath written for her a writing of divorce, and given [it] into her hand, and sent her out of his house,
24:2 and she hath gone out of his house, and hath gone and been another man's,
24:3 and the latter man hath hated her, and written for her a writing of divorce, and given [it] into her hand, and sent her out of his house, or when the latter man dieth, who hath taken her to himself for a wife:
24:4 `Her former husband who sent her away is not able to turn back to take her to be to him for a wife, after that she hath become defiled; for an abomination it [is] before Jehovah, and thou dost not cause the land to sin which Jehovah thy God is giving to thee -- an inheritance.
24:5 `When a man taketh a new wife, he doth not go out into the host, and [one] doth not pass over unto him for anything; free he is at his own house one year, and hath rejoiced his wife whom he hath taken.
24:6 `None doth take in pledge millstones, and rider, for life it [is] he is taking in pledge.
24:7 `When a man is found stealing a person, of his brethren, of the sons of Israel, and hath tyrannized over him, and sold him, then hath that thief died, and thou hast put away the evil thing out of thy midst.
24:8 `Take heed, in the plague of leprosy, to watch greatly, and to do according to all that the priests, the Levites, teach you; as I have commanded them ye observe to do;
24:9 remember that which Jehovah thy God hath done to Miriam in the way, in your coming out of Egypt.
24:10 `When thou liftest up on thy brother a debt of anything, thou dost not go in unto his house to obtain his pledge;
24:11 at the outside thou dost stand, and the man on whom thou art lifting [it] up is bringing out unto thee the pledge at the outside.
24:12 `And if he is a poor man, thou dost not lie down with his pledge;
24:13 thou dost certainly give back to him the pledge at the going in of the sun, and he hath lain

down in his own raiment, and hath blessed thee; and to thee it is righteousness before Jehovah thy God.

24:14 `Thou dost not oppress a hireling, poor and needy, of thy brethren or of thy sojourner who is in thy land within thy gates;

24:15 in his day thou dost give his hire, and the sun doth not go in upon it, for he [is] poor, and unto it he is lifting up his soul, and he doth not cry against thee unto Jehovah, and it hath been in thee -- sin.

24:16 `Fathers are not put to death for sons, and sons are not put to death for fathers -- each for his own sin, they are put to death.

24:17 `Thou dost not turn aside the judgment of a fatherless sojourner, nor take in pledge the garment of a widow;

24:18 and thou hast remembered that a servant thou hast been in Egypt, and Jehovah thy God doth ransom thee from thence; therefore I am commanding thee to do this thing.

24:19 `When thou reapest thy harvest in thy field, and hast forgotten a sheaf in a field, thou dost not turn back to take it; to the sojourner, to the fatherless, and to the widow, it is; so that Jehovah thy God doth bless thee in all the work of thy hands.

24:20 `When thou beatest thine olive, thou dost not examine the branch behind thee; to the sojourner, to the fatherless, and to the widow, it is.

24:21 `When thou cuttest thy vineyard, thou dost not glean behind thee; to the sojourner, to the fatherless, and to the widow, it is;

24:22 and thou hast remembered that a servant thou hast been in the land of Egypt; therefore I am commanding thee to do this thing.

25:1 `When there is a strife between men, and they have come nigh unto the judgment, and they have judged, and declared righteous the righteous, and declared wrong the wrong-doer,

25:2 then it hath come to pass, if the wrong-doer is to be smitten, that the judge hath caused him to fall down, and [one] hath smitten him in his presence, according to the sufficiency of his wrong-doing, by number;

25:3 forty [times] he doth smite him -- he is not adding, lest, he is adding to smite him above these -- many stripes, and thy brother is lightly esteemed in thine eyes.

25:4 `Thou dost not muzzle an ox in its threshing.

25:5 `When brethren dwell together, and one of them hath died, and hath no son, the wife of the dead is not without to a strange man; her husband's brother doth go in unto her, and hath taken her to him for a wife, and doth perform the duty of her husband's brother;

25:6 and it hath been, the first-born which she beareth doth rise for the name of his dead brother,

and his name is not wiped away out of Israel.
25:7 `And if the man doth not delight to take his brother's wife, then hath his brother's wife gone up to the gate, unto the elders, and said, My husband's brother is refusing to raise up to his brother a name in Israel; he hath not been willing to perform the duty of my husband's brother;
25:8 and the elders of his city have called for him, and spoken unto him, and he hath stood and said, I have no desire to take her;
25:9 `Then hath his brother's wife drawn nigh unto him, before the eyes of the elders, and drawn his shoe from off his foot, and spat in his face, and answered and said, Thus it is done to the man who doth not build up the house of his brother;
25:10 and his name hath been called in Israel -- The house of him whose shoe is drawn off.
25:11 `When men strive together, one with another, and the wife of the one hath drawn near to deliver her husband out of the hand of his smiter, and hath put forth her hand, and laid hold on his secrets,
25:12 then thou hast cut off her hand, thine eye doth not spare.
25:13 `Thou hast not in thy bag a stone and a stone, a great and a small.
25:14 Thou hast not in thy house an ephah and an ephah, a great and a small.
25:15 Thou hast a stone complete and just, thou hast an ephah complete and just, so that they prolong thy days on the ground which Jehovah thy God is giving to thee;
25:16 for the abomination of Jehovah thy God [is] any one doing these things, any one doing iniquity.
25:17 `Remember that which Amalek hath done to thee in the way, in your going out from Egypt,
25:18 that he hath met thee in the way, and smiteth in all those feeble behind thee (and thou wearied and fatigued), and is not fearing God.
25:19 And it hath been, in Jehovah thy God's giving rest to thee, from all thine enemies round about, in the land which Jehovah thy God is giving to thee -- an inheritance to possess it -- thou dost blot out the rememberance of Amalek from under the heavens -- thou dost not forget.
26:1 `And it hath been, when thou comest in unto the land which Jehovah thy God is giving to thee -- an inheritance, and thou hast possessed it, and dwelt in it,
26:2 that thou hast taken of the first of all the fruits of the ground which thou dost bring in out of thy land which Jehovah thy God is giving to thee, and hast put [it] in a basket, and gone unto the place which Jehovah thy God doth choose to cause His name to tabernacle there.
26:3 `And thou hast come in unto the priest who is in those days, and hast said unto him, I have declared to-day to Jehovah thy God, that I have come in unto the land which Jehovah hath sworn to our fathers to give to us;

26:4 and the priest hath taken the basket out of thy hand, and placed it before the altar of Jehovah thy God.
26:5 `And thou hast answered and said before Jehovah thy God, A perishing Aramaean [is] my father! and he goeth down to Egypt, and sojourneth there with few men, and becometh there a nation, great, mighty, and numerous;
26:6 and the Egyptians do us evil, and afflict us, and put on us hard service;
26:7 and we cry unto Jehovah, God of our fathers, and Jehovah heareth our voice, and seeth our affliction, and our labour, and our oppression;
26:8 and Jehovah bringeth us out from Egypt, by a strong hand, and by a stretched-out arm, and by great fear, and by signs, and by wonders,
26:9 and he bringeth us in unto this place, and giveth to us this land -- a land flowing with milk and honey.
26:10 `And now, lo, I have brought in the first of the fruits of the ground which thou hast given to me, O Jehovah; -- and thou hast placed it before Jehovah thy God, and bowed thyself before Jehovah thy God,
26:11 and rejoiced in all the good which Jehovah thy God hath given to thee, and to thy house, thou, and the Levite, and the sojourner who [is] in thy midst.
26:12 `When thou dost complete to tithe all the tithe of thine increase in the third year, the year of the tithe, then thou hast given to the Levite, to the sojourner, to the fatherless, and to the widow, and they have eaten within thy gates, and been satisfied,
26:13 and thou hast said before Jehovah thy God, I have put away the separated thing out of the house, and also have given it to the Levite, and to the sojourner, and to the orphan, and to the widow, according to all Thy command which Thou hast commanded me; I have not passed over from Thy commands, nor have I forgotten.
26:14 I have not eaten in mine affliction of it, nor have I put away of it for uncleanness, nor have I given of it for the dead; I have hearkened to the voice of Jehovah my God; I have done according to all that Thou hast commanded me;
26:15 look from Thy holy habitation, from the heavens, and bless Thy people Israel, and the ground which Thou hast given to us, as Thou hast sworn to our fathers -- a land flowing [with] milk and honey.
26:16 `This day Jehovah thy God is commanding thee to do these statutes and judgments; and thou hast hearkened and done them with all thy heart, and with all thy soul,
26:17 Jehovah thou hast caused to promise to-day to become thy God, and to walk in His ways, and to keep His statutes, and His commands, and His judgments, and to hearken to His voice.

26:18 `And Jehovah hath caused thee to promise to-day to become His people, a peculiar treasure, as He hath spoken to thee, and to keep all His commands;
26:19 so as to make thee uppermost above all the nations whom He hath made for a praise, and for a name, and for beauty, and for thy being a holy people to Jehovah thy God, as He hath spoken.
27:1 `And Moses -- the elders of Israel also -- commandeth the people, saying, Keep all the command which I am commanding you to-day;
27:2 and it hath been, in the day that ye pass over the Jordan unto the land which Jehovah thy God is giving to thee, that thou hast raised up for thee great stones, and plaistered them with plaister,
27:3 and written on them all the words of this law in thy passing over, so that thou goest in unto the land which Jehovah thy God is giving to thee -- a land flowing with milk and honey, as Jehovah, God of thy fathers, hath spoken to thee.
27:4 `And it hath been, in your passing over the Jordan, ye raise up these stones which I am commanding you to-day, in mount Ebal, and thou hast plaistered them with plaister,
27:5 and built there an altar to Jehovah thy God, an altar of stones, thou dost not wave over them iron.
27:6 Of complete stones thou buildest the altar of Jehovah thy God, and hast caused to ascend on it burnt-offerings to Jehovah thy God,
27:7 and sacrificed peace-offerings, and eaten there, and rejoiced before Jehovah thy God,
27:8 and written on the stones all the words of this law, well engraved.'
27:9 And Moses speaketh -- the priests, the Levites, also -- unto all Israel, saying, `Keep silent, and hear, O Israel, this day thou hast become a people to Jehovah thy God;
27:10 and thou hast hearkened to the voice of Jehovah thy God, and done His commands, and His statutes, which I am commanding thee to-day.'
27:11 And Moses commandeth the people on that day, saying,
27:12 `These do stand, to bless the people, on mount Gerizzim, in your passing over the Jordan: Simeon, and Levi, and Judah, and Issachar, and Joseph, and Benjamin.
27:13 And these do stand, for the reviling, on mount Ebal: Reuben, Gad, and Asher, and Zebulun, Dan, and Naphtali.
27:14 `And the Levites have answered and said unto every man of Israel -- a loud voice:
27:15 `Cursed [is] the man who maketh a graven and molten image, the abomination of Jehovah, work of the hands of an artificer, and hath put [it] in a secret place, -- and all the people have answered and said, Amen.
27:16 `Cursed [is] He who is making light of his father and his mother, -- and all the people have

said, Amen.
27:17 `Cursed [is] he who is removing his neighbour's border, -- and all the people have said, Amen.
27:18 `Cursed [is] he who is causing the blind to err in the way, -- and all the people have said, Amen.
27:19 `Cursed [is] he who is turning aside the judgment of fatherless, sojourner, and widow, -- and all the people have said, Amen.
27:20 `Cursed [is] he who is lying with his father's wife, for he hath uncovered his father's skirt, -- and all the people have said, Amen.
27:21 `Cursed [is] he who is lying with any beast, -- and all the people have said, Amen.
27:22 `Cursed [is] he who is lying with his sister, daughter of his father, or daughter of his mother, -- and all the people have said, Amen.
27:23 `Cursed [is] he who is lying with his mother-in-law, -- and all the people have said, Amen.
27:24 `Cursed [is] he who is smiting his neighbour in secret, -- and all the people have said, Amen.
27:25 `Cursed [is] he who is taking a bribe to smite a person, innocent blood, -- and all the people have said, Amen.
27:26 `Cursed [is] he who doth not establish the words of this law, to do them, -- and all the people have said, Amen.
28:1 `And it hath been, if thou dost hearken diligently to the voice of Jehovah thy God, to observe to do all His commands which I am commanding thee to-day, that Jehovah thy God hath made thee uppermost above all the nations of the earth,
28:2 and all these blessings have come upon thee, and overtaken thee, because thou dost hearken to the voice of Jehovah thy God:
28:3 `Blessed [art] thou in the city, and blessed [art] thou in the field.
28:4 `Blessed [is] the fruit of thy womb, and the fruit of thy ground, and the fruit of thy cattle, increase of thine oxen, and wealth of thy flock.
28:5 `Blessed [is] thy basket and thy kneading-trough.
28:6 `Blessed [art] thou in thy coming in, and blessed [art] thou in thy going out.
28:7 `Jehovah giveth thine enemies, who are rising up against thee -- smitten before thy face; in one way they come out unto thee, and in seven ways they flee before thee.
28:8 `Jehovah commandeth with thee the blessing in thy storehouses, and in every putting forth of thy hand, and hath blessed thee in the land which Jehovah thy God is giving to thee.
28:9 `Jehovah doth establish thee to Himself for a holy people, as He hath sworn to thee, when thou keepest the commands of Jehovah thy God, and hast walked in His ways;

28:10 and all the peoples of the land have seen that the name of Jehovah is called upon thee, and they have been afraid of thee.
28:11 `And Jehovah hath made thee abundant in good, in the fruit of the womb, and in the fruit of thy cattle, and in the fruit of thy ground, on the ground which Jehovah hath sworn to thy fathers to give to thee.
28:12 `Jehovah doth open to thee his good treasure -- the heavens -- to give the rain of thy land in its season, and to bless all the work of thy hand, and thou hast lent to many nations, and thou -- thou dost not borrow.
28:13 `And Jehovah hath given thee for head, and not for tail; and thou hast been only above, and art not beneath, for thou dost hearken unto the commands of Jehovah thy God, which I am commanding thee to-day, to keep and to do,
28:14 and thou dost not turn aside from all the words which I am commanding you to-day -- right or left -- to go after other gods, to serve them.
28:15 `And it hath been, if thou dost not hearken unto the voice of Jehovah thy God to observe to do all His commands, and His statutes, which I am commanding thee to-day, that all these revilings have come upon thee, and overtaken thee:
28:16 `Cursed [art] thou in the city, and cursed [art] thou in the field.
28:17 `Cursed [is] thy basket and thy kneading-trough.
28:18 `Cursed [is] the fruit of thy body, and the fruit of thy land, increase of thine oxen, and wealth of thy flock.
28:19 `Cursed [art] thou in thy coming in, and cursed [art] thou in thy going out.
28:20 `Jehovah doth send on thee the curse, the trouble, and the rebuke, in every putting forth of thy hand which thou dost, till thou art destroyed, and till thou perish hastily, because of the evil of thy doings [by] which thou hast forsaken Me.
28:21 `Jehovah doth cause to cleave to thee the pestilence, till He consume thee from off the ground whither thou art going in to possess it.
28:22 `Jehovah doth smite thee with consumption, and with fever, and with inflammation, and with extreme burning, and with sword, and with blasting, and with mildew, and they have pursued thee till thou perish
28:23 `And thy heavens which [are] over thy head have been brass, and the earth which [is] under thee iron;
28:24 Jehovah giveth the rain of thy land -- dust and ashes; from the heavens it cometh down on thee till thou art destroyed.
28:25 `Jehovah giveth thee smitten before thine enemies; in one way thou goest out unto them,

and in seven ways dost flee before them, and thou hast been for a trembling to all kingdoms of the earth;
28:26 and thy carcase hath been for food to every fowl of the heavens, and to the beast of the earth, and there is none causing trembling.
28:27 `Jehovah doth smite thee with the ulcer of Egypt, and with emerods, and with scurvy, and with itch, of which thou art not able to be healed.
28:28 `Jehovah doth smite thee with madness, and with blindness, and with astonishment of heart;
28:29 and thou hast been gropling at noon, as the blind gropeth in darkness; and thou dost not cause thy ways to prosper; and thou hast been only oppressed and plundered all the days, and there is no saviour.
28:30 `A woman thou dost betroth, and another man doth lie with her; a house thou dost build, and dost not dwell in it; a vineyard thou dost plant, and dost not make it common;
28:31 thine ox [is] slaughtered before thine eyes, and thou dost not eat of it; thine ass [is] taken violently away from before thee, and it is not given back to thee; thy sheep [are] given to thine enemies, and there is no saviour for thee.
28:32 `Thy sons and thy daughters [are] given to another people, and thine eyes are looking and consuming for them all the day, and thy hand is not to God!
28:33 The fruit of thy ground, and all thy labour, eat up doth a people whom thou hast not known; and thou hast been only oppressed and bruised all the days;
28:34 and thou hast been mad, because of the sight of thine eyes which thou dost see.
28:35 `Jehovah doth smite thee with an evil ulcer, on the knees, and on the legs (of which thou art not able to be healed), from the sole of thy foot even unto thy crown.
28:36 `Jehovah doth cause thee to go, and thy king whom thou raisest up over thee, unto a nation which thou hast not known, thou and thy fathers, and thou hast served there other gods, wood and stone;
28:37 and thou hast been for an astonishment, for a simile, and for a byword among all the peoples whither Jehovah doth lead thee.
28:38 `Much seed thou dost take out into the field, and little thou dost gather in, for the locust doth consume it;
28:39 vineyards thou dost plant, and hast laboured, and wine thou dost not drink nor gather, for the worm doth consume it;
28:40 olives are to thee in all thy border, and oil thou dost not pour out, for thine olive doth fall off.
28:41 `Sons and daughters thou dost beget, and they are not with thee, for they go into captivity;
28:42 all thy trees and the fruit of thy ground doth the locust possess;

28:43 the sojourner who [is] in thy midst goeth up above thee very high, and thou goest down very low;
28:44 he doth lend [to] thee, and thou dost not lend [to] him; he is for head, and thou art for tail.
28:45 `And come upon thee have all these curses, and they have pursued thee, and overtaken thee, till thou art destroyed, because thou hast not hearkened to the voice of Jehovah thy God, to keep His commands, and His statutes, which he hath commanded thee;
28:46 and they have been on thee for a sign and for a wonder, also on thy seed -- to the age.
28:47 `Because that thou hast not served Jehovah thy God with joy, and with gladness of heart, because of the abundance of all things --
28:48 thou hast served thine enemies, whom Jehovah sendeth against thee, in hunger, and in thirst, and in nakedness, and in lack of all things; and he hath put a yoke of iron on thy neck, till He hath destroyed thee.
28:49 `Jehovah doth lift up against thee a nation, from afar, from the end of the earth, as the eagle it flieth; a nation whose tongue thou hast not heard,
28:50 a nation -- fierce of countenance -- which accepteth not the face of the aged, and the young doth not favour;
28:51 and it hath eaten the fruit of thy cattle, and the fruit of thy ground, till thou art destroyed; which leaveth not to thee corn, new wine, and oil, increase of thine oxen, and wealth of thy flock, till it hath destroyed thee.
28:52 `And it hath laid siege to thee in all thy gates, till thy walls come down, the high and the fenced ones in which thou art trusting, in all thy land; yea, it hath laid siege to thee in all thy gates, in all thy land, which Jehovah thy God hath given to thee;
28:53 and thou hast eaten the fruit of thy body, flesh of thy sons and thy daughters (whom Jehovah thy God hath given to thee), in the siege, and in the straitness with which thine enemies do straiten thee.
28:54 `The man who is tender in thee, and who [is] very delicate -- his eye is evil against his brother, and against the wife of his bosom, and against the remnant of his sons whom he leaveth,
28:55 against giving to one of them of the flesh of his sons whom he eateth, because he hath nothing left to him, in the siege, and in the straitness with which thine enemy doth straiten thee in all thy gates.
28:56 `The tender woman in thee, and the delicate, who hath not tried the sole of her foot to place on the ground because of delicateness and because of tenderness -- her eye is evil against the husband of her bosom, and against her son, and against her daughter,
28:57 and against her seed which cometh out from between her feet, even against her sons whom

she doth bear, for she doth eat them for the lacking of all things in secret, in the siege and in the straitness with which thine enemy doth straiten thee within thy gates.

28:58 `If thou dost not observe to do all the words of this law which are written in this book, to fear this honoured and fearful name -- Jehovah thy God --

28:59 then hath Jehovah made wonderful thy strokes, and the strokes of thy seed -- great strokes, and stedfast, and evil sicknesses, and stedfast.

28:60 `And He hath brought back on thee all the diseases of Egypt, of the presence of which thou hast been afraid, and they have cleaved to thee;

28:61 also every sickness and every stroke which is not written in the book of this law; Jehovah doth cause them to go up upon thee till thou art destroyed,

28:62 and ye have been left with few men, instead of which ye have been as stars of the heavens for multitude, because thou hast not hearkened to the voice of Jehovah thy God.

28:63 `And it hath been, as Jehovah hath rejoiced over you to do you good, and to multiply you, so doth Jehovah rejoice over you to destroy you, and to lay you waste; and ye have been pulled away from off the ground whither thou art going in to possess it;

28:64 and Jehovah hath scattered thee among all the peoples, from the end of the earth even unto the end of the earth; and thou hast served there other gods which thou hast not known, thou and thy fathers -- wood and stone.

28:65 `And among those nations thou dost not rest, yea, there is no resting-place for the sole of thy foot, and Jehovah hath given to thee there a trembling heart, and failing of eyes, and grief of soul;

28:66 and thy life hath been hanging in suspense before thee, and thou hast been afraid by night and by day, and dost not believe in thy life;

28:67 in the morning thou sayest, O that it were evening! and in the evening thou sayest, O that it were morning! from the fear of thy heart, with which thou art afraid, and from the sight of thine eyes which thou seest.

28:68 `And Jehovah hath brought thee back to Egypt with ships, by a way of which I said to thee, Thou dost not add any more to see it, and ye have sold yourselves there to thine enemies, for men-servants and for maid-servants, and there is no buyer.'

29:1 These [are] the words of the covenant which Jehovah hath commanded Moses to make with the sons of Israel in the land of Moab, apart from the covenant which He made with them in Horeb.

29:2 And Moses calleth unto all Israel, and saith unto them, `Ye -- ye have seen all that which Jehovah hath done before your eyes in the land of Egypt, to Pharaoh, and to all his servants, and to all his land;

29:3 the great trials which thine eyes have seen, the signs, and those great wonders;

29:4 and Jehovah hath not given to you a heart to know, and eyes to see, and ears to hear, till this day,
29:5 and I cause you to go forty years in a wilderness; your garments have not been consumed from off you, and thy shoe hath not worn away from off thy foot;
29:6 bread ye have not eaten, and wine and strong drink ye have not drunk, so that ye know that I [am] Jehovah your God.
29:7 `And ye come in unto this place, and Sihon king of Heshbon -- also Og king of Bashan -- doth come out to meet us, to battle, and we smite them,
29:8 and take their land, and give it for an inheritance to the Reubenite, and to the Gadite, and to the half of the tribe of Manasseh;
29:9 and ye have kept the words of this covenant, and done them, so that ye cause all that ye do to prosper.
29:10 `Ye are standing to-day, all of you, before Jehovah your God -- your heads, your tribes, your elders, and your authorities -- every man of Israel;
29:11 your infants, your wives, and thy sojourner who [is] in the midst of thy camps, from the hewer of thy wood unto the drawer of thy water --
29:12 for thy passing over into the covenant of Jehovah thy God, and into His oath which Jehovah thy God is making with thee to-day;
29:13 in order to establish thee to-day to Him for a people, and He Himself is thy God, as He hath spoken to thee, and as He hath sworn to thy fathers, to Abraham, to Isaac, and to Jacob.
29:14 `And not with you alone am I making this covenant and this oath;
29:15 but with him who is here with us, standing to-day before Jehovah our God, and with him who is not here with us to-day,
29:16 for ye have known how ye dwelt in the land of Egypt, and how we passed by through the midst of the nations which ye have passed by;
29:17 and ye see their abominations, and their idols, wood and stone, silver and gold, which [are] with them,
29:18 lest there be among you a man or woman, or family or tribe, whose heart is turning to-day from Jehovah our God, to go to serve the gods of those nations, lest there be in you a root fruitful of gall and wormwood:
29:19 `And it hath been, in his hearing the words of this oath, and he hath blessed himself in his heart, saying, I have peace, though in the stubbornness of my heart I go on, in order to end the fulness with the thirst.
29:20 Jehovah is not willing to be propitious to him, for then doth the anger of Jehovah smoke, also

His zeal, against that man, and lain down on him hath all the oath which is written in this book, and Jehovah hath blotted out his name from under the heavens,
29:21 and Jehovah hath separated him for evil, out of all the tribes of Israel, according to all the oaths of the covenant which is written in this book of the law.
29:22 `And the latter generation of your sons who rise after you, and the stranger who cometh in from a land afar off, have said when they have seen the strokes of that land, and its sicknesses which Jehovah hath sent into it, --
29:23 ([with] brimstone and salt is the whole land burnt, it is not sown, nor doth it shoot up, nor doth there go up on it any herb, like the overthrow of Sodom and Gomorrah, Admah and Zeboim, which Jehovah overturned in His anger, and in His fury,) --
29:24 yea, all the nations have said, Wherefore hath Jehovah done thus to this land? what the heat of this great anger?
29:25 `And they have said, Because that they have forsaken the covenant of Jehovah, God of their fathers, which He made with them in His bringing them out of the land of Egypt,
29:26 and they go and serve other gods, and bow themselves to them -- gods which they have not known, and which He hath not apportioned to them;
29:27 and the anger of Jehovah burneth against that land, to bring in on it all the reviling that is written in this book,
29:28 and Jehovah doth pluck them from off their ground in anger, and in fury, and in great wrath, and doth cast them unto another land, as [at] this day.
29:29 `The things hidden [are] to Jehovah our God, and the things revealed [are] to us and to our sons -- to the age, to do all the words of this law.
30:1 `And it hath been, when all these things come upon thee, the blessing and the reviling, which I have set before thee, and thou hast brought [them] back unto thy heart, among all the nations whither Jehovah thy God hath driven thee away,
30:2 and hast turned back unto Jehovah thy God, and hearkened to His voice, according to all that I am commanding thee to-day, thou and thy sons, with all thy heart, and with all thy soul --
30:3 then hath Jehovah thy God turned back [to] thy captivity, and pitied thee, yea, He hath turned back and gathered thee out of all the peoples whither Jehovah thy God hath scattered thee.
30:4 `If thine outcast is in the extremity of the heavens, thence doth Jehovah thy God gather thee, and thence He doth take thee;
30:5 and Jehovah thy God hath brought thee in unto the land which thy fathers have possessed, and thou hast inherited it, and He hath done thee good, and multiplied thee above thy fathers.
30:6 `And Jehovah thy God hath circumcised thy heart, and the heart of thy seed, to love Jehovah

thy God with all thy heart, and with all thy soul, for the sake of thy life;
30:7 and Jehovah thy God hath put all this oath on thine enemies, and on those hating thee, who have pursued thee.
30:8 `And thou dost turn back, and hast hearkened to the voice of Jehovah, and hast done all His commands which I am commanding thee to-day;
30:9 and Jehovah thy God hath made thee abundant in every work of thy hand, in the fruit of thy body, and in the fruit of thy cattle, and in the fruit of thy ground, for good; for Jehovah turneth back to rejoice over thee for good, as He rejoiced over thy fathers,
30:10 for thou dost hearken to the voice of Jehovah thy God, to keep His commands, and His statutes, which are written in the book of this law, for thou turnest back unto Jehovah thy God, with all thy heart, and with all thy soul.
30:11 `For this command which I am commanding thee to-day, it is not too wonderful for thee, nor [is] it far off.
30:12 It is not in the heavens, -- saying, Who doth go up for us into the heavens, and doth take it for us, and doth cause us to hear it -- that we may do it.
30:13 And it [is] not beyond the sea, -- saying, Who doth pass over for us beyond the sea, and doth take it for us, and doth cause us to hear it -- that we may do it?
30:14 For very near unto thee is the word, in thy mouth, and in thy heart -- to do it.
30:15 `See, I have set before thee to-day life and good, and death and evil,
30:16 in that I am commanding thee to-day to love Jehovah thy God, to walk in His ways, and to keep His commands, and His statutes, and His judgments; and thou hast lived and multiplied, and Jehovah thy God hath blessed thee in the land whither thou art going in to possess it.
30:17 `And if thy heart doth turn, and thou dost not hearken, and hast been driven away, and hast bowed thyself to other gods, and served them,
30:18 I have declared to you this day, that ye do certainly perish, ye do not prolong days on the ground which thou art passing over the Jordan to go in thither to possess it.
30:19 `I have caused to testify against you to-day the heavens and the earth; life and death I have set before thee, the blessing and the reviling; and thou hast fixed on life, so that thou dost live, thou and thy seed,
30:20 to love Jehovah thy God, to hearken to His voice, and to cleave to Him (for He [is] thy life, and the length of thy days), to dwell on the ground which Jehovah hath sworn to thy fathers, to Abraham, to Isaac, and to Jacob, to give to them.'
31:1 And Moses goeth and speaketh these words unto all Israel,
31:2 and he saith unto them, `A son of a hundred and twenty years [am] I to-day; I am not able any

more to go out and to come in, and Jehovah hath said unto me, Thou dost not pass over this Jordan,
31:3 `Jehovah thy God He is passing over before thee, He doth destroy these nations from before thee, and thou hast possessed them; Joshua -- he is passing over before thee as Jehovah hath spoken,
31:4 and Jehovah hath done to them as he hath done to Sihon and to Og, kings of the Amorite, and to their land, whom He destroyed.
31:5 And Jehovah hath given them before your face, and ye have done to them according to all the command which I have commanded you;
31:6 be strong and courageous, fear not, nor be terrified because of them, for Jehovah thy God [is] He who is going with thee; He doth not fail thee nor forsake thee.'
31:7 And Moses calleth for Joshua, and saith unto him before the eyes of all Israel, `Be strong and courageous, for thou -- thou dost go in with this people unto the land which Jehovah hath sworn to their fathers to give to them, and thou -- thou dost cause them to inherit it;
31:8 and Jehovah [is] He who is going before thee, He himself is with thee; He doth not fail thee nor forsake thee; fear not, nor be affrighted.'
31:9 And Moses writeth this law, and giveth it unto the priests (sons of Levi, those bearing the ark of the covenant of Jehovah), and unto all the elders of Israel,
31:10 and Moses commandeth them, saying, `At the end of seven years, in the appointed time, the year of release, in the feast of booths,
31:11 in the coming in of all Israel to see the face of Jehovah in the place which He chooseth, thou dost proclaim this law before all Israel, in their ears.
31:12 `Assemble the people, the men, and the women, and the infants, and thy sojourner who [is] within thy gates, so that they hear, and so that they learn, and have feared Jehovah your God, and observed to do all the words of this law;
31:13 and their sons, who have not known, do hear, and have learned to fear Jehovah your God all the days which ye are living on the ground whither ye are passing over the Jordan to possess it.'
31:14 And Jehovah saith unto Moses, `Lo, thy days have drawn near to die; call Joshua, and station yourselves in the tent of meeting, and I charge him;' and Moses goeth -- Joshua also -- and they station themselves in the tent of meeting,
31:15 and Jehovah is seen in the tent, in a pillar of a cloud; and the pillar of the cloud standeth at the opening of the tent.
31:16 And Jehovah saith unto Moses, `Lo, thou art lying down with thy fathers, and this people hath risen, and gone a-whoring after the gods of the stranger of the land into the midst of which it

hath entered, and forsaken Me, and broken My covenant which I made with it;
31:17 and Mine anger hath burned against it in that day, and I have forsaken them, and hidden My face from them, and it hath been for consumption, and many evils and distresses have found it, and it hath said in that day, Is it not because that my God is not in my midst -- these evils have found me?
31:18 and I certainly hide My face in that day for all the evil which it hath done, for it hath turned unto other gods.
31:19 `And now, write for you this song, and teach it the sons of Israel; put it in their mouths, so that this song is to Me for a witness against the sons of Israel,
31:20 and I bring them in unto the ground which I have sworn to their fathers -- flowing with milk and honey, and they have eaten, and been satisfied, and been fat, and have turned unto other gods, and they have served them, and despised Me, and broken My covenant.
31:21 `And it hath been, when many evils and distresses do meet it, that this song hath testified to its face for a witness; for it is not forgotten out of the mouth of its seed, for I have known its imagining which it is doing to-day, before I bring them in unto the land of which I have sworn.'
31:22 And Moses writeth this song on that day, and doth teach it the sons of Israel,
31:23 and He commandeth Joshua son of Nun, and saith, `Be strong and courageous, for thou dost bring in the sons of Israel unto the land which I have sworn to them, and I -- I am with thee.'
31:24 And it cometh to pass, when Moses finisheth to write the words of this law on a book till their completion,
31:25 that Moses commandeth the Levites bearing the ark of the covenant of Jehovah, saying,
31:26 `Take this Book of the Law, and thou hast set it on the side of the ark of the covenant of Jehovah your God, and it hath been there against thee for a witness;
31:27 for I -- I have known thy rebellion, and thy stiff neck; lo, in my being yet alive with you to-day, rebellious ye have been with Jehovah, and also surely after my death.
31:28 `Assemble unto me all the elders of your tribes, and your authorities, and I speak in their ears these words, and cause to testify against them the heavens and the earth,
31:29 for I have known that after my death ye do very corruptly, and have turned aside out of the way which I commanded you, and evil hath met you in the latter end of the days, because ye do the evil thing in the eyes of Jehovah, to make Him angry with the work of your hands.'
31:30 And Moses speaketh in the ears of all the assembly of Israel the words of this song, till their completion: --
32:1 `Give ear, O heavens, and I speak; And thou dost hear, O earth, sayings of my mouth!
32:2 Drop as rain doth My doctrine; Flow as dew doth My sayings; As storms on the tender grass,

And as showers on the herb,
32:3 For the Name of Jehovah I proclaim, Ascribe ye greatness to our God!
32:4 The Rock! -- perfect [is] His work, For all His ways [are] just; God of stedfastness, and without iniquity: Righteous and upright [is] He.
32:5 It hath done corruptly to Him; Their blemish is not His sons', A generation perverse and crooked!
32:6 To Jehovah do ye act thus, O people foolish and not wise? Is not He thy father -- thy possessor? He made thee, and doth establish thee.
32:7 Remember days of old -- Understand the years of many generations -- Ask thy father, and he doth tell thee; Thine elders, and they say to thee:
32:8 In the Most High causing nations to inherit, In His separating sons of Adam -- He setteth up the borders of the peoples By the number of the sons of Israel.
32:9 For Jehovah's portion [is] His people, Jacob [is] the line of His inheritance.
32:10 He findeth him in a land -- a desert, And in a void -- a howling wilderness, He turneth him round -- He causeth him to understand -- He keepeth him as the apple of His eye.
32:11 As an eagle waketh up its nest, Over its young ones fluttereth, Spreadeth its wings -- taketh them, Beareth them on its pinions; --
32:12 Jehovah alone doth lead him, And there is no strange god with him.
32:13 He maketh him ride on high places of earth, And he eateth increase of the fields, And He maketh him suck honey from a rock, And oil out of the flint of a rock;
32:14 Butter of the herd, and milk of the flock, With fat of lambs, and rams, sons of Bashan, And he-goats, with fat of kidneys of wheat; And of the blood of the grape thou dost drink wine!
32:15 And Jeshurun waxeth fat, and doth kick: Thou hast been fat -- thou hast been thick, Thou hast been covered. And he leaveth God who made him, And dishonoureth the Rock of his salvation.
32:16 They make Him zealous with strangers, With abominations they make Him angry.
32:17 They sacrifice to demons -- no god! Gods they have not known -- New ones -- from the vicinity they came; Not feared them have your fathers!
32:18 The Rock that begat thee thou forgettest, And neglectest God who formeth thee.
32:19 And Jehovah seeth and despiseth -- For the provocation of His sons and His daughters.
32:20 And He saith: I hide My face from them, I see what [is] their latter end; For a froward generation [are] they, Sons in whom is no stedfastness.
32:21 They have made Me zealous by `no-god,' They made Me angry by their vanities; And I make them zealous by `no-people,' By a foolish nation I make them angry.

32:22 For a fire hath been kindled in Mine anger, And it burneth unto Sheol -- the lowest, And consumeth earth and its increase, And setteth on fire foundations of mountains.

32:23 I gather upon them evils, Mine arrows I consume upon them.

32:24 Exhausted by famine, And consumed by heat, and bitter destruction. And the teeth of beasts I send upon them, With poison of fearful things of the dust.

32:25 Without bereave doth the sword, And at the inner-chambers -- fear, Both youth and virgin, Suckling with man of grey hair.

32:26 I have said: I blow them away, I cause their remembrance to cease from man;

32:27 If not -- the anger of an enemy I fear, Lest their adversaries know -- Lest they say, Our hand is high, And Jehovah hath not wrought all this.

32:28 For a nation lost to counsels [are] they, And there is no understanding in them.

32:29 If they were wise -- They deal wisely [with] this; They attend to their latter end:

32:30 How doth one pursue a thousand, And two cause a myriad to flee! If not -- that their rock hath sold them, And Jehovah hath shut them up?

32:31 For not as our Rock [is] their rock, (And our enemies [are] judges!)

32:32 For of the vine of Sodom their vine [is], And of the fields of Gomorrah; Their grapes [are] grapes of gall -- They have bitter clusters;

32:33 The poison of dragons [is] their wine And the fierce venom of asps.

32:34 Is it not laid up with Me? Sealed among My treasures?

32:35 Mine [are] vengeance and recompense, At the due time -- doth their foot slide; For near is a day of their calamity, And haste do things prepared for them.

32:36 For Jehovah doth judge His people, And for His servants doth repent Himself. For He seeth -- the going away of power, And none is restrained and left.

32:37 And He hath said, Where [are] their gods -- The rock in which they trusted;

32:38 Which the fat of their sacrifices do eat, They drink the wine of their libation! Let them arise and help you, Let it be for you a hiding-place!

32:39 See ye, now, that I -- I [am] He, And there is no god with Me: I put to death, and I keep alive; I have smitten, and I heal; And there is not from My hand a deliverer,

32:40 For I lift up unto the heavens My hand, And have said, I live -- to the age!

32:41 If I have sharpened the brightness of My sword, And My hand doth lay hold on judgment, I turn back vengeance to Mine adversaries, And to those hating Me -- I repay!

32:42 I make drunk Mine arrows with blood, And My sword devoureth flesh, From the blood of the pierced and captive, From the head of the freemen of the enemy.

32:43 Sing ye nations -- [with] his people, For the blood of His servants He avengeth, And

vengeance He turneth back on His adversaries, And hath pardoned His land -- His people.'
32:44 And Moses cometh and speaketh all the words of this song in the ears of the people, he and Hoshea son of Nun;
32:45 and Moses finisheth to speak all these words unto all Israel,
32:46 and saith unto them, `Set your heart to all the words which I am testifying against you to-day, that ye command your sons to observe to do all the words of this law,
32:47 for it [is] not a vain thing for you, for it [is] your life, and by this thing ye prolong days on the ground whither ye are passing over the Jordan to possess it.'
32:48 And Jehovah speaketh unto Moses, in this self-same day, saying,
32:49 `Go up unto this mount Abarim, mount Nebo, which [is] in the land of Moab, which [is] on the front of Jericho, and see the land of Canaan which I am giving to the sons of Israel for a possession;
32:50 and die in the mount whither thou art going up, and be gathered unto thy people, as Aaron thy brother hath died in the mount Hor, and is gathered unto his people:
32:51 `Because ye trespassed against me in the midst of the sons of Israel at the waters of Meribath-Kadesh, the wilderness of Zin -- because ye sanctified Me not in the midst of the sons of Israel;
32:52 but over-against thou seest the land, and thither thou dost not go in, unto the land which I am giving to the sons of Israel.'
33:1 And this [is] the blessing [with] which Moses the man of God blessed the sons of Israel before his death,
33:2 and he saith: -- `Jehovah from Sinai hath come, And hath risen from Seir for them; He hath shone from mount Paran, And hath come [with] myriads of holy ones; At His right hand [are] springs for them.
33:3 Also He [is] loving the peoples; All His holy ones [are] in thy hand, And they -- they sat down at thy foot, [Each] He lifteth up at thy words.
33:4 A law hath Moses commanded us, A possession of the assembly of Jacob.
33:5 And he is in Jeshurun king, In the heads of the people gathering together, The tribes of Israel!
33:6 Let Reuben live, and not die, And let his men be a number.
33:7 And this [is] for Judah; and he saith: -- Hear, O Jehovah, the voice of Judah, And unto his people do Thou bring him in; His hand hath striven for him, And an help from his adversaries art Thou.
33:8 And of Levi he said: -- Thy Thummim and thy Urim [are] for thy pious one, Whom Thou hast tried in Massah, Thou dost strive with Him at the waters of Meribah;

33:9 Who is saying of his father and his mother, I have not seen him; And his brethren he hath not discerned, And his sons he hath not known; For they have observed Thy saying, And Thy covenant they keep.
33:10 They teach Thy judgments to Jacob, And Thy law to Israel; They put perfume in Thy nose, And whole burnt-offering on Thine altar.
33:11 Bless, O Jehovah, his strength, And the work of his hands Thou acceptest, Smite the loins of his withstanders, And of those hating him -- that they rise not!
33:12 Of Benjamin he said: -- The beloved of Jehovah doth tabernacle confidently by him, Covering him over all the day; Yea, between his shoulders He doth tabernacle.
33:13 And of Joseph he said: -- Blessed of Jehovah [is] his land, By precious things of the heavens, By dew, and by the deep crouching beneath,
33:14 And by precious things -- fruits of the sun, And by precious things -- cast forth by the moons,
33:15 And by chief things -- of the ancient mountains, And by precious things -- of the age-during heights,
33:16 And by precious things -- of earth and its fulness, And the good pleasure Of Him who is dwelling in the bush, -- Let it come for the head of Joseph, And for the crown of him Who is separate from his brethren.
33:17 His honour [is] a firstling of his ox, And his horns [are] horns of a reem; By them peoples he doth push together To the ends of earth; And they [are] the myriads of Ephraim, And they [are] the thousands of Manasseh.
33:18 And of Zebulun he said: -- Rejoice, O Zebulun, in thy going out, And, O Issachar, in thy tents;
33:19 Peoples [to] the mountain they call, There they sacrifice righteous sacrifices; For the abundance of the seas they suck, And hidden things hidden in the sand.
33:20 And of Gad he said: -- Blessed of the Enlarger [is] Gad, As a lioness he doth tabernacle, And hath torn the arm -- also the crown!
33:21 And he provideth the first part for himself, For there the portion of the lawgiver is covered, And he cometh [with] the heads of the people; The righteousness of Jehovah he hath done, And His judgments with Israel.
33:22 And of Dan he said: -- Dan [is] a lion's whelp; he doth leap from Bashan.
33:23 And of Naphtali he said: -- O Naphtali, satisfied with pleasure, And full of the blessing of Jehovah, West and south possess thou.
33:24 And of Asher he said: -- Blessed with sons [is] Asher, Let him be accepted by his brethren, And dipping in oil his foot.
33:25 Iron and brass [are] thy shoes, And as thy days -- thy strength.

33:26 There is none like the God of Jeshurun, Riding the heavens in thy help, And in His excellency the skies.
33:27 A habitation [is] the eternal God, And beneath [are] arms age-during. And He casteth out from thy presence the enemy, and saith, `Destroy!'
33:28 And Israel doth tabernacle [in] confidence alone; The eye of Jacob [is] unto a land of corn and wine; Also His heavens drop down dew.
33:29 O thy happiness, O Israel! who is like thee? A people saved by Jehovah, The shield of thy help, And He who [is] the sword of thine excellency: And thine enemies are subdued for thee, And thou on their high places dost tread.'
34:1 And Moses goeth up from the plains of Moab unto mount Nebo, the top of Pisgah, which [is] on the front of Jericho, and Jehovah sheweth him all the land -- Gilead unto Dan,
34:2 and all Naphtali, and the land of Ephraim, and Manasseh, and all the land of Judah unto the further sea,
34:3 and the south, and the circuit of the valley of Jericho, the city of palms, unto Zoar.
34:4 And Jehovah saith unto him, `This [is] the land which I have sworn to Abraham, to Isaac, and to Jacob, saying, To thy seed I give it; I have caused thee to see with thine eyes, and thither thou dost not pass over.'
34:5 And Moses, servant of the Lord, dieth there, in the land of Moab, according to the command of Jehovah;
34:6 and He burieth him in a valley in the land of Moab, over-against Beth-Peor, and no man hath known his burying place unto this day.
34:7 And Moses [is] a son of a hundred and twenty years when he dieth; his eye hath not become dim, nor hath his moisture fled.
34:8 And the sons of Israel bewail Moses in the plains of Moab thirty days; and the days of weeping [and] mourning for Moses are completed.
34:9 And Joshua son of Nun is full of the spirit of wisdom, for Moses had laid his hands upon him, and the sons of Israel hearken unto him, and do as Jehovah commanded Moses.
34:10 And there hath not arisen a prophet any more in Israel like Moses, whom Jehovah hath known face unto face,
34:11 in reference to all the signs and the wonders which Jehovah sent him to do in the land of Egypt, to Pharaoh, and to all his servants, and to all his land,
34:12 and in reference to all the strong hand, and to all the great fear which Moses did before the eyes of all Israel.

2011 edition published by TozMusic

Printed in the USA
CPSIA information can be obtained
at www.ICGtesting.com
LVHW080038190524
780607LV00007B/879